GUADALCANAL

Books by Eric Hammel

76 Hours: The Invasion of Tarawa
Chosin: Heroic Ordeal of the Korean War
The Root: The Marines in Lebanon
ACE! A Marine Night-Fighter Pilot in
World War II
Duel for the Golan: The 100-Hour Battle That Saved Israel
Guadalcanal: Starvation Island

GUADALCANAL
The Carrier Battles

CARRIER OPERATIONS
IN THE SOLOMONS
August–October, 1942

ERIC HAMMEL

CROWN PUBLISHERS, INC.
NEW YORK

FOR BARBARA

Published by Crown Publishers, Inc.,
225 Park Avenue South, New York, New York 10003 and in
Canada by the Canadian MANDA Group
CROWN is a trademark of Crown Publishers, Inc.
Manufactured in the United States of America
Library of Congress Cataloging-in-Publication Data
Hammel, Eric M.
Guadalcanal: the carrier battles

1. World War, 1939–1945—Campaigns—Solomon Islands—
2. World War, 1939–1945—Aerial operations, American. I. Title.
D767.98.H327 1987   940.54'26   86-32964
ISBN 0-517-56608-7
10 9 8 7 6 5 4 3 2 1
First Edition

GUIDE TO ABBREVIATIONS AND TERMS

ACRM	Aviation Chief Radioman
ACTG	Advanced Carrier Training Group
Adm	Admiral
Airacobra	Bell P-39 Army fighter
AM1	Aviation Metalsmith 1st Class
AMM3	Aviation Machinist's Mate 3rd Class
Angels	Altitude in thousands of feet
AOM2	Aviation Ordnanceman 2nd Class
AP1	Aviation Pilot 1st Class
ARM2	Aviation Radioman 2nd Class
AvCad	Naval Aviation Cadet
Avenger	Grumman TBF torpedo bomber
BB	Battleship
Betty	Mitsubishi G4M medium bomber
BGen	Brigadier General
BM1	Boatswain's Mate 1st Class
Bogies	Radio code for "enemy or unidentified aircraft"
Buntaicho	Japanese fighter-unit leader
Buster	Radio code for "immediate"
Butai	Japanese fighter squadron
CA	Heavy cruiser
CAP	Chief Aviation Pilot
Capt	Captain
Carp	Warrant Carpenter

v

Catalina	Consolidated PBY patrol bomber
Cdr	Commander
CEM	Chief Electrician's Mate
ChElec	Chief Warrant Electrician
ChMach	Chief Warrant Machinist
Chutai	Japanese bomber squadron
CinC	Commander in Chief
CL	Light cruiser
CLAA	Light antiaircraft cruiser
cm	Centimeter
CMM	Chief Machinist's Mate
CO	Commanding Officer
Col	Colonel
ComAirSoPac	Commander, Aircraft, South Pacific
Cox	Coxswain
CQM	Chief Quartermaster
CSF	Chief Ship Fitter
CTC	Chief Turret Captain
CV	Fleet aircraft carrier
CVE	Escort aircraft carrier
CVL	Light aircraft carrier
CWT	Chief Watertender
CXAM	Crosley experimental surface-to-air radar
CY	Chief Yeoman
Dauntless	Douglas SBD dive-bomber
DD	Destroyer
Devastator	Douglas TBD torpedo bomber
EM3	Electrician's Mate 3rd Class
Emily	Kawanishi H8K patrol bomber
Ens	Ensign
Exec	Executive Officer
(F)	Flagship
F3	Fireman 3rd Class
F4F	Grumman Wildcat fighter
FC3	Fire Controlman 3rd Class
FDO	Fighter Direction Officer
1stLt	First Lieutenant
(FF)	Fleet Flagship

Fulmite	Chemical fire retardant
GM2	Gunner's Mate 2nd Class
GySgt	Gunnery Sergeant
HIJMS	His Imperial Japanese Majesty's Ship
Hikokitai	Japanese carrier air group
Hikotaicho	Japanese air-group commander
HMAS	His Majesty's Australian Ship
HMS	His Majesty's Ship (Royal Navy)
IFF	Identification, Friend or Foe
Kate	Nakajima B5N torpedo bomber
LCdr	Lieutenant Commander
LSO	Landing Signal Officer
Lt	Lieutenant
Lt(jg)	Lieutenant Junior Grade
LtCol	Lieutenant Colonel
LtGen	Lieutenant General
Mach	Warrant Machinist
Maj	Major
Maru	Japanese transport or cargo ship
Mavis	Kawanishi H6K patrol bomber
Me-109	German Messerschmitt fighter
MG	Warrant Marine Gunner
MGen	Major General
mm	Millimeter
MM1	Machinist's Mate 1st Class
MoMM2	Motor Machinist's Mate 2nd Class
NAP	Naval Aviation Pilot (Enlisted)
OS2U	Vought Kingfisher observation scout
P-39	Bell Airacobra Army fighter
P-400	Bell Airacobra Army fighter (export model)
Pancake	Radio code for "Land immediately"
PB	Patrol boat

PBY	Consolidated Catalina patrol bomber
Pfc	Private First Class
PhM1	Pharmacist's Mate 1st Class
PhoM3	Photographer's Mate 3rd Class
PT	Patrol torpedo boat
RAdm	Rear Admiral
RBA	Rescue breathing apparatus
RE	Warrant Radio Electrician
RM3	Radioman 3rd Class
S1	Seaman 1st Class
SBD	Douglas Dauntless dive-bomber
2ndLt	Second Lieutenant
Shotai	Japanese fighter/bomber element
SM2	Signalman 2nd Class
SOC	Curtiss observation scout
TBD	Douglas Devastator torpedo bomber
TBF	Grumman Avenger torpedo bomber
TBS	"Talk Between Ships" radio
TM1	Torpedoman 1st Class
TSgt	Technical Sergeant
VAdm	Vice Admiral
Val	Aichi D3A dive-bomber
VB	Navy bombing squadron
VF	Navy fighting squadron
VMF	Marine fighting squadron
VMSB	Marine scout-bomber squadron
VP	Navy patrol squadron
VS	Navy scouting squadron
VT	Navy torpedo squadron
Wildcat	Grumman F4F fighter
WT1	Watertender 1st Class
Y2	Yeoman 2nd Class
Zero	Mitsubishi A6M fighter

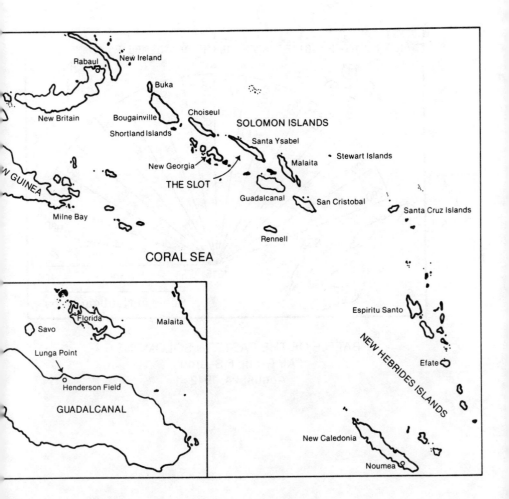

Rabaul · New Ireland · New Britain · Buka · Bougainville · Shortland Islands · Choiseul · SOLOMON ISLANDS · Santa Ysabel · Stewart Islands · New Georgia · Malaita · THE SLOT · Guadalcanal · San Cristobal · Santa Cruz Islands · N GUINEA · Milne Bay · Rennell · CORAL SEA · Espiritu Santo · NEW HEBRIDES ISLANDS · Efate · New Caledonia · Noumea

Florida · Savo · Malaita · Lunga Point · Henderson Field · GUADALCANAL

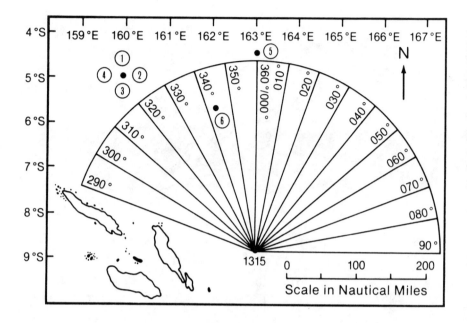

BATTLE OF THE EASTERN SOLOMONS
Air Group 6 Search
August 24, 1942

Sector	Pilots
235-250	Wakeham
	Stevens
250-266	Buell
	Wakeham
266-282	Welch
	McGraw
282-298	Burnett
	Miller
298-314	Lee
	Johnson
314-330	Ward
	Carmody
330-345	Strong
	Irvine
345-360	Ramsay
	Bloch

CONTACTS WITH JAPANESE SHIPS
by Air Group 10 Searchers

1. Welch and McGraw find Abe's surface force, 0717
2. Burnett and Miller find Abe's surface force 1740
3. Lee and Johnson find Nagumo's carriers, 0750
4. Ward and Carmody find Nagumo's carriers, 0820
5. Strong and Irvine find Nagumo's carriers, 0830

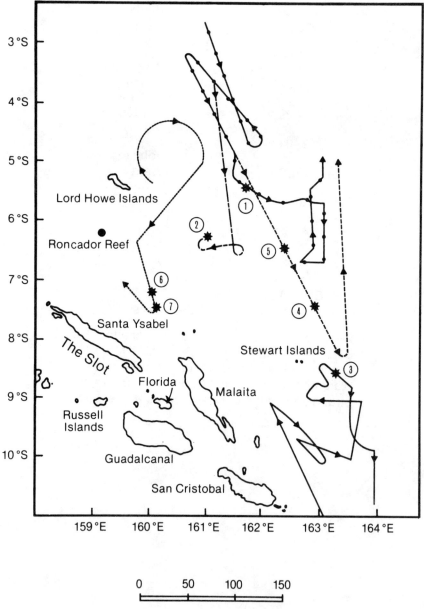

3°S

4°S

5°S

Lord Howe Islands

6°S

Roncador Reef

① ②

⑤

7°S

⑥

Santa Ysabel

⑦

⑦

The Slot

8°S

Stewart Islands

④

Florida

③

9°S

Malaita

Russell
Islands

10°S

Guadalcanal

San Cristobal

159°E   160°E   161°E   162°E   163°E   164°E

0   50   100   150

Scale in Nautical Miles

BATTLE OF THE EASTERN SOLOMONS
August 23-25, 1942

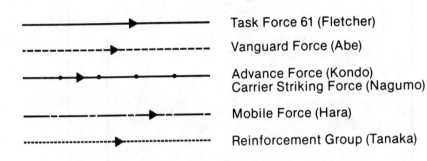

Task Force 61 (Fletcher)

Vanguard Force (Abe)

Advance Force (Kondo)
Carrier Striking Force (Nagumo)

Mobile Force (Hara)

Reinforcement Group (Tanaka)

August 24
1   1545 — Davis and Shaw find Nagumo.
2   1605 — Air Group 3 attacks **Ryujo.**
3   1712 — Japanese attack **Enterprise.**
4   1820 — U.S. torpedo bombers attack Kondo and Abe.
5   1820 — Elder and Gordon attack **Chitose.**
August 25
6   0835 — Cactus dive-bombers hit **Kinryu Maru** and **Jintsu.**
7   1015 — B-17s sink **Mutsuki.**

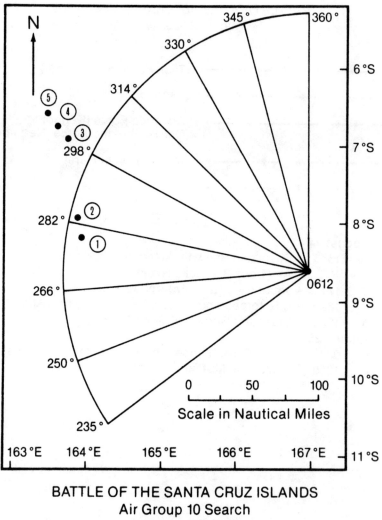

N

345° 360°

330°

314°

6°S

⑤ ④
③
298°

7°S

282° ②

①

8°S

0612

266°

9°S

250°

0   50   100
Scale in Nautical Miles

10°S

235°

163°E   164°E   165°E   166°E   167°E   11°S

BATTLE OF THE SANTA CRUZ ISLANDS
Air Group 10 Search
October 26, 1942

Sector	Pilots
290-300	Weissenborn
	Mears
300-310	Myers
	Corl
310-320	Jorgenson
	Bingaman
320-330	Jett
	Bye
330-340	Strong
	Richey
340-350	Davis
	Shaw
350-360	Lowe
	Gibson
360-010	Horenburger

CONTACTS WITH JAPANESE SHIPS
by Air Group 6 Searchers

1. Jett and Bye find **Ryujo**, 1440
2. Myers and Corl find **Ryujo**, 1500
3. Jorgenson and Bingaman find **Ryujo**, 1510
4. Strong and Richey find **Ryujo**, 1510
5. Lowe and Gibson find Abe's cruisers, 1510
6. Davis and Shaw find **Shokaku** and **Zuikaku**, 1545

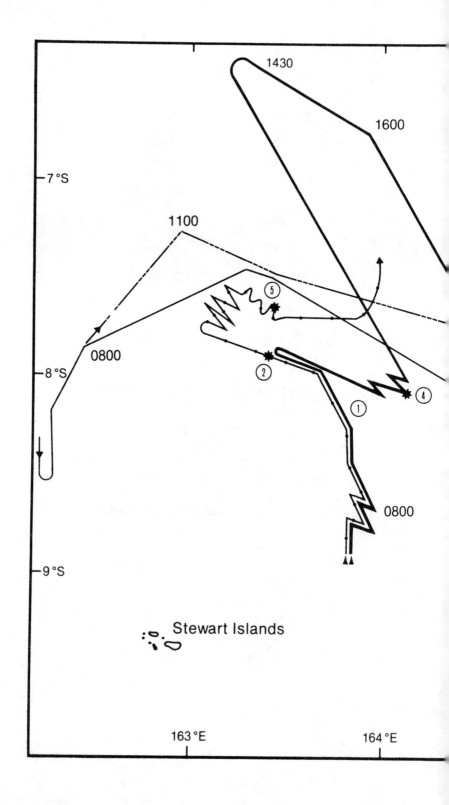

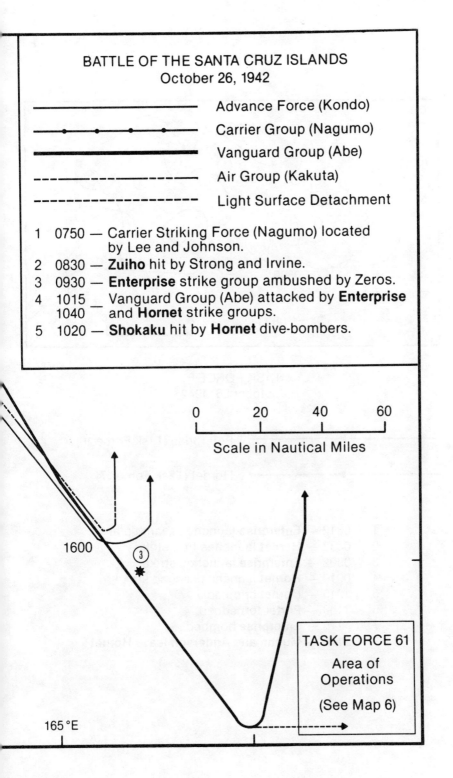

BATTLE OF THE SANTA CRUZ ISLANDS
October 26, 1942

——————————————— Advance Force (Kondo)

——•——•——•——•—— Carrier Group (Nagumo)

━━━━━━━━━━━━━━━ Vanguard Group (Abe)

— — — — — — — — Air Group (Kakuta)

- - - - - - - - - - - Light Surface Detachment

1 0750 — Carrier Striking Force (Nagumo) located
             by Lee and Johnson.
2 0830 — **Zuiho** hit by Strong and Irvine.
3 0930 — **Enterprise** strike group ambushed by Zeros.
4 1015 _ Vanguard Group (Abe) attacked by **Enterprise**
   1040   and **Hornet** strike groups.
5 1020 — **Shokaku** hit by **Hornet** dive-bombers.

0   20   40   60

Scale in Nautical Miles

1600

③
✳

165 °E

TASK FORCE 61

Area of
Operations

(See Map 6)

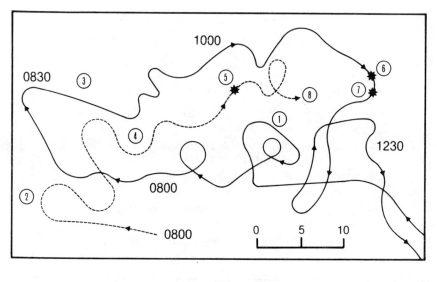

TASK FORCE 61
October 26, 1942

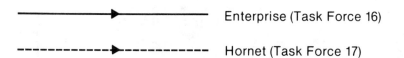

Enterprise (Task Force 16)

Hornet (Task Force 17)

1	0612 —	**Enterprise** launches search planes
2	0832 —	**Hornet** launches first strike
3	0902 —	**Enterprise** launches strike
4	0910 —	**Hornet** launches second strike
5	1015 —	**Hornet** crippled
6	1100 —	**Porter** torpedoed
7	1115 —	**Enterprise** bombed
8	2140 —	**Mustin** and **Anderson** leave **Hornet**

BOW

Port Bow 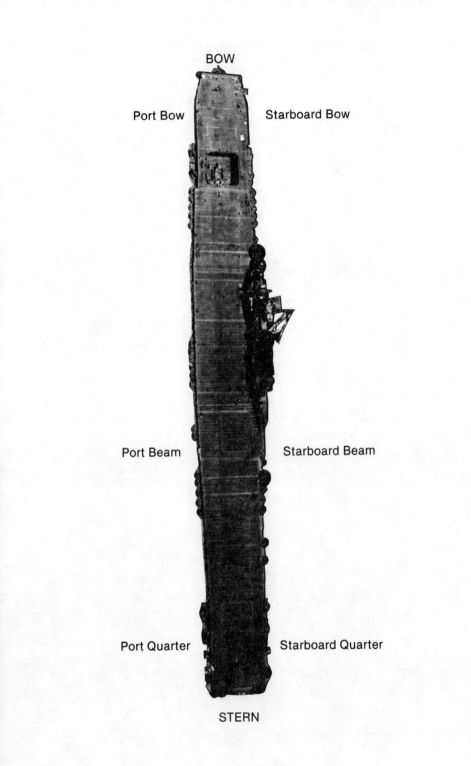 Starboard Bow

Port Beam   Starboard Beam

Port Quarter   Starboard Quarter

STERN

PART I

Invasion

I

The Japanese Pacific juggernaut that began at Pearl Harbor and the Philippines on December 7, 1941, rolled over the Australian- and British-mandated Bismarck Archipelago and Solomon Islands between late January and early May 1942. The occupation of the principal islands of both groups was undertaken by small naval surface forces and naval landing parties against almost zero opposition.

The occupation of the Solomon Islands was both beyond the scope of Japanese early-war aims and far ahead of schedule. While Japanese plans called for eventual seizure of the New Hebrides, New Caledonia, the Fijis, and the Samoan Islands, the need to rest and regroup resulted in a halt in the vicinity of Tulagi, an anchorage in the eastern Solomons capable of protecting a very large component of the Combined Fleet, the fighting arm of the Imperial Navy. There, at Tulagi, the Japanese decided to build fleet and air bases from which future operations to the south and east might be supported.

American senior naval strategists meeting in San Francisco in late June 1942 selected the Tulagi anchorage as the lead-off objective for their projected Pacific counteroffensive, which was to begin in midsummer. All the planners would have preferred a straightforward drive across the Central Pacific, an offensive carrier-supported surface-fleet operation that had been the basis of all United States contingency planning since the 1920s. But the danger lay to the south, across the vital shipping lanes linking Australia and New Zealand with the United States. Tulagi was simply the Japanese base closest to the shipping lanes and to the tiny island-bound Allied bastions guarding them.

After the objective had been selected, as the meeting was breaking up, news arrived from an Allied "coastwatcher"—a volunteer who had stayed behind when Crown forces retreated from the eastern Solomons—that the Japanese had crossed the 20-mile-wide channel from Tulagi to Guadalcanal Island to begin building a new airfield. The airfield immediately became the main objective of the first Allied Pacific counteroffensive, and the schedule was precipitously moved up. An amphibious landing force, guarded by numerous surface warships and all available American fleet aircraft carriers, was to be set in motion. The invasion was to take place in early August 1942.

A number of top-level strategists hoped, among other things, that Japanese fleet carriers would be drawn into the upcoming confrontation. Many of the airmen manning the American carriers wanted to follow up on their clear, tide-turning June victory at Midway.

But the main objective was stopping a renewed Japanese drive toward the New Hebrides before it started. The Americans were invading the eastern Solomons because they had to.

The Allied invasion fleet arrived in the eastern Solomons from its staging area in the Fijis in two parts. The troop transports carrying the reinforced 1st Marine Division were guarded by a mighty surface force composed entirely of cruisers and destroyers. The support force comprised three fleet carriers—*Enterprise*, *Wasp*, and *Saratoga*—and a screening force of a battleship, cruisers, and destroyers.

4

Despite realistic fears to the contrary, the approach of the invasion armada went completely undetected by the burgeoning Imperial Navy headquarters and air base complex in Rabaul, 600 air miles to the northwest. The Japanese defenders—little more than a battalion of bluejackets and the airfield construction and base forces it guarded—were to be taken completely by surprise.

The landing of Marines on Guadalcanal, Tulagi, and several nearby islands was to begin at 0800—eight o'clock in the morning—on Tuesday, August 7, 1942.

While surface warships attached directly to the invasion fleet were closing on darkened beaches on both sides of Sealark and Lengo Channels, the airmen of the three carrier air groups were preparing for their day's work. Air Group 3, *Saratoga's* strong arm—consisting of Scouting Squadron 3 (Scouting-3), Bombing Squadron 3 (Bombing-3), Torpedo Squadron 8 (Torpedo-8), and Fighting Squadron 5 (Fighting-5)—was to provide direct support for the Marines landing on Guadalcanal's northern shore. *Wasp's* Air Group 7—Scouting-71, Scouting-72, Torpedo-7, and Fighting-71—was to provide support for Marines landing at Tulagi and other islands on the north side of the channel. And *Enterprise's* Air Group 6—Scouting-5, Bombing-6, Torpedo-3, and Fighting-6— was to guard the carrier and surface invasion forces and to provide a ready reserve for its sister air groups.

卐

In sum, the three fleet carriers and their air groups comprised 75 percent of the aerial offensive striking arm of the entire U.S. Fleet.

The need to adequately support the first Allied counterstroke in the Pacific had been carefully weighed against ominous potential consequences. The Japanese strategy for the early phase of the war had been to draw out the American carriers and to destroy them. Thus far, two of only six U.S. fleet carriers that had been available at the start of the war had been destroyed. *Lexington*, *Saratoga's* sister ship, had been lost in the Coral Sea turning back a Japanese invasion fleet bound for Port Moresby, New Guinea. And *Yorktown*, sister to *Enterprise* and *Hornet*, had been lost at Midway. In return, however, the Americans had sunk one Japanese light carrier in the Coral Sea, and four Japanese fleet carriers at Midway. The odds had been made more nearly even at Midway, but the carrier force available to the Combined Fleet commander, Adm Isoroku Yamamoto, was by far more formidable than anything the Allies could maneuver in Pacific waters.

Still, because they enjoyed the fruits of two victories, a number of the American strategic planners who had conceived of the Guadalcanal invasion in San Francisco in June were not wholly averse to the notion of fighting the grand carrier battle Admiral Yamamoto apparently desired. So far as some of them were concerned, August 1942 was as good a time as any to decide the future course and possible outcome of the war.

But there were cautious dissenters who believed the United States needed to win time to fully engage her awesome industrial might in the building of an unstoppable war machine. These leaders often cited simple statistics: It would take until early 1943 to complete the first new carrier construction of the war. After that, carriers of all sizes and types would be joining the U.S. Fleet in accelerating numbers. Those in the know cited similar statistics to bolster the argument: Japanese industry had no hope of keeping pace with America's awakening industrial might and, indeed, would be hard-pressed simply to replace the losses sustained by the Combined Fleet at the Coral Sea and Midway. These strategists advised against initiating an early final confrontation. So long as some forward momentum could be maintained, they were all for awaiting the first fruits of the all-out wartime carrier construction program.

In the end, it came down to one man—the overall commander of the Allied Solomons invasion fleet, VAdm Frank Jack Fletcher. He was the man on the scene in the eastern Solomons. If the Japanese carriers sallied to rescue Guadalcanal's airfield, he would fight or withdraw, as *he* saw fit.

2

Guadalcanal. August 7, 1942.

Lt(jg) Smokey Stover, an element leader with *Saratoga's* Fighting-5, was to be among the first U.S. airmen launched against Japanese shore installations near Guadalcanal's Lunga Point. Though Stover had spent a sobering, pensive evening in his stateroom—writing his will and accompanying letters to his family—he did not really believe he was going to die in the morning.

The Fighting-5 pilots had attended lectures held every evening for the two weeks leading up to D-Day. Smokey Stover felt he was well acquainted with the squadron's targets and with the general situation at Guadalcanal and Tulagi. He was not certain about reports of possible opposition; some reports had placed land-based Zero fighters on Guadalcanal's new airstrip, but others claimed the runway was not yet operational; the latest report indicated that there were no Japanese land-based fighters in the eastern Solomons but that float fighters were definitely based at Gavutu, a tiny island seaplane base 20 miles north of Fighting-5's strike objective. This potential opposition seemed inconsequential to Stover because the float fighters were not nearly as maneuverable as the F4F Wildcat fighters he and his comrades would be flying.

Three four-plane divisions of Fighting-5—including Stover's—were to launch well before dawn and fly to Lunga Point in time to begin strafing airfield facilities by 0630, 15 minutes before sunrise. If reports of submarines and patrol boats based around Lunga were accurate, Fighting-5 was to help elements of the two *Saratoga*-based dive-bomber squadrons work them over. After that, the fighters would be free to use their remaining ammunition against targets of opportunity and then independently return to *Saratoga*.

Wasp's Air Group 7 was to carry out similar strikes against targets 20 miles to the north of Lunga—against Tulagi, Florida, Gavutu, and Tanambogo. And the bomber squadrons of *Enterprise*'s Air Group 6 were to lend a hand in general support, wherever needed, while Fighting-6 and elements of Fighting-5 maintained combat air patrols over the carriers and in the vicinity of the landing beaches. Torpedo bombers from all three carriers would be employed as on-call vertical bombers or on wide-ranging patrol missions throughout the eastern Solomons.

卐

The three fighter squadrons available in the eastern Solomons were each nominally composed of thirty-two Grumman F4F-4 Wildcat fighters. Each squadron was organized into up to eight four-plane "divisions" composed of two two-plane "elements." Each division was led by a senior fighter pilot, such as the squadron commander, the squadron executive officer, or the squadron flight officer. Each division's two two-plane elements, consisting of an element leader and his wingman, were normally led by the division's two senior pilots. The first-element leader was invariably the division leader. However, because some of the squadrons boasted enlisted, warrant, and newly commissioned former enlisted pilots with years of experience, the division and element leaders were not always pilots of senior rank. Indeed, a number of senior-ranked fighter pilots were relatively new to flying because of the Navy's policy of forcing its Regular officers to serve at least two years with the Fleet as surface line officers before being allowed to attend flight school. On the other hand, a program open to Reserve officers, beginning in 1935 and vastly expanded in 1940, had resulted in the nick-of-time appearance of many junior pilots beginning in mid-1941. By mid-1942, most of the pilots manning warplanes aboard fleet carriers were "AvCads"—Naval Aviation Cadets—with very junior Reserve commissions.

Smokey Stover had begun his military flying career on December 30, 1940, when he arrived at Pensacola, Florida, to attend flight school. He was designated a Naval Aviator and awarded his coveted Wings of Gold and a commission on July 2, 1941. He was subsequently assigned to *Hornet*'s Fighting-8, and went to sea for the first time aboard his brand-new carrier on December 27, 1941. He had been a bystander when Army Air Forces LtCol Jimmy Doolittle's Tokyo raid was launched from *Hornet*'s flight deck on April 18, 1942. He had come close to seeing first combat at Midway, but never saw an enemy airplane or any of the enemy carriers. The first time Ensign Stover fired in anger was on a strafing mission in which he undoubtedly killed survivors of a sunken Japanese cruiser.

The battle-depleted air groups of America's surviving carriers were extensively reorganized after Midway, and Lt(jg) Smokey Stover was reassigned to Fighting-5, formerly the sunken *Yorktown*'s fighter squadron. He reported to his new unit in Hawaii on July 3, 1942, just in time to prepare to ship out for the Solomons aboard *Saratoga*.

卐

Smokey Stover was awakened with all the other Air Group 3 pilots and aircrewmen at 0400, August 7. He had time to wolf down an unenjoyable breakfast, attend final briefings, and check out his Wildcat fighter before launching in the dark at 0530.

By manning their airplanes early, all of the strike pilots were able to become pretty well adapted to the darkness. The half-moon out in the predawn hours gave off a fair amount of light, but it was hidden by clouds part of the time. Smokey Stover's main concern was that there be enough moonlight to brighten the horizon. If not, he would have to resort to flying less certainly with the aid of instruments than by using direct sight.

When it was Stover's turn to launch—he was fairly far back in the fighter pack—he gave his engine full throttle and roared off into the darkness. As with all carrier launches, the heavy Grumman fighter dropped a bit as it cleared the end of the flight deck. Stover smoothly pulled back on his stick and followed the preceding fighter, which was marked by only a few faint lights receding into the dark sky.

There was a mix-up right behind Stover, whose wingman went astray. A division of Fighting-6 Wildcats freshly launched from *Enterprise* joined on the wingman, who then led them away from their objective. Someone else joined on Stover's wing, but he later disappeared.

Lt(jg) Slim Russell, a dive-bomber pilot with *Saratoga's* Scouting-3, was near the end of the string taking off from *Saratoga*. He noticed just before he taxied forward into his takeoff spot that a searchlight was playing from the carrier's starboard side. Russell fleetingly assumed the light was probing the darkness for a submarine, then forgot about it; submarines were not his immediate concern, a safe launch was.

Russell was flying the number two spot on Lt Ralph Weymouth, leader of Scouting-3's six-plane 3rd Division. The division rendezvoused ahead of the carrier at 500 feet and made two sweeping left-hand circles while it joined with the squadron's other divisions. Then Scouting-3 headed directly for its target at Kukum, 68 miles to the east-northeast. All the Dauntless pilots shut off their lights as soon as the squadron rendezvous had been completed—except for Slim Russell's wingman, the number three man on Lieutenant Weymouth's other wing. The dive-bombers were over Guadalcanal's southern mountain range—brightly marked by the set of lights on the one plane—before the green ensign was finally snapped from his reveries by the wild maneuvering of several other pilots, who eventually made him understand how he was endangering the entire formation.

☙

Fighting-5 flew in full darkness northwest toward Guadalcanal's western cape and did not turn off running lights until the fighters were 40 miles away from the carrier. The moon broke through the clouds as the Wildcats rounded the cape—Cape Esperance. In eerie moonlight, the fighters turned east and felt their way along Guadalcanal's northern coast. They were scheduled to arrive over Lunga at about the time the Scouting-3 Dauntlesses completed their direct hop over the island's interior.

Smokey Stover saw antiaircraft guns far ahead. He had expected to be tracked by shore-based guns, but these flashes appeared to be rising from the middle of the channel north of Lunga. After tense minutes, Stover realized that the flashes were from friendly warships, which were bombarding the beaches from Kukum eastward to the Marines' landing beach. Stover maintained formation while watching the colorful display. At regular intervals, bright yellow flashes flared from one of the now-visible dark splotches on the water. Each new bright flash soon resolved itself into three tiny white spots that soared aloft in long, glowing arcs before impacting among the coconut palms around Kukum.

At 20 minutes before sunrise, it was still so dark that Stover could see little more than the darker silhouette of the island. Far to the left, he could see warships bombarding Tulagi, where a row of five or six fires were evenly spaced along that island's dark shore.

Scouting-3's Lt(jg) Slim Russell, who was just then arriving from the south, could also see huge flashes of flame as the cruisers pounded the beaches. A large fire was raging beyond Kukum, but Russell could not see northward as far as Tulagi.

Upon arriving over the target area, the dive-bombers split up and individually circled. Russell flew in and out of the sparse cloud cover, which was at about 6,000 feet. He could easily see the airstrip behind Lunga Point. The dive-bombers had arrived a bit early, before the cruisers offshore had completed their scheduled bombardment. There was no sign of antiaircraft fire nor, for that matter, any other form of opposition. A vessel Slim Russell estimated to be 200 feet in length was burning in the water off Kukum, the apparent victim of the cruiser bombardment.

Then Russell saw that the fighters were going in.

卐

The three Fighting-5 divisions had been at about 5,000 feet when they had rounded Cape Esperance and started to descend toward Lunga. They had gained considerable speed between the cape and Lunga Point. Fighting-5's 1st Division, which was led by the squadron commander, LCdr Roy Simpler, pulled ahead of the pack, forcing the pilots in the rear divisions to add a lot of throttle to keep up. Smokey Stover had to race to keep sight of his own division leader, Lt Walter Clarke, who was only two planes ahead. Clarke momentarily disappeared from Stover's view whenever he got lower than Stover, and he was barely visible against the forest below when he was level with Stover.

The fighters swung a little south of where the cruisers were shelling Kukum and swept over the airfield from the west. A mile ahead of Clarke's 3rd Division, Simpler's 1st Division began firing. Smokey Stover could easily see Simpler's tracer ammunition ricocheting off the runway surface. At first, Stover thought the ricochets were the feared antiaircraft fire, but he observed the same effect as soon as Lieutenant Clarke opened fire and realized that he was in no immediate danger from guns on the ground. Each burst from the fighters' six .50-caliber wing-mounted machine guns—a mix of one tracer round in every four—slowly sank toward the buildings and partially completed revetments, then ricocheted up in red splashes as if from a Roman candle. It was still so dark that Stover could not use his Wildcat's electric gunsight, which reflected a bright calibrated ring on the fighter's windscreen. Even turned down to its lowest setting, the sight would have blotted out everything behind it.

To conserve ammunition, Stover initially fired only his four outboard machine guns. He aimed by firing short bursts, then corrected as he saw the fall of the bullets, which seemed to spray over half the field. Stover still expected return fire from the ground, so he pulled up in a climbing, twisting turn. But there was no answering fire.

The fighters returned again and again to fire at everything that possibly could have sheltered airplanes or men. Smokey Stover observed no human beings and no return fire. On one pass, he streaked at full throttle across the runway at only 50 feet to lay his gunfire beneath the roofs of several low metal-walled buildings, which appeared to have been abandoned by their Japanese landlords. In a way, it all seemed too easy.

While pulling out of one low pass to seaward, Stover saw in the gray dawn a moving mass in an open field. He fingered his trigger, ready to fire. Then he realized he was aiming at cows. Stover did not shoot, but several other fighter pilots did. The carnage disturbed Stover, though he was certain his comrades had fired in haste, too keyed up to stop themselves.

卐

As soon as the fighters had completed their strafing runs, Scouting-3's Douglas SBD Dauntless dive-bombers started dropping their 1,000-pound bombs along the coast and on the field. Many of the dive-bombers' rear gunners strafed buildings as the pilots pulled out of the bombing runs.

Lt(jg) Slim Russell watched the fighters leave and then pushed over against a dimly perceived gun emplacement 5,500 feet below.

As Russell dived, he fired his two cowl-mounted .50-caliber machine guns at the emplacement to suppress its return fire. As he neared the objective, however, he could see that there was no gun in the emplacement. The wind was blowing him away from his point of aim by then, but he decided to drop his 1,000-pound bomb anyway. Russell pulled the bomb-release toggle at 1,800 feet and pulled out. The bomb hit about 100 feet off the beach, in the water, causing no visible damage.

As Russell chastised himself for the bad drop, he circled and came back at about 60 feet over Kukum to strafe houses and presumed supply dumps with his forward machine guns. He was so intent upon strafing that he almost flew into the water.

Next, Russell joined several other SBDs over Lunga and strafed there. After the first pass at Lunga, as Russell flew back over the coconut trees, he saw streaks of red tracer coming at him from out of the trees. He pulled up and the tracer all fell behind and below his dive-bomber. He cautiously climbed and then dived again to strafe the spot from which the fire had come. No fire rose to meet Russell on the way down, but red tracer chased his tail as he pulled up. He expended a great deal of his ammunition strafing the coconut groves, but was unable to observe tangible results.

Russell finally had to quit at 0720 and return to *Saratoga*. When he glanced around, he saw that he was alone except for a cruiser-launched observation plane and several carrier fighters. He turned back over Guadalcanal and flew south to the ship. On the way, he noted how very rough the interior of the island appeared. Great rolling hills and mountains covered with dense green foliage were interspersed with occasional meadows beside which islanders had built tiny villages.

When Russell landed, everyone looked at him with wonderment. They all thought that he had spun into the water on takeoff. The searchlight Russell had thought was trying to pinpoint a submarine was actually trying to pinpoint a Dauntless that had indeed spun in. It turned out that an SBD two places ahead of Russell had been lost. Its pilot and radioman-gunner were never found.

࿕

Most of the early-morning aerial effort against Guadalcanal was wasted. Japanese laborers and a very small force of armed bluejackets drawn from the small naval-infantry force based at Lunga and Kukum ran from their bivouacs and the airfield construction site as soon as the shelling and strafing began. There were no land-based Japanese aircraft in the eastern Solomons; the Lunga airfield's first contingent of land-based warplanes was not due to arrive for another week. Air strikes from *Wasp* destroyed the only Japanese airplanes in the region, a few float fighters and amphibian reconnaissance bombers based at Gavutu.

Slim Russell grabbed a sandwich and a cup of cocoa while Scouting-3's twelve operational dive-bombers were being rearmed and refueled. After taking off at 0930 and circling over Kukum and Lunga for two hours, four Scouting-3 SBD dive-bombers struck an ammunition dump with 1,000-pound bombs and blew it up. Russell's second 1,000-pound bomb of the day was dropped into a wooded area, where it burned up two large tents and knocked down a frame building. Russell returned alone to *Saratoga* at about noon and turned in for a nap after eating lunch.

Smokey Stover returned to *Saratoga* from his early-morning strafing mission without incident at 0730. After his fighter was refueled and rearmed, he took off at 0930 to fly combat air patrol over the carriers. He thus missed the opening air battles over the eastern Solomons.

3

R abaul had little on which to go.

Moments before Allied cruisers opened fire on August 7, Tulagi Island's radio station transmitted a brief, perplexing message: "Large force of ships, unknown number or types, entering the sound. What can they be?"

RAdm Sadiyoshi Yamada, commanding the Imperial Navy's land-based 25th Air Flotilla, presumed that Tulagi was being raided, so he sent out a long-range reconnaissance bomber to investigate.

Before the reconnaissance could be completed, Tulagi sent a second—final—message: "Enemy forces overwhelming. We will defend our posts to the death, praying for eternal victory."

Bomber and fighter squadron leaders and air staff officers were summoned to Yamada's headquarters for a pre-strike briefing. LCdr Tadashi Nakajima, flight leader of the crack Tainan Air Group, perhaps the finest fighter unit Japan ever put into the air, vigorously protested that the 1,200-mile round trip to Tulagi and back was at the extreme range of his Mitsubishi A6M2 Type 0 ("Zero") fighters and could lead to the loss of half his command. A fierce argument ensued, but Admiral Yamada ordered the raid to commence: Twenty-seven twin-engine, land-based Mitsubishi G4M1 Type 1 ("Betty") medium bombers, which were scheduled to raid an Allied New Guinea base, would be sent against the mysterious invaders with eighteen of Nakajima's fighters.

The Tainan Air Group had been based at Lae, in northern New Guinea, for some months following its transfer from Formosa. There, the land-based naval aviators had honed their predatory skills against obsolete American fighters and bombers and their outclassed pilots and had moved to Rabaul only days earlier as a reward for their superlative performance. These were the men Lieutenant Commander Nakajima led down the dust-shrouded strip—an active volcano brooded nearby—on what was to be the longest round-trip fighter mission to that time.

卐

The Allied fleet in the eastern Solomons was amply forewarned. Paul Mason, a planter-turned-covert-observer, spotted the Japanese formation from his vantage point in southern Bougainville and radioed the news on a priority frequency: "Twenty-seven bombers headed southeast." The message was picked up at Port Moresby, New Guinea, and relayed to Townville, Australia, which boasted the strongest transmitter in the region. From Townville, the news was flashed to Pearl Harbor and, finally, to the fleet off Guadalcanal, which sprang to action.

卐

Seventeen Japanese fighters (one had aborted with engine trouble) and the twenty-seven Bettys came within range of American radars shortly after 1300, dead on time. While one "challenge" section of five Zeros led by Lt Shiro Kawai went in early to draw off the American fighter combat air patrol, the two remaining sections, under Lieutenant Commander Nakajima and Lt(jg) Junzo Sasai, remained impatiently tethered to the slower-flying Bettys, which were to execute high-level attacks on shipping with the 250-kilogram antipersonnel bombs meant for Allied ground targets in New Guinea.

Two four-plane divisions of Fighting-5 F4F Wildcats had been launched from *Saratoga* under the direction of Lt Pug Southerland at 1215 to relieve other fighters patrolling over the American invasion fleet anchorage between Guadalcanal and Tulagi. While Southerland was still enroute, four *Enterprise* Wildcats under Lt Lou Bauer, commander of *Enterprise*'s Fighting-6, were ordered by the fleet fighter direction officer (FDO) to fly to the northwest at an altitude of 8,000 feet; there were "bogies" out there, and Bauer was to intercept them as far from the anchorage as possible. Bauer did not know that the four F4Fs he left on station pending relief by Southerland were critically low on fuel and had to immediately depart. Other fighters were then being launched, but they were a half hour away.

Lieutenant Bauer's four F4Fs were nearing Savo Island—and heading toward the incoming Japanese strike—when they were ordered south, back toward the carriers. Bauer requested a confirmation, which he did not receive. Though puzzled, he had no choice but to comply.

Lieutenant Southerland's eight Wildcats arrived over the anchorage at about 1300 and at 12,000 feet. The sky above was overcast, all but precluding the visual sighting of the approaching Japanese, who were between 15,000 and 18,000 feet.

Minutes after reporting in to the FDO, Southerland's own four-plane division was ordered to the northwest. Minutes later, the second division, under Lt Pete Brown, was ordered to follow.

卍

Shortly after 1300, the Japanese bomber leader began a gentle descent through the clouds from 15,000 feet. He had been unable to see the transports, so decided to attack warships he and his bombardier could see near Savo Island. All twenty-seven bombers bellied through the clouds into clear daylight at about 1315. They were at 12,000 feet and only 500 yards from an astonished Pug Southerland, also at 12,000 feet and on a reciprocal heading.

"Horizontal bombers, three divisions, nine planes each, over Savo, headed for transports, Angels twelve [12,000 feet]," Southerland rattled off through his throat mike. "This division from Pug: Drop belly tanks, put gun switches and sight lamps on.

"Let's go get 'em, boys!"

The Bettys had opened their bomb bays, ready to attack the shipping below. Southerland dropped his fighter into a low-side run from the left and fired several bursts from his six .50-caliber wing guns at the leading bomber squadron. As he hurtled by, he aimed at the right nine-plane squadron and fleetingly fired into it from longer range. He was soon able to fix his aim upon a bomber in the rear squadron, to the left again, and saw his bullets start a fire in the fuselage just forward of the open bomb bay. Japanese bullets cracked the glass bulletproof windscreen in front of Southerland, and an incendiary round started a fire behind his cockpit. Southerland banked around to execute a low-side attack upon the trailing division. He used up all his remaining ammunition smoking another Betty, but he could not finish it off, nor could he hang around in his smoking F4F to see what happened to the Japanese bomber.

The other three Wildcats in Southerland's division were jumped by Lieutenant Kawai's five challenge fighters before they could attack the bombers. Kawai had missed seeing them as he passed over Savo at 15,000 feet, but he retraced his route just in time to catch them as they followed Pug Southerland against the Bettys. Ens Don Innis saw Kawai coming a split-second before the attack was sprung, and he took defensive action, shaking his assailants in the clouds after suffering some damage.

Lt Pete Brown's Fighting-5 division was moving to aid Southerland's two remaining F4Fs when Brown spotted the bombers, which were his primary targets. He was turning into a favorable attack position when his division was beset by at least five Zeros from Lieutenant Commander Nakajima's section, and possibly two from Lieutenant Sasai's. Meantime, however, Southerland's two remaining Wildcats were downed, their pilots lost.

While Brown and Ens Foster Blair parried the Zeros, Brown's second element pressed on after the Bettys. After becoming separated from Blair, Brown claimed two Zeros before damage to his Wildcat and a painful hip wound forced him from the sky. He barely made it home to *Saratoga*. Blair ran for cover in the clouds.

The Bettys released their bombs at 1320. As they did, Lt(jg) William Holt and Ens Joseph Daly, of Brown's division, roared through the Zeros and delivered a diving high-side attack upon the bombers, then pulled up to attack again. The Zeros, just barely under Lieutenant Commander Nakajima's control, regrouped and went after Holt and Daly. As they did, Ensign Blair rejoined the fight by attacking the bombers. Holt and Daly destroyed two of the Bettys, and Blair severely damaged another, but Holt and Daly were both downed by Zeros, and Blair was forced to run for home. (Daly, with nine bullet holes in his leg and second-degree facial burns, was rescued by cruiser *Chicago*, and Holt was picked up by destroyer *Jarvis*.)

The combination of the fighter attack, the altitude, and the number of moving targets below threw the Japanese bombardiers off their game. No real damage was done.

卐

Lt Pug Southerland was diving through 11,500 feet on his way out of the fight when he was attacked by a lone Zero. As the Japanese pilot executed repeated firing passes, Southerland cranked his seat down and hunched behind the armor plate at his back. Then he went to work on his guns, which he thought were empty, but which he hoped had merely jammed during his last firing pass on the Bettys.

By this time, the Zero was attacking from the starboard quarter, so Southerland pushed over as though diving to escape him, then immmediately pulled out, cracked his landing flaps, and pulled his throttle to low power. When the Zero overran the suddenly slowing Wildcat, as Southerland had hoped he would, the Japanese pilot made a climbing turn to the left. Southerland easily turned inside the Zero and saw that an aviator's dream had come true; he had a Zero at close range and perfectly lined up in his gunsight for an easy quarter-deflection shot. However, when Southerland pressed the trigger, nothing happened. He would have to fight the rest of the battle unarmed.

Then two fresh Zeros joined the attack on Southerland. The three Japanese repeatedly dived at Southerland in changing pairs,

firing first from one side and then from the other. Pug Southerland's job now merely consisted of determining which of the rotating pairs of Zeros attacking almost simultaneously on either quarter
was about to open fire first and then sharply turning toward it as it
opened up. This gave the firing Zero a full deflection shot so that it
invariably underled the Wildcat. Countless bullets struck the Wildcat's fuselage from cockpit to tail but did little serious damage. The
Wildcat's quick evasive turns also placed the second Zero directly
astern so that Southerland was adequately protected by the armored back of his seat. When the Zeros' runs were not quite simultaneous, Southerland would rely on his armor, placing the attackers
directly aft in succession as they made their runs.

APı Saburo Sakai was one of Japan's three top-scoring aces. It
was Sakai who had shot down the B-17 of U.S. Army Air Forces
Capt Colin Kelly eight months earlier in the Philippines, giving
America her first war martyr. This day, he was leading Lt(jg) Junzo
Sasai's second element above the Bettys.

As Sakai joined on Sasai at 12,000 feet, he noted that his two
brash, young wingmen were gone, no doubt drawn to the action
against Holt, Daly, and Blair. As Sakai scanned the sky in the hope
of spotting the errant pilots, he saw that three Zeros were trying to
down a lone American Wildcat. Sakai spotted the melee just as two
of the swift Zeros overtook and passed the slower Wildcat. It
seemed to the ace that the Wildcat was winning the fight, so he flew
up alongside Lieutenant (jg) Sasai and motioned for permission to
join the action. Sasai nodded.

Saburo Sakai fired his Zero's two 7.7mm cowl-mounted machine guns and two 20mm wing-mounted automatic cannon from
over 600 yards, more to distract Pug Southerland than in the hope
of destroying him. Southerland countered with a mock attack,
snapping into a tight left turn to disrupt Sakai's firing run.

Where the other three Japanese had hunted Pug Southerland
with superior firepower, Saburo Sakai hunted with his Zero's superior maneuverability. Two superb airmen were pitted against each
other, but the battle was unequal, for Sakai was armed and Southerland was not.

This was Sakai's first encounter with the F4F Wildcat. He had routinely been shooting down Chinese, Dutch, and American Army Air Forces pilots for five years—fifty-six kills claimed thus far—but he had yet to meet anything like the rugged Grumman carrier fighter he was taking on this day. He repeatedly maneuvered into superior attack positions only to find himself outmaneuvered by the slower but deftly handled Wildcat. Sakai pushed five separate attacks against Southerland but did not fire a round because he knew his bullets would not down him. Since Sakai did not know that Southerland had no bullets left, he remained cautious lest he fall under the Grumman's mangling .50-caliber guns. However, when Southerland tried to pull out of the fight after Sakai's fifth abortive attack, the Japanese pilot realized that the Grumman was not in fighting condition.

All Southerland wanted to do was get over friendly territory and bail out of his stricken fighter.

Sakai withheld his killing pass long enough to snap a photo of the Grumman with his Leica camera. Then he took careful aim and fired 200 7.7mm rounds from only 50 yards. Amazingly, though few of the bullets could have missed, and the Grumman seemed tattered and ripped to shreds, Southerland doggedly continued to fly toward Guadalcanal. Even more amazing, Sakai found himself hurtling over the suddenly slowing Grumman; Southerland was dead on Sakai's tail and could have destroyed the flimsier Zero if he had had bullets.

The riddled Wildcat was in bad shape but was still performing to Southerland's satisfaction. The F4F's landing flaps and radio had been put out of commission, a large part of its fuselage was like a sieve, and it was smoking from incendiary hits, though it was not on fire. All of the ammunition box covers on Southerland's left wing had been blown off, and 20mm explosive rounds had torn several gaping holes in the upper surface of the left wing. The instrument panel was badly shot up, the goggles on Southerland's forehead were shattered, the rearview mirror was broken, the windscreen was riddled, tiny drops of fuel were leaking onto the cockpit floor, and oil from the punctured oil tank was pouring down Southerland's right leg and foot.

At length, curiosity, along with his esteem for his dogged enemy, got the better of Sakai. He pulled up beside the American, whose rudder and tail were so much scrap. The two stared at each other as they flew straight and level, then Sakai surged ahead and signaled the American to come and fight if he dared. Pug Southerland shifted his stick from his right to his left hand and made what looked to Sakai like a plea for mercy. It was not. Southerland was preparing to bail out, and he needed his right hand to free his legs and body from his seat harness. Sakai chopped his throttle, dropped behind the American, and charged the pair of 20mm cannon in his wings. His finger lightly rested on the gun button, then pressed down.

The 20mm burst from Southerland's port quarter struck just under the Wildcat's left wing root. The fighter finally exploded, no doubt because of the gasoline vapor that had been collecting in the cockpit and fuselage. When Southerland felt and saw the flash below and forward of his left foot, he was ready for it. He dived headfirst over the right side of the cockpit, just aft of the starboard wing root. The holster of his automatic pistol caught on the canopy rail, but he immediately got rid of it without quite knowing how.

Saburo Sakai saw Pug Southerland fall away, trailing a huge silken canopy as he drifted toward the water. Seconds later, Southerland thudded to earth on Guadalcanal, several miles from the coast and many miles west of friendly lines.

卐

Lt(jg) Slim Russell, of Scouting-3, awoke at 1330 from his nap following two morning bombing missions and went up to *Saratoga*'s flight deck to see what was going on. Surprisingly, no one was working on the broad deck, and it took about a minute for Russell to find dozens of officers and sailors clustered around the carrier's antiaircraft gun galleries. Someone said that Zero fighters were overhead. *Saratoga* was nearing a storm front and the clouds were already very low, so Russell did not worry about Zero fighters. He walked past the Fighting-5 ready room and saw a naked form covered with blood. This was Fighting-5's Lt Pete Brown, who had just landed. Russell noted that Brown's Wildcat was badly shot up and that Brown had been hit in the fleshy part of the thigh and rump by an incendiary bullet. A medical corpsman told Russell that Brown's flesh was badly burned by white phosphorous. The corpsman opened up the inside of the pilot's leg, cut to the path of the bullet, and scraped out the fragments. It was a very messy job.

Of the eight Fighting-5 Wildcats in the two divisions Lt Pug Southerland had led off *Saratoga*, only three returned to the carrier: the severely wounded Lt Pete Brown, Ens Foster Blair, and Ens Don Innis. Two of the eight pilots were lost without a trace, Southerland was missing, and Holt and Daly were rescued by friendly warships. However, only Daly survived; Holt died when his rescue ship sank with all hands. Pug Southerland reached Marine lines with the help of an islander on August 10 and was air-evacuated to a rear-area hospital on August 12.

⇄

The fight over the fleet raged on as fresh American fighters came on station.

Lt(jg) Dick Gay, a former enlisted pilot with many years of military flying behind him, was leading his Fighting-6 division over Guadalcanal from the south when he was ordered by the FDO with the surface fleet to investigate antiaircraft bursts over the Tulagi anchorage. Gay's division was at 16,000 feet and flying northward over Guadalcanal's northern shore when all four pilots saw the telltale black puffs about 10 miles ahead and at about 13,000 feet.

Gay's wingman, Lt Vince DePoix, a sharp-eyed 1939 Annapolis graduate only a few months out of flight school, was the first to spot the riddled Japanese bomber formation over Florida Island as it was turning northwest for Rabaul. After trying unsuccessfully to attract the attention of his division leader, DePoix dived on several Zero escorts and the Bettys, which were at 12,000 feet. The interception was made over the center of Florida.

DePoix hurtled in at a relative speed of nearly 500 knots, fired a single burst while in range, sharply pulled up beneath the bombers, and pitched over to attack from astern. Another good burst struck one of the Bettys, which rolled away out of formation and crashed into the water north of Florida Island.

Meantime, Mach Howell Sumrall and his wingman, Mach Joe Achten, gained attack position over the bombers. Just as Sumrall commenced his attack, the light filament in his reflector gunsight burned out, forcing him to correct his fire on the fall of his tracer. Sumrall managed to smoke the port engine of the second bomber in the first section, and he caused extensive observable damage to the third bomber in the third section; he thought he might have severed the Betty's fuselage at the trailing edge of the port wing.

Sumrall pulled out directly below the bomber formation to throw off the aim of any belly gunners who might have been tracking him. As he recovered to get into position for another sweep through the bomber formation, he saw a Zero below, slightly to the left, and behind his Wildcat. It was clear to Sumrall that he would be under the Zero's guns before he could make the next run on the bombers. As the realization struck, the Japanese pilot opened fire. Sumrall kicked his F4F into a Split-S maneuver to force the Zero into a head-on run. However, one of the Japanese 20mm cannon rounds exploded in the Wildcat's fuselage just aft of the left wing. Sumrall immediately grabbed his microphone to alert the other Wildcat pilots, but the radio was dead. By then, Sumrall's cockpit was filled with smoke and he was unable to see a thing. Certain his fighter was on fire, he opened the cockpit canopy. The smoke immediately cleared to reveal that Sumrall was in the midst of four Zeros.

The four Japanese fighters worked Sumrall over for some moments, until Sumrall remembered hearing that a Zero's ailerons froze at speeds over 250 knots. To test the rumor, Sumrall went into a steep spiral to the left, which he reversed when his airspeed indicator nudged 250 knots. As Sumrall twisted to the right, he saw a huge cloud formation. Reasoning that the Japanese would assume he would make for the clouds, he pulled up into a climbing turn to the right from which he hoped to catch the Zeros as they passed his projected former diving turn. But the Zeros were gone; they had gone back to protect the bombers. By then, Machinist Sumrall was flying on his 27-gallon reserve fuel supply, so he headed toward *Enterprise* by the most direct route. He was concerned that solid 20mm hits in his wings—he could see great patches of ocean through the gaping holes—would affect the Wildcat's landing characteristics, but a quick test at altitude revealed that the abused fighter would behave.

In the meantime, Lt(jg) Dick Gay had smoked a Betty despite distraction from a pair of Zeros. Mach Joe Achten, Sumrall's wingman, got a good burst into one of the two Zeros from behind, but was prevented from seeing what happened because his F4F's wings and fuselage took solid hits from another Zero's 20mm cannon. Achten shook this assailant by diving for the thick cumulus clouds over Florida, but he eventually had to land his unflyable Wildcat in the water, from which he was plucked by a Navy transport. Gay's F4F was also shot up as he fled into the clouds. Lieutenant DePoix was wounded in the shoulder by a 7.7mm slug and his instrument panel was shattered as he, too, was driven into the clouds by swarming Zeros.

Gay and Sumrall safely landed aboard *Enterprise* and DePoix put down aboard *Wasp*.

रु

The next American aircraft to tangle with the Japanese attack group were five *Wasp* Dauntless dive-bombers that happened to be orbiting beneath the clouds above Tulagi Harbor. Ordered to top the clouds, see what was going on, and, if possible, break up the Japanese bomber wave, LCdr John Eldrige, commander of *Wasp*'s Scouting-71, pulled up. The mixed formation of Bettys and Zeros was climbing past 15,000 feet when Lt Dudley Adams, at the controls of the first Dauntless to top the clouds, fired on three Zeros from their left rear with the two .50-caliber machine guns mounted on his bomber's engine cowling.

The Zero-section leader was AP1 Saburo Sakai, just returned from his triumph over Pug Southerland. Sakai, whose fighter's glass canopy was punctured by one of Adams's rounds, whipped after the lone assailant and sent him down out of control. The Dauntless crashed into the waves. Adams was rescued by a nearby destroyer, but his radioman-gunner was killed. Lieutenant Commander Eldridge and the remainder of his flight withdrew back into the clouds before suffering further loss.

卐

Shortly after downing Adams, Saburo Sakai spotted eight *Enterprise* Dauntlesses under the command of Lt Carl Horenburger. The Dauntlesses were orbiting to provide on-call air support for Marines fighting on Tulagi and Gavutu.

Sakai and one of his wingmen mistook the distant dive-bombers for fighters, and they launched a stern attack, never suspecting that their quarry was armed with rear-firing twin .30-caliber machine guns.

Lieutenant Horenburger's radioman-gunner, AMM2 Herman Caruthers, was the first to see Sakai's approach. At that moment, he was passing the time communicating with AOM2 Harold Jones, another radioman-gunner, by means of Morse code hand signals—open hand, closed fist. When Caruthers signaled the approach of enemy aircraft, Jones spotted the Zeros 800 feet below and 3,000 feet astern his Dauntless. Suddenly, one of the Japanese fighters broke off, turned left, dived, and approached the Dauntless formation from underneath. Jones also saw a second Zero as it hurtled toward him from dead astern.

The Zero Jones saw approach the Dauntless formation from underneath was Saburo Sakai's wingman. The Japanese pilot approaching from astern—to within 300 yards—was Sakai. By the time Sakai had closed on Jones's dive-bomber, which was piloted by Ens Robert Shaw, he knew he had made an egregious error, but he was committed to the attack.

Ens Eldor Rodenburg was leading the first three-plane SBD section. As soon as he was made aware of the enemy fighters in the area, he closed up his formation as tightly as possible with a wingman on each wing and dropped back to a position slightly astern of and below the division leader. Lieutenant Horenburger was leading four wingmen—one on his starboard wing and three on his port wing. Both sections were in tight stepped-down formations. As soon as Rodenburg's move had concentrated the firepower potential of most of the Dauntless rear gunners, Horenburger led the formation in a gradual turn to starboard.

Sakai was coming in directly from astern, and he started firing when he was about 500 feet away from the rear SBD. A 20mm shell hit the vane of Ens Bob Gibson's 500-pound bomb, then ricocheted upward and exploded beneath Gibson's armored seat. To Gibson, the detonation felt like a swift kick in the pants, but he was unharmed. By then, several of the American gunners had responded with bursts from their twin .30-caliber machine guns. However, several others, including AOM2 Jones, could not initially bring their guns to bear on Sakai without shooting up the tails of their own bombers. When Sakai turned to the right and pulled up in order to avoid colliding with the SBDs, every rearseatman could safely fire. And all of them did.

At a distance of little more than 100 feet, AOM2 Jones saw Sakai's cockpit explode in a bright orange flame. The Zero's canopy appeared to be torn from its tracks, and Jones saw something fly out of the cockpit. He also got a clear look at Sakai's face, and saw that the Japanese ace's head had been forced back against the head rest. He had the distinct impression that the Japanese pilot had been wounded. The Zero pulled almost straight up and then fell away, trailing smoke, but Jones immediately lost sight of it as he swung his guns to bear on the Zero that was coming in from below.

Sakai's Zero began a vertical plunge toward the water. By incredible good fortune, Japan's leading ace overcame his severe head wounds and gravity to pull out at wavetop height and lurch for home. He later determined that the turbulence of the 7,000-foot dive must have extinguished the flames that threatened to consume his battered Zero fighter. Though severely wounded and nearly blinded from severe facial and eye injuries, Sakai struggled on to complete an epic 560-mile flight home in under 5 hours.

As AOM2 Jones fired at the second Zero, his attention was again refocused when his pilot, Ens Robert Shaw, announced over the intercom, "Stand by to bail out." Shaw told Jones that their Dauntless's controls were very sloppy and that he did not feel he could fly the airplane. Shaw fell out of formation and slowed the bomber while Jones surveyed the damage. He told Shaw with considerable relief that only the right half of the elevator was hit. Shaw decided to fly back to *Enterprise*, which was about 60 miles away. They made the slow return alone, and Shaw landed without incident.

Shaw and Jones were greeted by several medical corpsmen who had deduced from the condition of the Dauntless that they must have been badly wounded. The pilot and radioman-gunner climbed down to the flight deck without comprehending what the hubbub was about. The two extremely fortunate young men, who had not visibly suffered as much as a scratch between them, later learned that their SBD had been riddled by at least 232 rounds of 7.7mm ammunition. Three weeks later, Jones learned that a pain beside his left eye was caused by a pinhead-sized sliver of metal he must have acquired in his fight with Saburo Sakai.

卐

Six Fighting-6 fighters led by Lt Gordon Firebaugh, a former enlisted pilot with ten years' experience in fighters, had been launched from *Enterprise* at 1300, just as the Japanese formation was approaching Tulagi. Firebaugh's own four-plane division and a stray two-plane section found the retiring brown-green bombers as they passed over the southwest tip of Santa Ysabel Island, about 35 miles north of Savo. After a long, fuel-consuming chase to within attack range, Firebaugh split his force into two three-plane sections to mount simultaneous attacks on the bombers from the left and right.

RE Tommy Rhodes, Ens Bob Disque, and AP1 Paul Mankin attacked the Bettys from out of the sun, releasing their 30-gallon belly tanks as they approached. However, when Mankin discovered at the last moment that his vulnerable belly tank was still firmly affixed to his fighter, he stayed high to cover Disque and Rhodes.

After two runs—each of which caused a bomber to drop out of the formation but did not set it afire—Ensign Disque closed in on one of the Bettys again and got a solid hit on an engine or fuel tank. The bomber immediately trailed a long, bright orange flame with black smoke streaming behind it, but it continued on straight ahead in level flight.

Disque was so excited and entranced at the sight of *his* burning Betty that he pulled up parallel with it to look it over. He never thought about the nose, fuselage, and tail gunners, who were probably firing away at him. All he could think was, "If my dad could only see this!"

After a few moments, as Disque started to climb after the rest of the formation, he heard Mankin call out, "There's a Zero on your tail." Disque evaded the Zero's first pass and maneuvered him into a head-on run in which both pilots failed to score any hits. Then the Zero dived away and broke off.

Mankin and Disque headed back to the carriers on their reserve fuel. Disque landed aboard *Wasp*, which was the first carrier he came to and which, fortunately, was ready to recover planes. He ran out of fuel in the arresting gear. Mankin barely made it aboard *Enterprise* on the last of his fuel.

Radio Electrician Rhodes made one pass at the bombers, then continued through the formation to help Lieutenant Firebaugh and his two wingmen. The problem was that there was no sign of Firebaugh's element. Rhodes shot down one Zero in the course of some extremely frantic aerobatics and pulled his thoroughly riddled Wildcat into a friendly cloud until the heat died down. He later landed safely aboard *Enterprise*.

While the other three Wildcats had gone after the Bettys, Firebaugh and his wingmen, AP1 William Stephenson and Mach William Warden, had taken on three Zeros in a head-on attack. Firebaugh saw hits on one Zero's engine, then recovered to port in time to fire at a Zero that was chasing Stephenson. The Zero rolled away and Firebaugh was recovering in a near-vertical turn to the right when another, unseen, Zero put several rounds through his cockpit canopy and obliged him to pull away. As he did, he saw Stephenson crash into the sea. Suddenly, five new Zeros joined from starboard, and the Zero leader got onto Firebaugh's tail and repeatedly scored with heavy 7.7mm and 20mm bursts. Three more of the five new fighters attacked Firebaugh, and he returned fire in a wild melee, later claiming two kills. However, Firebaugh was burned when his cockpit was set ablaze, and he dived head-first out of the airplane. His spine was injured when his parachute deployed, and he landed in the water.

Machinist Warden had tried to follow Firebaugh through the initial attack, but his F4F sustained hits in the oil cooling system, which was soon ablaze. Warden dived to wavetop height and ran, but at least one Zero gave chase. Warden emptied his guns at the Zero, but his engine seized and he was obliged to land in the sea.

Firebaugh and Warden eventually reached safety, but nothing was ever again heard from Stephenson.

⁂

In the first aerial clash attending the first Allied offensive operation in the Pacific War, nine Wildcat fighters and one Dauntless dive-bomber were downed. A number of the Bettys that had been damaged but managed to fly away from Guadalcanal went down along the 600-mile return track.

⁂

A second attack developed at about 1430, when ten Rabaul-based Aichi D3A1 Type 99 ("Val") carrier-type dive-bombers went after the fleet. Four Fighting-6 fighters led by Lt Scoop Vorse caught three Vals on the way in and, though his wingmen were thrown off when the Vals dived, Vorse locked onto the tail of one dive-bomber and followed it down until it knifed straight into the channel.

Six other *Enterprise* fighters led by ChMach Don Runyon were on the way to Savo to take over the combat air patrol when black puffs from exploding antiaircraft rounds drew them toward Guadalcanal. Runyon dodged along the edge of the antiaircraft umbrella and fired at the nearest Val. He missed when the Val dived away, but one of his element leaders, AP1 Howard Packard, blew the flimsy fixed-gear warplane apart in midair.

Runyon leveled off almost immediately after passing the first Val and spotted another Japanese dive-bomber coming right at him. He fired as he pulled up his Wildcat's nose. At the same time, his wingman, Ens Dutch Shoemaker, launched a beam attack against the same target. The Val fell away, cartwheeled into the water, and brightly exploded on impact. Shoemaker relinquished full credit for the kill to Runyon, who next spotted a pair of Vals breaking into the clear at wavetop level. He got one and Ensign Shoemaker shared the second with Ens Earl Cook. Ens Harry March nailed a fifth Val east of Savo.

Two additional Vals were downed by antiaircraft fire from ships in the channel. Thus seven of ten Vals were downed over the anchorage. The three damaged survivors headed north, but all were too badly damaged or too low on fuel to save themselves.

Runyon, Packard, and March barely made it back to *Enterprise* on the last of their fuel. The other three pilots in Runyon's extended division—Shoemaker, Cook, and Mach Patrick Nagle—landed aboard *Saratoga*. Later that evening, Shoemaker, Cook, and Nagle were launched to help form a combat air patrol over the carriers. Shoemaker's Wildcat developed engine trouble and he was nearly shot down over *Enterprise* by a fellow Fighting-6 pilot who recognized his Wildcat at the last moment and led him to their ship. Cook and Nagle became lost and, though they both were reported as having completed successful water landings, neither was ever seen again.

۲۷

The only airstrike on August 8 comprised all of Rear Admiral Yamada's twenty-three remaining Bettys, nine Vals, and a strong Zero escort. The Japanese bombers, all armed with torpedoes, came in low and fast at 1156, evading American radar by dodging between high mountain ridges north of the target area.

Three *Enterprise* fighters led by ChMach Don Runyon picked up the first squadron of Bettys as it crossed the eastern tip of Florida so low that the propwash foamed the flat sea. Runyon dived on one Betty, which he missed, then pulled up and over to neatly drop another of the nimble bombers into the water. Ens Wildon Rouse got the Betty that Runyon had first missed, but was bounced by a Zero as he went after a second target. The Zero on Rouse's tail was itself chased by Ens Dutch Shoemaker. When the Zero veered to escape Shoemaker's guns, it flew directly into Runyon's sights and was hammered into the sea. Shoemaker immediately banked toward another Betty and downed it, bringing the score for the three fighters to five kills.

Warned that the Japanese were closing on the anchorage, four *Wasp* dive-bomber pilots prepared to meet them. However, a call for ground support left only one of them, Ens R. L. Howard, in a position to intercept. He dived through the Betty formation but forgot to turn on his gun switches, so could do no damage. When Howard turned back into the fight, his slow Dauntless was jumped by several Zero fighters. The Dauntless's radioman-gunner had a lively time keeping the other Zeros from his tail while Ensign Howard ran for cover. The remaining Bettys evaded fighter interception and pressed their attacks upon the shipping.

The crew of light antiaircraft cruiser *San Juan* at first mistook the Bettys for friendly planes, but gunners aboard *Canberra*, an Australian heavy cruiser, knew better and opened fire on them. Soon all the ships in the channel opened fire as the Bettys roared at them low over the water. The initial surprise was more than offset by the fact that the Bettys attacked the American fleet bunched up in one formation instead of from different angles.

For GM2 Jim O'Neill, aboard *San Juan*, the noise of the firing was almost overwhelming. From O'Neill's vantage point, the Japanese medium bombers were being shot down like ducks in a shooting gallery. *San Juan*, a modern antiaircraft cruiser, accounted for five of the Japanese warplanes. O'Neill clearly saw rounds from his own Oerlikon quadruple 1.1-inch pom-pom mount stitch a pattern across the Betty's fuselage, and then he saw the Betty explode.

At least thirteen Bettys and Vals were downed by the fleet before they could launch torpedoes. However, destroyer *Jarvis* was hit well forward by a torpedo, and a Zero damaged in the melee

33

dived into transport *Elliott*, setting her ablaze and causing her to drift aground.

In all, eighteen of twenty-three Bettys and at least two Zeros were downed without American loss. *Jarvis* was ordered to sail to safety alone under her own power. Lt Ralph Weymouth and Lt(jg) Slim Russell, of Scouting-3, flew over her just south of Guadalcanal's Cape Esperance on the morning of August 9, but she was never seen or heard from again. *Elliott's* crew was evacuated to a nearby transport and the ship was left to burn herself out.

卐

The bomber strength of the 25th Naval Air Flotilla—the only Japanese combat air unit in range of Guadalcanal—had been gutted in only two days of fighting. Though senior American air officers were proud of the showing, their aggressive young fighter pilots were generally downcast over allowing so many Zeros to escape, though the Wildcat was no match for the Zero and the Japanese fighter pilots were the best in the business.

卐

On the night of August 8, a Japanese surface force composed of seven cruisers and a destroyer attacked and thoroughly surprised two Allied cruiser-destroyer forces screening the invasion fleet from around Savo Island. In the resulting melee, four Allied heavy cruisers—*Canberra*, *Vincennes*, *Astoria*, and *Quincy*—were sunk or left in sinking condition, and a fifth heavy cruiser, *Chicago*, and several destroyers were damaged.

The Battle of Savo Island resulted in the precipitous withdrawal of the carrier task force and its escorts. And that obliged the amphibious flotilla and its escorts to withdraw to safer waters before as much as half of the supplies needed by troops ashore could be landed.

Though the invasion of Guadalcanal did not immediately set in motion the potential ultimate fleet confrontation of the war— desired by some and shunned by others, including the man on the scene, VAdm Frank Jack Fletcher—it did set in motion a series of stunning naval, land, and air confrontations. Among those were the third and fourth of history's five carrier versus carrier naval battles.

For the moment, however, all that was certain was that a reinforced division of U.S. Marines had been left ashore at Guadalcanal and Tulagi to fend for itself—without air or naval supports and within range of a major and burgeoning enemy aerodrome complex.

As a result of Admiral Fletcher's decision to avoid a confrontation he did not feel his warships or warplanes could win, the auspicious American aerial victory of August 7–8, 1942, was largely wasted.

PART II

Carrier Operations

4

The world's first true aircraft carrier, HMS *Furious*, launched the world's first carrier air strike against German Zeppelin sheds in northern Germany on July 19, 1918.

America's first true aircraft carrier, a converted collier, was recommissioned *Langley* on March 20, 1922, and designated CV-1 ("C" for carrier and "V" for heavier-than-air, a common designator for nongas-filled flying machines). During the six years it took the United States to build two additional carriers, *Langley* served as the test bed for the development of carrier-based air operations. Most of the techniques employed in launching and recovering carrier aircraft were developed and refined during *Langley*'s service as the U.S. Navy's only operational flattop.

While *Langley* pilots and aircrew were developing and learning their trade, the Navy was building two new fleet carriers. Both were converted from the newly built hulls of huge battlecruisers that were proscribed at the Naval Disarmament Conference held in Washington, D.C., in 1922. The first of the new electric-powered carriers to be launched was *Saratoga* (CV-3), which was commissioned on November 16, 1927. Less than a month later, on December 15, *Lexington* (CV-2) joined the U.S. Fleet. Both of the huge carriers were powered like the swift battlecruisers they were originally intended to be; both could run at nearly 35 knots (more than double *Langley*'s top speed of 14 knots). Moreover, both of the new carriers were large enough to operate at least seventy-five warplanes from their 800-foot-long, 160-foot-wide armored steel flight decks, and both were capable of moving huge distances between refuelings. Both were considered strategic weapons of the first order, and their appearance on the high seas carried the potential for U.S. naval aviation well into the late first half of the twentieth century.

Only two years after *Lexington* and *Saratoga* joined the Fleet, the Navy authorized construction of a small fourth carrier, *Ranger* (CV-4), which was to be the namesake of a line of inexpensive but numerous new constructions. Though *Ranger*, which was commissioned in 1934, was the first American carrier to be designed as such from the keel up, her marginal performance (top speed of 29 knots, deficient arresting gear, and elevators between the flight and hangar decks that did not quite fit the bill) forced naval architects to opt for larger, more expensive carriers that could do the job required of them.

The designers amassed all the information that could be gleaned from the four previous efforts and, in 1932, the Navy requested two new swift 20,000-ton carriers. Though the original request was turned down by Congress, the 1933 naval appropriations budget contained authorization for two slightly smaller but thoroughly modern fleet carriers.

The new ships, *Yorktown* (CV-5) and *Enterprise* (CV-6), were to be the prototypes for most of the fleet-type aircraft carriers that eventually carried the U.S. Navy through World War II. There were numerous changes made along the way, but the *Yorktown*-class carriers set the pace.

Each of the new carrier decks was constructed of teak or Douglas fir laid over a steel frame (similar to *Langley*'s and *Ranger*'s, but unlike *Lexington*'s and *Saratoga*'s armored steel flight decks). Both could get up to operational speeds of 32 knots, and both had plenty of built-in underwater antitorpedo protection. The underwater protection was considered crucial for avoiding and defeating submarine- or air-launched torpedoes, and the high speed would aid in the launch and recovery of airplanes as well as in the avoidance of torpedoes and bombs. Each new carrier had three built-in elevators to speed the stowing and readying of airplanes between the flight and hangar decks. And both were fitted out with numerous anti-aircraft weapons—up to 5-inch guns—mounted in gun galleries edging the flight deck. Each of the new carriers was capable of operating approximately seventy-five warplanes.

Langley was downgraded to tender status in 1934, which allowed the United States to replace her within the 135,000-ton allowance provided for fleet carriers under the 1922 arms-control treaties. The lobby that had brought forth *Ranger* as a precursor of small, inexpensive carriers got another chance. Thus the seventh U.S. carrier, *Wasp* (CV-7), was something of a throwback. She was a vastly improved *Ranger*-type carrier, capable of operating a full seventy-five-plane air group (the standard of the day) as efficiently as her larger sisters. Numerous delays and ongoing upgrades prevented *Wasp* from joining the Fleet until 1940.

The 1922 Washington Naval Disarmament Treaty lapsed at the end of 1936, but the U.S. Congress did not authorize any new carrier constructions until 1938, when a third *Yorktown*-class carrier, dubbed *Hornet* (CV-8), was more or less forced upon a Navy that, strangely, desired no new carriers. *Hornet* was commissioned on the eve of the Pacific War. A much improved ninth fleet carrier, *Essex* (CV-9), was authorized in 1938, but due to ongoing design changes she and the rest of her new class would not begin to appear until 1943.

The need for other types of carriers besides standard fleet carriers was seen, but little was done before the outbreak of the Pacific War to get the new types into service. One type was the "light" carrier (CVL), but none was in service by mid-1942. "Escort" carriers (CVE) were also authorized, and the first of these, *Long Island*, was commissioned in June 1941. She was seen as an aircraft ferry and convoy escort, and her type would have been useful on all the war-torn oceans from the first day of the war on. However, numerous delays associated with ironing out bugs in a new system resulted in a slow start on new construction.

Other world powers experimented with carriers during the interwar years. The Royal Navy, which was the first to use carrier air power, built just three carriers between the wars, but had four modern carriers under construction when war broke out in Europe in 1939. The Germans started to build one carrier, but she was never completed.

The U.S. Navy's only real competitor in the field of carrier-based aerial operations was Japan, a maritime nation whose position in the world depended utterly upon the strength of its Imperial Navy. Shackled like the U.S. Navy to the restrictions of the 1922 naval disarmament accords, Japan was allotted tonnage in each category of warship at a rate only 60 percent of that allotted the United States. Thus the Japanese concentrated on getting more bang for the ton than did the Americans.

Japan's first true carrier, tiny *Hosho*, which weighed in at only 7,470 tons, was commissioned in 1922. Like *Langley*, she served as the test bed for future constructions and the proving ground for Japanese carrier flight operations.

Japan's next two carriers—*Kaga* and *Akagi*—were built upon the incomplete hulls of proscribed battlecruisers—just like *Lexington* and *Yorktown*. *Kaga* weighed in at 38,200 tons and *Akagi* displaced 36,500 tons. (*Lexington* and *Yorktown* were each rated at 36,000 tons.) However, the Japanese announced that each of the new carriers was rated at 26,900 tons, thus saving the Imperial Navy 21,000 tons in its overall carrier construction allotment.

Neither of the big Japanese carriers had a superstructure, which was a familiar feature of nearly all American carriers. Both also featured innovative upper and lower flight decks, which allowed for more rapid or simultaneous launch and recovery of airplanes. On the negative side, the two giant Japanese carriers could each operate air groups of only sixty warplanes, as compared to the American standard of seventy-five warplanes per carrier air group. (*Kaga* and *Akagi* were both extensively remodeled between 1935 and 1937 to increase their capacities to ninety warplanes each.)

The fourth Japanese carrier, *Ryujo*, was completed in 1931. At 10,600 tons, she was rated a "light" carrier (CVL in U.S. naval jargon). She was capable of operating forty-six warplanes.

Hiryu and *Soryu* were authorized at 10,050 tons each when their keels were laid, but they wound up weighing in at 17,300 and 15,900 tons, respectively, when they were launched following the expiration of the terms of the 1922 naval disarmament accords. They were similar in many ways to their contemporaries, the American *Yorktown*-class carriers.

Following the termination of the naval construction accords, Japan went into the business of building floating gunnery platforms—battleships and large cruisers. She did so pretty much at the expense of new carrier constructions. While geared up to almost manic levels, the Japanese shipbuilding industry was severely limited in its ability to churn out new ships. Rather late in the game, when some spare capacity became available, the Imperial Navy placed orders for a pair of thoroughly modern new carriers. These were *Shokaku* and *Zuikaku*, both rated at 26,675 tons, about 5,000 tons larger than the American *Yorktown*-class carriers. Each of the new Japanese carriers could steam at 34 knots (versus 32 for the *Yorktown*) and could operate ninety-six warplanes (versus seventy-five for all the American fleet carriers). *Shokaku* was commissioned on August 8, 1941, and *Zuikaku* was commissioned on September 25—just months before their air groups participated in the Pearl Harbor attack along with the air groups from *Kaga*, *Akagi*, *Hiryu*, and *Soryu*.

Smaller Japanese carriers available on December 7, 1941, included light carriers *Hosho*, *Ryujo*, *Shoho*, and *Zuiho*, and escort carrier (CVE) *Taiyo*.

⛩

The United States began the war with six operational fleet carriers and one operational escort carrier—plus several hybrid conversions used for ferrying work. Japan opened the war with six fleet carriers, four light carriers, and one escort. The opponents traded light carrier *Shoho* for fleet carrier *Lexington* at the Coral Sea on May 7, 1942. That trade accrued some additional advantage to the Japanese side in numbers of carrier decks, tonnage, and numbers of operational carrier warplanes. Midway more than redressed the imbalance. There the U.S. Navy lost *Yorktown*, but Japan lost fleet carriers *Kaga, Akagi, Hiryu,* and *Soryu.*

The U.S. Navy was left with four operational fleet carriers and their air groups, and Japan was left with two fleet carriers, three light carriers, and one escort. Two new Japanese fleet carriers were about to be commissioned, but neither would be fully operational for some months. Similarly, several light and escort carriers under construction or about to be launched could not be operational before the end of the year.

5

U.S. and Japanese fleet carrier air groups in mid-1942 each comprised three basic warplane types: torpedo/vertical bombers, scout-/dive-bombers, and fighters.

The mix of airplanes within a fleet carrier air group reflected the similar—but not identical—offensive and defensive doctrines employed by the two warring powers.

The U.S. Navy's standard fighter of the period was the Grumman F4F-4 Wildcat. First employed at Midway as a replacement for the underpowered F4F-3 variant, the F4F-4 featured six .50-caliber wing-mounted machine guns, a fairly modern gunsight, diminished performance characteristics, and, as important as anything else, folding wings. While the enhanced fighting characteristics improved the chances of individual fighters to triumph and survive in aerial combat, the innovative folding wings simply allowed the U.S. Navy to pack more Wildcats aboard the fleet carriers of the day. On August 7, 1942, the three fleet carriers available at Guadalcanal operated a total of ninety-nine operational Wildcats.

Basically a defensive weapon, carrier-based Wildcats were designed to accompany carrier-launched bombers to their targets in order to fend off enemy fighters. They were also used to patrol above friendly carriers to fend off submarines and enemy air strikes. Providing ground strafing during hit-and-run raids of the type that had characterized carrier operations early in the war was a distinctly secondary role of the Wildcats, with an emerging role in the field of direct support for the forces ashore.

The U.S. Navy's standard scout- or dive-bomber of the day was the Douglas SBD-3 Dauntless, which entered active service with the Marines in mid-1940 and became operational in the Fleet in March 1941. It had a top speed of only 250 miles per hour, but it boasted a substantial search radius (350 nautical miles), and its strike radius was 300 nautical miles. Its payload was usually a 500-pound bomb or depth charge on patrol and a 1,000-pound bomb on a strike mission. The extremely maneuverable SBD-3 was well adapted to defending itself with two forward-firing, cowl-mounted .50-caliber machine guns fired by the pilot and two .30-caliber machine guns mounted on a free-moving frame fired by the rear-facing radioman-gunner.

Designed as an offensive dive-bomber and a long-range scout, the SBD was typically employed close to a friendly carrier deck for antisubmarine defense. In extreme cases it had been employed early in the war against incoming air strikes, as a surrogate fighter—a doctrine that was quickly dropped.

The third and newest U.S. carrier type was the Grumman TBF-1 Avenger torpedo bomber. The Avenger was just coming into operational service in early June 1942, so only six had been used at Midway, and they had all been land-based. By far the largest carrier-based airplane type of mid-1942 and indeed of the Pacific War, the TBF was sturdy and long-ranged. The first carrier pilots to fly the Avenger operationally loved it for its ability to get into the air fully loaded long before running out of flight deck. The crew of three had adequate, if not ample, defensive firepower; the pilot could fire one cowl-mounted .30-caliber machine gun through the propeller disk, the radioman could fire a single power turret–mounted .50-caliber machine gun, and the bombardier could fire a single tunnel-mounted .30-caliber stinger across the lower rear quadrant.

Used offensively, the Avenger could carry one aerial torpedo or up to four 500-pound bombs in its innovative internal bomb bay. It was also designed to fill in as a long-range scout and was often employed in tandem with SBDs. The TBF's only reasonable defensive role was on patrol against submarines, in which case it could carry up to four 500-pound aerial depth charges.

⚛

The Japanese fleet fighter of the day was the Mitsubishi A6M2 Zero. This fast but very small and lightly built long-range airplane was, in its early career, simply the finest fighter available to any of the world's military powers. Its edge was its extreme maneuverability and extremely high rate of climb. Simply stated, in a one-on-one fight, the Zero could almost always get away from nearly any adversary in the skies.

The Zero was armed with a pair of wing-mounted 20mm cannon and a pair of cowl-mounted 7.7mm machine guns. The two sets of guns could be fired separately or together. Usually, the cannon were used sparingly because of limitations in the number of 20mm rounds that could be carried and because of the weapon's relatively low rate of fire and low muzzle velocity. The 7.7mm guns were used at longer ranges while the 20mm cannon were used only for killing blows. In general, the carrier-based Zeros were used the same way as their American counterparts: for escorting bombers and to defend friendly warships under attack by enemy aircraft. However, because the Zero was longer ranged than the Wildcat, it almost always accompanied carrier-launched bombers while the Wildcat did so far less frequently.

The Japanese counterpart to the American SBD was the Aichi D3A1 Type 99 Val "carrier bomber." (Name designations such as "Val" were not universally employed until late 1942, but they are used here for convenience and familiarity.) The Val, which became operational in 1939, could lug a single exterior-mounted bomb of up to 370 kilograms (816 pounds) 1,250 miles at a cruising speed of just under 250 miles per hour. Unlike its American counterpart, the Val featured neatly spatted fixed landing gear. Its usual combat dive

47

was undertaken at an angle no greater than 60 degrees (as opposed to SBD's steeper, faster 70-degree dive).

Crewed by a pilot and radioman-gunner, the Val's defensive armament consisted of a pair of cowl-mounted 7.7mm machine guns and a single rear-facing flexible 7.7mm machine gun. Like the SBD, the Val was employed on scouting, dive-bombing, and anti-submarine missions.

The Nakajima B5N2 Type 97 Kate "carrier attack" bomber was accepted for fleet operations in 1937 and was thus a full generation older than its American counterpart, the TBF Avenger. A highly innovative model when first introduced, the Kate was a low-wing monoplane with retractable landing gear capable of lugging the superb 1,764-pound Type 91 21-inch aerial torpedo at relatively high attack speed. It had a 1,000-mile-plus range.

The Kate's three-man flight crew occupied a single cockpit covered with a distinctive, very long greenhouse canopy. The Kate's only defensive armament was a single 7.7mm flexible machine gun manned by the rear-facing radioman gunner. Neither the pilot nor the man in the middle, the bombardier, had anything with which to contribute to the defense of the airplane.

卍

Other naval aircraft types that might be available to either side were noncarrier-based scouts, bombers, and patrol bombers.

The American surface ship-based scout of the day was the flimsy, underpowered Curtiss SOC scout-observation plane. The SOC's main function was observing naval gunfire. Constructed mainly of fabric, and impeded in all but level flight by its bulky pontoon, the SOC was in no way qualified to defend itself against any form of aerial opposition.

The Consolidated PBY-5A Catalina amphibian patrol bomber, powered by a pair of powerful engines mounted on a distinctive "parasol" wing, had been successful thus far in the war—up to a point. This tender- or land-based patrol bomber could stay aloft at a cruising speed of 117 miles per hour over ranges of 2,550 miles. The PBY-5A was marginally capable of defending itself in a fight with its pair of .30-caliber bow-turret guns, a single rear-firing .30-

caliber stinger, and single .50-caliber machine guns mounted in each of two waist blister turrets. If nothing else, the Catalina had proven itself to be extremely rugged in the face of enemy attack, and it most often carried its crew—and vital information—home. When on patrol the Catalina could carry up to 4,000 pounds of payload, such as a pair of wing-mounted 500- or 1,000-pound bombs, or a pair of wing-mounted 500-pound depth charges, or a pair of wing-mounted aerial torpedoes.

The Japanese fielded a somewhat larger array of scouts, bombers, and patrol bombers, including several reliable, rugged reconnaissance floatplanes launched from surface warships or based alongside tenders. Several of the one- and two-place float fighters—including a nimble Zero variant—were capable of holding forth against Wildcats.

The Japanese premier long-range patrol bombers of the day were the Kawanishi H6K Mavis and brand-new H8K Emily four-engine flying boats. The Mavis featured single-mount 7.7mm machine guns in the bow, two side blisters, and an open dorsal position, and one 20mm cannon in a tail turret. The thoroughly modern Emily, which was just coming on the scene in mid-1942, could defend itself with five single-mount 20mm cannon—one each in bow, dorsal, tail, and two beam positions—and three 7.7mm machine guns—in two side hatches and a ventral hatch. The older Mavis was of startlingly flimsy, flammable construction while the Emily provided some armor protection, partially self-sealing fuel tanks, and a carbon dioxide fire-fighting system.

Unlike the U.S. Navy, the Imperial Navy made regular reconnaissance use of land-based bombers. Chief among these was the brand-new Mitsubishi G4M1 Type 1 Betty "land attack" bomber, which became available in very small numbers late in 1941 and which was only just coming into widespread use in mid-1942. The Betty—rated a medium bomber by Americans—was capable of carrying up to 1,000-kilograms of bombs (typically four 250-kilogram or two 500-kilogram bombs) or a single Type 21 aerial torpedo. The Betty had great range and speed and was extremely maneuverable. However, like most of the lightly constructed Japanese warplanes, the Betty was highly flammable and simply could not take much abuse in the form of a Wildcat's six .50-caliber machine guns. Its defensive armament consisted of two 7.7mm machine guns in the nose, one 7.7mm machine gun in each of two beam mounts, and a single 20mm cannon in a tail turret.

Thus, aside from scout types and the singular niche filled by the Japanese Betty, both navies deployed roughly equivalent aircraft in mid-1942. The Japanese had, by far, the better, more reliable aerial torpedo, and all of their carrier aircraft were faster and longer ranged than their American counterparts. On the other side, however, all of the American carrier models were by far and away more rugged and better armed than their Japanese counterparts.

卐

The organization of carrier air groups, squadrons, and smaller formations employed by the two sides was quite different.

American fighter squadrons, employing up to thirty-two airplanes each by mid-1942, were organized into more-or-less standing four-plane divisions of two two-plane elements each. Because of their limited range, Wildcat fighters were not ipso facto expected to undertake escort duties for air strikes; if enemy targets were well within the Wildcat's range, four or eight fighters might be sent along all or part of the way. Or none might be sent with the bombers. At all times during the day, four to eight Wildcats were aloft over the friendly carrier, and four or eight were ready to take off at short notice. Other fighters might supplement the bombers on antisubmarine patrol around the friendly carrier, though early in the war that standard practice had proven disastrous in a number of cases where there was a shortage of ready fighters to meet incoming attacks because of the attrition caused by using fighters for antisubmarine work.

American carriers depended mainly upon their own fighters to stave off enemy bombers. This meant that few fighters would be used to escort air strikes even against targets within the Wildcat's operational range. U.S. Navy surface ships accompanying the carriers could certainly put up formidable antiaircraft defenses, as could the carriers themselves, but the burden of defense fell upon a distant barrier of radar-vectored fighters whose primary mission was to fend off incoming enemy air strikes.

In the rapidly emerging, ever-changing doctrine of the period, the fighter division was to be the basic mutual-support element, its two two-plane elements operating as an integrated team, attacking enemy airplanes and defending themselves in tandem. The reality of swiftly moving aerial combat often resulted in the elements—and even the teams of element leader and wingman—becoming unglued. Training included all possible permutations, and every pilot could perform in every slot used in all formations up to a full squadron formation. No pilot was so senior that he could not take over the wing slot on a junior pilot if that was what the situation demanded.

SBD and TBF squadrons used as offensive strike forces were organized into flights of three planes each, and the flights were built up into six-, nine-, twelve-, fifteen-, or eighteen-plane units, depending on availability, the mission, and the array of targets. SBD airplanes and crews nominally organized into separate scouting and bombing squadrons were totally interchangeable. Since doctrine of the day called upon Dauntlesses to undertake arduous long-range search and close-in patrol missions, there was always a number of Dauntlesses that could not be launched for attacks either because they were busy elsewhere, had to be held back for other missions, or were down for maintenance. The same was essentially true for the less numerous Avengers.

The American scout and torpedo bombers were solid, maneuverable airplanes with enough firepower to hold off Japanese fighters, though not usually to defeat them. The standard stepped-down vee-of-vees formation employed on the way to and from strike targets was defensive in nature. Awesome firepower in the form of massed forward- and rear-firing machine guns presented attackers with a formidable deterrent. In a few cases, lone Dauntlesses had shot down Japanese fighters and bombers.

One overriding shortcoming of the U.S. Navy's carrier doctrine was that there had not yet evolved a means for smoothly combining and integrating the offensive *or* defensive capabilities of two or more carrier air groups operating together. Only the crudest control could be exerted by a carrier's fighter direction officer over his own defending fighter divisions. Handling more than one squadron at a time was simply beyond the capabilities of the crude radars and experimental fighter-direction systems then available. The same was true for coordinated air strikes. There was simply no means for having a designated strike commander oversee air strikes by more than a single carrier air group.

卍

The Japanese carrier air group (*hikokitai*) looked similar to its American counterpart, but it was doctrinally dissimilar in a number of ways, both in capabilities and outlook.

Japanese carrier-based fighters were organized into *chutai* of six to nine airplanes and then into *shotai* of three airplanes. The three-plane fighter *shotai* operated as a nearly inviolate unit, with a senior pilot and two wingmen. In most cases, one wingman was stationed off either of the senior pilot's wings, and just to the rear. Also, the *shotai* often operated in left or right echelon formations. In a left echelon, for example, the first wingman was stationed off and behind the leader's left wing, and the second wingman was stationed off and behind the first wingman's left wing. In most cases, also, the three launched coordinated attacks against targets selected by the senior pilot, and they operated as a team when on the defensive. However, defense was not one of the things the Zero fighter was built for, nor were Japanese pilots so much defense minded as they were finely honed predatory beasts.

In defense of their carriers, Japanese fighters did not have access to even the rudimentary carrier-based fighter direction enjoyed by the Americans. In general, their combat air patrols were smaller than the Americans' combat air patrols, but their deck-bound "ready" fighters could get to altitude a good deal more quickly than American ready fighters. Japanese carriers depended upon fighters to keep American bombers at a distance, but if the carrier group was away on a strike of its own, most of the fighters would be with the strike. Thus the burden of Japanese antiaircraft defense lay with the escort vessels. Strangely, the Japanese carriers themselves were grossly undergunned for a serious self-defense role, and few surface warships were ever designated to undertake close-in defense of the carriers.

Overall there were only eighteen to twenty-one Zero fighters available to each Japanese carrier air group, largely because there was no folding-wing variant available for denser storage. Offsetting this particular disadvantage was the habitual pairing of Japanese fleet carriers in offensive operations. Unlike their American counterparts, the Japanese fighter pilots were used to operating under the senior fighter command pilot—from any ship—in the air at the time of offensive or defensive operations. Only the smaller maneuver element, the three-plane *shotai*, was more or less structurally inviolate.

The Val and Kate squadrons were also organized into *chutai* of six to nine airplanes, composed of three-plane inverted vee-of-vees formations. As with the fighters—and unlike their American counterparts—Japanese offensive strike groups were highly flexible. Mixed groups from two or more carriers were often placed under the senior strike command pilot on the scene.

卐

In many ways, American fighter doctrine was superior in the defense and Japanese fighter doctrine was superior in the offense. And the more flexible Japanese strike doctrine was generally superior to American strike doctrine. Ultimately, however, any decision in a battle between carrier air groups would be determined by the size of the competing forces and by the staying power of the airplanes and the men who flew them.

6

Until 1935, all American officer pilots were Regular line officers, usually graduates of the U.S. Naval Academy, and all enlisted pilots (Naval Aviation Pilots, or NAPs—about 30 percent of all pilots) were specially selected from the Fleet. Since the U.S. Navy promoted only qualified pilots to command its carriers and carrier task forces, many senior officers, up to the rank of captain, attended flight school throughout the 1920s and 1930s.

When the Navy and Marine Corps vastly expanded their air strengths in 1934, it was realized that the pool of qualified Regular line officers could not fill all the available command billets, so the Aviation Cadet Act of 1935 provided for the selection and training of specially qualified Reserve pilots. Recruiting took place mainly among college graduates between the ages of twenty and twenty-eight. The initial AvCad course was extremely rigorous, including one year at flight school at Pensacola, Florida (465 classroom hours and 300 flight hours to qualify for wings). Once the AvCad earned his coveted Wings of Gold, he spent three years flying with the Fleet, ranked somewhere between warrant officer and ensign. The AvCad finally received his commission as a Navy ensign or Marine second lieutenant four years after qualifying for flight school. At the same time as he was commissioned, however, the early AvCad was placed on *inactive* status with the U.S. Navy or Marine Corps Reserve.

The AvCad program was substantially upgraded by the Naval Aviation Reserve Act of 1939. This provided for 6,000 trainees who would receive commissions upon completion of flight training at Pensacola and who would serve a total of seven years on active duty. AvCads who had earned their wings prior to the inception of the new act were immediately commissioned, and those who had gone on Reserve status were given the opportunity to return to active duty.

In 1940, Congress expanded the act to train enough pilots to man 15,000 Navy and Marine aircraft. On December 7, 1941, the Navy and Marine Corps had a total of 6,500 active-duty pilots. About half of them were AvCads trained at Pensacola or newer flight schools at Corpus Christi, Texas, and Jacksonville, Florida. In addition, many hundreds of AvCads were in the pipeline, days or months away from graduation.

As the AvCad program expanded alongside flight training programs for Regular officers and enlisted cadets, the vastly expanded needs of the day resulted in relaxed standards. Early in the program, only perfect physical specimens were selected (no dental fillings, no broken bones). This was to help reduce the pool of otherwise qualified applicants for a very small program. When more cadets were needed than the perfect-specimen pool could produce, some of the most extreme physical criteria were relaxed, and the educational requirement was rolled back to two years of college. As an added inducement, AvCads were to earn a bounty of $500 per year for four years, payable when they mustered out. Many a Depression-poor college sophomore signed up in the hope of earning enough in four years to pay his junior- and senior-year tuition bills.

At the same time that entry qualifications were being relaxed, cadets were required to weather fewer and fewer classroom and flight hours. Ultimately, the scaled-down 26-week course called for just 207 flight hours prior to commissioning and assignment to advanced specialized training. Even the speeded-up syllabus barely provided enough qualified—which is not to say "seasoned"—pilots to man the carrier air groups following the attrition resulting from the war's early carrier battles at the Coral Sea and Midway. Older AvCads, Regular officer pilots, and NAPs held the line as the new wave of AvCads, along with a sprinkling of qualified Regulars, learned the art of survival in the air—literally on the fly. In the weeks after Midway, more than one rookie pilot undertook his first real carrier landing as he was reporting in to his first operational squadron.

The American genius for mass training barely won the battle of time in the case of carrier-based combat pilots. But that particular genius had held the line. The same was not true for the Japanese survivors of the vicious early carrier battles.

卐

All Japanese officer pilots were graduates of Eta Jima, Japan's naval academy. However, since Japanese carrier captains and carrier-fleet commanders did not need to be qualified pilots, few older officers undertook the rigors of flight training. (A notable exception was Capt Isoroku Yamamoto, who was to command the Imperial Navy's Combined Fleet during the first eighteen months of the Pacific War.) Each young Eta Jima graduate was commissioned following a rigorous three-and-a-half-year course and before beginning flight training. Far from following the American model of decreasing flight training, the Japanese in 1940 lengthened their officers' course from about eight months to one full year. Also, whereas American pilots in the prewar years might be called upon to fly all types of airplanes available to the Fleet, most Japanese pilots specialized exclusively in fighters, single- or multi-engine bombers, or reconnaissance types.

Japanese enlisted pilots came either from the Combined Fleet, following several years' service, or they were recruited directly from the population. During the 1930s, the naval aviation community recruited many fifteen- and sixteen-year-olds, which obliged the Imperial Navy to undertake secondary education as well as flight training. An emphasis in selection was placed upon physical strength, coordination, and agility. Preflight training discipline was particularly brutal as a conscious means to weed out most candidates.

The selection, schooling, and training process was complete, but very slow. Belatedly, the Imperial Navy streamlined the system in August 1941, when it set a goal of training 15,000 pilots.

Most trained enlisted pilots entered an operational squadron with the rank Aviation Petty Officer 3rd Class (AP3). By the time the war started, some longtime enlisted pilots had been commissioned as special-duty ensigns, and many were warrant officers. By the time an Eta Jima graduate reached an operational squadron following theoretical and flight training, he was usually a newly promoted lieutenant junior grade.

By the time the Japanese enlisted pilot reached an air group, he had spent seven to nine months in flight training, including rudimentary instruction in his specialty. In that time, nearly two-thirds of his classmates had washed out of flight school. (Pensacola graduated about two-thirds of its cadets.)

⤵

The differences between the services became more pronounced at the operational level. Most American pilots were qualified to fly many aircraft types, though there was a trend toward placing an individual pilot in a specialty for which he had the most aptitude. The average Japanese pilot was specialized early in his training. American pilots were all selected for leadership traits while only Japanese officers and very senior enlisted pilots could lead other pilots into combat; the vast majority of Japanese enlisted pilots were merely taught to follow the leader.

The most important difference was the permanence of postings. Japanese rookie pilots were assigned to a particular air group, which served as his advanced training command. If the group happened to be engaged in combat, the rookie very often learned the finer points of his profession under the gun—or he died trying. If the rookie's air group had been gutted by combat losses—as was the case for many once the Pacific War got underway, but also during the long years of the so-called China Incident—there was a chance that he would rise to a key level of intermediate responsibility before he was quite ready. This tendency was not aided by the creation of many new carrier- and land-based air groups, which tended to siphon off many skilled senior pilots.

The rookie American naval aviator usually underwent advanced training in his specialty before joining an operational air group. For example, all fighter pilots honed their skills and flew the latest Fleet fighters at Opa-Locka, Florida. The fledgling bound for carrier duty would also train from several weeks to a month or two with an Advanced Carrier Training Group (ACTG). There he simply learned to take off from and land on a carrier deck (most often a simulated carrier deck superimposed on a land-based runway). If there was time, he stayed with the ACTG until he mastered carrier operations or, if he could not, until he was sent elsewhere, usually to fly multiengine planes.

As the competition for new pilots decreased after the Midway losses had been made good, the U.S. Navy began forming reserve carrier air groups. One of the first, Air Group 10, received a draft of battle-experienced veterans, some older pilots who had thus far missed combat (mostly due to training duties), and a large component of recent ACTG graduates. If everything went as planned, Air Group 10 would exchange places with a group already serving in the Pacific aboard a fleet carrier. There would always be a need to directly replace individual pilots lost in combat and operational accidents, but the reserve carrier air groups would provide young American rookies with the time and the place to learn the ropes from veterans. It was a golden opportunity most Japanese rookies missed.

The clear implication of the vastly different "polishing" phases was that the U.S. Navy was turning out pilots to spare while the Japanese were under the gun from the start. The Americans had staying power the Japanese lacked.

Of equal importance was that veteran American carrier pilots would eventually receive an opportunity to recuperate from the rigors of war cruises while the veteran Japanese carrier pilots would have to keep flying and fighting so long as their home carriers were in the war zone. Veteran American pilots could train rookies far from the sound of the guns, but Japanese veterans often could not. The potential for simple fatigue to have a negative impact on group operations was greater on the Japanese side. And, since the Japanese squadrons were manned by increasing numbers of raw fledglings, an increasing share of the burden inevitably fell upon the decreasing number of veterans. It was virtually impossible for the decimated carrier groups to draw experienced replacements—particularly command pilots—from land-based groups because of early and ongoing specialization in mission training.

If the war was not decided quickly—in a matter of months— the Japanese carrier air groups stood the better chance of simply being ground down.

7

The only reason for building, maintaining, and defending aircraft carriers was the mobility they afforded airplanes in moving across vast oceanic distances. The heart of the aircraft carrier and the carrier task force was air operations.

Prior to taking off on a typical search or combat mission, duty pilots gathered in their squadron ready rooms, which were steel cubes located in the deck just beneath the flight-deck level. They were like very small theaters with eight rows of four upholstered seats per row. On the forward bulkhead, to the left, was a teletype machine fitted out with a red typewriter ribbon. A large chartboard dominated the center of the forward bulkhead. On a table set against the rear bulkhead were a perpetually filled coffee urn and white enamel mugs. The room was perpetually hazy from cigarette smoke and was invariably dimly lighted. At night, the lights were red to prevent night blindness.

When a pilot was to leave for a search or patrol mission away from the fleet, the teletype clattered out a message to keep him abreast of the speed and planned course of the carrier, known magnetic variations, and other navigational data that would help him to a safe return.

If a long flight by all or most of the squadron was planned, the squadron engineering officer—a pilot with that additional squadron duty—might brief fellow pilots on how to get absolute maximum gas mileage by leaning out the fuel mixture to the point where engine temperature rose to the allowable limit.

In the event of a strike mission, the carrier's air officer—a senior pilot on nonflying duty as part of the ship's company—would usually come down from the bridge to cover special points and answer questions. As data continued to be updated via the teletype, individual pilots jotted down their own navigational notes on their plotting boards—16-by-18-inch navigational devices that fit under the airplane dashboard and that could be referred to and updated during flight.

Fighter pilots and the radiomen assigned to the bombers were given radio call signs and a schedule of frequencies and emergency bands for the mission and nearby bases.

When all had been said and done and it was time to leave, pilots and aircrewmen climbed from their separate ready rooms to the flight deck to man their airplanes—usually to the accompaniment of tinny voices sounding orders over the ship's public address system: "Pilots, man your airplanes."

卐

Once on the flight deck, a mission pilot might walk around his airplane to inspect it and the load of ordnance slung beneath it. Then he would climb aboard by way of the left wing. Once in the cockpit, the pilot shrugged into his seat and parachute harnesses, usually with a helping hand from his plane captain. Then he plugged in his helmet-mounted earphones and microphone. After a brief from the plane captain on quirks and potential problems—invariably followed by a thumbs-up for luck from the man who would stay behind—the pilot waited for clearance to run up the engine to check it and the magnetos. If there was a problem and the plane had to be scrubbed from the mission—the decision was the pilot's—the pilot had to signal the plane captain and then shut down the engine. If that happened, plane handlers would swarm around the airplane in a race to get it out of the way before the launch schedule was totally destroyed. If all seemed well with the power plant and the electrical system, the pilot waited his turn until signaled by the plane director or his assistant to taxi the airplane forward to the takeoff spot. Within a few seconds, as the engine wound up to full power, he had to get his fully loaded fighter or bomber from a standing start to fully airborne within a too-few hundred feet. As soon as the airplane was steady on the takeoff spot, the pilot pushed the brakes with both feet and nudged the throttle forward with his left hand until the engine achieved maximum takeoff power.

At a signal from the deck boss, the pilot lifted both feet simultaneously from the brake pedals. The plane was rolling. To keep it steady, the pilot alternately nudged first one brake pedal and then the other while holding the stick steady with his right hand and pushing the throttle forward with his left hand.

To increase the lifting power of aircraft wings, the carrier invariably raced at high speed directly into the wind during the launching operation. Depending on how full the flight deck was, any given airplane would be able to use more or less than one-half the total length of the flight deck for takeoff.

Predawn or evening launches were always a thrill because, in addition to normal perils, carriers in operational areas showed no lights whatsoever on the flight deck or superstructure. The total darkness did nothing to enhance depth perception ahead or to the sides. About all most pilots had to guide on in predawn or evening launches was the flickering blue flames emitted from the engine exhaust stacks of the airplane just ahead. The SBD that spun into the water during *Saratoga's* predawn combat launch on August 7 was a fairly typical example of the attrition problem faced because of operational accidents.

Seasoned pilots with a decade or more experience in carrier flight operations were only just slightly less prone to operational accidents than the rawest novice. In addition to inexperience and exhausting schedules that often muddled judgment or slowed reflexes, careworn airplanes and the relative inexperience among the burgeoning groundcrew population contributed to high operational losses.

A fully loaded SBD with a 1,000-pound bomb, 400 .50-caliber rounds and 1,200 .30-caliber rounds, plus a full load of gas had a tendency to waddle down the flight deck and more or less fall off the bow of the ship. If by that point the airplane had not powered up to 65 or 70 knots of air speed, it simply was not a flying machine and would fall into the water.

At a moment only the inner ear could gauge, the pilot smartly pulled the stick in his right hand toward the pit of his belly to get the nose up. He was committed to flight.

If the plane did become airborne, the pilot immediately had to pull up the landing gear and flaps. These tasks—coupled with keeping the nose high and turning leftward away from the ship—were made more difficult by the need to accomplish both jobs more or less simultaneously through cross-handed actuation or by shifting the stick from one hand to the other and back again. Carelessly dropping the left wingtip into the water was a fairly simple accomplishment while undergoing these gymnastics, and the sudden drag that mistake generated would easily flip a fully throttled airplane into the water.

The Wildcat pilots had to turn a hand crank twenty-six to twenty-nine times to pull up the landing gear while fighting their airplanes' marked tendency to pull to the left because of high engine torque. Turning the hand crank usually caused the newly airborne Wildcat to wobble across short arcs until the landing gear was safely up and secured.

The Avenger pilots had the best airplane by far for carrier takeoffs. The huge-winged TBF was often airborne long before it reached the bow, and it was usually uphill all the way.

⇄

A typical daily mission for carrier scout- and torpedo bomber crews was a dawn or afternoon search for enemy vessels. Each search sector usually consisted of a wedge of ocean 200–250 miles in length covering 10 degrees of a 360-degree circle centered on the

63

carrier. Depending on the needs of the moment, anywhere from eighteen to thirty-six 10-degree sectors would be searched. And depending upon the availability of SBDs and TBFs, each pie-shaped sector would be searched by one or two airplanes.

The searcher had to know his position at all times, both as a means for returning safely to his ship and in order to accurately report the position of whatever he might encounter. Each searcher was typically armed with a single 500-pound General Purpose bomb, though his mission was less to engage enemy ships than to find, track, and report on them. Only in extreme circumstances or if the opportunity was too good to pass up was a search pilot to launch an attack upon an enemy ship—preferably an enemy carrier—and only after he was dead certain he had made an accurate report that had been received by a friendly vessel.

Most of the hundreds of weekly search sorties were simply boring. Most of the search pilot's energy went into scanning the endless sea and checking his position relative to his carrier, which was usually on the move to a position far from the point at which the searcher had been launched.

Usually the search pilot flew out from the task force right on the surface because climbing to altitude used up a great deal of fuel. In any case, it was impossible for the pilot to read the play of the wind on the surface of the ocean at over 150 feet. By knowing the strength and direction of the wind, the pilot could determine which way and how far the airplane was being blown off course. This was the only way he could go out up to 250 miles and expect to find his way back home with reasonable assurance.

All carrier planes had small radio receivers that could pick up homing signals 15 miles in every direction from the carriers. Depending upon the code the pilot and radioman could hear, the pilot could fine-tune his final approach to the left or the right to find the carrier. If an airplane flew past the carrier in bad weather or at night, the homing radio would tell him—if he was in range. The key to the system was letter signals; the pilot knew which way to fly based upon which letter he was receiving on the radio.

Once settled on the first search leg, the pilot could stop watching his compass and airspeed indicator to the exclusion of all else and look around. Indeed, the search pilot's main purpose was looking far and wide to see what was out there. If he saw anything of note on the search leg or cross leg—enemy ships or an inbound hostile airstrike—he was to report all the details to his ship.

The third, or intercept, leg of the three-legged pattern was the crucial leg. If all the navigational computations—mainly direction and wind speed—had been correct, the search pilot would find his way home to Point Option—the place the carrier will be up to four or five hours after the searcher was launched. In the words of Ens Fred Mears, of Torpedo-3, "If he has done his navigation correctly and Point Option has not changed without his knowing it, the fleet will appear at the proper time. If not, there is still only water and more water."

Once the carrier pilot found the carrier, he had to undergo the stress of landing upon what invariably looked to him like a short, narrow flight deck that was moving *away* from him at high speed.

As soon as the returning pilot visually acquired the carrier, he would wheel into the imaginary oblong landing traffic pattern down the port side toward the stern of the ship. If landing operations were underway, the planes in the landing traffic pattern would pace themselves to begin final approaches at 40-second intervals. Airplanes with fuel or mechanical problems would receive priority clearance if there was time.

Each pilot in the landing traffic pattern would tick off his prelanding checklist: Canopy back and locked (for quick escape in the event he somehow hit the water), fuel on rich mixture (for immediate added power if he suddenly needed to fly away from "the groove"), fuel coming in from the fullest internal tank (so his engine would not suddenly die from fuel starvation while his mind was on other matters), cowl flaps partly open (to keep the engine cool), prop in low pitch (so he could bite the maximum amount of air at the low landing speed).

If the checklist checked, he was ready to land.

He next found the required lever and dropped the tail hook. He had by then slowed his fighter to an indicated air speed of 120 knots. Next, he lowered his landing gear and landing flaps; the latter caused a slight downward pitching motion. As he slowly flew up the carrier's wake, right in the groove, his airspeed indicator should have registered the desired 90 knots, and the fighter should have been in a perfect nose-high attitude. The experienced carrier pilot was able to fly by feel alone, which totally freed his eyes to follow the motions of, to all carrier pilots, the most important man in the world, his landing signal officer (LSO).

In essence, a carrier landing consisted of a sequence of these phases: While the carrier sailed at top speed into the wind, the pilot lowered his airplane's tail hook and approached the flight deck from dead astern; guided by the LSO, the pilot lined up on the flight deck at just the right altitude and speed; if the LSO was satisfied that the airplane was in the correct position relative to the deck, he signaled the pilot to land; if the airplane was not in the correct position and could not be guided into the groove in the time remaining, the LSO would wave it off for another try; if the pilot was allowed to land, he quickly dropped to the deck in what can only be described as a controlled stall with the intention of catching the extended tail hook on any of the dozen stout cables running the width of the deck; if the tail hook caught a cable, the cable gave a bit while the airplane was forced to a rapid stop; if the tail hook missed all the cables, and if the deck was clear, the pilot simply gunned the engine and took off for another try; if the tail hook missed the cable and the deck was obstructed, the nose of the plane was arrested by a flexible barrier, which usually ruined the propeller but prevented a flaming collision between the airplane and whatever obstructions lay ahead.

Only the LSO could determine when an approaching pilot was ready for the carrier. He would signal his opinions with his two outstretched luminous paddles.

By that time, the pilot was going over part of the litany again: A one-second delay in cutting the throttle makes the difference between a normal cable-arrested landing and a crash on the flight deck. Never touch the throttle until safely on the deck. If you miss the cables, immediately push the throttle forward to acquire lift-off speed. If the airplane is properly arrested, cut power to the absolute minimum and taxi off as soon as the hook and the cable have been separated by a deck crewman.

The pilot had to totally concentrate on altitude, attitude, propeller pitch, throttle setting, landing gear, flaps, tail hook, the rapidly approaching LSO, and the tossing, twisting, postage stamp-sized flight deck.

The LSO stood tall in front of his protective windscreen on the port aft corner of the flight deck. A pilot who had once naïvely asked the LSO what the screen was for had received a sarcastic answer that the ship would be doing 18–20 knots, which, combined with a wind-speed factor of anywhere from zero miles per hour to infinity, usually created enough of a breeze to pitch a sturdy LSO into the drink. The dark-colored screen also aided the pilot in finding and following the motions of the LSO, who was invariably clad in light-colored clothing.

On the far side of the screen was the LSO's assistant. It was his job to see if the tail hook, landing gear, and flaps of the approaching plane were down. If so, he would yell above the wind, right into the LSO's ear, "All clear." Then he would turn to watch the deck as the landing plane hurtled past the LSO platform into the cable.

Many LSOs waved their paddles with a great deal of energetic flair, but most passed the standard thirteen landing signals in the straightforward manner. Ten of the signals told the pilot of some specific error in technique or procedure—wrong height, wings not level, approach speed too fast or too slow, even that the tail hook was not deployed or the main landing gear was not down. The remaining three signals were "Roger," "Cut," and "Wave-off."

Pilots wanted a "Roger" on the first pass. If the plane was correctly lined up, the LSO would hold his paddles straight out in front of his shoulders to signify that the airplane was in the groove—that the approach was satisfactory.

Just as the pilot sensed that his plane's nose was hovering several feet over the fantail, the LSO dropped his left arm to his side. Then his right arm lifted and the right paddle abruptly slashed across his throat. That was "Cut."

The pilot immediately chopped back his throttle and held the stick rock steady. The airplane was now in a perfect three-point landing attitude, which meant that all three wheels would strike the deck at the same instant. Things happened fast from that point.

There was literally nothing for the pilot to do; the laws of physics were running the show.

The pilot next felt the shock of the landing gear as they hit the solid flight deck. Then he felt the tail hook grab hold of the wire. If it was the first wire, the landing was perfect. The mass of the fighter rapidly decelerated and came to an abrupt no-brakes near stop. Immediately, the tension on the arresting cable eased, and the fighter's remaining momentum pulled it forward about 40 feet with the hook still attached. This brought the fighter to a slow, controlled stop. At that point, the pilot came under the direction of the deck crew and plane handlers. No more than five seconds had passed from "Cut" to the rolling stop.

Once the pressure was off the tail hook, the pilot and his airplane became the center of furious activity. A quick glance into the rearview mirror would reveal a deck crewman ducking beneath the tail to release the hook from the cable. At almost the same instant, another deck crewman took charge of the taxi routine by passing up his unique set of signals. First, on signal, the pilot retracted the tail hook. Then he had to get lined up with the centerline of the deck to get into taxi position. The vertical barrier, which looked like a large tennis net and was raised for all landings, was dropped as soon as the tail hook caught the cable. The instant the tail wheel was clear of the barrier, the obstruction was raised again in preparation for the next landing.

As soon as the airplane cleared the barrier, the LSO's assistant, who was standing with his back to the LSO, turned aft and yelled "All clear" into the LSO's ear.

If the recovery operation was perfect, the succeeding airplane was in position to take the "Cut" just as the previous airplane cleared the deck barrier.

Often, in a large landing operation, the LSO had to pass the "wave-off" signal to two or three pilots as they felt their way into the groove one after another. To pass this signal, the LSO simply waved both paddles over his head. The "wave-off" had the force of absolute law. Even if the pilot was in fact right in the groove and lined up for a perfect landing, he had to obey the "wave-off" signal, as there might be an emergency beyond his knowledge or range of senses—such as an imminent enemy attack.

On the way north to the Solomons, Ens Fred Mears, of Torpedo-3, had had to make an emergency landing aboard *Enterprise*. He was just completing an exercise torpedo run on the ship when his engine began to cut out for a second or two and then catch again. Mears thought there was a clog in the fuel line. After circling the ship twice trying to make the engine run true by adjusting the controls and having no success, Mears made an emergency pass down the starboard side of the ship with his tail hook down—the signal for a "delayed forced landing." The ship did not clear the flight deck so Mears circled again and passed down the port side, which is the signal for an "immediate forced landing." Only then did *Enterprise* swing into the wind. Ensign Mears got into the landing circle and began his approach. As Mears came up the groove, he was given a "Low" signal by the LSO. He added throttle, but the engine conked out again astern of the ramp. Then it came to life again just in time. The LSO gave Mears the "Cut," and the motor died as soon as the pilot chopped the throttle. The mechanics later told Mears that there was a stoppage in the carburetor. It was fortunate for Mears and his two crewmen that they were not hundreds of miles away over open sea when the engine began acting up. Too many of Mears's contemporaries had disappeared without a trace, no doubt because of "routine" malfunctions like the stopped carburetor.

⌇

Maintaining and servicing the warplanes of a carrier air group required endless hours of work by the dedicated ground crew.

AMM2 Bernard Peterson, who was awaiting word on his application for flight training, was in charge of the aircraft hydraulic and rigging crew for all of Torpedo-3's Grumman TBF Avengers. He had four seamen strikers working for him; they were younger seamen working their way up the rungs of the promotion ladder, trying to get their aviation machinist's mate ratings.

The permanence of the flight crews was fairly well established during a combat situation. However, during routine operations, many of the senior ground crew flew on training missions to qualify for standby air crew duty and to enable them to receive flight pay, a sort of reward for extra services. AMM2 Peterson had been trained as an alternate air crewman, but his maintenance specialty required that he spend far more time taking care of the TBFs than flying in them.

Typically, the commanding officer, executive officer, and flight officer of a carrier squadron had their own personal airplanes and crews. The junior officers usually flew any airplane assigned to them, often with a strange crew.

Each plane had its own plane captain assigned. That was *his* plane, and his plane only. He and the pilots who flew it would call upon the ordnance, engineering, and radio sections of the squadron for corrective action or maintenance, as required. The ship's company did the plane handling on the hangar and flight decks, plus refueling and respotting airplanes.

Most of the air crewmen in the torpedo, scouting, and bombing squadrons held radioman ratings, but a small percentage were aviation machinist's mates or even aviation ordnancemen.

Torpedo-3 consisted of approximately twenty-four pilots, fifty aircrew, four ground officers, and a nucleus of twelve ground crew. The scouting and bombing squadrons were slightly smaller because they rated fewer air crewmen. In addition to flying duties, everyone had certain ground or shipboard duties.

Nearly all the torpedo, bombing, and scouting squadrons had between twelve and eighteen operational airplanes at any particular time. Attrition usually occurred because of accidents and maintenance problems.

PART III

Preliminaries

8

Lt(jg) Slim Russell
Scouting-3

Diary entry of August 11, 1942

Yesterday we heard the Japs really pulled a fast one at 0300, August 9. The cruisers and destroyers of our outfit were convoying the transports out of the harbor. Suddenly, seaplanes were heard. They dropped flares around our fleet and enemy cruisers and destroyers pounded torpedoes into our outfit.

We had word that on August 8, at noon, an enemy fleet was approaching Guadalcanal from the northwest. At that time, it was only 240 miles away. Why our three carriers ran southeast—away from our fleet in harbor— is something I can't understand.

The cruisers *Vincennes*, *Astoria*, *Quincy*, and *Canberra* were sunk. The Jap losses? We have not heard a word and probably never will.

I believe there are too many heads running this show.

And too-old heads at that. Let's kick them out. A dark page in U.S. Navy history.

We have pulled back to a spot halfway to New Caledonia to refuel. The [heavy cruiser] *Chicago*, with fifteen troopships, etc., is somewhere to the westward. Our next move? Probably back to Guadalcanal. I feel confident a Jap landing will be attempted soon on Guadalcanal.

On August 12, Ens Bob Gibson and Ens Jerry Richey, of *Enterprise's* Bombing-6, took off on antisubmarine patrol at dawn and almost immediately surprised a Japanese fleet submarine as it lay on the surface about 20 miles ahead of *Enterprise*. Gibson went straight into a bombing run and dropped his SBD's 500-pound bomb within 50 feet of it. Richey followed Gibson in and placed his 500-pound bomb within 20 feet of the hull. The target, which was down by the bow, lay on the surface for five or six minutes while both pilots made repeated strafing attacks; Gibson and Richey each fired their .50-caliber forward guns on the inbound runs, and their rearseatmen fired their twin .30-caliber free guns while the planes were outbound. Richey later claimed to have seen several Japanese sailors lying wounded or dead on the deck while other Japanese struggled in the water. At length, both pilots observed the submarine, which remained down by the bow and stationary throughout its ordeal, slip beneath the surface. Gibson and Richey received official credit for sinking the submarine, but Japanese records fail to confirm the loss.

卐

LT(JG) SLIM RUSSELL
Scouting-3

Diary entry of August 14, 1942

Well, we're on our way back to Tulagi, back to hit at the Japs. Since the tenth, we've drifted southward,

74

fueling, consolidating. The battered *Chicago* and fifteen transports passed quite near us on the eleventh.

Hear that the Japs are really laying for Tulagi. Hope we catch a big part of their fleet there. Would really be wonderful to let them have about forty 1,000-pound bombs down their stacks. Am anxious to get there, do a good job, and then head for home.

LT(JG) SMOKEY STOVER
Fighting-5

Diary entry of August 16, 1942

We have been circling around north of New Caledonia and about 300 miles from Tulagi, waiting for the Japs to make a counterinvasion, I suppose. They have been bombing there about every other day, with no opposition since we left.

AOM2 ALFRED CAMPBELL
USS Enterprise

Diary entry of August 16, 1942

Yesterday Tulagi was attacked by high horizontal Jap bombers. The damage was very small. The Marines had consolidated their beachhead positions and there is little resistance left in the rest of the islands. Bombers from Australia have been bombing Rabaul very regularly.

We are topping off fuel for the destroyers. And we are about 100 miles from Tulagi. At the present time we are protecting the supply line from Australia to the Solomons from attacks from the east and south. Cruisers are up north.

⚡

Also on August 16, Lt(jg) Bill Henry and Ens R. E. Pellesier, of *Saratoga*'s Scouting-3, were assigned a long-range patrol mission that would take them north toward Guadalcanal and Savo by way of Malaita Island. Normally, the two SBDs would have flown with

75

500-pound General Purpose bombs aboard, but, while the pilots were checking out their airplanes, the ordnancemen removed the bombs without explanation.

As the Dauntlesses were flying north of Florida Island, Henry and Pellesier both sighted a Japanese two-stack destroyer steaming north-northeastward at about 20 knots. At 1106, as Henry led Pellesier abeam the enemy ship, Japanese gunners aboard the destroyer opened fire on both American warplanes. The initial bursts were extremely close, but neither airplane was hit. Henry motioned to Pellesier to prepare to attack, then led the way up to 5,000 feet and ahead of the destroyer, wishing all the while he had contested the decision to remove the bombs.

Halfway through the initial strafing run, Henry's .50-caliber machine guns jammed after firing only 20 rounds each. Pellesier fired approximately 400 .50-caliber rounds at the destroyer's stacks. Neither pilot observed damage to the destroyer, and neither plane was damaged.

After recovering at low altitude, Henry turned south for home. Pellesier was well off to his left, attracting close antiaircraft bursts until out of range of the Japanese guns.

Because strict radio silence had been imposed to mask the presence of the carriers so close to Guadalcanal, Henry could not transmit a fix on the enemy destroyer. He had to wait to fly all the way back to the fleet and drop a message to *Saratoga*'s deck. A follow-up attack was not launched.

The cat-and-mouse game could be played by both sides.

On August 17, Ens H. H. Coit, of *Wasp*'s Scouting-71, ran into a Japanese Mavis four-engine flying boat about 30 miles from his ship. He made several runs on the vulnerable patrol bomber in the face of heavy machine-gun and cannon fire but was unable to hit it in a vulnerable spot. The Mavis escaped as Coit rushed to *Wasp* to make an emergency landing. The Dauntless was full of holes and the hydraulic system was out of commission, but neither Coit nor his gunner had been hit.

AOM2 ALFRED CAMPBELL
USS Enterprise

Diary entry of August 17, 1942

About 300 miles south of Tulagi.

Allied planes are patrolling around Tulagi and the other Solomon Islands, so we are in a position to intercept anything they pick up.

Cool weather.

The *Astoria, Vincennes,* and *Quincy* are three cruisers that, according to scuttlebutt, have been sunk by the Japs at Tulagi in the skirmish that took place a few days ago. No official information, though. Also, it is believed that *Chicago* got her bows blown off.

Diary entry of August 19, 1942

Launched SBDs and TBFs to scout over Tulagi. Returned about noon. Had General Quarters about 1400. Reported enemy aircraft, but turned out to be a PBY. Took bombs off TBFs and put on torpedoes.

The [TBF] scouting unit found a Jap cruiser but did not bomb it as the mission was scouting. So they said. But the truth is the pilots didn't know whether they had bombs or torpedoes. The Jap cruiser put up a heavy but inaccurate antiaircraft fire.

[Scouts] found a Jap sub, but it crash-dived before the planes could attack it. One pilot dropped a bomb, but it wasn't armed so it didn't go off.

LT(JG) SMOKEY STOVER
Fighting-5

Diary entry of August 19, 1942

Plan of the Day for tomorrow says, "Clear Ships For Action." We're going North!

LT(JG) SLIM RUSSELL
Scouting-3

Diary entry of August 20, 1942

Tulagi bearing 303 [degrees], distance 228 [miles].
On August 18, we fueled from tanker *Platte* and
received mail. The mail was from June 21–July 7.

Yesterday morning, three destroyers and one
submarine were reported to have shelled Tulagi.

This past week we have done little except go around
in circles. Yesterday, I flew 9 hours. One 200-mile
search with Ens Bob Balenti, and I flew on [the wing of]
Lt M. P. MacNair for a 250-mile hop in the afternoon.
Supposedly an enemy force out there, but no could find.
Did sight two islands. Also two PBYs.

This morning we had battle stations and stripped the
ship for action. One heavy cruiser, one light cruiser, and
three destroyers were reported shelling Tulagi at 0600.
Wasp sent search planes out at 0800. Three destroyers
and one light cruiser reported 30 miles, bearing 270
[degrees], from Savo Island on course 330 degrees at a
speed of 25 knots. Leaving us in a hurry! We were then
258 miles from them. A heavy cruiser was reported in
Tulagi Harbor, possibly damaged by a B-17. Since that
time, I have not heard anything more. The ship has
been at General Quarters all day.

Long Island, a small converted carrier, joined us last
evening and is with us now. She has nineteen fighters
and twelve dive-bombers with her. Marine planes. She
is to send them into Lunga Field soon.

This afternoon, we had quite a few bogies reported.
Believe at least one of them was a Jap floatplane.

Lt(jg) Smokey Stover
Fighting-5

Diary entry of August 20, 1942

At General Quarters all day from 0900. Quite useless
and tiring for everyone, in my opinion. Came up to
about 190 miles from Tulagi.

We had a couple of alarms and manned our planes,

and *Wasp* fighters went out after a Jap seaplane. [The FDO] broke radio silence, but he got away.

Turned at about 1600 to course 100 [degrees] at 14 knots. Running away again!

Long Island launched Marine fighters and some SBDs going to Lunga Field on Guadalcanal.

AOM2 ALFRED CAMPBELL
USS Enterprise

Diary entry of August 20, 1942

Sent out scouts early in the morning. They spotted some Jap ships. They came back and were rearmed with 1,000-pound bombs. We stood by to launch an attack group. We speeded up to better than 20 knots but decided to discontinue until tomorrow.

LT(JG) SMOKEY STOVER
Fighting-5

Diary entry of August 21, 1942

I hear the Japs have made a landing on Guadalcanal to the east of our Marines, who are hollering for help. Don't know if we will go in.

卐

On an August 21 scouting hop that covered the Santa Cruz Islands, Scouting-71's Lt(jg) Charles Mester and Ens R. A. Escher discovered a seaplane tender, two destroyers, and several patrol planes in a bay at Ndeni Island. Upon receiving no recognition signals from the vessels and identifying them as Japanese, the two SBDs initiated a bombing and strafing attack.

When already well into his dive, Mester saw stars on the wings and fuselages of the patrol planes. They were friendly PBYs! Mester immediately pulled clear, but Escher did not recognize them as friendly and carried out his attack. His 500-pound bomb landed just off the beam of the seaplane tender and he retired under heavy antiaircraft fire from the ships.

The seaplane tender was *Mackinac*. Ensign Escher soon learned that his well-placed bomb had wrecked two OS2U scout-observation planes, damaged the tender's gasoline system, and injured several islanders who happened to be nearby in canoes.

⤵

ENS FRED KRUEGER
USS Enterprise

Diary entry of August 21, 1942

It has been a good day. Our scouts have begun to run into enemy units. It looks like something might be brewing. Several single units seem to be starting down this way, and it looks like we will get a crack at them after all. Everything seems to point at their trying to retake Tulagi and Guadalcanal.

⤵

August 22, 1942, was a busy, exciting day.

The day began with an inspirational message from Adm Chester Nimitz, Commander-in-Chief of the U.S. Pacific Fleet, which was published in *Saratoga*'s Plan of the Day: "Our prime objective is enemy ships. Surely we will have losses, but we will also destroy ships and be that much nearer the successful conclusion of the war."

The first excitement of the day began when a bogey was picked up on *Enterprise*'s radar at 1048. Immediately, the carrier's FDO vectored out a division of Fighting-6 under Ens Red Brooks. However, no one in Brooks's division received the message because they were flying through a heavy rain squall at that moment.

The FDO next ordered ChMach Don Runyon's Fighting-6 division to investigate the bogey, but neither Runyon nor his three wingmen received this message.

Finally, the FDO reached Lt Scoop Vorse's Fighting-6 division, which proceeded at 1055 on vector 270 degrees at 10,000 feet. After Vorse had flown about 15 miles, the vector was changed to

200 degrees at 8,000 feet. Moments later, the course was again corrected to 180 degrees.

Lt(jg) Slim Russell, who was monitoring the *Enterprise* fighter-frequency transmissions in Scouting-3's ready room aboard *Saratoga*, heard one of the American fighter pilots report, "Looks like a big combination." And then, "It's a Jap Kawanishi four-engine scout P-boat." And then, "I'm going after him."

At this time, the Japanese snooper was only 15 miles from the carriers but was unable to see them because of poor visibility.

Lieutenant Vorse and Ens Dick Loesch climbed to deliver an overhead attack while Lt(jg) Howard Grimmell and Ens Francis Register proceeded to the same altitude to deliver a below-opposite attack.

Vorse executed his overhead run at 1105. He had fired only twenty-five rounds from each of his six .50-caliber wing guns when the flimsy Mavis burst into flames. He immediately pulled clear. Ensign Loesch was preparing to open fire when the big patrol bomber erupted in flames, so he never completed the act.

CAP Wilhelm Esders, of Torpedo-3, was returning to the task force from his morning scouting mission when he glanced to the north and saw the fighters chasing the large seaplane. Within moments, the seaplane disintegrated.

The fire started in the fuselage and quickly spread to the mid-wing section. A moment later, the giant parasol wings collapsed upward, and the fuselage and wings fell separately into the sea.

CAP Esders saw parts of the fuselage, wings, engines, the contents of the fuselage, and what looked like people fall from 8,000 or 9,000 feet. Esders did not see any parachutes blossom, but someone else reported seeing one man jump from the burning plane without a parachute.

Slim Russell and the other Scouting-3 pilots heard Vorse's report: "Red Base [*Enterprise*] from Red-5 [Vorse]. Enemy plane shot down in flames." The scout-bomber pilots cheered and commented that the experimental radar fitted to all the carriers was proving to be a real a lifesaver.

Also on August 22, Torpedo-8's Ens J. H. Cook was taking off to proceed on inner air (antisubmarine) patrol. Just before his TBF got to *Saratoga*'s bow, it went off the left side of the deck, left wing down, and plunged into the water. The radioman and a passenger got out, but Cook and his bombardier were lost when the torpedo bomber sank.

And on the morning of August 22, Cdr Don Felt, the commander of *Saratoga*'s Air Group 3, flew to Guadalcanal's Henderson Field—the newly operational runway that his own air group had strafed and bombed on August 7. While Felt was completing his business with Marine aviation officers, Japanese bombers struck the field from 22,000 feet. The Japanese bombs holed the packed-earth runway, but repair crews quickly filled in the craters and Marine air operations quickly resumed. Felt later reported to his pilots that he saw one Japanese bomber trailing smoke from a 90mm antiaircraft hit as it left the area. Four Marine F4F fighters were shot up trying to get through the bombers' Zero escorts, but no Marine pilot was injured. However, one of the precious Marine F4Fs cracked up on landing.

Commander Felt's big news was about a 1,000-man Japanese infantry force that had been defeated in a daylong battle on August 21. Felt heard that 769 Japanese bodies were piled up on the beach and along the stream guarding the eastern flank of the Marines' Lunga Perimeter.

Finally, at 1745, August 22, heavy cruiser *Portland*, on the starboard hand of *Enterprise*'s Task Force 16, reported a torpedo passing her from port to starboard. The torpedo was first seen broaching about 1,700 yards off *Portland*'s starboard beam at 240 degrees. At the same time, destroyers of *Wasp*'s Task Force 18 reported a sonar contact and dropped depth charges. An investigation by ships of Task Force 16 and Task Force 18 failed to produce any hard submarine targets, but Japanese submarines were most certainly shadowing the American carriers.

9

The Battle of Midway was not, as historians of the period like to proclaim, the beginning of the end for the hegemonous empire of Japan. She was defeated there, it is true, but America could yet have lost the Pacific War. No. Midway was not the beginning of the end for Japan.

Midway was the beginning of the beginning for the United States. It tested her will, found her airmen sound of the sort of stamina it would take to win the war. It gave America the opportunity to defeat Japan, the will to defeat Japan, the means to defeat Japan.

The beginning of the end for Japan arrived on August 7, 1942, when nearly 20,000 U.S. Marines assaulted Guadalcanal and neighboring islands at the periphery of the empire of Japan. A war thoroughly defensive became a war haltingly offensive.

In only two days marked by heavy—but by no means universally heavy—fighting, the U.S. 1st Marine Division and attached combat units achieved every one of their immediate objectives in the eastern Solomon Islands. Chief among their accomplishments was the virtually bloodless seizure of an uncompleted airfield about midway along Guadalcanal's northern shore. This airfield—its pre-servation, its destruction, its defense, its seizure—would be the focal point of all that followed in an incredible six-month air, land, and naval campaign upon which both sides committed more than either could really afford.

But those first days were heady. All two of them. For, on the second night following the landings, a Japanese naval surface battle force, incredibly outnumbered but bolstered by utter surprise, sank one Australian and three American cruisers. The Battle of Savo Island annihilated what confidence the Battle of Midway had instilled in the otherwise defeat-weary U.S. Fleet. Originally scheduled to withdraw from the Guadalcanal area on the fifth day because of an imagined fuel shortage, the three American carriers assigned to cover the Marine landings were ordered by their com-mander, VAdm Frank Jack Fletcher, to run from the range of imag-ined Japanese carriers late on the second day. Fletcher's precipitous withdrawal obliged the transports and their supporting surface warships to retire, and they did, with at least 40 percent of the Marines' supplies and ammunition still in their holds.

In only two weeks, as unskilled young American warriors struggled to overcome the psychological defeat brought on by Fletcher's ignominious departure, elements of the Imperial Army and Imperial Navy all but won back the initiative they had lost by being defeated at the Coral Sea and Midway and by allowing American ground units to seize occupied territory in the Solomons. In the two weeks following the Savo debacle, Japanese cruisers and destroyers—and even surfaced Japanese submarines—bombarded American installations in the Guadalcanal area with complete im-punity. Though the three American carriers idled away those weeks almost, but not quite, within bomber range of Guadalcanal and Tulagi, Japanese bombers and fighters encountered zero op-position over the islands, and they bombed and strafed almost at will, kept wary by only a few antiaircraft guns.

The American decision to remain on station but out of range was just that, a decision, consciously made at the highest levels of the American Pacific Fleet command. The precious carriers would be used only if the Guadalcanal garrison fell into dire straits or if Japanese carriers sailed into range.

Suffering only from despicable intelligence evaluations, which underrated the American landing force by a factor of one to ten, Japanese destroyers landed several hundred infantry-trained naval bluejackets and just over 1,000 crack Imperial Army infantrymen —again, without any opposition, or even the knowledge of the Marines ashore. These slim units, with rear echelons yet to be landed, were to assault the Marine perimeter screening the just-completed runway during the last week of August 1942. The *only* problem was that there would be little more than 2,500 Japanese to assault a perimeter held, in total, by well over 10,000 Americans.

The only other problem, which occurred after the Japanese advance detachments had been landed, was the arrival on August 20, 1942, of nineteen Marine F4F-4 Wildcat fighters and twelve Marine SBD-3 Dauntless dive-bombers at Guadalcanal's newly completed Henderson Field.

On August 19, the day before the arrival of the Marine aircraft, approximately thirty-five officers of the Imperial Army advance echelon moved up to scout the Marine perimeter defenses. They were discovered by a Marine patrol, and many were killed in a wild gunfight. Fearful of being attacked himself while awaiting his second echelon and the unfolding of an intricate area-wide plan slated to defeat the American carriers, Col Kiyano Ichiki, the Japanese commander, ordered an immediate night assault upon the unassessed Marine defenses.

On August 21, in a tough, nightlong free-for-all fought with fists, hand grenades, bayonets, and swords as much as with rifles, machine guns, and artillery, nearly 800 of his 1,000 first-line soldiers were killed and Colonel Ichiki took his own life.

IO

I t is a common impulse for practitioners of the military sciences to draw upon the lessons of the past while planning the battles of the future.

When one gets to the core of military history and the exercises in manipulation that spring from it, one finds that all strategies and all tactics remain more or less ageless: One side attempts to mass its manpower and weapons in such a way as to defeat the other in the attack or in the defense. This is true for land armies, and it is true for navies.

Military science is largely the art of the known coupled with human audacity, intuition, and luck.

The beginning of World War II saw the addition of an element of warfare whose consequences upon the modern battlefield were not yet known. Theory, audacity, intuition, and luck would play their roles in the new war, but air power would forever change the nature of war on land and at sea. Even by mid-1942, three years into the new war, no one had quite synthesized the lessons of air power, no one yet knew quite how to use it, what might happen as a result of its presence over the battlefield, its full impact upon strategies and tactics.

For men inculcated in the traditions and lessons of nineteenth century warfare—and that included every man who had, by mid-1942, attained flag rank—air power was a chimera.

࿄

One of the most overrated characters of modern military history is Isoroku Yamamoto, commander-in-chief of the Combined Fleet, the Imperial Navy's operational arm.

Not quite the visionary extolled by his countrymen nor quite worthy of the almost unseemly posthumous praise heaped on him by the men he defeated (a convenient impulse—raising the vessel of defeat to godlike stature), Yamamoto was a bright, forceful leader, but he was no innovator. The surprise-attack strategy he forced upon his service and nation was cribbed from his hero and mentor, VAdm Heihachiro Togo, who launched surprise war upon the Russians at Port Arthur in 1904. A late-blooming pilot, Yamamoto was no air-power strategist, and certainly no air-power innovator. The innovators were on his staff or, more correctly, on the staffs of his subordinates.

Yamamoto loved the *idea* of aerial warfare—particularly carrier-air warfare—but when it came time to play his hand, this inveterate gambler always hedged.

Yamamoto drew the wrong lessons from his youthful experience at Port Arthur, and he drew the wrong lessons from Midway, a defeat he, as much as anyone, brought upon his nation. As had Togo at Port Arthur, Yamamoto spurned the concept of the second—killing—strike. He had tacitly withheld permission for a death-dealing second strike at Pearl Harbor, a strike that certainly would have destroyed the bulk of American reserve fuel stocks in the Pacific and undoubtedly would have prevented American warships, particularly American carriers, from carrying out spoiling raids and the strategic actions at the Coral Sea and Midway. Firm orders against launching a second strike against Midway had been issued by Yamamoto's chief of staff well in advance of that action, again with Yamamoto's *tacit* approval. At odds with reality, sowing the seeds of confusion among Yamamoto's obedient subordinates, that order set in motion a string of events that brought on the destruction of four first-line Japanese carriers by American naval aviators.

In the final analysis, Yamamoto, whom history has labeled a carrier-warfare genius, was the overseeing technician of rather standard battleship strategies. There is ample evidence to support the view that he mistrusted the ability of his carrier squadrons to play a strategic role or misunderstood their worth.

卐

The strategy Isoroku Yamamoto and his staff cobbled together in the face of the Allied incursion into the Eastern Solomons had one aim, never before successful: To place Japanese *surface* forces in contact with the American carriers and their escorts. This was the vaunted Midway strategy coupled with the tactics of the Coral Sea draw. It was used and used again, in draws and defeats, because it was the pet theory of Japan's most revered naval leader after Togo, Isoroku Yamamoto.

The actual form of the Japanese plan in the maturing Solomons action was an amalgam of the Coral Sea and Midway plans. A convoy of vulnerable troop transports would move on Guadalcanal accompanied by a surface bombardment force whose task it was to damage Henderson Field, Guadalcanal's newly completed runway. One light carrier, escorted by several surface warships, was to mount a strike or strikes against Henderson Field in support of the troops ashore. Two fleet carriers and a fairly large force of escorts was to sail behind the light carrier and launch surprise strikes against American carriers drawn into range by the activities of the light carrier. A very powerful battleship-cruiser-destroyer force—positioned yet farther from the light carrier—was to dash in against the American carriers and their surface escorts, and destroy them by gunfire.

The role of the Japanese carriers—as at Midway—was to support a landing operation; attract and hold the attention of American carriers; attack and damage (sink, if possible) the American carriers; and, ultimately, support the operations of Japanese surface forces against American carrier and surface forces.

The upcoming battle was to be a slightly smaller version of the cataclysmic surface engagement between the main components of two modern fleets that was to have taken place at Midway. It was to be the battle Japanese naval strategists had been planning for two decades. Indeed, it was to be Japan's third attempt in four months to bring to reality a set-piece battle that had been drawn and re-drawn for endless map-table battles throughout the 1920s and 1930s. Above all, it was to be Isoroku Yamamoto's vindication for the defeat he had suffered at the hands of the Fates—and not at the hands of the United States—at Midway.

It was to be the final battle of the Pacific War.

卍

What can be said of Yamamoto's adversaries?

Fate, and little else, prevented the U.S. Navy from following Yamamoto's cherished ideals of carrier-surface strategy. In the greatest irony of modern warfare, carrier forces operating under Yamamoto's subordinates destroyed the prime ingredients of iron-clad American surface strategy. The battleships severely damaged or permanently sunk by Japanese carrier strikes against Pearl Harbor compelled the weakened U.S. Navy to undertake four carrier versus carrier clashes in the Pacific from May to October 1942. And the aggregate outcome of those clashes—not foresight—suggested the carrier-based strategy that eventually contributed so heavily to Japan's maritime defeat.

The American focus upon carriers at the Coral Sea and Mid-way did not, in the minds of the leaders of the time, constitute a new broad-based naval strategy. Rather, it signaled the paucity of American battleships in the combat arena. So-called "black-shoe" battleship-cruiser admirals dominated the U.S. Navy of 1942 and would continue to dominate it well into 1943. Indeed, most of the leading "carrier" admirals of 1942 were, in fact, cruiser and battleship admirals, not aviators at all. And many of them were serving in jobs well beyond their grasps.

Yamamoto's imperfect carrier-surface amalgams—lightly screened multi-carrier task forces operating in conjunction with and usually acting as bait or advance strike forces for distant battleship-cruiser-destroyer maneuver forces—were based upon the overwhelming superiority the Combined Fleet enjoyed in surface assets.

Far from being the products of a perfect vision of how war should be waged in the vast Pacific, American carrier task forces—groupments of single carriers, each surrounded by its own screen of defending surface vessels—operated the way they operated because of a keenly felt scarcity of both carriers and screening warships. The first three weeks in the Guadalcanal arena cost the Allies—chiefly the United States—four cruisers and several destroyers. All of these ships but one destroyer were sunk by Japanese surface forces operating virtually within sight of Marine positions on Guadalcanal. Such losses appreciably added to the pressure already heaped upon the carrier task forces to achieve some lasting results in a type of warfare by then demonstrably more prone to the vagaries of Fate than most.

⇜

All but ignoring the avowed purpose of the late-August exercise—landing troops on Guadalcanal and supporting their assault against what its intelligence service labeled "about 2,000 Marines"—Combined Fleet managed to amass a staggering array of nearly sixty warships, plus transports and submarines. The intention was to destroy any carriers the Americans sent to support the Marines on Guadalcanal.

The top Japanese admirals feared American carriers far more than they respected their own. Those few American carriers loomed larger in Japanese minds in August than they had even in May, before the crushing humiliation of Midway.

Americans certainly feared risking their few carriers in action against Japanese carriers. But they had won big at Midway so knew well the potential fruits of carrier versus carrier warfare. More important, however, they *had nothing else but their carriers* with which to counter the Japanese carriers—nothing at all but their carriers to parry Japanese moves and buy time for the hurried, harried builders of yet more carriers and a new generation of . . . battleships!

II

The Japanese battle plan—dubbed "KA" after the first syllable of "Guadalcanal" rendered in Japanese—was promulgated in its entirety by August 21. By that date, the Japanese naval force gathered at Truk, the main Japanese fleet anchorage in the Central Pacific, included two fleet carriers, one light carrier, five cruisers, eight destroyers, a seaplane tender, and numerous fleet auxiliary vessels. Also on that date, 8th Fleet, at Rabaul, counted four cruisers and five destroyers. There were one hundred Imperial Navy warplanes based at Rabaul, chiefly Betty medium bombers and land-based Zero fighters. Numerous long-range patrol aircraft were operating from Rabaul as well as from a newly established forward patrol base at Rekata Bay, on Santa Ysabel.

The putative centerpiece of the Japanese operation, the "Reinforcement Group," was commanded by RAdm Raizo Tanaka, a hero of the Battle of the Java Sea, and composed of one large troop transport and three small patrol boats that had been rigged out to carry their share of the 1,500 Japanese infantrymen bound for

A6M Zero fighter. *(Official USN Photo)*

B5N Kate torpedo bomber. *(Official USN Photo)*

F4F Wildcat fighter makes an arrested carrier landing. *(Official USN Photo)*

Top: TBF Avenger torpedo bomber in action. *(Official USN Photo)*

Above: LSO In Action   Lt Dave McCambell, of *Wasp*.
(Official USN Photo)

Left: SBD Dauntless dive-bomber. The pilot is Lt(jg) Slim Russell and the photographer is Cdr Don Felt, both of *Saratoga*'s Air Group 3.   *(Compliments of A. G. Russell)*

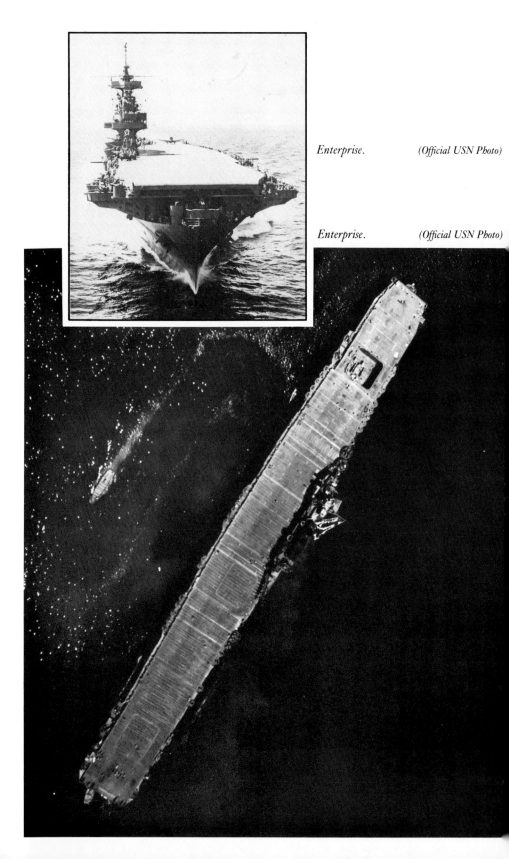

Enterprise.   (Official USN Photo)

Enterprise.   (Official USN Photo)

VAdm Frank Jack Fletcher.
(Official USN Photo)

Lt(jg) Slim Russell
(Compliments of A. G. Russell)

Fighting-5 Wildcat Pilots: *(left to right)* Lt.(jg) Smokey Stover, Lt Sandy Crews, Lt Pete Brown, Lt Pug Southerland, Lt Chick Harmer, LCdr Roy Simpler, Lt Dave Richardson. *(Official USN Photo)*

Torpedo-3 Flight Leaders: *(left to right)* Lt Johnny Myers, LCdr Charlie Jett, and Lt Rube Konig, of Torpedo-3. *(Compliments of J. N. Myers)*

Ryujo. (Official USN Photo)

Above: Lt Syd Bottomley. (Official USN Photo)

Left: Cdr Don Felt. (Compliments of H. D. Felt)

Top: Ens Roger Crow (on Guadalcanal in September 1943). Note makeshift armor seatback of Crow's SBD, S-13.

(Compliments of R. C. Crow)

Above: A Fighting-6 Wildcat Division: (*left to right*) Mach Don Runyon, AP1 Howard Packard, Ens Dutch Shoemaker, Ens Bill Rouse. *(Official USN Photo)*

Top: *Enterprise* sailors and Marines practice firing their 20mm antiaircraft guns.

(*Official USN Photo*)

Above: *Enterprise*'s port aft 5-inch antiaircraft gun group. Note the LSO platform at the aft edge of the flight deck.

(*Official USN Photo*)

Guadalcanal. The transports were escorted by a light cruiser and six destroyers. Much as he had been doing for some weeks, and with staggering results, Tanaka was to land the infantry and then seek out targets of opportunity afloat in the narrow channel between Guadalcanal and Tulagi or bombard Marine shore installations or the air base facilities and Marine warplanes at Henderson Field, which was located directly behind Lunga Point.

The Japanese fleet carriers—*Shokaku* and *Zuikaku*—and their escorts were organized into the "Carrier Striking Force" and commanded by VAdm Chuichi Nagumo, who had led the Japanese carriers to Pearl Harbor. It was Nagumo's understanding that he was to attack and destroy, if possible, the three American fleet carriers that Japanese reconnaissance aircraft had first pinpointed east and southeast of the Solomons on August 20.

Temporarily attached to Nagumo's Carrier Striking Force was RAdm Chuichi Hara's "Mobile Force," the diversionary group composed of light carrier *Ryujo*, a heavy cruiser, and two destroyers. Kate torpedo bombers and Zero fighters based aboard *Ryujo* were to cover the approach of Rear Admiral Tanaka's Reinforcement Group by mounting a diversionary air strike against the newly landed Marine air group at Guadalcanal's Henderson Field.

Running interference for the two fleet carriers was RAdm Hiroaki Abe's "Vanguard Group," with its two battleships—*Hiei* and *Kirishima*—three heavy cruisers, one light cruiser, and six destroyers. Abe, who had seized Wake Island for Japan, was to finish what the carriers were to start, namely the destruction of American surface vessels accompanying the American carriers.

VAdm Nishizo Tsukahara's 11th Air Fleet, which had just moved forward to Rabaul with fresh groups to supplement the battered 25th Air Flotilla, was to mount bomber strikes against Henderson Field and generally oppose any attempts by American land-based or carrier-based aircraft to strike Japanese forces ashore or afloat in the Solomon Islands.

Other Japanese forces in the area included three roving and nine picket submarines, a heavily escorted group of fleet oilers stationed north of the Stewart Islands, and the Rabaul-based cruisers of 8th Fleet—the same force that had struck the U.S. invasion fleet and sunk four cruisers on the night of August 8.

❀

Including the three carriers that Admiral Fletcher had led from the Guadalcanal area on August 9, the Americans had thirty warships, organized into three carrier task forces, with which to counter the main strength of Yamamoto's Combined Fleet. In addition, the U.S. fielded nineteen Wildcat fighters and twelve Dauntless dive-bombers, newly arrived at Guadalcanal; just over a dozen Catalina patrol bombers operating out of Graciosa Bay, Ndeni, in the Santa Cruz Islands; and a small group of Army Air Forces B-17 heavy bombers, which were running long-range search patrols out of Espiritu Santo, in the New Hebrides. A fourth U.S. carrier, *Hornet*, was enroute from Pearl Harbor with its covering force of cruisers and destroyers. Finally, far from the scene, two new fast battleships, a new light antiaircraft cruiser, and several destroyers were making for the Panama Canal from East Coast ports.

❀

The main body of the Combined Fleet sortied from Truk on the morning of August 23, a Sunday. Its track was southeast by south, which would carry the Japanese ships well to the east of the Solomon Islands. The U.S. carrier task forces were approximately 150 miles east of Malaita, heading north by northeast, more or less in the direction of the Japanese fleet.

Rear Admiral Tanaka's Reinforcement Group left Rabaul before sunrise on August 23.

That morning, the Japanese counted fifty-eight warships and 177 carrier-based warplanes ready for battle against thirty U.S. warships and 259 warplanes.

❀

The first brush occurred at 0950, when a Ndeni-based PBY Catalina patrol bomber found the Japanese transports and their escorts heading toward Guadalcanal at 17 knots. The sighting was reported to *Mackinac*, at Ndeni, and relayed to Vice Admiral Fletcher, aboard *Saratoga*, at 1012. Fletcher ordered *Saratoga*'s skipper, Capt DeWitt Ramsey, to prepare Cdr Don Felt's Air Group 3 to strike Rear Admiral Tanaka's troop-laden transports.

At 1510, *Saratoga* began launching thirty-one SBDs and six TBFs under Commander Felt to locate and attack an enemy force Felt understood to be composed of two cruisers, three destroyers, and four transports. The Japanese reportedly were then 275 miles from the American task force. Felt was also ordered to return to Guadalcanal after the attack, before sunset if possible, and to rendezvous with *Saratoga* next morning.

The estimated point of contact Felt was given had been deduced from the assumption that Tanaka would hold to the course and speed he was maintaining at the time of the PBY contact. However, Felt's doubts in that regard grew as his air group formed up and headed north.

The weather was not good. Visibility was poor because of rain showers and heavy cloud cover. Dead ahead was a heavy weather front. To cope with the situation, Commander Felt spread the group into a line of three-plane sections at 100 feet over the sea and set their course. They flew into the weather front one hour after launch, section leaders on instruments, wingmen tucked in tight on their leaders. Because of the weather, it was difficult to maintain the integrity of the line of planes.

For Lt Paul Holmberg, a 1939 Naval Academy graduate and a relatively inexperienced member of Bombing-3, staying in formation and avoiding flying into the ocean while trying to keep track of his position and navigation was most difficult. Like many of his comrades, Holmberg flew with his cockpit open in order to see the Dauntless on which he was flying formation. It was flown by LCdr DeWitt Shumway, the Bombing-3 commander. Rain entered the open cockpit and added considerably to Holmberg's discomfort.

Even the experienced pilots were having trouble. Lt Syd Bottomley, the Bombing-3 executive officer, remarked to his rearseatman about what a nerve-racking flight it had turned out to be, flying in formation with so many planes, in and out of showers, under low clouds, with poor visibility.

The pilots frequently lost sight of one another.

When the *Saratoga* strike group flew out of the weather an hour after flying into it, Commander Felt noted with considerable satisfaction and relief that everybody was still in line.

The search continued for about 275 miles with no contact. The Japanese transports had reversed course.

Finally, Commander Felt passed the word by radio: "Return to base," which meant Guadalcanal's Henderson Field. The strike group still faced a flight of about 250 miles through bad weather in decreasing afternoon light. At length, the American warplanes broke out of the bad weather in three-quarters moonlight as they were making landfall on Malaita Island. When the Navy bombers finally arrived over Henderson Field it was fully dark, and the pilots had to turn on their running lights. The duration of the flight was 4.3 hours.

The Marine and Navy air base units servicing Henderson Field lined up several captured Japanese trucks along the edge of runway and turned on the truck lights so the *Saratoga* pilots could see to land.

As Bombing-3 was coming in to land, Lt Syd Bottomley's radioman-gunner, AMM1 David Johnson, told Bottomley that he could see fireflies in the mahogany trees to port. Lt(jg) Slim Russell, of Scouting-3, immediately understood that he was being fired on by machine guns in the trees. But Russell was strangely unconcerned. Rather, he thought about how pretty all those tracers were as they rose toward his SBD. LCdr Bullet Lou Kirn, the Scouting-3 commander, felt the gunfire might have been the result of the tension and uncertainty that prevailed at Henderson Field—that the antiaircraft fire was from *friendly* guns. Fortunately, no damage was done, although several Navy pilots landed in the wrong direction—ostensibly to fool the gunners.

In view of the previous limited experience of a majority of the pilots under such trying conditions, Cdr Don Felt believed Air Group 3 had accomplished some marvelous flying. More than ever, he had complete faith in the ability of his group's experienced section leaders under extremely difficult instrument flying conditions, and in the apparent fine discipline of all his subordinates.

Once on the ground, Slim Russell and several other Scouting-3 pilots were led through a coconut grove to a tent about a mile from the runway. There, Russell and the others were given a mess kit apiece piled high with stew, hardtack, peas, and pears. Though the Navy pilots were used to dining off of china and being served by mess stewards aboard ship, they were all extremely glad to get at the Marines' hearty fare.

LCdr Bullet Lou Kirn was less fortunate than many of his young pilots. After seeing to the dispersal of the Scouting-3 Dauntlesses, which had to be refueled by hand from 55-gallon fuel drums, Kirn broke away long after the Marine air group's messing facilities had closed down. All he received was some Japanese hardtack.

After eating cold Marine K-rations, Lt Syd Bottomley was able to sample a form of boilermaker consisting of a small bottle of California Lejon brandy and captured Japanese Asahi beer.

Later that evening, Slim Russell's group listened with rapt attention as their Marine hosts told stories about the August 7 landings. According to the storytellers, the Japanese had not realized that American troops were landing. When the Japanese had run for the bush just ahead of the advancing Marines, they had left their radios on, food on the tables, fires in the stoves. Though the Marines had quickly taken control of the area around the air base, they were still having problems rounding up Japanese snipers. Russell and his fellow aviators also heard details of the heavy battle that had raged on the east flank of the Marines' Lunga Perimeter only three nights earlier.

It started raining late in the evening, but all the *Saratoga* pilots and aircrew had to sleep in or beside their planes in case the Japanese mounted an early-morning attack. Slim Russell could not get to sleep, so he sat around talking with the Marines. He was surprised to learn that his countrymen slept in foxholes, which looked to Russell like graves, with only one blanket over them, a fern under them, and their clothing and helmets on.

Before the night was over, Russell learned why the Marines settled for such stark sleeping conditions: A Japanese destroyer or submarine closed on the beach at about 0200, August 24, and dropped about fifteen 3-inch or 5-inch rounds in the direction of the parked TBFs and SBDs. The shelling was close, but it did no damage. After recovering from his initial shock, Russell thought it was kind of fun to listen to the shells whistling through the air. But he slept very little the rest of the night.

Air Group 3 was held at readiness to launch a morning strike against the Japanese transports it had missed the previous afternoon. While Marine SBDs searched northward along New Georgia Sound, between the double chain of the Solomon Islands (soon to be named the Slot), Marine ground crew finished the laborious task of refueling the thirty-seven Navy carrier bombers from 55-gallon fuel drums. Each Dauntless required the contents of five fuel drums, all of which had to be pumped by hand. Marine mechanics and Navy aircrew tinkered with engines and other systems in the waiting airplanes.

Lt(jg) Slim Russell and his buddies got up at 0700 and went down to the beach to look at dead Japanese. When the pilots had seen their fill of decomposing battle-ravaged corpses, they stopped in at the base quartermaster's office, where a Marine captain gave Russell a Japanese bolt-action rifle, a new Japanese gasmask, and some chopsticks. Later, a Marine sergeant gave Russell a Japanese bayonet to fit the rifle, which was very rusty and full of sand. The rifle's former owner was reputed to have been bayoneted by a Marine. When Russell pulled back the rifle's bolt, he found an expended cartridge in the chamber.

While awaiting orders, Lt Syd Bottomley and several other Bombing-3 pilots were given a tour by their Marine hosts, including a look at the Japanese prisoner stockade. There, for the first time, Bottomley and the other carrier pilots saw their enemies at close hand. They also visited the Tenaru River battlefield of August 21. Unlike many of the younger pilots, Bottomley thought "it was a sickening sight, with Japanese bodies all over the place putrefying in the heat."

The Marine dawn air search turned up no sign of Admiral Tanaka's transports or of any Japanese ships. Air Group 3 was released to return to *Saratoga,* which was nearly two hours away. To reciprocate for the hospitality and fuel it had received at Henderson

Field, the Air Group 3 strike bombers left behind all the bombs they had so circuitously lugged from *Saratoga*.

It turned out that one of the Bombing-3 SBDs had not been fueled during the night. Its pilot, Lt(jg) Bob Elder, discovered this condition minutes after joining the formation. He could not go on, so a second Bombing-3 plane was detailed to escort him back to Guadalcanal. The two were to fly to *Saratoga* as soon as the Marines had corrected the fueling error.

Action around the American fleet on August 23 consisted of several contacts between *Enterprise* scout-bombers on air patrol and at least two Japanese submarines.

At 0725, August 23, Lt Turner Caldwell, the Scouting-5 commander, sighted a surfaced submarine as it bent on all speed along a due southerly course. Caldwell dropped his SBD's 500-pound General Purpose bomb close aboard the submarine, but he was unable to observe any results before the Japanese boat dived.

At 0815, in a nearby search sector, the Scouting-5 flight officer, Lt Birney Strong, and his wingman, Ens John Richey, surprised a second surfaced submarine running at full speed on a course a bit west of south. Once again, the American 500-pound General Purpose bombs caused no observable damage. Though this Japanese submarine also crash-dived, it surfaced twice and was strafed both times by Strong and Richey.

Enterprise's routine afternoon search turned up no enemy surface warships, but at 1530 Ens Glenn Estes and Ens Elmer Maul, of Scouting-5, sighted and attacked a surfaced Japanese submarine as it raced on a course a bit east of south. Both airmen claimed near hits with their 500-pound General Purpose bombs, and both reported sighting a large oil slick after the submarine had disappeared from view. Though Estes and Maul were credited with damaging the enemy warship, there are no Japanese records to support the damage claim.

The repeated sightings of enemy submarines was troubling, but not particularly alarming. The American carriers had been patrolling the same area for two full weeks, so it was expected that the

Japanese had sent submarines to shadow or attack the American fleet.

⇌

When word of the abortive *Saratoga* strike reached Task Force 61 late on the afternoon of August 23, VAdm Frank Jack Fletcher consulted with his staff and reached a decision he had been putting off for some days.

Eager and ready to meet the oncoming Japanese carriers, which he knew he outnumbered in serviceable warplanes, Fletcher had for some days put off the routine refueling of his fleet, particularly of the carriers. When it appeared on August 23 that the overdue Japanese sally was not taking place—a feeling bolstered by a late-arriving message from Pacific Fleet Intelligence that placed the Japanese carriers well to the north of Truk—Fletcher ordered *Wasp* and her accompanying Task Force 18 to steam southward to rendezvous with fleet oilers. The refueling operation, which obliged all ships to steam at very low speeds, had to be undertaken well out of range of both enemy scouts and carrier attack aircraft. This meant that *Wasp's* Air Group 7 would be beyond supporting range of the *Enterprise* and *Saratoga* air groups for at least two days.

Fletcher's decision, which was seen as a prudent precaution in light of information pointing to a confrontation in several days' time, left the American fleet in the vicinity of Guadalcanal with a combined total of 177 operational Dauntlesses, Avengers, and Wildcats to take on VAdm Chuichi Nagumo's 176 Vals, Kates, and Zeros.

PART IV

The Battle of the

Eastern Solomons

I 2

The Japanese and American carrier task forces were approaching one another. A clash that seemed improbable to VAdm Frank Jack Fletcher seemed a certainty to VAdm Chuichi Nagumo. Indeed, the certainty was enhanced by Fletcher's unwitting action during the night of August 23–24, when, after releasing *Wasp* to refuel in the south, he kept his Task Force 61 steaming northward through the night. By 0800, the American carriers were about 150 miles due east of Malaita. Nagumo's Carrier Striking Force—including fleet carriers *Shokaku* and *Zuikaku*—was about 250 miles to the north-northwest.

Twenty *Enterprise* Dauntlesses were launched, beginning at 0630, to undertake a dawn search covering a fan from 290 degrees (north of west) to 070 degrees (north of east).

Air Group 3, under Cdr Don Felt, which had launched from Henderson Field at 0900, was expected to begin landing back aboard *Saratoga* at around 1100.

At 1017, *Enterprise* picked up a report from the Noumea-based headquarters of RAdm John McCain, the commander of all Allied aircraft in the South Pacific area (ComAirSoPac). The report relay stated that a Ndeni-based PBY patrol bomber had sighted a Japanese task force 220 miles north of Malaita at 0930. The report cited the presence of a carrier, two cruisers, and a destroyer. In fact, this was RAdm Chuichi Hara's Mobile Force: light carrier *Ryujo*, heavy cruiser *Tone*, and destroyers *Amatsukaze* and *Tokitsukaze*.

The PBYs tended by *Mackinac* had been flying all night trying to fix the position of the Japanese forces between Truk and the Solomons. On the basis of one fleeting contact report, five of the PBYs had even braved the darkness to deliver a night torpedo attack. Fortunately, perhaps, they had been unable to find targets. In addition to the Catalinas trying to find the Japanese carriers, PBYs were trying to relocate the Reinforcement Group commanded by RAdm Raizo Tanaka. It would be some time before Tanaka was found again, but one of these PBYs was attacked at 1028 by three float-observation planes tended by auxiliary light carrier *Chitose*. According to a report by *Chitose*'s captain, another PBY unwittingly got to within 25 miles of the *Ryujo* force before being forced to jettison its bombs and flee three other *Chitose*-based float-observation planes.

Also at 1017, an *Enterprise* TBF filling in as part of *Saratoga*'s inner air patrol sighted a Japanese submarine running southeastward on the surface at 12 knots. The submarine crash-dived before the search plane could mount an attack.

The *Enterprise* dawn search, which had flown out to 200 miles, found nothing but empty sea. All planes safely returned to their carrier by 1050.

At 1105, Lt Rodger Woodhull, the Scouting-5 exec, was on inner air patrol when he found a surfaced Japanese submarine northwest of Task Force 61. The Japanese submarine, which was making full speed on a due southerly course, crash-dived while Woodhull was still three minutes away. The search pilot dropped his 500-pound bomb 1,200 feet along an extension of the submarine's wake, but neither he nor his rearseatman saw any signs of damage.

All of *Saratoga*'s airplanes that had left Henderson Field were safely aboard their home carrier by 1130. Upon arriving aboard

Saratoga, Cdr Don Felt, the Air Group 3 commander, was told, "Get ready to take off immediately. There's another enemy outfit." "How far away?" Felt asked. He was given the position and replied, "No. That's beyond our range. Let's just take it easy. This gang has flown all day yesterday, spent the night in their planes, and flown back here to the ship. They need just a bit of rest. Keep getting intelligence and when those ships are within our range we'll go get them."

The returning *Saratoga* SBDs and TBFs had all left their 1,000-pound bombs for the Marine SBDs at Henderson Field. Thus, in addition to needing to be fueled to capacity for the upcoming flight, all the Air Group 3 strike aircraft had to be armed—1,000-pound bombs for the Dauntlesses and aerial torpedoes for the Avengers. While armorers, fueling crews, and mechanics swarmed over, under, and through each of the planes, the tired pilots and aircrew dispersed to their staterooms and berthing spaces for showers and fresh clothing. Sandwiches and coffee would be awaiting them in the squadron ready rooms.

卐

Responding to orders from the *Saratoga* FDO at 1143, Lt Dave Richardson, of Fighting-5, led his four-plane Wildcat division 50 miles out from Task Force 61 and encountered a four-engine Emily patrol bomber that was heading straight for the American carriers. As soon as the four Wildcats roared into view, the big amphibian dived for the relative safety of the surface, leveled off at 50 feet, and flew flat out toward Rabaul. The four American fighters made one firing pass apiece, chipping pieces and parts from the Emily's airframe. The big amphibian finally fell into the waves during Lieutenant Richardson's second firing pass, and he was given full credit for the kill.

卐

At 1158, *Enterprise* intercepted another ComAirSoPac sighting report from a Ndeni-based PBY: One carrier, two heavy cruisers, and one destroyer had been sighted at latitude 04°40' south and longitude 161°15′ east, heading due south. This appeared to be a repeat of the 1017 message. *Saratoga* received yet another repeat of this message at 1203.

The morning's action had revealed a number of things to the American leadership afloat with Task Force 61. The numerous sightings of doggedly determined *surfaced* Japanese submarines on August 23 and thus far on August 24 made it clear that the American carriers were being systematically shadowed. No doubt position reports were being sent by the surfaced submarines to ships and bases throughout the region.

Task Force 61 was by then under almost constant observation by Japanese search planes. Several in addition to the downed Emily were picked up by radar during the morning. As in the fleet confrontations at the Coral Sea and Midway, the Japanese searchers demonstrated a marked aptitude for locating and tracking the American force virtually without being detected or, at least, directly challenged. Since there were also Japanese submarines in the vicinity in the early morning of August 24, Fletcher's staff conceded that the Japanese commander probably had full and frequent reports regarding the location, speed, and heading of Task Force 61.

As the number of contacts with Japanese submarines and search aircraft mounted, it became increasingly clear that Fletcher's gamble to release Task Force 18 and *Wasp's* entire Air Group 7 had come acropper. There was definitely one Japanese carrier out there, and no telling what else. If, indeed, a Japanese carrier or carriers meant to draw Fletcher into battle on August 24, there was a very strong probability that it or they would have closed to within range of American search—and strike—aircraft by midafternoon.

At 1210, Vice Admiral Fletcher, who was aboard *Saratoga*, ordered *Enterprise's* Air Group 6 to mount its second long-range search of the day "as soon as possible." The searches would be conducted across a fan of 10-degree sectors from 290 degrees (west-northwest) to 90 degrees (due east).

A mixed bag of twenty-two SBDs from Bombing-6 and Scouting-5 and seven TBFs from Torpedo-3 were readied for the searches. *Enterprise* turned into the wind at 1229 to begin the launch.

⁂

As soon as the search aircraft were away, Fletcher decided with great reluctance to get Cdr Don Felt's rearmed, refueled, and refreshed Air Group 3 into the air as soon as the pilots could be briefed.

Fletcher's extreme reluctance arose mainly from the fact that contact reports were vague and, as far as he could tell, incomplete. Hours had passed since Task Force 61 had received any fresh news about the small carrier task force that had been found in the morning by the Ndeni-based PBY. Fletcher and most of the senior officers around him intuitively believed that other carriers had to be lurking undetected in other quadrants; Japanese performance at the Coral Sea and Midway made that surmise a virtual certainty.

Another important consideration in launching Air Group 3 was the virtual certainty that Task Force 61 had been pinpointed by the Japanese submarines and reconnaissance aircraft. Fletcher had won big at Midway by catching the Japanese air groups aboard their carriers. Indeed, the crippling destruction of the Japanese fleet carriers at Midway could be largely laid to the presence of volatile deck-bound armed and fueled attack aircraft when the American strike force pounced. Fletcher vaguely hoped to repeat that stroke, and he undoubtedly feared being caught in a surprise attack with Don Felt's armed and fueled SBDs and TBFs on *Saratoga*'s flight deck. There was certainly no harm in trying to hit the enemy before he had an opportunity to launch his strike.

However, the immediate impetus for Fletcher's decision to launch Air Group 3 was dictated by the lateness of the hour. The day was dwindling away. Better, he and his senior staff thought, to get the strike group underway against the known enemy carrier group to the northwest; Felt could easily be diverted if the *Enterprise* searchers found the anticipated larger carrier force in that general direction or to the north.

Thirty-one SBDs and eight TBFs would undertake the strike.

The very few remaining Air Group 3 bombers—including Lt(jg) Bob Elder and his wingman, who had just arrived from Henderson Field following Elder's refueling snafu—were either out of commission or needed to conduct air patrols around *Saratoga's* Task Force 11. In addition to two fighter squadrons, then, Fletcher had a total of fourteen SBDs and twelve TBFs remaining on hand for antisubmarine patrols or follow-on strikes. Beginning at 1326, immediately after the launch of a dozen freshly fueled Fighting-5 Wildcats to relieve the combat air patrol over Task Force 11, Commander Felt led the Air Group 3 strike aircraft aloft.

At the precise minute in which Felt's group began launching, Lt Dick Gray's Fighting-5 division was vectored out by the *Saratoga* FDO to investigate a radar bogey. Gray found a four-engine Mavis flying boat—undoubtedly out of Rabaul—and shot it down in flames at 1329 only seven miles off *Saratoga's* starboard beam. No one doubted but that the Mavis had been shadowing Task Force 11 for some time and that its crew had had plenty of time to report *Saratoga's* position to its base and possibly to Japanese carriers.

Once Felt's attack group had flown from sight, and until the *Enterprise* searchers reported in, control of events had passed from Frank Jack Fletcher's hand.

13

☀

Marine 2ndLt Mel Freeman was serving as the junior lieutenant with Marine Fighting Squadron 212 (VMF-212) at Espiritu Santo when Guadalcanal was invaded. Within a few days of the invasion, higher headquarters put out the word that five or six reserve fighter pilots were needed at Guadalcanal to serve with Capt John Smith's VMF-223, which was then on its way to the island and which would be flown off escort carrier *Long Island* as soon as the captured airstrip could be put into service.

VMF-212's skipper called all the pilots together and assured them that he knew everyone in the squadron would want to go. That being the case, he said, everyone would have to draw a card for the honor. Mel Freeman had never won a thing in his life, but he drew one of the lucky cards that time. The other winners were four other green second lieutenants and one well-seasoned warrant officer. The lucky six went on standby, and from that time until they left a few days later, they could head into town on liberty anytime they wanted. The recipients of the permissive liberty felt it was like a last favor for the condemned.

The news back from Guadalcanal in the first few weeks after the invasion was grim. The VMF-212 pilots heard reports of constant bombings and shellings, and they knew that the efforts to build the airfield were being hampered by a lack of equipment as well as the fact that the runway and air-base facilities were the main targets of the bombardments.

On August 21, the reserve pilots were finally put aboard an old World War I–era destroyer-transport loaded with aviation gasoline, bombs, and bullets for the Marine fighter and bomber squadrons that had arrived at Henderson Field two days earlier.

It was quite a trip. As the unescorted ship neared Guadalcanal and began cutting big circles in the water, Second Lieutenant Freeman saw several bombers high overhead. The bombers no sooner passed the ship—no one aboard had any idea whose they were—then the lookout yelled, "Torpedoes!" Immediately, the ship picked up so much speed that it went down by the bows just as the torpedo passed close astern.

It turned out that the destroyer-transport was waiting for the sun to go down so that it could sneak up to Kukum and land the munitions, fuel, and reserve pilots. After sunset, the vessel sailed along the beach for a time and then came to an abrupt stop. The reserve pilots climbed over the side into rubber boats. All they had with them was a parachute bag apiece filled with some clothes and their toothbrushes.

The six fresh fighter pilots did not get five yards up the beach before they heard some shooting. A dark form grabbed Mel Freeman and pushed him down. After the shooting stopped, the pilots were hustled into a vehicle and driven to a pitch-dark coconut grove. Sentries kept stopping the truck until someone finally told the driver he could not go any further in the dark. The pilots settled in for the night right there, falling asleep on their parachute bags.

In the morning, it was revealed to the VMF-212 aviators that they had come ashore the night after the big battle by the Tenaru River. Everyone on the island was jumpy and expected Japanese raiders to land on the beach—just like the reserve pilots had—or that infiltrators were trying to penetrate the coconut grove in order to get at the airplanes lined up near Henderson Field—just like the reserve pilots had.

Mel Freeman flew his first combat mission the next day, August 22, but did not encounter any Japanese warplanes. Freeman was also bombed for the first time that night when Japanese nuisance bombers randomly dropped bombs along the beach, runway, and coconut grove.

卍

RAdm Chuichi Hara's Mobile Force—10,150-ton *Ryujo*, the smallest Combined Fleet carrier, heavy cruiser *Tone*, and destroyers *Tokitsukaze* and *Amatsukaze*—was to attack Guadalcanal and draw off the American task force reportedly heading north against Bougainville. At the same time, VAdm Chuichi Nagumo's Carrier Striking Force, with its nucleus of two fleet carriers, was directed to turn northeastward and flank the enemy ships as they pursued Rear Admiral Hara's decoy force.

Rear Admiral Hara's Mobile Force set off from Truk at 26 knots on August 23. Cdr Tameichi Hara, *Amatsukaze*'s skipper, was glad to be going into his first really big mission of the war under Rear Admiral Hara, whom many considered to be a brilliant leader. However, Commander Hara was deeply troubled by the presence of the antiquated and diminutive *Ryujo* because "The best pilots were never assigned to older ships, and, after losing so many flyers at Midway, I was positive that *Ryujo* aviators were sadly inexperienced."

Mobile Force's first enemy contact came at 0913, August 24, when lookouts spotted an American scout—undoubtedly the Ndeni-based PBY that first reported *Ryujo*'s position. The PBY doggedly followed Mobile Force for many miles but eventually turned away, presumably because it was running low on fuel.

Mobile Force proceeded as planned for four more hours without sighting another enemy searcher. The sea in which *Ryujo* sailed that morning was extremely calm, but thick cloud cover obscured the sun and sky except at brief, infrequent intervals. The cloud conditions favored lurking snoopers, if there were any, and could mask enemy bombers as they maneuvered to deliver an attack.

At 1300, Mobile Force was 200 miles north of Guadalcanal. At that hour, *Ryujo* launched six Kate torpedo bombers and fifteen Zero fighters, which were to raid Henderson Field. Then *Ryujo* turned westward toward the spot at which she was scheduled to rendezvous with the attack group.

Everything appeared to be going according to plan.

卐

Perhaps unbeknown to RAdm Chuichi Hara, the Mobile Force commander, 11th Air Fleet, at Rabaul, launched a force of Betty medium bombers in time to meet *Ryujo's* Kates and Zeros as they approached Henderson Field from the direction of Malaita. It is not known if the projected confluence of the two attack forces was intentional or accidental.

The Bettys flew, as always, straight down the Slot on their way to Guadalcanal. This flight path took them directly over several hidden camps manned by British, New Zealand, and Australian coastwatchers who had remained in the Solomons following the Japanese occupation in order to man radios and monitor the comings and goings of warships and warplanes through the area. Late on the morning of August 24, 1942, the coastwatchers flashed warning messages to Henderson Field as the Bettys flew over them.

卐

From the moment of their arrival at Henderson Field only five days earlier, the Guadalcanal-based Wildcats of VMF-223 had been totally dependent upon coastwatcher sighting reports to place themselves in good position at ample altitude to intercept the almost daily air strikes by Rabaul-based bombers. Extremely slow climbers, the heavy, slightly underpowered F4Fs had to allow just enough time between takeoff and the appearance of the incoming strike to attain a height advantage over the attackers. If the slow-climbing Marine fighters arrived on the scene only a minute or two late, they might not be able to launch attacks against the bombers—

or penetrate phalanxes of swifter defending Zeros—until after the bombs had already fallen.

The fourteen alert fighters that were scrambled shortly before 1400 on the afternoon of August 24 were led by Capt Marion Carl, who had scored his first kill at Midway. In fact, Carl was one of the few Marine fighter pilots to survive Midway.

At 1420, the *Ryujo* Kates, which had been neither reported nor picked up by the crude radar available at Henderson Field, were streaking toward Savo Island from the direction of Malaita at 9,000 feet. The Bettys, coming from the northwest, were somewhat higher, and the Zeros accompanying the bomb-equipped Kates were higher still.

As soon as the Marine fighter pilots got the scramble order, the idea was to take off in order of divisions and sections behind the flight leader. However, in practice, everyone rushed to get the altitude advantage over the incoming bombers. Since some of the fighters could outperform others, the system of elements and divisions invariably broke down and everyone usually just joined up on whoever was closest.

VMF-212's Mel Freeman was pretty far back in the pack. For one thing, he was the junior lieutenant, so he started back in the pack on the ground. Also, he never got any of the better airplanes available, and that conspired to make him trail behind the leaders once he did get rolling.

The word was a bit late in arriving so, by the time the lead Wildcats had struggled to altitude, the Bettys had already dropped their bombs and were turning away to the northwest to head home to Rabaul. They were nose-down and *moving*.

The bombers were on the Marines' left as the Wildcats were completing the long climb. Capt Marion Carl was leading the pack, quite a bit above Mel Freeman, and very far ahead. There were Zeros flying toward the Wildcats from the far right. Several of the Grummans peeled off to meet them, but Carl held steady to catch up with the Bettys. Lieutenant Freeman kept his eyes on Carl as the flight leader "peeled off and delivered one of the most *beautiful* overhead runs I ever saw!"

It was by then time for Freeman to make his run on the Bettys.

He picked out one of the bombers and fired. It was an easy 45-degree deflection shot, but Freeman was rattled and misjudged. He was eventually able to pull the bullets from his six .50-caliber wing guns ahead of the right motor. Freeman was fairly certain he hit the Betty's fuselage, and he saw the engine start to smoke, but he dived through and did not see whether or not the Betty blew up.

Freeman passed right underneath the Betty and tried to get more speed to come back up and around. However, down below, he saw that he was overtaking a single-engine airplane with a big greenhouse canopy as it flew directly away from him. He instantly decided to go for the Kate, so he opened fire while still following through on the Betty. Freeman was certain he shot the rear gunner but was going so fast he had to pull up to get over the Japanese airplane. The gunner was just hanging over the side and the pilot and bombardier were looking up at the passing Wildcat. They had no defensive armament; there was nothing else they could do. Freeman stared back, trying to see their faces. He was sure that he would overrun the Kate and that the pilot would pull up behind him and fire imagined nose guns into the hurtling Wildcat; a fighter would have done so. Freeman pulled up to the left and turned so he could loop back behind the Kate.

Before Freeman could complete his maneuver, however, he looked up and saw a Japanese fighter really bearing down on him. He pulled around to go for the Zero head-on, and the two fighters exchanged shots. The Zero flew right over Freeman's head and kept going. Freeman lost track of him.

Lieutenant Freeman happened to be looking straight ahead when he saw one of the Grumman fighters spinning toward the earth right in front of him. The Wildcat was smoking, and Freeman thought he saw flames. He kept hoping that the pilot would get out, but the Marine rode his Wildcat all the way into the water. It turned out that the dead pilot was probably Freeman's roommate.

By the time Freeman saw the Wildcat go in, he could not find anyone else in the sky, so he flew back to the field and landed. He did not know if he had shot any of the Japanese planes down, but he did know that he had killed the Kate's rear gunner. "He was the first man I ever killed. Until then, I had not really thought much about killing anyone. I had survived. The killing felt weird, but the survival part was exhilarating."

⇄

A second phalanx of American fighters was represented by a pair of Army Air Forces pilots flying P-400 fighters—an inadequate Lend Lease version of the Bell P-39 Airacobra. Five of the long-nosed P-400s—which were armed with four .30-caliber and two .50-caliber wing-mounted machine guns and a 20mm cannon that peered out from the center of the propeller spinner (the engine was behind the pilot)—had flown into Henderson Field on August 22. Interception of the August 24 raid was the combat debut of the P-400 and the Army's 67th Pursuit Squadron over Guadalcanal.

The 67th Pursuit's skipper, Capt Dale Brannon, and his regular wingman, 2ndLt Deltis Fincher, saw the black Condition I flag go up over the air operations radar van and ran for their fighters. By the time the P-400s' engines had been started, both Army pilots could hear the drone of aircraft engines overhead. Bombs began hitting the runway as Brannon and Fincher turned off the taxiway and raced in echelon along the wide main runway. As the two lifted off and retracted landing gear, a fighter swooped low to strafe the runway.

After all the trouble Brannon and Fincher had gone to getting aloft, they missed out on the main action because of a previously unperceived altitude limitation imposed by their squadron's inability to charge the high-pressure British oxygen systems that had been installed in the fighters in anticipation of their being shipped to Britain. The P-400s got to 16,000 feet, but both pilots became woozy and had to drop back down to 14,000 feet to fully regain their senses.

As it was, a lone *Ryujo* Zero—undoubtedly attracted by the strange airplanes—flew into range. Brannon and Fincher pounced. They turned into one another and let fly with everything—a total of twelve machine guns and two 20mm cannon. The Zero disintegrated.

⇄

Capt Marion Carl destroyed one Betty, a second Betty was claimed by 2ndLt Gene Trowbridge, and 2ndLt Zenneth Pond claimed two. Mel Freeman claimed only a probable for the Betty he smoked, but he could very well have destroyed it.

With the arrival of the *Ryujo* Kates and Zeros, the Marines' attack on the Bettys broke up. The surviving medium bombers were allowed to fly from the area as all hands raced to stop the Kates or challenge the Zeros. In the ensuing wild melee, 2ndLt Gene Trowbridge claimed a Zero in addition to his two Bettys, TSgt Johnny Lindley thought he got another Zero, and VMF-212's MG Tex Hamilton claimed two Zeros destroyed. Capt Marion Carl shot down a Betty and two of the Kates and triumphed over a Zero—which, in addition to his Midway kill, made him the first Marine Corps fighter ace in history.

VMF-223 claimed twenty confirmed kills, but the Japanese lost, at most, three Kates, five Bettys, and four Zeros, including the one that fell to the Army P-400s.

At 1430, Cdr Tameichi Hara's *Amatsukaze* picked up a message from the only *Ryujo* Kate equipped with a radio. It claimed that the Guadalcanal bombing had been successful, but Commander Hara wondered just how effective the six-plane raid could have been.

Capt Tadao Kato, *Ryujo*'s captain, recorded that his six carrier attack planes and fifteen fighters "delivered a strong attack on the airfield at Guadalcanal, destroying fifteen enemy fighters in the air and bombing antiaircraft and machine-gun emplacements and silencing them." More to the point, Captain Kato's combat report claimed that "having been thoroughly deceived by this maneuver, the enemy believed this small force to be our main strength."

In fact, the *Ryujo* Kates and Rabaul-based Bettys caused negligible damage on the ground. Three Marine Wildcats were destroyed in the air, and their three pilots were killed.

14

Cdr Charlie Jett, the Torpedo-3 commander, and Ens Bob Bye, also of Torpedo-3, were sent to the northwest of Task Force 61 to search on the 320–330-degree sector. Everyone seemed to feel this was the most promising direction for finding the Japanese carrier pinpointed by the morning PBY searches out of Graciosa Bay. Jett was convinced that he and his young wingman really would find the carrier.

Shortly after Jett and Bye took off from *Enterprise*, ARM2 Dewey Stemen, Bye's radioman-turret gunner, spotted a Japanese reconnaissance plane—perhaps a Zero float fighter out of Rekata Bay. For a few moments, since the TBF was still climbing toward its search altitude of about 1,500 feet, Stemen thought that Bye was trying to intercept the snooper. Apparently the Japanese pilot thought the same thing—perhaps that the TBFs were F4Fs, which looked the same but were smaller. In any case, the snooper was soon lost in the clouds as he climbed away from Bye and Jett.

卐

The barely wavering drone of the single huge engine had been numbing the edge of his mind for what seemed like eons, and the gray haze blurred the image of the sea below as far as his hooded, steel-blue eyes could see. The crow's-feet at the edges of his eyes pulsed as he squinted into the uneven gray light. The sweaty, rubber-cushioned earphones constraining his close-cropped light brown hair snapped and whined at odd and infrequent intervals, but they had uttered no words since take-off. His eyes, aching from the watchfulness, darted across the horizon in long, practiced sweeps. He counted the whitecaps to test the speed and course of the otherwise unperceivable wind.

They could be there, LCdr Charlie Jett thought. The enemy carriers he had been stalking since the word reached him in San Diego that December Sunday, eight months earlier. If they were there, he mused . . . well, he'd report back and then attack them, hit them. Likely die trying. There seemed to be no other alternatives. They were out there. The carriers. Somewhere. In this sector, or the next one.

Charlie Jett quickly glanced aft over his right shoulder. Bye was still there, holding formation. Another young kid, as prepared for the war as any of Charlie Jett's seemingly aged contemporaries. Bye, the wingman, had it a tad tougher, Jett knew; he had to search as well as hold formation on his squadron commander. But the airplanes were good, responsive, forgiving of the gaffes the ensigns who filled Jett's torpedo-bomber squadron were prone to make. Hot kids, Jett knew; fighter pilots, most of them, dragooned to the torpedo squadrons to help make good the astounding losses sustained at Midway. God, Jett thought, so many dear friends lost in a matter of minutes!

Today was going to be the day Charlie Jett paid the killers back in kind. Not the actual killers, Jett knew; most of them had been lost in June, along with the torpedo crews with whom he had cruised and trained and partied in peacetime. But the same *kind* of killer was out there: the enemy carriers and the men who flew from them.

He looked once more to the left as he planned far in advance his turn across the end of the search sector and the long, fruitless flight back to the friendly carriers.

And that's when he thought he saw them, looming gray shapes

hundreds of feet down and to the left—roughly to the west. All he could see were their foaming wakes streaking the dull surface of the ocean.

It was 1440.

Within seconds, Jett was certain that one of them was a carrier, but he was unable to identify the other two or three ships.

The flight commander looked over at Bye, who was on his right wing. He was fairly certain the younger pilot had seen the ships, too. Bye stayed right with Jett, who flew on straight ahead while his radioman, ACRM I. H. Olson, broke radio silence to report the sighting and Jett's best reckoning of his position. The searchers' main job was to report back.

After reporting to base, Jett's first thought was that he controlled four 500-pound bombs—two in Bye's bomb bay and two in his own. He figured they were already out there, so he and Bye might as well try to damage the carrier.

Jett was sure that the searchers in neighboring sectors would be vectored over to his sector to pick up the trail or to mount attacks.

After the two torpedo bombers had observed the Japanese force for a while, ARM2 Dewey Stemen, Bye's radioman, transmitted an amplifying report to base. Stemen thought the TBFs would return to Task Force 61, so he was surprised when he noticed that they were still climbing and had turned toward the enemy ships. As Stemen was pondering these events, his earphones crackled as Bye informed the bombardier, AMM3 W. E. Dillon, that the torpedo bombers were going to attack the enemy carrier. Stemen riveted his attention to the search quadrants behind his airplane, looking for Japanese fighters.

The TBFs could not go in low, as they would have if they had had torpedoes aboard. Charlie Jett knew that the best altitude for a level bombing attack was 8,000 feet. He continued flying northward, slowly climbing all the way to conserve fuel.

卐

Lt(jg) Weasel Weissenborn and Ens Fred Mears were in the 290–300-degree sector—the westernmost sector, three sectors west of Jett and Bye. Both pilots heard some muttering over the air—Jett's report—but neither could quite make out the words. The mere fact that radio silence had been broken should have put the two on alert, but they overlooked the obvious and turned back to *Enterprise* at the end of their sector's short cross leg.

卐

Cdr Tameichi Hara, commander of destroyer *Amatsukaze*, had just finished eating his lunch on the bridge when one of his lookouts called, "A plane, looks like the enemy, coming from 30 degrees to port." Through binoculars, Hara indeed saw an airplane slipping in and out of the distant clouds.

Immediately, signal flags went up, ships' whistles blew, and antiaircraft guns were trained out to track the American airplane.

As the first airplane approached RAdm Chuichi Hara's Mobile Force, a second one emerged from the clouds. Cdr Tameichi Hara turned toward *Ryujo* and stared openmouthed, for the carrier was taking no precautionary action whatsoever.

Commander Hara ordered his antiaircraft guncrews to open fire, although the American bombers were well beyond range. Heavy cruiser *Tone*, the Mobile Force flagship, and destroyer *Tokitsukaze* also began firing—no doubt in reaction to *Amatsukaze*'s lead.

After an interminable delay, two Zero fighters took off from *Ryujo*. No other Japanese planes were aloft. The Zeros rapidly climbed toward the intruders, but their quarry flew into the clouds. Both fighters gave up the chase and flew back to take up station directly over *Ryujo*.

Commander Hara was astonished at *Ryujo*'s lack of aggressiveness in her own behalf. He was both worried and furious at the lackluster performance of the carrier's captain and the two fighter pilots. He felt that *Ryujo* would be helpless in the event a full-blown American air strike appeared, so he wrote out a note and gave it to his signal officer to transmit to the carrier by semaphor flags: "From Commander Tameichi Hara, *Amatsukaze* CO, to Commander Hisakichi Kishi, *Ryujo* Executive Officer: Fully realizing my impertinence, am forced to advise you my impression. Your flight operations are far short of expectations. What is the matter?"

The message was extraordinarily rude and audacious for a Japanese officer. Indeed, Hara was certain he was the first Japanese naval officer ever to have sent such a message during an operation. He had addressed the message to Commander Kishi because the two had been classmates at the Eta Jima Naval Academy. Hara knew that his classmate was not responsible for *Ryujo's* flight operations, but he wanted to make his feelings and fears understood; he was reasonably sure that Kishi would wield his influence with the carrier's master, Capt Tadao Kato.

The response was quickly transmitted by semaphore flags from *Ryujo's* bridge: "From Kishi to Commander Hara: Deeply appreciate your admonition. We shall do better and count on your cooperation." Minutes later, *Ryujo* began launching her entire remaining air complement of seven Zero fighters.

卐

Lt John Myers, the Torpedo-3 executive officer, was flying with Mach Harry Corl, also of Torpedo-3, in the 300–310-degree search sector—two sectors to LCdr Charlie Jett's left. The two had clear weather in their sector so Myers had elected to conduct his search from about 9,000 feet. It thus is quite possible that unperceived wind conditions at the higher altitude caused the two to drift off course well to the north of their intended route.

Lieutenant Myers did not hear Charlie Jett's position report at 1440. He and Corl had already turned on the cross leg of their search pattern, and they were about to turn again for the return leg. As they did, Myers spotted a Japanese heavy cruiser. That was at about 1500 hours. He first saw *Tone* from a distance of about eight miles at about one o'clock on his starboard bow. There was a cloud bank in the direction of the zigzagging ship.

Myers ordered his radioman to break radio silence and report the enemy position to *Enterprise*. Meanwhile, though the two Avengers were already at 9,000 feet, Myers and Corl spiraled higher, to 10,000 feet, to get above the antiaircraft fire. The fire from the cruiser was accurate and rising in steps from 7,000 to 9,000 feet. Myers absently noted that the cruiser sported five antiaircraft batteries—two on the port side, two on the starboard side, and one forward. There was no antiaircraft fire aft. The cruiser herself was a bit strange, for all four of her 8-inch gun turrets were forward of the bridge.

卐

As LCdr Charlie Jett finally neared bombing altitude at about 1500, he curved back around toward the carrier, west of it. This placed him in a favorable up-sun position relative to *Ryujo*, which he could now see was a very small carrier.

All four ships, which had been able to track Jett and Bye during the long climb, turned toward the torpedo squadron commander to present the smallest possible targets. When Jett and Bye got within range, all four ships began shooting at them. Despite the fire, Jett rigidly led Bye along the bombing line.

Jett was fairly certain he saw other airplanes a long way off during the early part of the bomb run, but he was also surprised that he had not encountered a Japanese combat air patrol. If there had been fighters up, he would never have had a chance to drop his bombs as he and his bombardier-gunner would have had their hands full defending themselves.

AMM2 Dewey Stemen, Ensign Bye's radioman-gunner, was also surprised that he had not seen any enemy aircraft during the climb or initial approach on *Ryujo*. As Stemen peered beyond the intense but very inaccurate antiaircraft fire, he noticed that there were no airplanes on the carrier's flight deck. He thought the absence of aircraft around the Japanese task force was very strange until he realized that *Ryujo* had probably already dispatched an attack force against an American target—presumably Task Force 61.

Jett began his bombing run at about 1510 from 12,200 feet. His bombardier, AMM2 Herman Calahan, was manning the Norden bombsight, which was located forward in the airplane, right beneath and behind the cockpit. Calahan, who by then had lined up the crosshairs of the bombsight on the carrier's deck, was in charge; he directed Jett on the final approach. Jett assumed that Bye was still with him, but he could not divert his attention from the target.

The antiaircraft fire from all four Japanese warships remained heavy, but it was all well below the two Avengers.

As soon as bombardier Calahan released the bombs, Jett dived away from the carrier at full power. *Ryujo* sharply turned to starboard as soon as the bombs were released. Charlie Jett saw all four bombs—Bye's and his own—simultaneously burst in the wake of the ship, about 150 feet astern, and very close together.

Jett kept diving away from the gunfire and leveled off again at full speed—about 250 miles per hour—at about 150 feet. He had done his job; it was time to head for home.

卐

As Lt John Myers and Mach Harry Corl started their horizontal bombing run on *Tone*, Myers's radioman-gunner reported at least three Zeros overhead. With that hint in mind, it was only a moment or two before Myers spotted the carrier and what appeared to be two destroyers.

One of the Zeros approached Myers's TBF from the port quarter, rolled over on its back, and fired. He missed, but two more Zeros dived on Myers's starboard beam. They both fired, but their tracers were low.

Myers radioed Corl to tell him to take independent evasive action and try to take cover in a cloud bank in the direction of the surface force. Myers reached the safety of the clouds, and made a position report to *Enterprise*. He found *Ryujo* again and attempted a low-level bomb run on her, but with no apparent results.

Next, Lieutenant Myers tried to radio Corl with orders to rendezvous for their return to base, but Corl did not respond. Myers's gunner told the pilot that he believed Corl's plane had been hit but that he was not sure. Further attempts to contact Corl failed, so Myers had his radioman transmit his last position to *Enterprise*. Then he turned for home alone.

(About six months later, one of Corl's crewmen, ARM3 Delmer Wiley, was picked up by an Allied coastwatcher and eventually returned to safety. Corl and his other crewman perished.)

卐

Ens H. L. Bingaman, of Torpedo-3, and Ens John Jorgenson, of Scouting-5, were flying together in the 310–320-degree sector, to the west of and immediately adjacent to Jett's sector. Bingaman was supposed to have flown with another TBF, but it had been grounded with a mechanical problem and Jorgenson's SBD had been substituted.

ARM3 Paul Knight, Bingaman's radioman-gunner, spotted the *Ryujo* force at about 1510. However, Bingaman descended to about 500 feet and to within about 5 miles of the enemy ships before ordering Knight to transmit a position report. Knight, who was scanning the entire sky from his power turret, saw no other planes in the area, but someone in the two-plane section, probably Jorgenson, later reported seeing two TBFs make a horizontal bombing run and two other Avengers being chased by a Zero. After Knight made his report, Bingaman and Jorgenson turned back for *Enterprise*.

卐

The last search team to find *Ryujo* was composed of two Dauntlesses flown by the Scouting-5 flight officer, Lt Birney Strong, and Ens John Richey. As Strong led Richey down the inbound leg of their 330–340-degree sector at 1,500 feet, he saw at least three ships about 15 miles ahead and to starboard. That was at 1510—the same time that Jett and Bye were dropping their bombs, Myers and Corl were being attacked by Zeros, and Bingaman and Jorgenson were approaching *Ryujo*.

Strong led Richey in a shallow dive to investigate. As the two SBDs flew through the haze, Strong counted three surface warships. He did not at first see *Ryujo*, but the haze before him shifted a bit as he came to within five miles of the Japanese task force. There was *Ryujo!*

Immediately, Strong's radioman, ARM2 Gene Strickland, telegraphed a message to *Enterprise*: "Position lat[itude] 06-25 S, longi[tude] 161-20 E, course 180, speed 15 [knots]." Though Strickland keyed the message over and over in plain language for six straight minutes, *Enterprise* did not acknowledge.

Their job done as well as they could do it, Lieutenant Strong and Ensign Richey turned for home.

A total of five TBFs and three SBDs flew at least to within sighting distance of RAdm Chuichi Hara's Mobile Force. At least five separate sighting reports were transmitted by the American searchers beginning at 1440. However, the first report—Jett's—did not reach Task Force 61 until 1548. The reasons for the delay were purely technical: The fleet fighter directors were making heavy use of the frequency they shared with the searchers during the period of the numerous *Ryujo* sightings; and local radio disturbances were created whenever the fleet had to operate at high speed to launch or recover aircraft, as it was doing throughout that hour.

Earlier receipt of the *Ryujo* sightings would undoubtedly have cleared the air around the Task Force 61 flag deck of the fog of war that was created by other reports involving the location of VAdm Chuichi Nagumo's anticipated Carrier Striking Force.

卐

The first Americans to see Nagumo's Carrier Striking Force were the crew of a Ndeni-based PBY searching in what, for carrier-based searchers, would have been the 340–350-degree sector—a little west of due north of Task Force 61. The time of the crucial sighting was 1500.

At 1505, only five minutes after the fresh PBY sighting, Com-AirSoPac reported the find to Task Force 61. The position report placed "one carrier" about 60 miles northeast of the position reported in the morning by the first PBY to sight *Ryujo*. It was felt by Fletcher's staffers that the new sighting was merely the *Ryujo* task force. In the absence of reports from Jett, Bye, Myers, Corl, Bingaman, Jorgenson, Strong, and Richey the surmise was reasonable.

It seemed that the launch of Air Group 3 toward the early *Ryujo* sighting had been the best possible decision after all.

卐

Air searchers normally went out 200 miles, flew a cross leg, and then flew back 200 miles to base. However, on August 24, Lt John Lowe, the Bombing-6 executive officer, and Ens Bob Gibson, also of Bombing-6, were ordered to fly out 50 miles farther than usual in the 350–360-degree search sector. Lowe and Gibson flew at 1,000 feet and navigated by dead reckoning.

The two were nearing the tail end of their extended search sector at exactly 1500 when they ran into what appeared to be five heavy cruisers and three destroyers bearing 180-degrees and sailing at 20 knots. The position was almost due north of the spot where Lowe and Gibson had launched from *Enterprise*. There appeared to be other ships far to the northwest.

Lowe's radioman immediately transmitted a contact report, but he received no response. Lowe led Gibson up to a higher altitude and tried to send the report again. Still no answer.

Next, the two Dauntlesses circled to the east—up-sun and away from the cruiser force—and climbed to 11,000 feet. Lowe had decided to bomb the largest cruiser.

The U.S. Navy dive-bombers pitched over into their dives at 1510. As they dived, the cruiser turned her beam to them. As they neared the end of the dive, the cruiser abruptly swung to starboard and skidded around to reverse course. Most of the antiaircraft gunfire was falling away well short of the dive-bombers.

Lowe and Gibson both released their 500-pound bombs at 2,500 feet, glided the rest of the way down to 20 feet off the water, and retired to the south at full throttle. On the way down, Lowe's radioman-gunner saw his bomb strike the water about 20 yards off the cruiser's port quarter. Ensign Gibson's bomb hit within 25 feet of the cruiser's port bow; its blast sprayed seawater over the cruiser's bows, but did no apparent damage.

Lowe had had the impression that the cruiser fired her main guns at him as he was leaving the area with Gibson.

Lowe and Gibson had found part of RAdm Hiroaki Abe's Vanguard Force, which was serving as the outer screen protecting Nagumo's Carrier Striking Force from surface attack. Abe's Vanguard Force was also on alert to deliver a surface attack against the American carrier task force if they sailed within striking range of one another.

As Lieutenant Lowe feared, neither of his sighting reports reached Task Force 61.

Lt Ray Davis, the Bombing-6 commander, and his wingman, Ens Robert Shaw, were flying a 250-mile search in the 340–350-degree sector. They were at 1,500 feet and flying on the outbound leg of the search when they both sighted a large Japanese task force. Initially, Davis saw only cruisers and destroyers, and he decided to attack one of the two leading light cruisers. As Davis's radioman-gunner, AOM1 John Trott, transmitted the sighting report, the Dauntlesses went into a steep, spiraling climb to about 14,000 feet.

During the climb, Ray Davis detected a carrier of about 20,000 tons behind the light cruisers. Another carrier was a little further off. The near carrier—Davis identified it as *Shokaku*—had a flight deck full of planes. She became Davis's priority target.

AOM1 Trott's sighting report to *Enterprise* identified two large carriers with full flight decks, four heavy cruisers, six light cruisers, and eight destroyers on course 120 degrees—southeast—at a speed of 25 knots.

Davis and Shaw began their dives from upwind and down-sun at 1545. Davis noted that the target carrier was turning to starboard when he began his dive. In the time it took Davis and Shaw to drop from 7,000 feet to 2,000 feet, the carrier completed a 60-degree turn.

Heavy antiaircraft fire was bursting at all levels up to and beyond the diving Dauntlesses. The larger caliber fire seemed to be inaccurate, but many of the smaller weapons seemed to be right on target. As Davis was bounced all over the sky by near misses, he felt he would be extraordinarily lucky to survive.

The American pilots released their 500-pound bombs at 2,000 feet, followed through into low pull-outs, and withdrew at high speed more or less in the direction of the easternmost light cruiser.

Trott reported to Lieutenant Davis that his bomb hit no more than 5 feet off the carrier's starboard side, aft of amidships. Shaw's bomb hit no more than 20 feet off the carrier's starboard quarter, close to Davis's. Both SBD gunners saw two splashes of water where the bombs struck, and a single column of smoke.

Shaw's gunner, AOM2 Harold Jones, observed eight planes amidships and a dozen more spotted aft on the carrier's flight deck. The ordeal was far from over.

Accurate antiaircraft fire from the easternmost light cruiser struck both dive-bombers as they passed over that ship. And there were seven or eight planes in the air over the carrier. One, a Zero, began a run on the retiring Dauntlesses. Fortunately—miraculously—antiaircraft fire from the forward light cruiser brought the Zero down.

AOM1 Trott and AOM2 Jones repeatedly broadcast contact reports as Davis and Shaw flew back to *Enterprise*.

卍

Neither *Saratoga* nor *Enterprise* picked up Lt Ray Davis's contact report, but several screening vessels did, and the news was immediately relayed to *Saratoga's* flag bridge. As VAdm Frank Jack Fletcher and his staff pored over their charts, they saw the outlines of the massive Japanese trap. It was clear from Davis's contact reports that the big Japanese carriers—which were only 198 miles to the north—were on the verge of launching a killing blow against Task Force 61. It was also clear that *Ryujo* was the bait, precisely as Fletcher had feared she might be.

Fletcher ordered the immediate transmission of a message aimed at diverting Cdr Don Felt's Air Group 3 strike force away from *Ryujo* and toward *Shokaku* and *Zuikaku*.

15

Soon after launching, and not many miles away from *Saratoga*, S1 Bob Hansen, a Scouting-3 radioman-gunner, became aware of a worsening stomachache and shooting pains in his groin. Hansen at first thought he had come down with appendicitis, or something worse, and became extremely agitated about his possible fate. The pains increased until he became too uncomfortable to sit still or concentrate on scanning his dive-bomber's rear quadrants for enemy fighters. Soon Hansen found himself internally debating about whether or not he should ask his pilot, Ens Jim Sauer, to turn back because he was too ill to go on. While trying to arrive at a decision, Hansen continuously squirmed around in his seat trying to contrive a position that would permit him to relieve the stress in his guts. He hated to ask Sauer to turn back on a combat hop the pilot had been looking forward to during two years of training and operational flying and wondered if he could suffer in silence until his Dauntless returned to *Saratoga* hours later.

As Seaman Hansen shifted around in search of a comfortable position, he unbuckled the leg straps of his constraining parachute harness to give himself a little added freedom. Immediately he noticed a marked improvement in the aches and pains, so he began searching for the secret of such welcome relief. After almost completely recovering from the distress, he realized that, in his haste to put on his parachute, he had unwittingly strapped his left testicle to his left leg.

Ensign Sauer was permitted to undertake his maiden combat flight without interruption. The only strike plane to abort was one of eight TBFs, which had an engine malfunction.

☡

At 1548, Cdr Don Felt's radioman intercepted a contact report stating that one carrier, one cruiser, and two destroyers were at latitude 06° 25' south, longitude 161° 00' east on course 270 degrees at a speed of 20 knots. Felt immediately shifted his heading northward to make for the indicated position. However, when the *Saratoga* strike bombers did not make contact as expected, Felt turned back to a westerly heading.

At this point, Felt's command radio receiver failed, and he had to turn the lead over to LCdr Bullet Lou Kirn, the Scouting-3 commander.

No one in the strike group received VAdm Frank Jack Fletcher's message to divert from the *Ryujo* fix and attack *Shokaku* and *Zuikaku*.

☡

RAdm Chuichi Hara's Mobile Force was sighted by the *Saratoga* strike group at 1605 near latitude 06° 32' south, longitude 160° 40' east. *Ryujo* and her consorts were on a southwesterly course and running at high speed. At the time of the sighting, the American bombers were at 14,500 feet and southeast of *Ryujo*. High scattered clouds bordered the enemy task force. The surface wind was estimated to be 8 knots from out of the southeast.

As the strike group closed on Mobile Force, Commander Felt directed that Scouting-3, the 1st Division of Bombing-3, and five of the seven remaining Torpedo-8 TBFs attack *Ryujo* while Bombing-3's 2nd Division and the two remaining TBFs attack cruiser

Tone. Upon the order "Execute," the strikers climbed away to the north and began the final approach from the northeast at 16,000 feet.

During the climbing approach, *Ryujo* was observed turning into the wind and launching one or two Zeros.

彁

While *Ryujo* was launching her ready fighters, her surface escort—cruiser *Tone* and destroyers *Amatsukaze* and *Tokitsukaze*—moved to protect the minuscule carrier with a ring of antiaircraft fire. One of the destroyers took up station on the starboard beam of the carrier, the other destroyer was ahead on the port bow, and *Tone* was ahead on the starboard quarter and about three miles away.

At the same time, *Ryujo* frantically radioed her returning Guadalcanal strike force to order the Kates and Zeros to fly directly to an emergency airstrip at Buka, about midway between Guadalcanal and Rabaul.

彁

Scouting-3's attack commenced at 1620 from 14,000 feet, with dives initiated from the northwest quadrant. Several Japanese planes were observed circling the carrier at low altitude, and light, ineffective antiaircraft fire from the carrier was encountered by the plummeting dive-bombers.

LCdr Bullet Lou Kirn's own five-plane 1st Division of Scouting-3 was the first to push over into near-vertical dives. Kirn was the leader. All five pilots dropped their 1,000-pound bombs from about 2,500 feet but scored no hits.

Next up was Scouting-3's 2nd Division, led by the squadron executive officer, Lt Robert Milner. Lt(jg) Bill Henry's rearseatman told Henry that his bomb landed close to the ship, inside the carrier's turn.

Another member of Milner's division, Ens Roger Crow, had mastered a unique dive-bombing technique while still in training early in the war. When Crow's dive-bomber—number S-13—went into the dive, Crow not only flipped open his dive flaps, he also flipped the adjacent landing-gear control. So, instead of diving at a rather breathless 240 knots, he went down at about 160 knots. With the wheels and flaps slowing Crow, all the trailing Scouting-3 bombers soon passed him.

Crow's airplane was shaking violently, something he had not learned to overcome in his ongoing experiments. When he looked down at the deck of the carrier and saw all the ships shooting at him, he naturally thought he was being hit. He looked around for fighters, but did not see any.

While Ensign Crow hung as if suspended in midair, the four members of Scouting-3's 2nd Division who had started out behind him dropped their 1,000-pound bombs—and missed.

The five Dauntlesses of Scouting-3's 3rd Division, led by Lt Ralph Weymouth, also passed Ensign Crow in their dives.

卐

Ens Jim Sauer called back to his radioman-gunner, S1 Bob Hansen, over the phones, "Are you ready, Hansen?"

"Ready as ever."

"Here we go, then."

Their SBD assumed the vertical.

In all dives, the man in the rear cockpit dives backward. His primary purpose is to protect the pilot and plane from enemy fighters. Thus Seaman Hansen caught only a fleeting, furtive look over his shoulder at the target. The flight deck was painted a dull orange color. Near the bow was a large red circle; he presumed it was for identification purposes. Hansen thought the sight of the colorful warpaint contrasting with the bright blue of the water and the foaming, silvery-white wake was rather pretty. So far as he was concerned—war or no war—the Japanese had built a beautiful ship.

Sauer's and Hansen's dive was uneventful. Their Dauntless was not hit by antiaircraft fire, and the expected Zeros did not materialize. After Ensign Sauer released his 1,000-pound bomb, he pulled out of his dive, which allowed Hansen to take a good long look at the beautiful warship. As Sauer leveled off just above the water, Hansen saw bullets kicking up tiny fountains of spray alongside the plane, and an occasional burst of antiaircraft from *Tone* soared over their heads, but without effect.

࿕

Lt Syd Bottomley, whose Bombing-3 division was flying into position to attack *Tone*, watched in amazement as Dauntless after Dauntless dived on *Ryujo*—as 1,000-pound bombs fell all around her without any direct hits. *Ryujo* was circling at high speed, a tactic Bottomley had seen Japanese destroyers use at Midway with astounding success.

Lt Gordon Sherwood, a senior member of Bottomley's division, also watched in amazement as all those dive-bombers peppered the water all around the carrier with their bombs. Like Syd Bottomley, Sherwood ascribed the misses to *Ryujo*'s speed and her seemingly endless skidding turn.

࿕

All but one of the Scouting-3 bombers assigned to *Ryujo* had released their 1,000-pound bombs and missed.

The last man to reach drop altitude was Ens Roger Crow. Because of his slow speed, he had a dead easy shot at the carrier.

Dive-bomber pilots normally gauged their bomb drops on the leader's bomb. When Crow saw where the bombs of every man in front of him missed, he made the needed correction. It was good enough. Crow's 1,000-pound bomb went straight down *Ryujo*'s forward elevator.

S1 Bob Hansen was riding Ens Jim Sauer's Scouting-3 Dauntless away from *Ryujo* when he definitely saw Crow's bomb strike the carrier. Smoke and debris ascended several hundred feet in the air, and an open fire broke out. That was Scouting-3's only hit.

As the Scouting-3 Dauntlesses ran from the immediate vicinity of *Ryujo* and her consorts to a predetermined rendezvous point, LCdr Bullet Lou Kirn's radioman-gunner, ACRM C. E. Russ, definitely saw a Zero fighter destroyed when it flew over an exploding bomb on the water. When there was a moment to look back, Kirn himself saw that *Ryujo* was heavily smoking from Ensign Crow's solitary hit.

卐

Bombing-3's 1st Division, led by LCdr DeWitt Shumway, made diving attacks on *Ryujo* from 15,000 feet. The planes dived from various directions in an attempt to counteract the expert ship handling that had thrown off the aim of all but one of the preceding Scouting-3 pilots.

Lt Paul Holmberg, who was following Shumway at about a 10-second interval, had difficulty picking up the carrier in his bombsight because the dive-bomber division was badly out of position for making a good dive on the carrier. *Ryujo* was steaming in a tight circle and Holmberg noticed that *Tone* was in a bigger circle surrounding the carrier. He had to rotate his airplane's wings counter-clockwise about 60 degrees and pull up the nose a little to move the crosshairs in his bombsight "on top" of the carrier's flight deck. Holmberg saw Shumway's bomb leaving his aircraft at about 2,000 feet, and he could see that it was going to miss the target. As a result of his observation, Holmberg tried to skid his airplane around to get his bomb to hit, or at least drop closer to the target than Shumway's. He did so by depressing his left rudder pedal. Holmberg did not see his bomb hit *Ryujo*, but shortly after he pulled out of the dive, he looked back and thought he saw a tall geyser of water alongside the starboard quarter of the carrier. How much damage Holmberg's near miss caused is problematic.

Though hits were claimed by several members of Bombing-3's 1st Division, it is virtually certain that, of twenty-one 1,000-pound bombs dropped thus far, only Ens Roger Crow's had actually struck *Ryujo*.

卐

While the twenty-one Scouting-3 and Bombing-3 SBDs assigned to attack *Ryujo* were mounting the main attack, Bombing-3's seven-plane 2nd Division, under the squadron exec, Lt Syd Bottomley, was on its way northward to get into the best position from which to attack heavy cruiser *Tone*. Bottomley deliberately took his time getting lined up for his dive against the cruiser because the antiaircraft fire was light and only three or four fighters were observed in the air. An extremely skilled veteran dive-bomber leader, Bottomley felt he had all the time in the world to do it right.

Farther out, the leader of Bottomley's second element, Lt Gordon Sherwood, could see a pair of TBFs circling near the edge of a cloud, waiting until Bottomley's division began its attack to begin their own runs against *Tone*.

At length, Bottomley's Dauntlesses arrived in position to dive on *Tone*. As Bottomley pushed over, he kept *Ryujo* in sight out of the corner of his eye. Dauntlesses were still diving on her, but there were as yet no hits. At last, after losing several thousand feet of altitude in his 60-degree dive, Lieutenant Bottomley precipitously pulled out and closed his SBD's dive brakes. He radioed Lt Gordon Sherwood, "Hey, Gordon, belay that. Come over and hit the carrier."

At just that moment, Cdr Don Felt noted that nothing better than very close misses were being obtained by the first ten dive-bombers, so he radioed Bottomley to countermand his original order; everything was to be put on the carrier.

When what Felt thought was the last dive-bomber had gone into its dive, he too pitched over and attacked *Ryujo*. According to Felt's radioman-gunner, who took a photograph as they pulled out of the dive, Felt obtained a hit slightly to the left and abaft the center of *Ryujo*'s flight deck. As Felt pulled out, he took a quick look back and then strafed a destroyer that suddenly loomed in his gunsight.

卐

While Commander Felt was making his solitary dive, Lt Syd Bottomley's seven-plane Bombing-3 division picked up a little of its lost altitude as it got into position to get the carrier.

Prior to a combat dive, there were several things to be taken into consideration. The most important was the direction of the surface wind. It was preferable for the dive-bombers to work their way upwind of the target to a point where their angle to the target from the horizontal is about 70 degrees. This diminished the effect of the wind in deflection errors, right or left. On the other hand, it steepened the dive toward the vertical, if they were diving downwind, and increased the possibility of throwing the bomb over the target. It was much more difficult to hit a target if the wind moved the dive-bomber right or left and if the path of the plane turned into a corkscrew. Diving upwind flattened the dive, which lessened the vertical speed and kept the bomber in its dive longer.

The speed and direction of the carrier was a factor that was best compensated for during the dive by estimating where the helpful red ball at *Ryujo*'s bow was going to be at the time the bomb would hit. So far as Syd Bottomley was concerned, this was the factor that would separate a hit from a near miss.

With the carrier slightly forward of the beam, Bottomley waggled his wings and peeled out of the formation, followed by his wingman and the rest of his division. As Bottomley pushed over for the second time in a matter of minutes, he vowed to himself to flame the carrier with his bomb or plummet all the way into the flight deck. Fortunately, the only opposition was from antiaircraft gunfire; not one Zero had approached in Bottomley's sector at altitude.

As Bottomley's nose tipped all the way over, he acquired the carrier's flight deck in his optical bombsight. He opened the dive brakes and throttled the engine back, pushing the fuel mixture control forward to "automatic rich" while putting the propeller in low pitch and the blowers—air intakes—in low. He could still adjust the trim tabs as needed and concentrate on the dive maneuver.

Bottomley pointed the crosshairs of the sight at the position where he expected the carrier to move and momentarily held them there to see how the wind was affecting the dive and whether the target was moving as he had estimated.

On the way down, while the carrier was still in her turn, Bottomley tried to visualize the advance and transfer vector that the carrier's bridge was making. He twisted his airplane toward the projected aiming point.

Bottomley's rearseatman, AMM1 David Johnson, sang out the altimeter readings as they descended. Bottomley constantly corrected all the way down. He knew that he had to be steady on by

4,000 feet; last-minute corrections before hitting the release point were futile.

Shortly after Johnson called out 3,000 feet, Bottomley felt he was in position. He pressed the electric bomb-release button on the top of his stick to release his 1,000-pound bomb. Immediately, he reached forward under the instrument panel to pull the manual bomb release—just to make sure. Due to altimeter lag, he knew he must have been at about 1,200 to 1,500 feet when the heavy bomb fell away.

Lt Gordon Sherwood saw Syd Bottomley's bomb strike *Ryujo* squarely amidships.

Due to the excitement of the pull-out—closing dive brakes, putting on full throttle, getting down on the water, heading for the nearest opening between the screening ships, jinking and turning to avoid antiaircraft fire—Bottomley was unable to see what followed. But AMM1 Johnson could. He reported at least three more hits before he was no longer able to follow the action.

Lt Gordon Sherwood carefully watched his altimeter before releasing his bomb. His rearseatman and others saw it hit a little behind Bottomley's. As Sherwood pulled out, he saw Lt(jg) Roy Isaman get a hit, too.

By this time, *Ryujo* was smoking badly. Flames were soaring from beneath the flight deck on both sides and down her entire length.

As S1 Bob Hansen's Scouting-3 Dauntless ran from the Japanese task force, Hansen's only thought was to look for fighters. He scanned the sky and water for aircraft. Since all Hansen could see was clear sky except for two friendly torpedo bombers that were just going into the attack, he peeked at the carrier: "The ship appeared in black silhouette. Heavy black smoke was curling from the sides and rolling over the deck in a streaming curtain. An occasional lick of flame appeared from amidships. The water cut by the bow was high enough to attract my attention from the ship itself. I surmised that her skipper was turning his speed up to full. From out of the smoke near the after end, flickering spurts of rapid-fire antiaircraft were showing. I marveled at the pluck and downright guts of the gunners sticking to their tasks against such strong and horrible odds."

Cdr Tameichi Hara, captain of destroyer *Amatsukaze*, saw nearly the same sights as Seaman Hansen: "Two or three enemy bombs hit [*Ryujo*] near the stern, piercing the flight deck. Scarlet flames shot up from the holes. Ominous explosions followed in rapid order. Several more bombs made direct hits. Water pillars surrounded the carrier, and it was engulfed in thick, black smoke. This was no deliberate smoke screen. Her fuel tanks had been hit and set afire."

卐

The TBFs of Torpedo-8 were up next.

Many of the Avenger pilots over Mobile Force had personal scores to settle that day. Torpedo-8 had been virtually wiped out at Midway, all but one attacking pilot slaughtered in a suicidal torpedo attack. Several Torpedo-8 pilots had been detailed to bring new TBFs out to the Pacific from the States to replace the slow Douglas TBD-1 Devastators in which the main body of the squadron had flown to its death at Midway. The new TBFs and their crews had arrived too late to depart for the battle aboard their carrier, so they had flown to the Midway airstrip. From there, several had delivered an attack on the Japanese fleet. Of that contingent, only Ens Corwin Morgan and his crew had survived. Morgan was leading the two-plane element assigned to attack *Tone*.

The larger Torpedo-8 contingent—the five TBFs initially assigned to launch an attack against *Ryujo*—began encountering antiaircraft fire while gliding downward from 12,000 feet. Despite the gunfire, the flight leader, Lt Bruce Harwood, proceeded with the attack. The bulk of the antiaircraft fire was behind the Avengers, which employed their high speed and jinking maneuvers to evade it. However, most of *Ryujo*'s surviving Zeros were spotted between sea level and 7,000 feet.

As the TBFs passed 2,000 feet, they were attacked by several Zeros. Ens Gene Hanson, Harwood's second-element leader, was facing Zeros for the first time; he found them to be very fast and maneuverable. Two or three of them attacked Harwood, but they did not stay with his element very long. One started to make a run on Ensign Hanson, who ordered his turret gunner to track it. However, as Hanson saw the Zero above start to dive on his TBF, he pulled the huge carrier bomber up on its tail and headed straight for it. The Zero immediately veered away. Hanson's turret gunner got off a couple of rounds at it as he went by. Ens Aaron Katz, who was behind Hanson, radioed to say that the Zero's bullets went way above Hanson's airplane. For some reason, Ensign Hanson alone was singled out for attack by the Zeros. He was strafed three more times, but succeeded each time in scaring the enemy fighters away.

The truth is that the *Ryujo* fighter pilots did not press their attacks with much determination. Many of the TBF gunners reported hitting the Zeros, but no kills were claimed.

The Zeros disappeared altogether when the torpedo bombers broke into two sections ahead of *Ryujo* to deliver simultaneous hammer-and-anvil torpedo attacks against both of the carrier's bows. At that point, Gene Hanson noted, the carrier, cruiser, and destroyers were throwing everything they had at the TBFs. He was sure that the antiaircraft fire was the major factor in the withdrawal of the Zeros.

Lieutenant Harwood's section of three TBFs took the starboard bow, and Ensign Hanson went after the port bow along with Ensign Katz. The Scouting-3 attack, which had been going on throughout the approach of the torpedo bombers, was by then concluded. It was necessary for both Harwood and Hanson to postpone their attack three separate times due to the smoke obscuring the carrier from Ens Roger Crow's hit, and perhaps Cdr Don Felt's as well. There was a large fire amidships coming from beneath the flight deck. During one abortive approach, the TBF pilots saw at least three more definite bomb hits on the carrier—all by Lt Syd Bottomley's Bombing-3 division.

In that time, Lieutenant Harwood estimated, the carrier made two complete circles. When he could finally see her again with some clarity, she was still moving, but slowly—at less than 10 knots—and apparently losing speed fast. At that moment, *Ryujo* was broadside to Harwood's approach and in an ideal position for a torpedo run. Harwood released his torpedo.

On the opposite bow, Gene Hanson had identical difficulties getting into a good attack position. By the time he did, *Ryujo* appeared to be completely ablaze from bomb hits. Hanson released his torpedo at about 1,200 yards, but was unable to see if he scored as he immediately made a left turn to dodge the heavy antiaircraft fire.

S1 Bob Hansen, of Scouting-3, saw a huge column of water appear from the far side of the ship—Ensign Hanson's side. He was certain that at least one of the torpedo bombers had scored a hit. Moments later, Seaman Hansen saw several more columns of water, more smoke, and more debris rise all around *Ryujo*.

Nearby, Cdr Don Felt's radioman-gunner observed a torpedo hit on the starboard bow of the carrier—Harwood's side. It lifted the bow out of the water and set it over to the left.

Lt Gordon Sherwood, of Bombing-3, saw one perfect torpedo hit that threw water high into the air. To Sherwood, it appeared that the carrier was jarred from her course upon impact.

Ryujo lost headway and soon lay dead in the water.

Torpedo-8 claimed one certain and two probable hits on *Ryujo*. It is possible—even probable—that still other torpedoes struck the light carrier's hull but failed to detonate.

卐

The attack on *Tone* as originally ordered by Cdr Don Felt was to be a coordinated attack by Lt Syd Bottomley's Bombing-3 division and two TBFs under Ens Corwin Morgan, the Midway survivor. The attack order was countermanded by Commander Felt, but the TBFs did not get the countermand order and proceeded with their attacks on the cruiser.

During the final approach on *Tone*, Ensign Morgan's wingman, Ens Robert Divine, was repeatedly attacked by Zero fighters. Divine's plane was struck by bullets from one Zero while he was making his torpedo run, but he persisted in his attack. Morgan and Divine released their torpedoes on the starboard quarter, but, though a hit was claimed, both missed.

卐

Cdr Tameichi Hara, of destroyer *Amatsukaze*, watched in stupefaction as the long lines of American bombers turned from *Ryujo* and headed for the carrier's three surface consorts: "All guns opened fire as the planes swooped on us. My ship was making 33 knots and zigzagging frantically. Tremendous bow waves kicked up by the speeding destroyer drenched me on the bridge."

If Commander Hara was made to feel uncomfortable by the American airmen, it was more or less unintentional. All the U.S. Navy pilots and aircrewmen had one basic impulse once their bombs and torpedoes had been dropped: Escape!

卐

Ens Bill Behr, a Bombing-6 pilot who had been swept into Scouting-3 for the strike, had been the third American pilot to release his bomb over *Ryujo*. Behr was pulling out at 1,200 feet when a pair of Zeros took up station on his SBD, one on either side. Sensing that the Zeros were about to initiate simultaneous firing passes on his plane, Behr turned into the right-hand fighter. But he was a little too late; fourteen 7.7mm rounds fired by the left-hand Zero struck the evading Dauntless. Ensign Behr next pushed the stick in his right hand all the way to the firewall and dived away from the Zeros, which completed several more firing passes apiece before they drew off. After turning toward *Saratoga*, Behr climbed back to 1,000 feet, where he met three more Zeros. Without waiting for any prompting, Behr pointed his Dauntless's nose back toward the waves. The Zeros followed, but they could not get in any good firing passes so close to the water, and they soon departed.

As Lt(jg) Bill Henry, of Scouting-3, pulled out of his dive low on the water, he passed too near a Japanese destroyer. Henry was sure the destroyer's gunners would fill his SBD with antiaircraft rounds, but the gunfire seemed to be passing him in favor of another target farther to the right. Henry nervously glanced in the direction of the heaviest fire and saw that Ens Roger Crow was flying with his wheels down and that he was the main target for all the antiaircraft gunfire.

The Japanese were apparently concentrating on Crow because

he was the slowest target in the sky. By the time he got his speed up, the gunners had him zeroed in, so they kept after him. All the gunfire was hitting the water close to Crow's SBD Number S-13, but instead of turning tail—as he would have been expected to do—he flew up through the funnels of bullets. So long as the gunfire hit the water, he knew, he could safely gain altitude to miss the deadly trajectories. It was a good theory; he did not get a single hole in the airplane. After a long solitary escape, Crow caught up with the rest of his squadron.

After pulling out of his dive, Lt Paul Holmberg, the second member of Bombing-3 to drop his bomb, saw a Japanese fighter up ahead making a pass at LCdr DeWitt Shumway's airplane. Next, the Zero turned to make a pass at Holmberg, who turned toward the fighter in a such a way as to force him to turn into a tighter circle if he expected to shoot Holmberg down. Apparently, the Zero pilot was out of ammunition or did not want to wrap up in a tight turn that close to the water—they were at less than 100 feet—so he broke off the attack.

After getting clear of the screening vessels, Lt Syd Bottomley headed for Bombing-3's rendezvous point and made one or two orbits to allow other members of his squadron to join on him. Then they headed straight for Task Force 61.

🜨

AOM1 Ervin Wendt, Lt Bruce Harwood's TBF tunnel gunner, could not use his single ventral .30-caliber machine gun until after Harwood had dropped his torpedo, made a left turn, and swung away from *Ryujo*. At that point, Wendt was free to strafe the burning ship's flight deck.

As Harwood was retiring, one Zero followed him. Harwood managed to turn his large but highly maneuverable torpedo bomber under the nimble Zero. Then ACRM G. J. Sullivan drew a bead with his single turret-mounted power-operated .50-caliber machine gun and let fly. The Zero pulled out before coming close enough to hurt Harwood's airplane, although Harwood saw bullets hitting the water ahead of his wing. When the Zero returned for another pass, AOM1 Wendt looked up through ACRM Sullivan's turret in time to see the Japanese attack from overhead at a 45-degree angle. Wendt saw Sullivan's tracer rounds fall into the Zero's nose and knock off part of the engine cowling. Then the evasive motion of the TBF caused Wendt to lose sight of the Japanese plane, which did not make another attempt to duel Chief Sullivan.

As Ens Gene Hanson was retiring in the direction of *Tone*, his TBF was hit in the tail by a small-caliber explosive round, which tore loose part of the vertical fin and peeled off a large portion of fabric from the rudder.

卐

The last sight any of the American pilots and aircrew had of *Ryujo* was a huge pillar of oily black smoke billowing skyward and spreading across the horizon.

卐

As the American warplanes flew from sight, *Tone* signaled, "Destroyers, stand by *Ryujo* for rescue operation."

Cdr Tameichi Hara's *Amatsukaze* immediately dashed toward the sinking carrier but was delayed from approaching when three airplanes suddenly appeared from the clouds. As the distant airplanes drew nearer, they were identified as *Ryujo*'s returning Zero fighters. The Zeros slowly circled over the sinking carrier, then one of them slowly glided toward the water and ditched beside *Amatsukaze*. Commander Hara did not see what became of the other Zeros—they ditched near *Tokitsukaze*—for he was obliged to redirect his attention to rescuing the pilot of the first Zero. All three pilots were rescued, but their fighters had to be abandoned in the water, there being no means for hoisting them aboard the destroyers.

The rescue of the three ditched pilots took valuable time from setting up the rescue of the survivors among *Ryujo*'s 700-man crew. It seemed to Commander Hara that *Ryujo* would sink at any moment, but the flame-engulfed, smoke-shrouded carrier with many gaping holes remained afloat. In time, the flames subsided—possibly, Commander Hara surmised, because of the thousands of tons of seawater flowing into her.

Amatsukaze was closing on *Ryujo* again when a new alert brought Commander Hara's attention skyward once again. Two large airplanes—Hara correctly identified them as U.S. Army Air Forces B-17s—emerged from the clouds. The alert obliged *Tone* and *Amatsukaze* to zigzag away from the crippled carrier at high speed lest the heavy bombers engulf them in their anticipated pattern of bombs. *Tokitsukaze* had to back away from *Ryujo* at high speed to gain sea room. As the surface warships scattered, all three opened fire at the two bombers with all the antiaircraft guns that could bear. The two bombers dropped bombs from high altitude, and all fell into the sea wide of any possible target.

It was nearing dusk by the time the two bombers flew from sight. There was barely enough light left to conduct the long overdue rescue operation.

Ryujo was still afloat, but she had no power. As *Amatsukaze* drew near, Commander Hara was struck by the amount of damage he could see. The fires had gutted the vessel. Hideous, grotesque corpses were strewn everywhere. The carrier had a 40-degree list to starboard and was visibly sinking further into the sea with each passing minute.

Hara saw one of the light carrier's signalmen waving semaphore flags, which read: "We are abandoning ship. Come alongside to rescue crew." The destroyer captain ordered his ship to close on *Ryujo*'s lower starboard flank, though he was risking the loss of his ship if the heavier carrier suddenly heeled over and locked *Amatsukaze* in a death grip.

Long rolling waves caused *Ryujo*'s canted superstructure to brush against *Amatsukaze*'s exposed bridge, which sent a trickle of cold sweat down Commander Hara's back. Many of the destroyer's strongest seamen were sent to the port side of the ship and outfitted with long poles with which they held *Amatsukaze* off *Ryujo*. Long planks were run out to link the two vessels and, soon, the first of 300 wounded and able-bodied survivors filed across to *Amatsukaze*'s deck. Among those killed in the bombing attack had been Commander Hara's Eta Jima classmate, Cdr Hisakichi Kishi.

Suddenly, as the flow of survivors waned to a trickle, *Ryujo*'s list dramatically increased. She was definitely about to go under. "Evacuation finished?" Commander Hara shouted.

An officer at the end of the plank nodded and answered, "Yes, sir! Please cast off. It's getting dangerous."

Amatsukaze's powerful turbine engines roared to full power and the lithe warship pulled away from *Ryujo's* looming flank. The destroyer had bounded forward barely 500 meters when *Ryujo* slipped beneath the surface.

Amatsukaze immediately joined *Tokitsukaze* and *Tone* to help rescue swimmers. As wounded, oil-stained survivors climbed aboard the surface vessels, *Ryujo's* surviving attack planes returned from the strike on Guadalcanal. Clearly confused by the absence of their carrier, the raid survivors circled overhead. One of the warships tried to raise the flight leader by radio, but he had been lost and none of the others had a radio aboard. This alone explained why the Kates and Zeros had failed to heed orders to proceed to the emergency airstrip at Buka.

A quick count revealed that seven of twenty-one Kates and Zeros had failed to return. The survivors had to ditch. All the pilots and aircrew were saved, but all the warplanes were lost.

As the last rays of sunlight receded in the west, *Tone, Tokitsukaze,* and *Amatsukaze* turned eastward. They had been ordered by VAdm Chuichi Nagumo to join his Carrier Striking Force.

16

I t is a hard rule of war that you go with what you have when you have it. The rules of chance and opportunity do not allow for missing the moment.

Thus it was that VAdm Frank Jack Fletcher had to make an immediate decision to launch his meager reserve of strike aircraft against RAdm Hiroaki Abe's surface Vanguard Group when its location was reported by Lt John Lowe and Ens Bob Gibson at about 1500. (He had not yet received word of Lt Ray Davis's discovery of the carriers.) For Fletcher to have waited would have amounted to no offensive effort at all against what then appeared to be the heart of the Japanese battle fleet.

Fletcher's ready reserve aboard *Saratoga* consisted of just five Torpedo-8 TBFs that had not gone out against *Ryujo* with Cdr Don Felt's strike group. The launch of the little *Saratoga* reserve strike group was precipitous. The Avenger pilots were given a vector, but there was no opportunity for them to collect charts or flight gear; they simply started going.

The Torpedo-8 skipper, Lt Swede Larsen, initially missed out on claiming an airplane because he ran below to collect his gear. He emerged on the flight deck as the very last available TBF was taxi-ing into the launch position. Larsen, who had commanded Tor-pedo-8's land-based contingent at Midway, was not about to miss this strike. He sprinted to the moving airplane and stopped the launch. He then unceremoniously ejected the pilot, CAP Red Dog-gett, and climbed behind the controls.

The last flyable strike aircraft left aboard were two Bombing-3 SBDs. These were in the care of Lt(jg) Bob Elder, who had had fueling problems at Henderson Field in the morning, and Elder's wingman, Ens Bob Gordon. The two had arrived home too late to rearm and refuel in time to launch with Commander Felt's strike group. As soon as Swede Larsen's TBFs were away, Elder and Gordon were called to the flight deck to taxi their rearmed and refueled dive-bombers forward to make room aft for returning fighters. The next thing either of them knew, they were motioned into taxi position and shown terse chalkboard notes that provided them with little more than a vector. Then they were launched. Nei-ther of them had his navigation board or charts of any sort. As soon as Elder and Gordon were airborne, they raced to catch up to Swede Larsen's TBFs.

卐

Shortly after the last *Saratoga* strikers were away, Admiral Fletcher received Lt Ray Davis's chilling sighting report: the two Japanese fleet carriers had been found and unsuccessfully attacked, and all indications were that they had both launched and were con-tinuing to launch strike aircraft. Davis was unable to elaborate, so Fletcher was left to decide for himself how much time he had to counter the incoming strike.

It soon became certain that Fletcher's gamble that Air Group 3 could be diverted from the bait to the main target had come acrop-per. In very basic terms, Fletcher had traded a potentially decisive follow-up on Midway for one expendable Japanese light carrier.

By the time Lieutenant Davis's sighting report arrived and was assessed, *Enterprise* ground crew had managed to rearm and refuel eleven Air Group 6 morning-search and air-patrol bombers. These SBDs were hastily organized into a strike force. The pilots—some of whom had flown grueling morning searches and the rest of whom were on the day's "battle bill" as reserve attack pilots—were hurriedly briefed on the carrier targets and prepared for launching.

The launch was to take place nearly at the maximum range for combat-loaded strike aircraft, over 250 miles from *Shokaku* and *Zuikaku*. The first SBD off *Enterprise*'s flight deck was flown by Lt Turner Caldwell, the Scouting-5 commander. The remaining Dauntlesses—a total of eight from Scouting-5 and three from Bombing-6—were hastily launched. They joined up on Caldwell as they arrived, without much concern for organization by rank or formal division assignments. The three Bombing-6 pilots, who received no briefing at all, joined up wherever they could.

卐

As soon as Caldwell's mixed strike force—recorded in the log as Flight 300—had cleared *Enterprise*'s deck, six pilots from Torpedo-3 were called from their squadron ready room and ordered to taxi their Avengers forward to make room for the afternoon searchers, who were due back within minutes. That was at about 1625. At 1632, *Enterprise*'s crude long-range radar first picked up the incoming Japanese strike at extreme range.

The precise motivation for the launch has been lost. It is most probable that the command wanted the armed and fueled TBFs in the air to prevent them from being blown up with potentially catastrophic results by the incoming Japanese strike bombers. (Under normal circumstances, unmanned ready aircraft would have been jettisoned over the side at the first word of an incoming strike.) It is also likely that their immediate readiness presented Fletcher with the very last weapon he could employ against the Japanese carriers. Whatever the motivation, Lt Rube Konig, the Torpedo-3 flight officer, was thoroughly surprised when he heard the flight-deck loudspeaker blare, "This is a launch." He was also advised that, since the task force's future course could not be remotely predicted, the Avenger pilots should try to land at Henderson Field. Saying so and doing so were two different things, however, for neither Konig nor any of the other Avenger pilots had their mapboards or charts with them. The dismay was just setting in when Konig saw a flight-deck crewman approach his airplane and hold up a chalkboard reading, "Enemy bearing 330. Approx. distance 300 miles." With that, Konig and the other five Torpedo-3 pilots were launched.

The last *Enterprise* pilot to launch was LCdr Max Leslie, the Air Group 6 commander, who was flying a long-range TBF he had had specially modified with extra fuel tanks and radios to serve as a strike-control plane. Because of the weight of the extra fuel, Leslie had to begin his launch from the after elevator. By the time he reached the launch position, *Enterprise* was zigzagging at high speed to throw off incoming Japanese dive-bombers. Leslie was set to go but was ordered to cut his engine and stand by at the last moment. He had no idea why. A few minutes later, the Air Group 6 commander was ordered to get airborne.

The launch was smooth, but upon making the normal left turn, Leslie found himself facing a sky full of outgoing antiaircraft gunfire. His earphones crackled, full of sighting reports and tally-hos from the fighters. Many of the screening surface warships were obviously firing at Leslie's fuel-laden Avenger. The air-group commander dived toward the water and weaved around battleship *North Carolina* as her antiaircraft gunners filled his right wing with shrapnel holes. Once free of friendly fire, Leslie shaped course for the reported enemy carriers and flew alone after the SBDs and TBFs that had by then receded from sight. He had no way of knowing if he would have a ship to come home to.

17

☀

The defense of aircraft carriers in mid-1942 was conducted across three interlocking spheres. The first defense was by fighters, whose primary mission was to intercept and engage incoming enemy bombers as far from the friendly carrier deck as possible. Next, any incoming bombers that got past the fighters were to be engaged by relatively long-range heavy-caliber anti-aircraft gunnery put up by the carrier herself and the warships accompanying her. The final defense lay in the hands—literally in the hands—of gunners manning medium- and light-caliber automatic weapons aboard the escorts and the carrier herself.

Task Force 61's first line of defense—the distant fighters— were to be controlled by radar-guided FDOs based aboard the two carriers. On August 24, 1942, the most experienced FDO in the Fleet was LCdr Ham Dow, of *Enterprise*, a 1926 Naval Academy graduate and pilot who had overseen the defense of his carrier at Midway. Assisting Dow on August 24 was Lt Hank Rowe, a 1937 Annapolis graduate and pilot who had been seconded to the Royal Air Force in early 1941 to learn the rather eclectic art of controlling fighters at a distance by means of radar. Rowe had attended all the

British schools on the subject and, because the British were the world's leading experts in radar-guided fighter direction, Rowe was considered one of the U.S. Navy's leading lights. He had helped establish the Navy's Fighter Direction School in Hawaii directly under Pacific Fleet auspices and then had been temporarily assigned as a working evaluator to the *Enterprise* fighter direction staff for the Guadalcanal invasion.

Given the combined expertise of Ham Dow and Hank Rowe, *Enterprise* was the obvious choice to serve as the central clearing house for radar-assisted fighter direction on August 24. Thus the combat air patrols and ready fighters of both Fighting-6 and Fighting-5 came under Dow's and Rowe's direction at 1632, the moment the first radar contact with enemy warplanes was made.

卐

The radar-assisted fighter-direction capability of the day was both experimental and crude. Indeed, it was Hank Rowe's specific job to act as a participating observer as a means of finding specific ways to improve sighting, tracking, communications, control, and interception techniques.

The system was based on the experimental CXAM radars, built by Crosley Corporation. Since the operating end of the device looked to many like a bedspring, all of the thirteen sets in the U.S. Fleet were familiarly known as "bedspring" radars.

LCdr Ham Dow was assigned to a small compartment known as Radar Plot, which was located on the third deck of the carrier's island structure. Armed with only a microphone on a long cord, Dow stood over a plotting table. On the far side of the table were two junior FDOs—two of the six trainees who comprised the backup pool of FDOs aboard the carrier. The two assistants were equipped with earphones and chest-supported sound-powered microphones connected to the radar communications frequency. Their job was to plot the progress of the incoming enemy flights, along with the relative positions of gaggles of friendly fighters, on the polar chart located on the table. A fourth member of the team was the gunnery liaison officer, who coordinated moves by fighters with the ship's gunnery department—to help friendly fighters stay clear of friendly fire, it was hoped. The gunnery liaison officer was the only member of the team who had access to eyeball information from outside the windowless Radar Plot compartment. Lt Hank Rowe was also squeezed in around the table, serving as an immediate backup for Dow as well as an evaluator of the system.

The radar repeaters were located in an adjacent compartment, so information was passed to the junior FDOs only by means of their sound-powered battle phones. Three radiomen and their radio receivers were also crammed into Radar Plot; one each of the radios was devoted to incoming traffic from the torpedo bombers, scout bombers, and fighters, which all usually operated on separate frequencies. A fourth radio was used to monitor talk between the task force commander and all the ships in the task force. These radios were the FDO's only means for following the changing scene of the battle outside on the constantly revised and updated polar chart.

In theory, the fighter-direction operation provided a controlling influence over defensive fighter operations, which tended to become diffused as action drew nearer and eventually erupted. Just as the Landing Signal Officer's observations morally outweighed the observations of the pilot coming in for an arrested landing, so the FDO's instructions outweighed the on-the-spot deployment decisions of the fighter leaders until the point the battle was actually joined. In essence, the FDO was the commander of fighters and the orchestrator of defensive fighter tactics.

That was the theory. The reality was that the crude CXAM had limited range, and there were gaps in its vista.

Though the CXAM was designed to "see" a single airplane 50 miles out in any direction, it was known that it could pick up larger formations of incoming aircraft at ranges of up to 90 miles—if the airplanes were high enough and if the air was humid enough. (Moist air is a better conductor than dry air.)

As soon as the first radar sighting was made, the CXAM— rotating high atop a special mast over the island superstructure— was to be routinely stopped for a better fix and then rotated some more to search for other targets. All the enlisted radarman answering to the FDO had to go on was a fuzzy sort of inverted V-shaped interruption in an otherwise level horizontal white line running the width of his radarscope. The bearing of the target was easily determined by a gyro-controlled bearing indicator located right over the radarscope.

As soon as the radar sighting, bearing, and time of sighting had been confirmed, the information was fed to the junior FDOs, who marked each sighting report on the large polar chart. The center of the chart represented the carrier, and each new mark represented the progress of various groups of aircraft. Enemy or unidentified "bogies" were marked *x* and friendly aircraft were marked *o*. The progress of each was represented by lines drawn between each new time-annotated mark and the previous time-annotated mark. The polar chart was calibrated by means of degree-marked radii emanating from the center of the chart and concentric distance-marked circles.

The only way to separate enemy aircraft from friendly ones was by means of the IFF (Identification, Friend or Foe) transmitter carried aboard every U.S. carrier-based fighter or bomber. Whereas each group of enemy or unidentified aircraft on the radarscope registered above the line as an inverted V, IFF registered as a V below the line.

The size of a gaggle of incoming airplanes had to be estimated from the size of the V. Exhaustive testing had been run over the preceding year, and the experienced radarmen manning the scopes aboard *Enterprise* and *Saratoga* were considered so well versed in their arcane trade that their judgments were not questioned. As a matter of fact, their estimates proved to be remarkably accurate.

The speed of radar-sighted aircraft was easily determined by the time it took the incoming or passing airplanes to get from one point on the polar chart to another.

The only variable that had to be based on pure estimate was the altitude of the incoming gaggles. Until incoming planes flew to within the 12-mile range of standard gunnery radars, there was no way to provide hard information regarding this vital statistic. The CXAM had no means for providing an explicit altitude reading. However, it had been noted that there were reliably permanent gaps in the readings of each individual radar set. These gaps had been calibrated by exhaustive use of friendly target planes flying at known altitudes and distances from the ship. Thus, each time a bogey disappeared, the "fade" chart that had been specially prepared for each radar was supposed to yield a confirmatory altitude. However, the charts had been drawn up in calm seas; thus any roll experienced by the ship heavily impacted upon the accuracy of the implied readings. In fact, the *only* way to be certain that friendly fighters had an altitude advantage over the incoming enemy was to direct the Wildcats to sufficient altitudes without recourse to radar estimates. It was easier for fighters to dive from above than to try to climb from below.

Another dangerous gap in the system was the inability of the CXAM to spot low-flying bogies at distances in excess of 12 miles. This was caused simply by the effect of the curvature of the earth upon a line-of-sight technology.

卐

LCdr Ham Dow swung into action as soon as *Enterprise's* 1632 radar sighting had been confirmed by *Saratoga's* radar. First, Dow took stock of all the fighter assets arrayed on the plotting board. He had to decide whom to send where, and whom to hold back in reserve. Such variables as time aloft—which is to say fuel supply, which is to say range, which is to say duration of fighting ability— and who was leading what division had to be factored into the equation.

Almost as soon as the initial sighting had been made and evaluated, all the incoming airplanes faded from the radarscopes.

卐

The first bogies—unidentified aircraft—were spotted 88 miles out on bearing 320 degrees, which was a straight line from Task Force 61 back to VAdm Chuichi Nagumo's Carrier Striking Force. The target faded at 85 miles, which, when everything was factored into the equation, yielded an estimated altitude of 12,000 feet— which was very much on the low side.

Ham Dow began moving the fighters he had aloft, and both carriers came into the wind to clear their flight decks of all airplanes—the ragtag SBD and TBF formations—and numerous reserve fighters, which were launched at 10-second intervals until a total of fifty-three Wildcats—twenty-five from Fighting-5 and every one of Fighting-6's twenty-eight operational fighters—were clawing for altitude over the fleet or moving to the northwest, toward the periphery of the arena.

卐

For Lt Sandy Crews, of Fighting-5, August 24 had started out rather tamely. Crews was the second-section leader in a four-plane division led by Lt Chick Harmer, the Fighting-5 exec. Harmer's division was launched on an early combat air patrol, in which not a thing happened and not a word was spoken. The four Wildcats routinely landed after 3.2 hours in the air.

Harmer's division was again launched on a routine combat air patrol a little after 1400 and flew to 20,000 feet. As the uneventful patrol entered its fourth hour, Sandy Crews began thinking it was time to return to *Saratoga* for the day. However, Chick Harmer began to sense that a sudden upturn in radio traffic might lead to an exciting delay.

The issue was decided when *Saratoga's* FDO radioed to ask Harmer if his division could delay landing for a while. The communications were terrible, but Harmer was able to gather from the parts of the FDO's transmission that got through that the radars had just picked up a large bogey at some distance. At that moment, Harmer's four Wildcats each had an average of 70 gallons of fuel remaining, but the division leader felt it was enough to warrant their remaining aloft.

Ens Bob Disque, of Fighting-6, was a member of the division led by Lt Dick Gay, which had also flown a four-hour morning mission before being recovered by *Saratoga* at 1530. While Gay's Wildcats were being refueled, the pilots first heard that friendly scouts had sighted a Japanese carrier, had made uncoordinated bombing attacks with unobserved results, and had observed a large flight of enemy aircraft headed toward Task Force 61.

Gay's Fighting-6 division, and others from both Fighting-6 and Fighting-5, began launching after the last of the TBFs and

SBDs had been cleared from the flight deck. By the time Bob Disque was airborne at about 1655, radio silence had been broken and everyone was chattering on the air.

By the time LCdr Roy Simpler, the Fighting-5 commander, was launched, communications between the FDOs and the fighters were in a state of total confusion. To Simpler's immediate and immense chagrin, his division was vectored in the opposite direction—away from the enemy strike—to identify a target flying at about 12,000 feet.

Mach Howell Sumrall was the number-two element leader in the Fighting-6 division led by Lt Scoop Vorse. In an unusual departure from routine so close to a fight, Vorse and Sumrall relinquished the lead of their elements to their relatively green wingmen—a rather brave means for giving the two young ensigns some supercharged on-the-job training. Vorse's division was initially vectored away from the enemy gaggle to investigate a bogey at 1,500 feet which turned out to be a pair of TBFs approaching the fleet with their IFFs turned off. The friendly bombers were very likely flown by Lt(jg) Weasel Weissenborn and Ens Fred Mears, the first all-TBF afternoon search team to have turned for home.

卐

The big bogies reappeared in the *Enterprise* radarscope at 1649. Their range was firmly fixed at 44 miles, half the initial distance to Task Force 61 at which they had originally been sighted 17 minutes earlier. LCdr Ham Dow used the brief minutes remaining to vector four Fighting-6 divisions directly against the largest formation.

Lt Scoop Vorse's division, which was at 2,000 feet following its contact with the friendly TBFs, was the lowest of the four first-line fighter divisions. However, the four Wildcats were sent racing by Dow's abrupt order: "Vector three-two-zero, angels twelve, distance thirty-five [miles]. Buster [full speed]."

As the division climbed through 8,000 feet, Vorse spotted eighteen brown-and-tan Vals arrayed in a perfect vee-of-vees formation against the clear blue sky. It was the first human sighting of the afternoon. The division leader yelled "Tallyho" into his throat mike at precisely 1655 and steeply climbed toward the approaching Japanese dive-bombers.

As Mach Howell Sumrall hung his tail-end Wildcat on its propeller to match Vorse's full-throttle climb, he spotted a dozen Zeros. From three to six of the Japanese fighters appeared to be using their considerable altitude advantage to close on the Wildcat division.

The Wildcats weaved and maneuvered as they climbed toward the Vals. So did the Zeros, but the Japanese pilots declined to attack. Soon, Sumrall noticed that the last man in the Japanese formation was getting very restless; he continued to roll upside down to look at Sumrall, who was flying the tail-end position, which is usually the realm of the least qualified junior pilot. Sumrall guessed that the Japanese pilot was hoping he would straggle, so he accommodated him by dropping back. The Japanese pilot waggled his wings to indicate he was attacking, a foolish and unnecessary display.

While the Zero was losing altitude, Sumrall kicked full right rudder, pulled his F4F's nose as high as possible, and fired a short burst to make the Zero pilot steepen his dive. The Japanese obliged and dived away underneath Sumrall. The veteran U.S. Navy pilot dropped his fighter's nose. Sumrall's .50-caliber bullets blew off the rear end of the Zero's belly tank and passed through the Zero's fuselage. The Japanese fighter entered a long, shallow dive and flew all the way into the ocean.

As Sumrall was drawing off his Zero, Scoop Vorse and his wingman, Ens Dick Loesch, matched altitude with the nearest nine-plane Val *chutai*, which had by then entered a long, shallow dive toward *Enterprise*. As Vorse reversed his heading to go after the Vals at 12,000 feet, he and Ensign Loesch were overtaken by several Zeros. Vorse immediately whipped into a low-side attack on the nearest Zero. Flames streamed out behind the Zero's cockpit for a moment, then nearly died out. Suddenly, the stricken Zero turned its nose straight down and crashed in flames into the ocean.

Loesch, who stuck with Scoop Vorse during the entire action, was given an assist on another Zero, on which he fired at long range at the same time another unidentified Wildcat also hit it.

Machinist Sumrall's wingman, Ens Francis Register, took on a Zero in a wild melee lasting only a few seconds. As Register emerged from the fight, he saw the Zero smoking, burning, and diving away out of control toward the sea. Suddenly, a large bundle detached itself from the burning cockpit. The pilot, who wore no parachute, fell flailing all the way to the surface. As Register recovered altitude, he came upon an alien fighter he took to be a German-built Messerschmitt Me-109. Whatever it was—undoubtedly a Zero—he shot at it and watched it fall in flames.

🜨

Scoop Vorse's early "Tallyho" upon sighting the Vals was the last clear transmission of the battle. Immediately, the fighter-direction channel manned by LCdr Ham Dow was literally squelched off the air as the additional direct sightings of Japanese aircraft was reported by overexcited Wildcat pilots. Since all fifty-three American fighters were obliged to operate on the single frequency available to Dow, it was absolutely assured that two or more of them would be transmitting at the same moment—and that caused a painfully audible squeal across the entire network. At those odd intervals where the squeal abated, the elated cries of "Tallyho" and worried warnings of "There's a Zero on your tail" thoroughly cluttered the air waves.

Within minutes, as the first U.S. fighters pitched into the oncoming Japanese formations, Ham Dow was bathed in sweat as he vainly exerted physical and psychic energy to try to reestablish needed radio discipline. The fighter-direction system fell apart when the communications link was utterly overwhelmed at the outset of the defensive fighter attacks.

🜨

One of the last clear orders Ham Dow was able to transmit went to the Fighting-6 division led by Ens Red Brooks, a recently commissioned former enlisted pilot with many years of flying in carrier-based fighters. While most attention was firmly riveted on the rapidly approaching high Val and Zero formations, Dow's radarman fortuitously noticed a small bogey approaching virtually at wavetop height. Ensign Brooks was ordered to investigate just before Dow was overwhelmed by a flood of radio calls.

Brooks's division—which picked up a fifth member, a stray Fighting-5 Wildcat piloted by Ens Mark Bright—flew out 60 miles along its vector and found nine Vals and two Kates streaking along a reciprocal heading. The American division leader immediately delivered a high-side run on one of the lead Vals and hammered it into the water. As Red Brooks pulled up, he found himself directly on the tail of one of the Kates, which sustained numerous solid hits from Brooks's six .50-caliber wing guns and cartwheeled into the water.

Ens Harry March took out the second Kate at long range from dead astern.

AP1 Paul Mankin dived straight down upon the rear Val, which his wing guns tore apart. Then Mankin nudged the nose of his Wildcat toward the next-to-last Val, but the Japanese pilot evaded with a quick left turn. When Mankin got on the Val again, the Japanese pilot again flicked his lithe dive-bomber hard to the left, away from the danger. And again. At last, Mankin approached the bomber from above and behind. The Japanese pilot's next left turn brought him directly into the cone of .50-caliber bullets Mankin sent out just in time. The Val dropped its left wing, which connected with the water, and knifed right into the sea. Mankin buzzed the grave for a few moments to see if the pilot or gunner escaped, but he saw no sign of life.

RE Tommy Rhodes shot down a fourth Val, while Ens Mark Bright claimed a fifth and won an assist on a sixth before the surviving Japanese aborted their attack and flew off at high speed in the direction of their own distant carriers.

⚛

Ens Bob Disque, of Fighting-6, began hearing reports from fighters farther out that flights of nine or twelve Val dive-bombers were coming in at about 17,000 feet. Frequent reports of "Splash one" were heard. There were also quite a few excited calls of "Zero on your tail." A quick look down revealed that the ships beneath Disque's Wildcat had begun serious evasive maneuvers. Disque was able to see their long curving white wakes on the dark blue water. Soon, he saw orange flashes brighten the gray outlines of the ships, and black puffs appeared in the bright blue canopy over the fleet.

〄

Lt Chick Harmer, the Fighting-5 exec, never did receive a vector from the FDO because the volume of traffic on the channel was so great—almost a steady roar—that Harmer could not make out a complete message to or from anybody. What galvanized Harmer to take independent action was the sight of an entire Japanese airgroup formation silhouetted against the backdrop of a large cloud on the opposite side of the task force from his patrol station. He headed for the intercept at full bore.

The air group Harmer spotted was about 15 to 20 miles away. The four Fighting-5 Wildcats and the Japanese warplanes were heading directly toward each other. As far as Harmer could see, the Japanese were not under attack by any American fighters.

The lead Japanese formation was a nine-plane Val *chutai*, which Harmer's division eventually joined right over *Enterprise*. The Japanese *chutai* leader—who might have been the Japanese *hikotaicho*, the strike commander—started his dive just as Harmer started his approach from above against the lead three-plane Val *shotai*.

At this point, in Harmer's view, his pilots blew everything that they had been trained to do. Instead of following the division leader against the lead Val *shotai*, they broke formation and went off singly on their own.

Harmer stuck to the Japanese *chutai* leader right through the beginning of his vertical dive. The Japanese rear gunner fired a few bursts but was evidently silenced by the initial burst from Harmer's machine guns. Though the Val did not burn, as Harmer was sure it must if it had sustained fatal damage, it suddenly steepened its dive. There was no way Harmer's Wildcat could match the dive, so Harmer pulled out. Observers on *Enterprise* later reported that the lead Val dived straight into the water.

Despite Harmer's misgivings about his subordinates, Lt Sandy Crews managed to attach himself to the back of the third Val and give it two or three good bursts. Crews was unable to see anyone in the Val's rear seat, and there was no return fire. As with Harmer's Val, Crews's target did not begin to burn by the time the anti-aircraft fire from *Enterprise* and supporting warships got too thick to breast. Crews pulled out at about 3,000 feet and started to climb back up toward the stream of incoming planes. He was able to make one opposite-course pass at another Japanese plane, but without any observed results.

Ens John McDonald, Harmer's wingman, claimed one Val destroyed before it went into its dive. On the other hand, Ens Ben Currie, Crew's wingman, could not get a piece of any of the Vals entering the cone of heavy antiaircraft fire, but he dived toward the water and arrived in time to catch a Val as it retired after dropping its bomb.

卐

Lt Howard Jensen's three-plane Fighting-5 division took on what appeared to be the second Val *chutai* 15 miles out as it began diving on *Enterprise* from 16,000 feet. In a scorching action, Jensen claimed three of the Vals before he was run off by four Zeros, which he evaded by diving. He got back into the fight just in time to damage a fourth Val. Meantime, Ens John Kleinman tangled with two Vals and a Zero, all of which he claimed as kills. The third man in Jensen's division, Lt(jg) Carleton Starkes saw two Vals fall from the sky before he shot a Zero off the tail of an unidentified American fighter.

卐

Lt Jim Smith, of Fighting-5, was launched from *Saratoga* with Ens Horace Bass and Ens Charles Eichenberger during the last mad scramble aloft at 1645. As did so many other Fighting-5 pilots, the three made contact as the Vals reached their pushover point. Eichenberger followed one of the Vals right through the antiaircraft fire. The Val was destroyed during the chase. Though Eichenberger manfully admitted that it might have fallen to surface gunfire, he was nevertheless given credit for the kill because his superiors felt that any antiaircraft round that could have destroyed the Val would have destroyed the closely following F4F as well. As it was, Eichenberger's Wildcat emerged from the flight through friendly fire without a nick or a dent.

Not so for Eichenberger's two wingmen. Neither Lt Jim Smith nor Ens Horace Bass emerged from the cauldron, and neither pilot was ever seen again.

卐

ChMac Don Runyon had cunningly led his all-veteran Fighting-6 division up-sun as soon as it was assigned to a station close in to *Enterprise*. The ploy worked, for Runyon was able to jump a Val leader at 1705 from out of the blinding orb as it passed the 5-mile mark on the way in. The Val simply disintegrated and exploded at an altitude of 15,000 feet. Runyon followed through and used his diving speed to resume his up-sun position in time to catch an unwary Val *shotai*. He selected one of the three fat targets and fired all his guns. The Val flared up in a spectacular blaze and fell smoking and burning all the way into the distant water. Runyon again used his diving speed to regain altitude, and he was into his third attack when a stream of tracer passing from high and astern alerted him to some unanticipated danger. Runyon immediately chopped his throttle to slow his Wildcat and was handsomely rewarded when his assailant, a Zero, shot into view from overhead—right in front of his gunsight pipper. A little squirt of .50-caliber bullets sent the Zero pilot diving to his death. By then, Runyon had overshot the dive-bombers, so he again used his diving speed to good advantage, this time to climb up directly beneath one of the Vals, which he easily dispatched with a killing belly shot. No sooner done than Runyon was again assailed by a diving Zero, which he pulled up to meet. Following a quick exchange, the Zero turned for home trailing a stream of black smoke.

In the meantime, AP1 Howard Packard, Runyon's wingman, took on a Val, which he claimed as a probable.

Ens Dutch Shoemaker chased the surviving Vals straight down through the funnel of *Enterprise*'s own antiaircraft fire. He overran the Val he had selected to shoot down, but managed to get on the tail of a second dive-bomber about halfway down in its dive.

Though Shoemaker was certain he hit both Vals, he saw neither of them burn or fall into the sea and thus made no claims.

Mach Beverly Reid, Shoemaker's element leader, also entered the antiaircraft cauldron in pursuit of a Val. He was never seen again, presumably the victim of friendly fire.

⚛

A four-plane Fighting-5 division led by Mach Doyle Barnes was launched from *Saratoga* at 1615 and went into action at about 1710, as yet another Zero-escorted nine-plane Val *chutai* tipped over against *Enterprise*.

Ens Ram Dibb attacked one of the dive-bombers at 14,000 feet and succeeded in downing it in flames. He then surged through friendly antiaircraft fire to get at a Zero, which twice maneuvered into superior attack positions from which Dibb emerged following violent evasive maneuvers. The last successful evasion carried Dibb almost to the surface, where he opportunistically downed a Val as it was recovering from its bombing run. At that point, Dibb had to leave the fight because his Wildcat's engine had been struck by small-caliber rounds; there were also bullet holes in the carburator intake and exhaust manifold from antiaircraft shrapnel.

Another member of Barnes's division, Gunner Charles Brewer, intercepted the Vals at 15,500 feet—just before they pushed over—and made repeated firing runs on them right through the friendly antiaircraft fire. He claimed two Vals shot down in flames plus one Zero destroyed.

Ens Douglas Johnson made a firing pass at one of the Vals at 14,000 feet, missed, and came back to execute a high-side pass on the same Japanese bomber at 10,000 feet. The Zero flamed and rolled away. Johnson's attention was immediately diverted from the flaming Val when he was challenged by a Zero. The two fighters exchanged several bursts on the way down before Johnson went into a controlled full-power spin to evade the nimble Mitsubishi. As Johnson pulled out low over the sea, he got a good burst into a retiring Val and saw it stagger into the water.

Machinist Barnes was seen following a Val into the antiaircraft curtain, but he never regained altitude and was not seen again.

By then—only minutes into the Japanese attack—U.S. fighters operating close in to Task Force 16 were facing columns of antiaircraft fire from the water to 20,000 feet and 5 miles out from *Enterprise*. It was an awesome display, and most of the converging Wildcat divisions kept their distance.

卍

Fighting-5's Lt Dave Richardson had been launched from *Enterprise* at about 1615 with Lt Marion Dulfiho and Ens Leon Haynes, neither of whom usually flew with Richardson. During the launch preparation, Richardson was briefed on a mission to escort the eleven-plane SBD strike that had been sent after the Japanese carriers. The three Wildcats were ready to launch when Richardson was ordered by means of a chalkboard message to simply climb to 10,000 feet and orbit until contacted.

Upon reaching their orbit altitude, the three *Saratoga* Wildcat pilots spotted the attack waves of Vals as they passed through 15,000 feet on their way toward *Enterprise*. Dave Richardson immediately executed a climbing turn toward the dive-bombers, but all three Wildcats of his makeshift division, which were flying in loose echelon, were simultaneously bounced by six or eight Zeros.

Ensign Haynes reflexively turned in to meet the attack, and he managed to make a head-on run at one Zero as it leveled off. After passing the first Zero without sustaining hits, Haynes maneuvered onto the tail of a second Japanese carrier fighter. Though Lieutenant Richardson made an unsuccessful attempt to support Haynes by attacking the Zero in a "scissors" maneuver (a brand new unofficial tactic later known as the Thach Weave), Haynes managed to shoot down the enemy fighter himself.

The third member of the Richardson trio, Lt Marion Dulfiho, a seasoned veteran, mysteriously disappeared and was never seen again. Apparently he was downed by a Zero.

It is possible that this melee was witnessed and joined by Fighting-5's Lt Dick Gray and Ens Frank Green, who had been launched from *Enterprise* at 1445 and who had been vectored toward the center of the action just before the fighter-direction channel went awry. In any case, Gray—who earlier in the day had overseen the downing of a Japanese four-engine patrol bomber—joined a swirling fighter versus fighter action already in progress and claimed the destruction of one Zero. Though no one definitely saw Gray's Zero crash, he got so many rounds into it at such close range that he was able to see the pilot slump forward. The last he saw of the Zero it was spinning away, violently out of control. Gray was given credit for killing the pilot and thus for destroying the Zero.

۩

It was a *good* day for the U.S. Navy fighters. More than half of the fifty-three Wildcat pilots aloft engaged Vals or Kates before they could attack *Enterprise*, and many of the Japanese bombers were actually downed—as opposed to claimed—before they could launch their attacks. But the heroic fighter effort proved to be too little and too late.

Enterprise was in for some heavy damage, and her crew of 3,000 was in for some heavy losses.

18

*

AMM2 Bernard Peterson, a member of the Torpedo-3 ground crew, had been on *Enterprise*'s flight deck watching the distant opening air battle when his section chief suggested they head for the protection of the hangar deck. Once below, the two joined a group of sailors in the open boat pocket and continued to eye the air battles, which seemed to be closing in.

About 1,800 yards off *Enterprise*'s port quarter, Lt(jg) George Hamm, destroyer *Monssen*'s first lieutenant, saw the sunlight glint off a glass canopy as the Vals emerged from a puff of high cumulus cloud at about 1710. First one tiny dot appeared, then another. Within moments, Hamm saw six or seven of the Vals lined up in single file. At first, they moved so slowly that they appeared to be hanging in midair.

The first man aboard *Enterprise* to actually *see* one of the Japanese dive-bombers was a Marine sergeant manning one of the 20mm automatic antiaircraft batteries located on catwalks around and just below the edge of the carrier's flight deck. In accordance with standing orders, the sergeant immediately opened fire.

It was 1711—39 minutes after *Enterprise*'s first radar contact.

Seconds after the Marine sergeant's sighting, *Enterprise*'s loud-speakers boomed the warning: "Enemy aircraft overhead."

⚛

Enterprise's gunnery department, which was essentially devoted to antiaircraft gunnery, oversaw three types of weapons. The most powerful and longest ranged were eight 5-inch .38-caliber guns (hereafter designated merely as "5-inch" guns) mounted in pairs at each corner of the flight deck. Four medium-range quadruple 1.1 inch Oerlikon pom-poms were located in pairs at flight-deck level just ahead and just aft of the superstructure, and a fifth quad 1.1-inch mount was located at the bows just beneath the leading edge of the flight deck. Finally, thirty 20mm cannon—with several .50-caliber machine guns thrown in—were located on the catwalks just below and virtually all the way around the flight deck.

The gunnery department was in the hands of the carrier's gunnery officer, LCdr Orlin Livdahl, a 1926 Naval Academy graduate. His key assistant, the antiaircraft gunnery officer, was LCdr Benny Mott, of the Annapolis class of 1930.

All defensive fires were formally coordinated by the gunnery and antiaircraft gunnery officers and their assistants from Sky Control, which was atop the island 110 feet above the waterline. They acted on the basis of what they saw for themselves, or from reports from the gunnery liaison officer manning the plotting table in Radar Plot, and from the 105 officers and sailors of L ("Lookout") Division, who were manning posts all around the flight deck and throughout the tall island on the starboard side of the flight deck. L Division was an integral part of the gunnery control system. Its lookouts had been painstakingly trained to keep their eyes riveted to particular sectors—no matter what was going on elsewhere.

Gunnery control was exercised largely by means of sound-powered battle phones once the sound of gunfire drowned out the ship's loudspeakers. Each battery had at least one talker connected to the primary and secondary gun-control centers. The gunnery officer's and antiaircraft gunnery officer's talkers could cut into any fire-control circuit by means of a rotary switch. When the gunnery officers or lookouts reporting to them saw airplanes approaching, they deployed their forces in proportion to the threat and tried to hold something back for new threats. If no battery was firing at a new target, the gunnery officers, from their Sky Control vantage points, ordered particular batteries to switch targets.

Since the start of the war, Lieutenant Commander Livdahl and Lieutenant Commander Mott had been unrelenting in their quest for perfect defensive gunnery. An analysis early in the war had revealed to Livdahl that 96 percent of all rounds fired fell behind the target. His reaction was to train his gunners to lead their targets—to take into account the forward momentum of the target and to visualize a point ahead where the line of flight and the line of tracers would converge. In addition, he spread the word that the pointer of any gun who missed astern of a target would be replaced. This, more than anything, assured a climbing rate of hits. When the rate of hits among formally assigned gun pointers rose to near perfect, Livdahl concentrated on cross-training every other member of every gun crew and then raising their accuracy to near-perfect levels. Whenever possible—most days—gunners aboard *Enterprise* spent the noon hour firing at target sleeves towed by Air Group 6 airplanes.

One dubious advantage Orlin Livdahl counted on was the probability that *Enterprise* would be the main focus of most or all of the Japanese attackers. If that was so, he reasoned, the task of his gunners would be made easier, for there would be no need to lead airplanes that were heading straight for them.

A real problem with the gunnery program lay in the fact that only a relatively small percentage of the gun crews were composed of full-time gunners, who were also primarily responsible for maintaining the guns. The majority of sailors assigned to the gun crews normally worked at a wide range of jobs in the ship's company or the various air departments. Shooting and learning to shoot was a vital but secondary duty.

There were many problems inherent in the system, not the least of which were the possible speed and accuracy of the 5-inch and 1.1-inch guns. Early in the war, a full-time gun captain in charge of one of the quad 1.1-inch mounts had been asked by LCdr Benny Mott how he would go about shooting down an airplane.

The gunner replied that he would quickly traverse the mount back and forth and quickly raise and lower the four barrels to put out a lethal area barrage that incoming aircraft would have to fly through. Since the four 1.1-inch mounts were entirely hand-operated and without any automatic guidance system, the gunner's answer was about the best Mott was going to get at that time. Mott was certain that a lethal dose of 1.1-inch ordnance would be more a matter of luck than skill. In fact, in training exercises conducted in the days before the August 24 action, the 1.1-inch guns had merely fired at target sleeves pulled along at low speed by TBFs. All the guns around the island—sixteen barrels—had fired at once, and, though the sleeve had been hit, no one considered the exercises to be remotely realistic.

The 1.1-inch guns and projectiles aboard *Enterprise* were crude and outmoded. Each round's point detonator, which was armed as soon as it emerged from the gun barrel, was so sensitive that it could be detonated by a raindrop. A "tracer" effect for each round was gained by attaching a small strip of silk that was ignited by the detonation of gunpowder when the round was fired.

Keeping the gun on target by means of the crude tracer or keen eyesight was the job of the pointer, who was assisted in this task as well as target selection by the battery officer, who was responsible for two mounts, and the gun captain, who was responsible for just one mount.

The job of the loaders for each 1.1-inch Oerlikon mount was to extract empty magazines and replace them with full magazines. The chamber serving the four guns in one mount held two magazines, so quick loaders could assure that the guns were always armed. However, old ammunition frequently jammed and had to be extracted by hand, thus appreciably slowing the rate of fire or silencing the mount altogether.

The 5-inch guns were more reliable, but they were hampered by a very much slower rate of fire. Each round, with its premeasured powder charge, had to be loaded by hand. Though the guns were controlled at long range and high altitude by a relatively sophisticated director, the system was fairly crude and quite slow in its own right. At low altitude and short range, the guns went on local control, which slowed them even more. About the best a 5-inch crew could hope for was a near miss that blossomed into a lethal burst of shrapnel in proximity to a diving or oncoming airplane.

The last line of defense lay in the hands of the 20mm gun crews. Each gun was manned by two trained gunners. One, the senior gunner, was strapped into a shoulder harness right behind the gun. The other, the loader, worked at his shoulder and stood ready to take over the firing if the gunner was injured or killed. The gun was fixed on a highly flexible mount that was welded to the flight-deck catwalk; it operated as an extension of the man to which it was mated. Capable of putting out many rounds in short bursts, the 20mm guns—which were grouped in four-gun batteries—were far more responsive and reliable than the 1.1-inch guns and generally more useful weapons than either the 5-inch or 1.1-inch guns.

One important innovation undertaken by Lieutenant Commander Livdahl was the transfer of Marines from the 5-inch guns to the 20mm cannon. Livdahl felt that Marines had the basic know-how to make the best use of the lighter weapons, which had to be fired with great reliance upon precisely the sort of hand-eye coordination they had mastered on rifle ranges during and after boot camp. Since there were not enough Marines to go around, sailors manned many of the 20mm cannon.

Of course, *Enterprise*'s fate was largely in the hands of gunners aboard the six destroyers, one light antiaircraft cruiser, one heavy cruiser, and one battleship of Task Force 16, all of which had gone into a circular defensive deployment around the carrier at the first news of the incoming airstrike.

The ship's crew had been on duty since an hour before sunrise. By the time the Japanese air strike appeared on the carrier's CXAM radar, the sailors on deck—who were *not* told of the new development—were bored and restless.

BM2 Arthur Davis, the air group master-at-arms, was just leaving an hours-long game of acey-deucey—he was the big loser—when he decided to share a dire premonition with BM1 Al Gabara, captain of the Number 4 1.1-inch gun mount, the sternmost Oerlikon. Though distant air battles and infrequent loudspeaker reports had alerted the crew, it was by no means certain that a major air strike was closing in from the north. Thus Davis simply told Gabara that he had a "bad feeling" and bet that an attack against *Enterprise* herself would soon be mounted. Gabara told Davis that, in that event, he would finally have an opportunity to fire his guns, to get paid off for the long hours of training and the many longer hours of unrelieved boredom.

No sooner said than the Marine sergeant sighted a glint of sunlight off the lead Val as it tipped over to begin its dive against the port side of the ship. Davis and Gabara turned, and Davis shouted, "Here they come" as he pointed skyward.

Immediately, all the guns that could bear were trained around to the port side of the ship. They immediately opened fire—whether or not the gunners had targets in sight.

⚛

For all the boredom they had endured, the officers and sailors on and around the flight deck could at least react to what they could see with their own eyes. Sailors and officers below decks, busy or not, had to rely upon other senses, and that tended to raise the levels of fear in closed areas.

AM3 Ed Krzeminski was on the hangar deck when the guns over his head began firing. Since Krzeminski could not see anything, he reflexively dropped to the steel deck in a little passageway with a ladder leading up to the island. There was little more he could do than hope for the best. Suddenly, a great wash of seawater all but carried him away from his place at the foot of the ladder. The great ship had swerved so hard that water had been washed up as high as the hangar deck. Thoroughly rattled, Krzeminski crawled out onto the deck of the cavernous hangar and lay on his stomach near the forward elevator. Better, he felt, to be exposed in the open than drowned—or worse—in a tight little steel vault.

From his standpoint about 1,800 yards out, Lt(jg) George Hamm, of destroyer *Monssen*, felt that he was looking down upon the carrier's flight deck from a great height, so far did she heel over in her turn.

High up on the third deck of *Enterprise*'s island, the force of the hard turn to port and an attendant 28-degree list was magnified to awesome proportions. The five officers huddled around the FDO's plot table in Radar Plot were sure the big ship was capsizing. Consequently, the battle was momentarily abandoned by a rather panicked exodus toward the nearest hatchway. LCdr Ham Dow was so rattled that he grabbed the D-rings on his Mae West lifejacket and inflated the vest before leaving the table. The two junior FDOs threw their pencils on the plot board, executed smart about-faces, but came up short when the gunnery liaison officer blocked the route to the outside. Ens George Givens was brought back to earth when he heard the grinning gunnery liaison officer, who was the only one of the group with outside communications, announce that all was well with the ship. All hands sheepishly returned to their work.

High above in Sky Control, LCdr Orlin Livdahl noticed that the butterflies that had been plaguing him since the first radar sighting at 1632 had suddenly flown away. He was dead calm.

⇌

Enterprise was making 27 knots when the Vals started down on her port side and port quarter at 1710. The first Vals that survived the fighter onslaught spiraled down from about 18,000 feet, entered steeper dives at about 15,000, and finally dropped their bombs from 1,500–2,000 feet.

The Val pilots clearly attempted to follow the carrier through her radical evasive maneuvers in the last seconds before dropping, but they were off the mark.

From his vantage point in Sky Lookout Forward, about 100 feet above the flight deck, directly above the captain's bridge, Ens Ross Glasmann, the L Division junior officer, clearly saw the Vals passing through 15,000 feet and heading straight toward him from off the port bow. At that instant, a Zero with a Wildcat firmly attached to its tail flitted into view. As the Zero tried to dive away from the pursuing U.S. Navy fighter, Glasmann saw its twin cowl-mounted 7.7mm machine guns wink at him. He instinctively ducked as a stream of bullets buzzed close by Sky Lookout Forward and impacted far below on the surface of the ocean. When Glasmann looked back around for the Zero, all he could see was a flaming wreck as it fell into the water. A moment later, the pursuing Wildcat also burst into flames under the impact of numerous antiaircraft rounds. It knifed straight into the water.

Glasmann returned his gaze to the lead Val just as it swung from off the port bow to off the port beam to release its 500-kilogram bomb. From his high vantage point, he was able to see the bomb as it fell toward the flight deck.

Lt Robin Lindsey, the carrier's senior Landing Signal Officer, was on the tiny LSO platform at the port after corner of the flight deck when the first bomb raised a huge geyser of seawater almost directly beneath his feet. Lindsey jumped down to the walkway next to the exposed LSO platform and yanked out his .45-caliber pistol—more a totem than a suitable weapon for staving off enemy dive-bombers.

Lt(jg) Ed DeGarmo, the nearest 20mm battery officer to the blast, was painfully wounded by a hot sliver of steel deep in his right foot, but he refused relief. One of his gun captains took a sliver of steel that would render him blind in one eye, but he too refused to relinquish his battle station. And a loader on one of the aft sponson 20mm guns was lifted right out of the sponson and tossed up onto the flight deck. He was so dazed that he climbed down to the 20mm gun nearest his resting place and reloaded it before realizing it was not his own.

Adding immeasurably to the excitement were streams of 7.7mm machine gun bullets fired by Val pilots in their dives or Val reargunners retiring from the vortex of the attack. Angered beyond reason, Lt Robin Lindsey sighted down the barrel of his automatic pistol and cranked off several rounds at a departing Val gunner who was firing at the ship.

One Marine 20mm loader had a full magazine of 20mm rounds blown up in his hands by a 7.7mm round. Live rounds cooked off in all directions, but no one, not even the loader, was hurt.

Each near miss slewed around the stern and staggered Marine

Pfc Robert Lee, who was manning the portside stern 20mm cannon. And several bombs fell close enough to the ship to dash cold seawater over Lee, his loader, and nearby gunners. The noise of the gunfire was so overwhelming that it continued to ring in Lee's ears even when he momentarily ceased firing so his loader could change ammunition drums.

Burning airplanes seemed to be falling all around *Enterprise*. Over 100 feet above the waterline, in Sky Lookout Forward, Ens Ross Glasmann and his lookouts felt the heat of flames on their upturned faces as the second Val recovered right over them, faltered, and then plunged on into the sea.

The third Val in line dived obliquely past Sky Lookout Forward and straight into the water with its bomb still aboard. The impact of the speeding airplane set off the big bomb, which threw up a huge geyser of water and a smelly black substance that fell over Sky Lookout Forward, one of the highest points on the nearby carrier.

As the attack developed, the array of Vals moved clockwise from the port bow and on down the starboard side. LCdr Benny Mott, the antiaircraft gunnery officer, was initially elated because the carrier's greatest array of firepower was concentrated on the starboard side. But the ship continued to swing around and the Vals were soon diving on the ship from astern, and then from the port quarter.

Pfc Robert Lee, who was manning the portside stern 20mm cannon, immediately felt that his first exposure to combat was much easier than the long hours of training he had endured over many months. The plunging Vals obliged by diving straight at him. All Lee had to do was lean back in his harness, flex his knees to tilt the barrel of the gun straight up, draw a bead, and put out a few tracer rounds to see how close to the target he could come. The zero-deflection corrections from that point were simple. Lee had been trained to concentrate on one target at a time until it dropped its bomb, disappeared from his ring sight, or blew up.

卐

Though destroyer *Grayson*, which was 1,800 yards off *Enterprise*'s starboard beam, had no firm targets in sight, she opened fire at 1711 when *Enterprise*'s Marine sergeant set off the antiaircraft conflagration. The first view *Grayson*'s gunners had of the Vals was when they were ahead of and high over *Enterprise*. Thus all of *Grayson*'s guns, including her 5-inch main battery, were redirected from a bearing on the starboard quarter—upsun—to port and well ahead. Cdr Harold Holcomb, the commander of Destroyer Division 22, who was aboard *Grayson*, saw the first three Japanese planes shot from the sky. Lt(jg) George Hamm, aboard destroyer *Monssen*—1,800 yards off the carrier's starboard quarter—also distinctly saw the first three Vals crash into the sea.

The best antiaircraft gunship in the array around *Enterprise* was light cruiser *Atlanta*, a swift new vessel that had been specially designed for a fleet antiaircraft role. *Atlanta* did a superb job of following *Enterprise* through her radical turns, but since she was sailing off the carrier's starboard bow and the Vals were attacking from port, her sixteen radar-controlled 5-inch rapid-fire guns mounted in eight dual mounts could not provide cover at intermediate or low altitudes. The best *Atlanta* could do was fire across *Enterprise* at Vals as they entered their dives or wait until retiring Vals flew past the carrier. *Atlanta* was further prevented from making the most of her deadly guns because friendly vessels kept showing up in her sights.

Heavy cruiser *Portland*, which maintained station more or less off *Enterprise*'s port bow, had better clearance for her 5-inch batteries, but she had only four such guns on a side. These were controlled by slow, antiquated gun directors and took far longer to get rounds out than *Atlanta*'s modern batteries. Thus, while *Portland*'s numerous lighter weapons contributed to the destruction of the Japanese dive-bombers, she was not the best ship in the best spot.

North Carolina, a thoroughly modern "fast" battleship, brought up the rear of the formation. As soon as the action started, she had increasing amounts of difficulty keeping station or keeping up. At 27 knots, she was fast for a battleship, but she was slower than any of the carrier's other escorts, and even *Enterprise* was able to grind out 30 knots of speed once she got going.

The battleship's antiaircraft firepower was awesome. LCdr John Kirkpatrick, the antiaircraft gunnery officer, personally controlled forty .50-caliber machine guns, forty 20mm cannon, four Oerlikon 1.1-inch quadruple mounts, and twenty 5-inch twin-mount dual-purpose guns. As had LCdr Orlin Livdahl aboard *Enterprise*, Kirkpatrick, a 1931 Naval Academy graduate who had served in the Reserves from 1935 until recalled in 1941, had overseen a strict training program that had brought his gun crews to high proficiency for their first battle.

The first time *North Carolina* fired off her entire antiaircraft array at once was when the first Vals tipped over above *Enterprise*. Even Lieutenant Commander Kirkpatrick was shaken by the volume of noise, smoke, heat, and smell of burning materials. As did many others aboard the ship, Kirkpatrick briefly wondered if all that gunfire had set the battleship ablaze. It seemed so to Lt(jg) George Hamm, who was abeam *North Carolina* aboard destroyer *Monssen*. Indeed, the Task Force 16 commander, RAdm Thomas Kinkaid, radioed from *Enterprise* at the height of the attack to inquire if *North Carolina* was afire.

Moments after the attack commenced to port, AOM2 Lester Tucker, the gun pointer manning *North Carolina*'s sternmost starboard 20mm cannon, spotted what appeared to be a half-dozen high-altitude bombers passing overhead just as a spread of bombs struck the surface of the water nearly 1,000 yards away from the nearest ships. Though this flight's passage and drop was noted by other members of the battleship's topside crew, and in her action report, there is no other mention of high-level bombers of any type by either of the U.S. carrier fighter squadrons or other Task Force 16 warships. (One possibility is that recovering Vals were mistaken for another type of airplane, but this does not account for the pattern of bombs. Also, just as the dive-bomber attack began, LCdr Max Leslie, the Air Group 6 commander, passed close to *North Carolina* and his command TBF was struck by a round from her very first antiaircraft salvo. However, this hardly explains the consistent reports of six or eight bombers by *North Carolina* gunners.)

卐

At 1712, a Val that could not seem to get lined up on *Enterprise* went after destroyer *Balch*, which had been putting out maximum antiaircraft fire for a full minute in support of the carrier. Observers occupying numerous vantage points saw the Val stagger in mid-flight under the impact of *Balch*'s guns and then alter course as if to crash into *Enterprise*'s flight deck. It barely missed. LCdr Orlin Livdahl, in Sky Control, tucked his head into his shoulders as the flaming dive-bomber passed within 20 feet of his perch. The Val slid by just off the the starboard bow before plunging into the water and exploding.

At almost the same moment, a wingless, tailless dive-bomber fell burning from high altitude into the water off *Balch*'s port quarter. It disintegrated upon impact but did not catch fire. And, as a Japanese warplane turned toward *Balch* with a Wildcat in hot pursuit, *Balch*'s guns opened fire and riddled it. (No doubt the Wildcat pilot also claimed credit for the kill.)

Observers and ready gunners aboard *Saratoga* and her consorts were mildly elated to see that the full weight of the air strike was falling elsewhere. Though *Saratoga*'s Task Force 11 was only 10,000 yards behind Task Force 16 and firing in support of it, the Japanese pilots were apparently intent upon crippling one carrier before going after the other.

卐

Capt Edward Sauer, who was embarked in *Balch* with the staff of his Destroyer Division 6, observed as many as fifteen 500-kilogram bombs detonate in the water near *Enterprise*. As destroyer *Monssen* was radically shifted from the port quarters to the starboard beam as a result of the carrier's wild evasion maneuvers, Lt(jg) George Hamm saw several bombs harmlessly fall into *Enterprise*'s wake. Then it looked to Hamm like the next bomb would certainly strike the carrier.

Indeed. The first bomb ever to strike *Enterprise* did so at precisely 1714. The 500-kilogram delayed-action bomb angled into the teak flight deck at the forward starboard corner of the after elevator and penetrated 42 feet through three steel decks before detonating in the chief petty officers' quarters. The entire ship whipsawed from the shock of the blast, which jerked hundreds of sailors and Marines from their feet.

The immediate area of the detonation, including the chiefs' quarters and a metal shop, was devastated. An entire damage-control party, an ammunition-handling detail, and the detail manning the elevator pump room were instantly consumed. Thirty-five men were killed outright and as many as seventy were injured. The steel deck beneath the detonation was left with a 24-foot crater, and the overhead had a bulge 24 feet in diameter. The flight deck, three levels up, was left with a 2-foot-high bulge and the after elevator was rendered inoperable—fortunately while flush with the flight deck. Several large storerooms at or just below the waterline were holed; several of the holes were 6 feet in diameter.

Two precautions had been taken that probably prevented the ship from being rapidly engulfed in flames: Flammable paint had been chipped from the compartments around the impact zone, and just before the attack Mach Bill Fluitt, the ship's gasoline officer, oversaw the draining and venting of nearby aviation fuel lines, which were all filled with inert carbon dioxide moments before the bomb struck.

The steeply angled path of the bomb had carried it through the sponson supporting Lt John Williamson's Gun Group 3—the aft starboard pair of 5-inch guns—where it started several small fires. Williamson secured the entire crew of Number 5 5-inch gun to fight the fire.

The ship settled on a minor starboard list as fires broke out in all the affected berthing and storage areas. As the flames quickly spread through mattresses, clothing, and stores, thick, blinding smoke choked off the entire area. Several key electrical cables and mains were destroyed or shorted out, and water pressure in nearby firefighting mains dropped off to useless levels.

There was no time to recover from the first bomb when, only 30 seconds later, a second 500-kilogram bomb landed only 15 feet away from the first hit.

࿕

Each of *Enterprise's* eight 5-inch gun mounts was manned by a crew of twenty-four, including one officer, and each of the two-mount gun groups was under the supervision of one battery officer.

Thus there were forty-six enlisted sailors and three officers manning Lt John Williamson's Gun Group 3—the two after starboard 5-inch mounts. In addition, the after-battery troubleshooter, GM1 William Powell, ran to Gun Group 3 from the port aft 5-inch guns when the first bomb set off the ready powder. Powell had just dropped into the gun gallery from the flight deck when the second 500-kilogram bomb detonated at deck level and right on top of the guns.

Observers on other ships or elsewhere on *Enterprise*—including a movie cameraman who caught the whole thing on film—noticed that the bomb blast was instantly followed by a secondary blast of very large magnitude. The secondary blast was the sympathetic detonation of Gun Group 3's ready powder casings—perhaps as many as sixty-five that early in the action. Tremendous heat coupled with the shattering explosion and release of a huge orange ball of flame and voluminous black smoke assured the instantaneous death of forty-one of Gun Group 3's forty-nine gunners and officers—including Lt John Williamson and GM1 William Powell. All of the surviving gunners and at least four bystanders were severely injured. Indeed, all of the fatalities who were not ripped to shreds by the force of the blast were burned beyond easy recognition; many were little more than small, grotesque charcoal caricatures of the men they had once been.

The terrific blast threw large chunks of metal and pieces of human bodies out as far as destroyer *Monssen*, which was at least 1,500 yards off the starboard quarter endeavoring to follow the carrier through its radical turns. As debris struck the destroyer and the water around her, Lt(jg) George Hamm saw that someone aboard *Enterprise* had had the presence of mind to throw out a smoke marker and life rafts in the event live crewmen had also been blown overboard.

卐

It was coming up 1516. BM1 Al Gabara, the Number 4 1.1-inch gun captain, happened to be looking at his friend, BM2 Art Davis, when the third bomb was stopped by a structural member of the after elevator. The bomb was probably defective, as it went

179

off at flight-deck level in a relatively low-order detonation. Davis, who was standing in the open next to the Number 2 elevator, was simply blown apart by the force of the blast. A large chunk of him landed in the after 1.1-inch gun pointer's lap.

BM1 Gabara went into shock for a few seconds, until one of the loaders yelled into his ear, "Gabby, you're hit." He did not feel a thing, but he followed the loader's gaze until he found that a steel sliver had punctured his right arm just below the elbow. He also found that he had spent a few lost moments absently sweeping shell casings from the mount.

PhoM3 Robert Read, one of three photographers who had been charged with recording the defense of the ship on film for later study, was standing tall in an exposed vantage point on the island as he followed the third bomb in his viewfinder all the way to impact. Read got his superb shot, but shrapnel from the blast killed him.

S1 Willie Bowdoin, a member of the Number 3 1.1-inch gun crew, was wounded in the leg and posterior by tiny steel shards and knocked to the flight deck. When Bowdoin recovered his senses, he saw that a small fire had broken out behind the gun, so he moved to grab a fire extinguisher to put it out. He was arrested in his tracks by the screams of S1 Joyce Lamson, the Number 3 gun pointer, who had also been thrown to the deck. Lamson's abdomen had been torn open by bomb shrapnel and his intestines were exposed. One of his legs also appeared to be shredded.

AMM2 Joe Greco, a Fighting-6 mechanic who had played in BM2 Art Davis's acey-deucey game, was kneeling behind the flight-deck crane when Lamson fell to the deck beside him. There was an interminable moment of silence before the injured sailor pleaded for help. S1 Willie Bowdoin passed him by; he had no idea how he could help, and he was intent upon saving the gun from the fire that seemed about to engulf it. Almost without thinking, AMM2 Greco and another aviation groundcrewman gingerly lifted Lamson and carried him to the aid station located just beneath the flight deck.

Meantime, S1 Willie Bowdoin fought the fire, and won.

As BM1 Al Gabara's circle of attention widened beyond his own injuries, he saw that every man in the gun crew had been peppered and slightly injured by flying steel slivers. It took several more moments for Gabara to notice that the starboard after 5-inch gun gallery was a smoking ruin.

$$\text{卍}$$

AMM2 Bernard Peterson owed his life to a prescient warning from his section chief. Peterson, among many other onlookers, had been standing in the open hangar deck boat pocket and watching the air action when the bombing attack began. The section chief warned the dozen or so sailors to stand clear only an instant before the first bomb exploded below decks and only 20 feet away. The explosion caused the entire after section of the hangar deck to bulge upward, and that actually popped several onlookers clear up to the overhead. Most of the men in the area suffered flash burns and shrapnel wounds, but none was as seriously injured as they all might have been had they remained in the exposed boat pocket.

Moments after AMM2 Peterson's hearing returned, a 20mm gunner on the after catwalk complained that he had something in his eye and needed relief. Peterson, who had qualified as a TBF .50-caliber turret gunner and whose friends among the 20mm gunners had given him a little practice, strapped into the harness and immediately began firing at a diving Val. *Bonk . . . Bonk . . . Bonk.* Peterson was at first surprised by the 20mm gun's low rate of fire, but he quickly settled in. A real sense of power suffused him as his gun's bright popcorn balls of tracer stitched the Val's body. The airplane blew up. Before Peterson could come onto a new target, a second Val appeared to be struck from the air by other guns. His stream of tracer joined others on yet another Val, and that too fell out of the sky.

$$\text{卍}$$

When Ens Ross Glasmann, over 100 feet above the waterline in Sky Lookout Forward, realized that many of the Vals were bound to recover right over his station, he drew out his .45-caliber automatic pistol, held it in both hands at arm's length, and deliberately squeezed the trigger in the hope of placing at least several rounds into the cockpit area of each passing dive-bomber. He was only 30 or 40 feet from each of the dive-bombers. He felt collected and in full control, even when he found himself staring right into the eyes of a passing Val pilot who appeared to be growing a beard. Glasmann saw one of his rounds hole the cockpit right in front of the bearded pilot, and this Val peeled off to the left and plunged into the ocean. As Ensign Glasmann fired, he was completely oblivious of the angry taunts that he shouted at the passing dive-bombers and would be quite taken aback by his outspoken enmity when one of his lookouts later commented on it.

A Val that still had its bomb aboard was passing by higher overhead than the other Vals when a 20mm round from one of the escorts impacted right on the nose of the lethal projectile. There was a terrific dark blast right over Sky Lookout Forward and slivers of the bomb and parts of the vaporized Val rained down on the tiny exposed nest. Several large pieces and numerous tiny pieces struck the helmets of men in exposed positions throughout the island, but no one was noticeably injured. Fortunately, the momentum of the diving Val impelled the worst part of the detonation out over the water.

Well before Ensign Glasmann's ears cleared from the blast, he returned his attention to sighting in on other passing Vals with his automatic pistol. In all, three of his targets dived on into the ocean, and his lookouts later swore that his marksmanship was the cause. However, Glasmann could plainly see numerous tracer-marked streams of 20mm and .50-caliber from many sources enter the wings, fuselage, and cockpit area of each passing dive-bomber; he knew that his contribution was only a small part of the total impact. Glasmann fired two seven-round clips in about three minutes.

卐

The first four Vals to survive their dives were obliged to re-cover along a path directly between *Grayson* and *North Carolina*. All four airplanes flew very low and very slow, at no more than 130 miles per hour. They were thus superb targets.

The first such Val crossed over the destroyer from starboard to port at an altitude of about 300 feet. The pilot incurred the wrath of all hands by opening fire with his cowl-mounted 7.7mm machine guns. A shower of bullets struck *Grayson*'s Number 3 5-inch gun, an adjacent 20mm battery, and the aft torpedo mount. Eleven men were wounded. As *Grayson*'s after 20mm gun groups trained onto the passing Val and poured out a lethal concentration, the Val staggered and fell away into the water off the destroyer's port bow.

The next three Vals to get away from *Enterprise* flew up *Grayson*'s starboard side. The first was clearly downed by *North Carolina*'s port guns. The second drew the wrath of *Grayson*'s starboard 20mm battery; repeated hits at close ranges caused it to side-slip and crash 100 yards off *Grayson*'s port bow. The last of the four Vals was engaged by only one 20mm gun as all the other starboard guns had been directed against distant targets over *Enterprise*. This Val jinked away from *Grayson*'s gun and flew directly into the immense cloud of low-level fire *North Carolina*'s port batteries were putting out.

卐

One Val banked sharply away from *Enterprise* and pulled out of its dive just a few feet above the water before zooming right over destroyer *Monssen*. In that fleeting instant, Lt(jg) George Hamm managed to look the begoggled Japanese pilot right in the eyes. As Hamm turned to follow the Val away, he looked straight down the barrel of a 20mm gun that was also tracking the warplane. Many streams of 20mm tracer crossed behind, ahead, and right through the receding dive-bomber. The airplane briefly smoked and streamed a flame, but Hamm saw the fire go out as the Val flew on out of sight. It was one of only a half dozen Vals Hamm saw get away.

卐

Though *North Carolina* continued to fall further and further behind *Enterprise*, her guns were able to bear on many Vals as they recovered from dives on the carrier.

Late in the attack, at about 1715, just as *North Carolina* was struck by several errant rounds from other ships, she became the exclusive target of at least six Vals that detached themselves from the main attack force diving on *Enterprise* and came up the battleship's stern to deliver relatively low-level glide-bombing attacks.

AOM2 Lester Tucker and other members of the starboard aft 20mm gun battery spotted several of the low-flying glide-bombers as *North Carolina* turned hard to port—either to evade the imminent attack or to follow *Enterprise* into an evasive turn. One group of starboard twin 5-inch mounts dropped their barrels from high-altitude targets but were prevented from firing at the oncoming Vals beause the gun-target line passed right through the stern catapults, each of which sported a fully fueled SOC floatplane armed with light bombs. The only opposition *North Carolina* could offer was from several of her sternmost 20mm guns.

The glide-bombing technique uses the momentum of a shallow dive to throw the bomb at the target. It is an inexact science requiring immense skill. The Japanese gliding down on *North Carolina* were not skilled enough. All six 500-kilogram bombs missed the ship, but one struck abreast the port catapult close enough to knock down gun crews, dent the side of the ship above the waterline, and raise a column of seawater that drenched several after 20mm gun crews. Most of the Val pilots and gunners strafed the battleship's deck and upper works as they dived and recovered.

As the Vals were passing overhead, Lester Tucker's loader became mesmerized by the sights of the battle and forgot to replace the gun's expended ammunition drum. Tucker pulled himself from his harness to give the awestruck loader a swift kick in the rear. Just as the surprised loader turned, a passing Val unleashed a stream of 7.7mm bullets. One round barely missed the loader's head before passing between Tucker's legs and on into a bag of expended 20mm cartridges, which spilled out over the deck. Another 7.7mm round from the same burst passed through the abdomen and out the back of AMM3 George Conlon, the loader on the next gun forward. Conlon, who had just made his rate that morning, sat down heavily on the deck behind his gun and fell over backward.

As Tucker's revitalized loader threw in a fresh ammunition drum, one of the last Vals to dive on *Enterprise* recovered and flew down the starboard side of the battleship close enough for FC3 Larry Resen—in Sky Control, 120 feet above the water—to see the pilot's face. Resen was certain that the pilot wanted to carry home detailed information about the first modern U.S. fast battleship to weather combat in the Pacific. When AOM2 Tucker and nearby gunners saw the last Val fly by only 150 feet away with its canopy thrown back and the pilot and gunner staring at them, they took revenge for George Conlon by blasting it into the sea.

AMM3 Conlon was carried by stretcher to the aid station set up in the aviation storeroom by the fantail aircraft catapults, but he expired before the corpsmen could begin treating him. He was the battleship's only fatality of the day.

↺

All ships ceased fire between 1719 and 1720. For most of the officers and men topside in Task Force 16, the abrupt silence was almost painful.

19

Carrier pilots in the air over their own flight decks are motivated at several levels: There is the thrill of the hunt, which tends to block out a lot of other matters; there is the sense of duty to the living souls stranded in the friendly ships; and there is the pragmatic realization that a severely damaged or sunken flight deck cannot be used for a safe landing.

These three motivations are precisely the forces that carried so many Wildcat pilots against the diving Vals and on into the cones of friendly anitaircraft fire. At least one, and possibly four, of the five Wildcat pilots lost in the opening melees were brought down by friendly fire.

The motivation for the hard fight the Wildcat jocks—and other U.S. Navy pilots—gave the *retiring* Vals was pure revenge.

After the Japanese dive-bomber leader pulled away from Lt Chick Harmer, the Fighting-5 exec, Harmer peeled out of his own dive and found another Val in his sights. The Val appeared to Harmer to have already dropped his bomb, but Harmer followed him anyway, though his Wildcat sustained several hits from 7.7mm machine gun fire put out by the Val's rear gunner. Suddenly, the Val pulled up right in front of Harmer's Wildcat—it looked like he was trying to loop—and Harmer had to pull out in a steep right bank to miss colliding with him. As the fighter-squadron exec completed a 180-degree turn, he saw a huge splash below the wings of his fighter. He was thus credited with a probable kill.

Harmer was by then at less than 500 feet, and not another F4F was in sight. All the other aircraft in sight were Japanese. He had evidently flown into their rendezvous area.

Chick Harmer immediately lost interest in the last Val's possible crash sight when a blast of tracer passed his fighter. He had a Zero on his tail!

Harmer's F4F-4 could not outturn or outclimb the Zero. The Zero was able to hang quite comfortably on Harmer's tail and follow his every evasive maneuver while letting the Wildcat have it with repeated 7.7mm bursts. One burst penetrated the canopy, struck the instrument panel, and injured Harmer in both legs. The Wildcat pilot did the only thing he had left in his bag of tricks—he turned the armor-plated back of his seat to the Zero's guns and did his best to keep it there. He could hear and feel the gunfire for long, long seconds, but then it abruptly stopped. Harmer had no idea what spared him as he rather gingerly flew from the area.

卐

One of the day's most surprising engagements took place as Lt Rube Konig's tiny strike force of six Torpedo-3 Avengers circled the task force to gain altitude and find the mixed group of eleven Scouting-5 and Bombing-6 SBDs sent out following the last-minute launch from *Enterprise*. The SBDs never joined up. As Konig finally turned north, toward the last known position of the Japanese carriers, a lone Val joined up on his formation. Clearly, the Japanese pilot was looking for some help navigating home, though it is doubtful he initially realized he had joined a U.S. Navy formation.

In the second or two it took the U.S. airmen who noticed the intruder to figure out what to do, the Japanese pilot woke up and opened fire on Mach John Baker's TBF from 500 yards astern and off Baker's port quarter. Immediately, Baker's turret gunner, ARM3 C. L. Gibson, returned the fire. The first burst, a short one, struck the Val's fuselage. A longer second burst fell between the Japanese warplane's cockpit and engine. The Val, which had been closing in on Gibson, dropped away in flames and appeared to dive all the way into the ocean.

🌀

Lt(jg) Dick Gay's unengaged Fighting-6 division, which had been among the last Wildcats to launch, climbed away from the task force to about 12,000 feet and was just turning back to get closer to *Enterprise* when it was suddenly taken on by an unknown number of Zeros. Dick Gay went into a tight turn onto the tail of one Zero, flamed it, and continued on in the turn behind another Zero.

Ens Bob Disque, the division's tail-end Charlie, was in a tight turn, following the other three Wildcats. As Disque watched Gay go after the second Zero, he was rudely made aware that he had become the target of another Zero he never really saw. Disque heard what sounded like someone throwing a handful of gravel against the side of a tin barn. At that, he instinctively knew that his fighter had been hit, and he tightened up his tall body to present as small a target as possible to the next burst. But the next burst did not come.

Disque continued around in his tight turn and, within seconds, came upon the second Zero Gay had been chasing. He poured bullets into the Japanese fighter in an almost head-on pass.

By the time Disque completed his firing pass, he had lost sight of Gay and found himself alone in the sky. His fighter had a multitude of neat, clean holes in the wing roots alongside the cockpit, a number of grooves in the covering for the oxygen bottle down by the right rudder pedal, and two holes in the canopy track by the pilot's right shoulder. Though severely chastened, Disque silently gave credit to the Japanese pilot, whom he felt had to be a superb gunner to have put all of his burst right into the Wildcat's cockpit area at a nearly 90-degree angle. Disque would later learn that his fighter had received about 110 rounds in the cockpit and wing-root area. It all happened so fast there had been no time for Disque to think about it.

⌇

Lt(jg) Weasel Weissenborn and Ens Fred Mears, of Torpedo-3, returned to the task force in clear skies just after 1700 and made a recognition signal before completing their approach on *Enterprise*. All of a sudden, Mears saw light cruiser *Atlanta*, which was guarding *Enterprise*'s starboard flank, become immersed in a great cloud of gray-black smoke. Mears was at first sure the cruiser had been struck by something—a bomb or a torpedo—but he quickly realized that she had opened fire with her antiaircraft batteries. Farther on, *North Carolina* lit up from stem to stern as all her light, medium, and heavy antiaircraft batteries seemed to open fire at once.

As all the ships turned in unison, Mears looked up and saw three Vals, lined up one after the other, slowly dive on the nearby carrier. At the same instant, Mears's earphones crackled with an urgent warning: "All friendly planes keep clear during the attack."

The two TBFs turned away and circled beyond the rim of the fight. Mears became so engrossed in watching the colorful action that he all but forgot to fly his Avenger. There were masses of flame as burning airplanes dodged in and out of the antiaircraft cloud. Nearby, shrapnel from bursting 5-inch anitaircraft rounds were falling in patches like heavy rain. Near *Enterprise*, Mears saw great white geysers marking the spots where Japanese 500-kilogram bombs struck the water.

⌇

As Ens Bob Disque flew alone around the edge of the main action, he saw a TBF low on the water, banking and turning, trying to evade a Zero that was making repeated firing passes at it. This could very well have been the Torpedo-3 search plane flown by Ens H. L. Bingaman.

Bingaman had returned to the task force in the company of an SBD flown by Ens John Jorgenson, who had accompanied him on the search hop. Moments after discovering the task force, which appeared to be under attack, Bingaman's TBF was attacked by three Zeros, and Jorgenson's SBD disappeared from sight, perhaps because it too was attacked.

Ensign Bingaman, a fighter pilot who had been dragooned into torpedo bombers following the Midway massacre, allowed his killer instincts to prevail over his good sense. He immediately began challenging the three Zeros by maneuvering into direct head-on passes. This effectively negated the defensive capabilities of his two crew gunners—AMM3 Calvin Crouch, who was manning the TBF's .30-caliber tunnel stinger, and ARM3 Paul Knight, who was manning the .50-caliber power-turret gun.

Finally, after what seemed like ages to the gunners, Bingaman leveled off right over the sea and flew straight ahead at top speed. Apparently, the now-certain kill was left to just one of the Zeros, which made a rear approach ARM3 Knight saw as being right out of the gunnery school manual. At the precise moment the Zero flew into range, Knight plinked out a short burst and saw his tracer going just a hair over the Zero's starboard wing. Knight also saw a thin wisp of yellowish smoke curl back over each of the Zero's wings—the telltale signature of 20mm cannon fire.

From Ens Bob Disque's high vantage point, the Zero and TBF appeared to be so close to the surface of the ocean that the Zero's 7.7mm and 20mm rounds were kicking up a visible pattern in the water.

ARM3 Paul Knight nudged his power turret over just a hair and resumed firing. It was a long burst. Knight was gratified to see that his tracers were falling right across the top of the Japanese fighter's engine cowling.

At this moment, Ensign Disque dropped down and caught the Zero from behind.

ARM3 Knight did not see the friendly Wildcat, but he saw essentially the same thing Bob Disque saw from his totally different vantage point: The Zero dropped its right wing, as if peeling off to the right, and flew straight into the water.

Though Disque passed close to the TBF, Knight never saw him. He had other matters to contend with. At the precise moment the Zero staggered to the right in its death throes, a 20mm cannon round—or perhaps a .50-caliber round from one of Disque's guns—struck the Plexiglas power turret. Everything seemed to explode in Knight's face.

Seconds later, before Knight could recover, Ensign Bingaman announced that he was ditching the bullet-riddled TBF. AMM3 Crouch climbed out of the gun tunnel and strapped into a seat facing the rear of the crew compartment right behind the cockpit. Knight, who was strapped into his turret seat, merely braced himself for the shock of the imminent contact.

The Avenger slid into the water at a fairly high speed and came to an abrupt stop, the shock from which momentarily knocked Paul Knight unconscious. When Knight fully regained his senses, he found that the airplane was well down by the nose and that he was in the process of ejecting the side escape hatch. As the radioman-gunner attempted to crawl through the hatch, however, he felt something holding him back by the left ankle. There was a momentary fit of panicked kicking, which seemed to free the foot, and Knight left the airplane.

By the time Knight left the sinking Avenger, Bingaman and Crouch had deployed a life raft. Knight kicked across the few yards of water separating him from the raft and was helped aboard by his crewmates. It was only then discovered that the explosion in the power turret had left Knight with lacerations in the forehead, face, left leg, and left hand.

Moments later, the TBF sank. Ensign Bingaman, who had a small laceration between his eyes, announced that it was 1715.

卐

Shortly after helping knock down the Zero that had been menacing Ens Bingaman's TBF, Ens Bob Disque sighted a Zero low on the water, apparently headed for home. He approached the Zero from above and camped on his tail before firing every .50-caliber round he had left. Then Disque had to watch the Zero slowly pull away and disappear over the horizon.

卐

Lt Walter Clarke led his Fighting-5 division around the friendly antiaircraft fire, but Lt(jg) Smokey Stover and his wing-

man, Ens Mortimer Kleinmann, separated from Clarke—more or
less accidentally—and started to enter the snarling Wildcat versus
Zero melee at the top of the antiaircraft curtain. Immediately, a
Zero zoomed them. Stover and Kleinmann gave chase and repeatedly fired at the Zero but with no apparent results. The Zero was
faster than the Wildcats. The two U.S. Navy pilots chased the
Imperial Navy pilot for five minutes but could not gain on him even
after dropping their belly tanks.

No member of Clarke's division claimed a kill.

᛭

Ens Wayne Presley and Ens Melvin Roach, of Fighting-5,
were launched from *Saratoga* at 1700 among the last Wildcats to be
sent aloft. By the time the two got to within range of the swirling
dogfights, *Enterprise* was well under attack. Too low to have an effect on the incoming Japanese bombers, the two were moving to
take on retiring Vals when Presley spotted a parachute shroud just
over the water at some distance. He led Roach out to investigate,
but diverted when he saw a low-flying Val leaving the area. Presley
set up a head-on approach and hammered the Val into the waves.

᛭

Lt Lou Bauer, the Fighting-6 commander, had launched with
his division from *Saratoga* at 1630 and had been vectored away from
the fight during the brief period the FDOs had had control of the
fighter deployment. As the battle over *Enterprise* heated up, Bauer
led his division around to intercept follow-on Japanese strike forces,
if there were any, or to block the escape routes he felt would be
used by retiring Vals and Zeros. The move paid off at 1715 when
Bauer found a Val heading northward, away from Task Force 61, at
high speed. Bauer set up a high-side attack and both he and his
wingman, Ens Wildon Rouse, put many rounds into the Val before
it splashed into the water.

Some minutes later, as Bauer led his intact division to higher
altitude, a Zero passed close enough to draw deadly attention. The
Zero took absolutely no evasive action as Bauer fired into it for
some moments before giving way to his second-section leader, Ens

James Halford, who finished the sluggish enemy fighter off at extremely low altitude with a final burst that sent it plunging to destruction.

⚜

Lt Vince DePoix's six-plane Fighting-6 combat air patrol division was heading into the fight at 17,000 feet a bit late because it had been guarding a distant sector. Suddenly, the division leader saw a lone Zero passing in the opposite direction at what he estimated to be 12,000 feet. As DePoix dived at full speed after the Japanese fighter, he saw markings on the Zero's tail slowly resolve themselves into a pattern that identified the Japanese pilot as a *buntaicho*, a fighter-group commander. At that, DePoix poured on so much power that his Wildcat began vibrating. So intent was DePoix on scoring against a senior Japanese pilot that he entered the awesome curtain of antiaircraft gunfire *North Carolina* was putting out. The Zero disappeared without DePoix's having had an opportunity to fire, and DePoix roared into a turn to avoid the sheets of gunfire that were rising to meet him.

⚜

The Fighting-5 and Fighting-6 Wildcats were by no means the only U.S. warplanes operating in proximity to Task Force 61 during the fateful minutes of the Japanese attack. In addition to *Enterprise* SBDs that were conducting routine air patrols when the Japanese began their approach, the fates conspired to bring numerous *Enterprise* scouts back home in time to watch or become embroiled in the swirling action.

Ens Howard Burnett and another Scouting-5 Dauntless pilot got back to *Enterprise* only minutes after she had launched the last of her fighters and several minutes before the Japanese attack started. Burnett was in the landing pattern when his gunner, ARM2 Harold Wilger, saw the pilot of the other SBD point up over the carrier. Wilger turned in his seat to see what was going on just as the first two Vals completed their dives. This was also the first Wilger saw of the rising antiaircraft curtain.

Ensign Burnett immediately broke away from the traffic circle, rolled over, and dived for the surface—right onto the tail of a retiring Val. As the SBD flew on, ARM2 Wilger, who was looking back over his gunsight for targets, saw a plane—presumably the one Burnett had chased—create a great plume of water as it skidded into the sea.

By then, Burnett was flying through the task force, heading in the opposite direction of the ships. The SBD passed down *North Carolina*'s starboard beam, which scared ARM2 Wilger nearly to death when he realized that his ride was as good a target as any Japanese plane in the vicinity.

Burnett flew right up the tail of a retiring Val and followed it for many miles, well beyond the range of friendly antiaircraft fire, but he could not get close enough to hit it. The task force was long out of sight when Burnett decided to break off. He saw a small island on the horizon, from which he took a bearing, and turned back to join numerous other U.S. Navy warplanes milling around the edge of the fight. By then, ARM2 Wilger's biggest fear was that he would not have a ship to go home to. He had served with Scouting-5 aboard *Yorktown* at the Coral Sea, where she had been damaged, and at Midway, where she had been sunk.

⁂

LCdr Charlie Jett, the Torpedo-3 skipper, and Ens Bob Bye did not quite have Task Force 61 in sight when they heard the order to bombers to keep clear of the area. Jett led Bye in a turn and climbed to 3,000 feet to circle well away from the action. The antiaircraft barrage was seen clearly by the crews of both TBFs, and RM3 Dewey Stemen, Bye's radioman-gunner, saw several Japanese bombs nearly miss or actually strike *Enterprise*. Stemen also noticed that the *Saratoga*'s Task Force 11 was slowly putting distance between itself and the Japanese main effort.

Two retiring Vals found the two TBFs and made abrupt firing passes that caught both Avenger crews by surprise. Lieutenant Commander Jett was not sure the Avengers could put out enough firepower to scare off the Vals, but he knew that the TBF's big wings made for slower, tighter turns than any other warplane in the air. It was possible for the TBFs to chop speed back to a grindingly slow 70 knots at low altitude, well below the stalling speed of the Vals. So, unable to outgun the Vals, Jett led Bye around in an effort to outmaneuver them.

While the TBF pilots tried to outfox the Vals, the TBF gunners tried to shoot them down. Dewey Stemen, who was manning Bye's turret-mounted .50-caliber machine gun, tracked and fired at two Vals in quick succession as they passed overhead from nose to tail. Stemen locked onto a third dark blur—and barely held his fire when it registered as a Dauntless dive-bomber. The stray SBD briefly joined up on Bye's wing, but he soon flew off on his own. Bye was particularly incensed by the SBD's departure; he and Jett needed the extra firepower the dive-bomber's twin .50-caliber and twin .30-caliber guns could have provided. He testily asked Stemen if he had noted the airplane's number, which he intended to report, but Stemen had not.

RM3 Stemen went back to searching for approaching Vals and picked up one as it came storming in directly from starboard. This was the best target Stemen had had thus far, and he took his time getting his gunsight on the largest feature, the engine cowling. Bye was moved by the long silence to urge Stemen to open fire, but the gunner would not be rattled, even when the Val's guns twinkled with red and yellow flame. When Stemen was finally set, he fired, but all his tracer rose to a point just over the Val's starboard wing root—a shade high and a shade to the left. The Val veered away around and below Bye's tail and then came up right into the notch between the TBF's tail and starboard wing—just a hair too low and too close to be endangered by the TBF's turret or tunnel guns. Stemen stared at the Japanese pilot and rear gunner in stark disbelief until the pilot dropped down and away. Stemen was so amazed by the close encounter that he did not get his turret around in time to fire so much as a parting salute.

Neither side drew blood, and all the Japanese soon left. By that time, however, Bye had become separated from Jett. Unable to locate any other U.S. planes, he flew on alone until he encountered three more Vals. Another of the many fighter pilots who had been sent to reman the torpedo squadrons after Midway, Bye reflexively selected the Val that seemed the least aware of goings on around him and approached from starboard. The Val pilot saw Bye at the last instant and foolishly maneuvered directly into the TBF's line of fire. Bye fired the single .30-caliber popgun mounted on the cowling in front of the cockpit. As soon as Bye completed the burst, he turned his big torpedo bomber back toward the two remaining Vals and fired his nose gun at medium range into the port beam of a second Val. Then Bye turned away again to pursue his first target, which he shot full of holes from dead astern. By then, however, three other Vals swarmed over Bye to protect their victimized comrade. Bye and the Vals broke off the action by tacit mutual consent.

卐

At length, the bomber command channel resounded with a fierce order: "SBDs, attack the torpedo planes." Though he was flying a TBF, Ens Fred Mears, of Torpedo-3, reacted by leaving his element leader, Lt(jg) Weasel Weissenborn, and flying straight toward *Enterprise*, into the circle of fire. On the way, he met two Japanese warplanes recovering from steep dives. At first, Mears was convinced that he was being bounced by Zeros, which was a jolt. But a second look convinced him that he had luckily encountered a pair of Vals. Chastened, Mears banked away from the Vals, as much to give his turret gunner an easy shot as to rejoin Weissenborn in the safe zone. However, the Vals followed the Avenger and opened fire. By the time Mears found Weissenborn again, Weissenborn had joined up on the wing of LCdr Charlie Jett, who had been searching for his lost wingman, Ens Bob Bye.

As Mears nudged up beneath Jett's left wing, one of the pursuing Vals prudently withdrew. However, the other flipped in a fast head-on firing pass at Mears, who could easily see the long yellowish streamers of smoke curling back over the Val's engine from the twin 7.7mm machine guns. As the Val was about to pass over the top of Mears's TBF, Mears pulled up and fired his cowl-mounted .30-caliber machine gun. Then the Val was gone, chased off by the Avenger formation's three turret-mounted .50-caliber machine guns.

卐

Lt Johnny Myers, the Torpedo-3 exec, who had lost his wingman, Mach Harry Corl, to Zeros over *Ryujo*, made it to within 25

196

miles of *Enterprise* when he was bounced by a lone Zero, which made a wide sweep from the port side before passing from sight astern. Four of the Zero's 20mm cannon rounds detonated on or in Myers's already-damaged TBF—one in each wing, one in the fuselage, and one in the rudder. At least fifty 7.7mm rounds also struck the Avenger. When the smoke cleared, Myers discovered that his radioman-gunner and bombardier had both been hurt.

Myers fought his sluggish controls and turned away from the battle to find a safe place to hide out until it was time to land—or ditch, whichever came first.

彁

Lt Carl Horenburger, of Bombing-6, was approaching the fleet in the quadrant assigned for recognition of friendly warplanes when he first noticed the heavy volume of antiaircraft fire rising from over the horizon. Horenburger prudently aborted his approach and began cutting lazy circles in the air well beyond the intensifying action. One lazy pass brought him within sighting distance of four Vals, which were circling at 200–300 feet prior to retiring to their own carriers.

Horenburger, who had been leader of the SBD flight that had swatted AP1 Saburo Sakai from Tulagi's skies on August 7, picked up the scent and roared after the four Vals. However, his efforts to place the fire of his cowl-mounted .50-caliber machine guns was significantly hampered by the weight of the 500-pound bomb he had lugged on his long search flight and which he was loath to jettison just then. Sheer persistence brought Horenburger's laden Dauntless within range of the Vals. He saw his tracers strike at least one of them, and he felt 7.7mm rounds strike his own airplane before the Vals completed their rendezvous maneuvers and rapidly drew away from the slower SBD.

彁

Bombing-6's Lt Ray Kline returned from an uneventful solo search mission at about 1725, just in time to spot five Vals as they were retiring from the scene of their air strike. Kline jerked his

Dauntless into a pass on the rear Val, but he could not get the Japanese bomber to stay in his sights long enough to get a shot off. At length, Kline's rearseatman, ARM1 Edward Garaudy, was able to get off a burst with his free guns, and he saw some of his tracers strike the Val. By then, however, Kline was far from home and low on fuel, so he gave up the chase.

⚛

Among the first Air Group 3 strike bombers back from sinking *Ryujo* was an element of three SBDs led by LCdr DeWitt Shumway, the Bombing-3 commander. The three, and several others strung out farther behind in loose formation, sighted Task Force 61 while there was still plenty of antiaircraft fire in the air, so Shumway led them away a bit to the north to ride out the storm.

After a long look at the conflagration over *Enterprise*, Lt Paul Holmberg glanced across to the airplane flying off Shumway's other wing and was stunned to see two fixed-gear dive-bombers—Vals!—slip into formation on the other SBD off Shumway's wing. Holmberg immediately grabbed his intercom microphone and ordered his rear gunner, ARM2 C. W. Albright, to open fire on them. Albright was apparently enthralled with the big show over *Enterprise*, so did not bring his guns to bear in time. No doubt embarrassed and frightened when they noticed their egregious error, the two Japanese broke off and dived away from the Dauntlesses.

⚛

When the Zero that had been shooting up Lt Chick Harmer's F4F from behind disappeared, Harmer found he was headed in the direction of Task Force 61. He could easily see the smoke from burning *Enterprise*, and quickly spotted *Saratoga*, which was about 10 miles behind her. He passed the burning carrier, though she appeared ready to take on airplanes, and flew on at 1,000 feet, intent upon landing aboard his own home.

Harmer saw that his was the only airplane in *Saratoga*'s landing pattern. He made an approach he felt was a really good one, but, just as he leveled his wings in anticipation of the "Cut," the LSO, Lt Walter Curtis, gave him a "Come on" followed an instant later by the expected "Cut." The little extra throttle Harmer had to give in response to the "Come on," along with his airplane's being light because it was nearly out of fuel and ammunition, sent Harmer into a thoroughly embarrassing barrier crash that flipped his fighter over on its back. Harmer was not hurt, but his F4F was wiped out—along with his pride.

It turned out that leg wounds Harmer had acquired in his last fight with a Zero were minor, but the doctor routinely gave him a stiff jolt of morphine and sent him to bed.

卐

In the chatter and excitement following the first collision of American and Japanese warplanes, the FDOs forgot or could not get through to the Wildcat division led by Fighting-5's skipper, LCdr Roy Simpler, which they had vectored out after a bogey in the opposite direction of the Japanese air strike just before the start of the action. Simpler dutifully remained on his vector for more than a half hour before he was able to break into the communications net with a request for instructions. The FDO with whom he spoke ordered his immediate return.

By the time Simpler reached Task Force 61, all the attackers were retiring at high speed and low altitude. The Fighting-5 commander immediately flew down to low altitude in the attack area, but the fight was all over by the time they arrived. He was furious with the foul-up that had kept him from the fight.

卐

At 1725, LCdr Bullet Lou Kirn, of Scouting-3, was leading a large part of Air Group 3 back from the *Ryujo* strike at 500 feet when he chanced to see a fresh Japanese strike group flying at 8,000 feet and on a parallel course, more or less in the same direction as the U.S. Navy bombers. Sensing that his group had not yet been spotted by the Japanese, Kirn ordered his radioman, ACRM C. E. Russ, to break radio silence to warn the friendly vessels of a possible impending follow-on strike. The message was repeated twice more.

Fortunately for all parties concerned, the Japanese follow-on strike of eighteen Vals, nine Kates, and three Zeros—which had been preparing to launch when Lt Ray Davis found their carriers— had been given an incorrect position report before leaving their ships under the leadership of the *Zuikaku hikotaicho*. Thus the group entirely missed Task Force 61.

At 1737, Bullet Lou Kirn again spotted other airplanes at a distance. These turned out to be four U.S. Army Air Forces B-17 heavy bombers that had been sent out from Espiritu Santo to join the search for Japanese ships. The B-17s approached the starboard quarter of Kirn's group from the southwest. Kirn assumed the recognition had been reciprocal until, at a range of only 500 yards, the nose gun of one of the B-17s was seen to open fire. The fall of the tracer indicated that the stream of bullets was well short, but the carrier bombers took evasive action and flew on.

At 1740, several of Kirn's pilots simultaneously spotted four Vals slightly to starboard and racing on an opposite heading at 1,000 feet—500 feet higher than the SBDs. Once again, ACRM Russ sounded the alarm, and Lieutenant Commander Kirn led his group down to 200 feet to meet the Vals from dead ahead. As the Vals passed right over the Dauntlesses, all the American pilots lifted their noses to climb in unison and simultaneously cut loose with their nose guns. All the radioman-gunners who could bring their guns to bear also fired straight up at the passing Vals.

As the Vals flew by overhead, Ens Alden Hanson and Lt(jg) R. K. Campbell, both of Bombing-3, left Kirn's formation to deliver individual attacks on the Vals. Hanson pressed home a high-side attack at low altitude and observed a large volume of smoke issuing from his target as it crashed into the sea. Meantime, Campbell flew to a position 2,000 feet above and just astern of the Japanese group and delivered a high-side attack on another Val. He saw his rounds strike the Val's right wing tank, which was immediately ignited by the .50-caliber tracer rounds. Campbell claimed to have seen his Val crash into the sea within five seconds of Hanson's Val.

In all, three of the brown-and-tan survivors of the strike on *Enterprise* were counted off as they splashed into the waves, and the fourth Val was smoking when it flew from sight.

Finally, at 1814, three more Vals were spotted to starboard by members of Kirn's mixed group at a distance of five miles. There is no information available to explain why they were still in the vicinity of Task Force 61 a full hour after the strike, but it is reasonable to assume that they had become disoriented and could not find their way back home. Perhaps they were errant members of the follow-on strike, or perhaps they were members of the initial strike group that had hung around on the reasonable assumption that they could join the survivors of the follow-on strike for the trip home.

Several of the eager U.S. Navy pilots broke formation to give chase. The Vals apparently noticed the danger, so they turned southward and highballed away on a long, curving course. One of the six or seven U.S. dive-bombers was number S-13, the airplane in which Ens Roger Crow had delivered his successful slow-motion attack against *Ryujo*. Crow well knew that he could not catch the Vals in a tail chase, so, while the other Dauntless pilots tried to overtake the Japanese at high speed, he flew across the chord of the Vals' curving course, directly to the point at which he anticipated the Vals would straighten out. The result was that Crow's S-13 beat the other SBDs to the Vals.

Crow positioned himself up-sun and high in such a way as to force the Vals to come at him from the port side. Certain he had not been seen, he alerted his gunner, ARM3 T. H. Miner, that a target would soon appear low and to port and that "You better get it." That said, Crow opened fire with his cowl guns on the number two Val and immediately saw the Japanese rear gunner catapulted from his seat into midair. Crow coolly raised the nose of his dive-bomber to correct his aim and sent out more half-inch bullets. This burst fell flightly over the Val's nose, so Crow dropped his nose just a hair and prepared to fire again. Before he could, however, the rear plane pulled straight up into ARM3 Miner's gunsight; quite clearly, the tail-end pilot had tumbled to the ambush and had panicked. Then the lead Val pulled up to the left. At that instant, the second Val—Crow's initial target—blew up. The rear Val flew straight into the fireball and also blew up. Meantime, the lead plane, which was pulling up to the left, flew right in front of Crow's cowl guns. As soon as Crow resumed firing, the left gun jammed. But the right gun blew a cylinder head off the Val's engine, then holed the cowling and riddled the engine block.

Crow was thoroughly drained, and so were his fuel tanks. When he saw Lt Ralph Weymouth pull up, he signaled that he needed an escort. The two SBDs turned toward *Saratoga* and, when they arrived, Weymouth signaled the ship that Crow needed to make an immediate landing. Crow was recovered on the last of his fuel without incident.

In Ens Roger Crow's two big fights of the day—the slow dive and wheels-down recovery over *Ryujo* and the split-second triple kill—not one bullet or piece of shrapnel struck his lucky airplane, S-13.

卐

In all, U.S. Navy aviators and gun crews from every ship in Task Force 16 claimed seventy of thirty-six Vals as confirmed kills. And more Zeros and Kates than had been in on the air strike were also credited as confirmed.

The real total of kills—shared by many—was more like twenty of thirty-six Vals definitely destroyed, plus six or eight Zeros and a Kate or two. Even these numbers are in dispute, for Japanese records vary widely.

In addition, an estimated six Kates from the abortive second strike became lost in the darkness and buzzed around some distance from Task Force 61 until they apparently ran out of fuel and ditched. This estimate is consonant with a clear uncoded voice-radio message intercepted by *Enterprise* and interpreted on the spot by a Japanese linguist.

Returning Japanese pilots made equally outlandish claims. They reported hitting two carriers with bombs and leaving both burning and sinking. They also claimed hits on a battleship, which was also left burning. Zero pilots reported downing many more than the five Wildcats that were actually shot down. As it was, at least one of the Wildcats—and as many as four—succumbed to ship's fire.

20

Ships at sea that are on fire are in mortal danger.

From the standpoint of fire alone, *Enterprise* had sustained about the worst sort of hit imaginable. The only things that saved her from immediately blowing up were the timely flooding of vulnerable aviation fuel lines with inert carbon dioxide gas; the coolmindedness of a sailor who jettisoned a huge detachable low-octane fuel tank into the sea; and a dazed storekeeper who emerged from the eye of the blast, made his way to the paint and pyrotechnic storerooms, and set off the system that smothered vulnerable compartments with carbon dioxide.

As it was, however, the first bomb had detonated in a berthing space, with ample bedding and clothing to feed the flames, and in a metal shop, where tiny pieces of scrap could become molten harbingers of the ultimate fate of the rest of the steel ship. The blast threw out or severed electrical circuits that controlled lighting and firefighting pumps, while several key water mains serving that part of the ship were also destroyed or disabled. Moreover, most of the nearest damage-control men in the after repair party—Repair IV— were killed or injured in the blast.

Deaths and destruction notwithstanding, nearby damage-control teams from Repair III, the midships repair party, swung into immediate action toward the vortex of the 500-kilogram bomb blast. First, an investigation team from the nearest surviving damage party—men who had been trained for the eventuality of key fatalities felt its way along intervening passageways and compartments. It arrived almost before the effects of the initial blast had dissipated.

Upon inspecting the damage, the team reported via its sound-powered battle phone to the ship's first lieutenant, LCdr Herschel Smith, and his assistant, Lt George Over, who were running the damage-control effort out of a compartment beneath the island known as Central Station. Smith already had a pretty good idea that the damage control party in the immediate vicinity of the blast had been gutted; he had not been able to establish contact with it. After checking with other damage parties nearby, Smith swung his resources into action. Initially, Smith and Over pored through engineering diagrams of the ship to find and suggest useful alternatives to men on the scene for the best ways to reestablish communications, electrical power, and water pressure in the bomb-damaged sectors. As soon as Smith had definitive reports, he would place the orchestration in Lieutenant Over's hands and proceed to the scene of the major conflagrations to personally assess damage to the ship and directly control firefighting and repair efforts.

卐

The first task was to contain and control the fires that were in danger of consuming the innards of the ship. Electricians ran out emergency power cables for lighting and firefighters ran hoses aft from the nearest undamaged fire main forward. Sailors wearing gas masks and wielding flashlights headed into the murk at the outer edges of the smokey blaze and felt their way inward toward the center, checking and reporting on damage as they moved. They could not go far, however, because the gas masks could not filter out choking smoke and fumes. To do so, they needed special Rescue Breathing Apparatus (RBA) vests, which filtered and refiltered air sealed from outside contamination.

Right behind the scouts were corpsmen, also rigged out in gas masks and carrying flashlights in addition to medical-aid bags. If there were living men in the shambles, the corpsmen would carry them out and treat them. In fact, there were ninety-five officers and sailors who needed treatment for everything from smoke inhalation to traumatic amputations of arms and legs.

卐

Before the repair parties below decks could even begin to deploy to fight fires in and around the chiefs' quarters and metal shop, the second bomb took out Gun Group 3. In its way, the blast on the after starboard quarter was as threatening to *Enterprise* as the fires below decks.

As had happened below, damage parties immediately converged on the conflagration, though the danger from exploding ordnance was acute and approaches were made with a good deal of extra caution. LCdr Slim Townsend, the carrier's flight deck officer, took charge of the topside damage control efforts. Townsend's immediate concern, beyond controlling the intense blaze in Gun Group 3, was to repair the flight deck so *Enterprise* could begin landing planes at a moment's notice.

Ens Jim Wyrick, a junior gunnery officer, was among the first men into the gun group. Together with three enlisted firefighters, Wyrick heaved burning and flammable material right over the side of the ship. The heat around the quartet was so intense that they would have succumbed had not a nearby firefighter played a stream of water directly on them.

Lt Robin Lindsey, the ship's senior LSO, first realized that there was something amiss when he heard an unusual crackling sound from Gun Group 3, which was located directly across the flight deck from the catwalk beneath the LSO platform on which Lindsey had taken cover. Once the thought of a fire penetrated Lindsey's numbed brain, he sprang to action with nearby sailors and helped haul a hose hooked up to a fulmite fire-retardant generator across the after flight deck to the fiercely burning 5-inch gun gallery. The smoke in the gun gallery obscured all sights, and the heat was intense. Lindsey was certain that he would be roasted alive if the ready ammunition detonated.

As the smoke slowly dissipated, Lieutenant Lindsey looked down and found that one of his feet was firmly implanted in the open stomach cavity of a roasted sailor; ribbons of guts were spread in all directions. Though sickened, Lindsey carrried on.

Moments later, the sailor with whom Lindsey was controlling the high-pressure nozzle of the fulmite hose blurted out, "I can't hang in any longer. Do you think you can handle the hose?" Lindsey said he could and the sailor left. Immediately, the LSO was knocked off balance by the pressure from the hose and thrown up against a bulkhead at his back. He could barely move until someone stepped in and helped.

Meantime, Ens Jim Wyrick had discovered a locker filled with unexploded 5-inch rounds and powder charges. He quickly organized a fifteen-man detail from among volunteers and oversaw the jettisoning of every potentially lethal round into the sea.

One ongoing problem was a jet of flame shooting out one side of the gun gallery that no amount of fulmite could put out. It later was revealed that the bomb had nicked a steel line carrying hydraulic oil to the after elevator. The oil was under 820 pounds of pressure, so the tiny rent had the effect of a blowtorch. Until the chief machinist's mate in charge of the after elevator came topside to see if his elevator was flush with the deck, no one knew what the source of the dangerous blast of flame might be or how to defeat it.

࿔

The third bomb, a 250-kilogram device that struck at 1716, was of relatively low order and unquestionably defective. Withal, it blew a 10-foot hole in the flight deck and shut down the midships elevator. The area was sprayed down and shipfitters went right to work fashioning a metal plate to cover the yawning gap.

࿔

One of the top men on the scene of the firefighting below decks was CSF Jim Brewer, of the Construction and Repair Department. As each new compartment in the vicinity of the below-decks blast was reached, Brewer was among the first—if not the first—to enter. His job was to locate the source of each individual blaze and to tell hose teams the best means for beating it down. If equipment or supplies had to be removed from the compartment, Brewer pointed it out and allocated the manpower to undertake the job. In time, Brewer was overcome by smoke and heat and had to be ordered from the scene by the ship's executive officer. His loss was felt, but there were other good men to step into his shoes.

While the fight to save *Enterprise* was focused on the metal shop and chiefs' quarters, CMM Reuben Fisher took charge of a hose that had been brought aft from a working fire main and entered a storeroom that led directly to an ammunition hoist loaded with 5-inch powder charges on the way up to Gun Group 3 from the magazine. If the fire reached the ammunition, Fisher knew, there was no telling what lethal chain of events might be set off.

As Fisher opened the door to the compartment, he was greeted by heat, smoke, and flame. The fire hose was trained into the compartment and the fire was slowly beaten back. The hose team advanced behind Fisher into the darkened space, where smoldering racks of dry provisions were sprayed and sprayed again. The ammunition hoist was reached in due course and the dangerously hot powder cans were cooled with water from the hose.

A fire in the highly flammable parachute loft was also quickly extinguished, as was a blaze that threatened the torpedo storage magazine.

Fulmite foam, oil from ruptured tanks, blood, seawater, and debris made footing particularly precarious in unlighted, smoke-filled compartments. Ventilation often fed fires as much as it cleared smoke. Portable blowers had to be used to selectively ventilate numerous blind spaces, and gasoline-fueled handy-billy portable pumps had to be used to lower water levels in others. The work was treacherous, tiring, and generally a threat to the lives and health of the firefighters and the shipfitters and carpenters who moved directly in their wake.

By the glow of emergency lights, several carpenters had to wade into armpit-deep water to caulk a number of gashes—the largest was six by two feet—left below the waterline by the bomb.

Using emergency supplies of heavy lumber stored in strategic places throughout the ship, the carpenters built a cofferdam to contain the flooding. Then they used wire mesh to bind bedding and pillows into the tears in the carrier's side. Once the cofferdam was filled with the bedding and wedged in place, emergency pumps went to work emptying the affected compartments. Nearly 250 tons of seawater were pumped from one larger storeroom alone.

卐

At 1819—65 minutes after the first bomb tore its way into *Enterprise*'s innards and while firefighting and repair efforts frantically continued below—the carrier majestically turned into the wind at 24 knots and began the routine recovery of her warplanes.

21

ollowing two contacts at the start of the Japanese strike, Lt Sandy Crews, of Fighting-5, chased after a few planes, but they all turned out to be friendlies. The sky was full of bursting antiaircraft shells and burning and exploding planes, and airplanes and bombs were crashing into the water. The Fighting-5 element leader could not help musing that this day real life was just like the movies.

All the diving, twisting, turning, and shooting Crews had done since spotting the first *chutai* of Vals on the way in toward *Enterprise* had long ago separated him from the rest of Lt Chick Harmer's division, and his wingman had long ago separated from him. Crews's fuel supply was critically low, so he headed back for *Saratoga* and made a wide approach to the carrier with his wheels down because he knew a lot of people were trigger-happy; the last thing he wanted was to look like a Japanese plane to ships' gunners. Crews's approach was made without incident, and he landed on the last of his fuel at about 1740. He had been in the air 3.6 hours.

All four Wildcats of Lt Scoop Vorse's intact Fighting-6 divi-

sion were on reserve fuel when the fight ended, so they headed for
Saratoga, which was amply protected from the brunt of the Japanese attack by concealing low clouds. Three of the Wildcats safely
landed aboard the big steel-decked carrier at 1740, but Lieutenant
Vorse ran out of fuel as he flew up the groove, and he had to settle
for a neat landing right in the carrier's wake. He was picked up by a
guard destroyer after only moments in the water.

卍

At 1756, destroyer *Grayson* was ordered to sail 40 miles to the
northwest to stand by to pick up returning scouts and strike aircraft
that were by then running low on fuel. She was to remain on station overnight and catch up with the departing Task Force 16
around noon the next day, August 25. *Grayson* turned to her new
heading only one minute after receiving the order and proceeded
from sight at a speed of 25 knots.

卍

The returning *Enterprise* scouts, which had been in the air far
longer than any other U.S. warplanes, were made especially vulnerable to the rigors of ditching because they were also kept from
landing aboard either carrier the longest. When Lt Carl Horenburger, of Bombing-6, approached *Enterprise* following his inconclusive duel with rendezvousing Vals north of the task force, he
joined up with numerous fighters and bombers that were forced to
wait while the battle damage was repaired. Fuel was getting to be a
problem for Horenburger, who had been on a long search hop and
who had used a great deal of what he had brought back trying to
engage several Vals at high speed. He used the last of the fuel in his
SBD's four 50-gallon tanks and was well into his 18-gallon reserve
when the landing signal was hoisted over the damaged carrier.
When Horenburger's turn to land finally came and he was entering
the groove off *Enterprise*'s stern, another carrier bomber broke in
from the starboard quarter—a highly unorthodox approach, to say
the least. Horenburger stubbornly held to his course; he was angry
for one thing and did not feel he had enough fuel left to go around
again. The intruder veered off and made a water landing just as

Horenburger safely reached the ramp and took the "Cut" from the carrier's senior LSO, the incomparable Lt Robin Lindsey.

Lt John Lowe, the Bombing-6 exec, and his wingman, Ens Bob Gibson, returned from the discovery of and attack on the Japanese surface Vanguard Group while the air attack was underway. Lowe thought that *Wasp* might be undergoing her refueling close enough to Task Force 61 to risk a flight south to find her. However, *Wasp* was well beyond range, as Lowe eventually realized, and he and Gibson returned to the task force on the last of their fuel. Gibson was just turning upwind at 1810 to begin his approach on *Saratoga* when his engine died. He ditched dead ahead of cruiser *Minneapolis*, and he and his radioman-gunner climbed out onto one wing. Both airmen were neatly plucked from the water by destroyer *Farragut*. Lieutenant Lowe landed aboard *Enterprise* at 1830 without difficulty.

☈

Cdr Don Felt's Air Group 3, which had not lost a single airplane during the strike or numerous air battles, began landing aboard *Saratoga* at 1815. Despite her many injuries, *Enterprise* began routine recovery operations at about the same time.

Six Torpedo-3 searchers had managed to join up on the squadron commander, LCdr Charlie Jett, by the time *Saratoga* was ready to begin landing the large torpedo bombers. First, the Avengers were ordered to jettison their bombs. Only four of the seven still had their bombs aboard; the other three—Jett, Ens Bob Bye, and Lt Johnny Myers—had all dropped theirs on *Ryujo* hours earlier. Lieutenant Myers, whose TBF had been riddled by Zeros over *Ryujo* and close to home, was the first of the group to land aboard *Saratoga*. Indeed, he signaled that his would be an emergency landing; his controls had been damaged by Japanese 7.7mm and 20mm rounds, and Myers was not sure they or he would withstand the demands of a precision carrier recovery.

While warplanes on *Saratoga*'s flight deck were being respotted to accommodate Myers's damaged TBF, Ens Fred Mears and Ens Bob Divine, a member of the Torpedo-8 group that had struck *Ryujo*, opted to fly 25 miles to *Enterprise*, which had no planes in her landing pattern just then. LCdr Charlie Jett followed Mears and Divine aboard *Enterprise* a few minutes later.

Myers made his delicate approach and managed to get aboard *Saratoga* on his first pass, which was fortunate. As soon as the tired pilot gave his engine a bit of throttle to clear the arresting wires, the engine died. No gas.

Ens Bob Bye, who had used up a great deal of fuel keeping station on LCdr Charlie Jett's wing during the long patrol—a wingman's occupational hazard—and still more fuel in a series of running fights with Vals, could not keep his TBF airborne long enough to take his turn landing aboard *Saratoga*. He flew off to the side of the big carrier at 1832 and told his aircrew to prepare for a water landing. RM3 Dewey Stemen, who was manning the turret gun, locked up the turret armor plate, put his feet on the footrest, and leaned back hard into his seat back, praying he would not be knocked unconscious by the sudden stop and thus left to go down with the airplane. The sea was dead calm and Bye made a smooth water landing—only two or three little bounces. As the Avenger settled in, Stemen popped the turret's port escape hatch and climbed out onto the wing, from which he slipped and fell into the water. By the time Stemen climbed back aboard the wing, the bombardier, AMM3 W. E. Dillon, was at work on the other wing trying to release the life raft from its outside compartment. Stemen opened the compartment from his side and pushed the raft bundle while Dillon pulled. When the raft was free, Stemen crawled over the top of the fuselage to join Dillon. They inflated the raft and then went forward to find out why Ensign Bye had not joined them. The pilot was in the cockpit, busily attending to a last-minute scavenger hunt. As soon as Bye had retrieved everything he wanted—and at the insistent urging of his crewmen—he climbed to the wing. The three airmen jumped into the raft just as the TBF slipped beneath the waves. In time, Bye, Stemen, and Dillon were rescued by destroyer *Balch*, which sank their trusty life raft with machine-gun fire.

⁂

RE Werner Weis, also of Torpedo-3, had been launched from *Enterprise* with Lt Rube Konig's tiny strike group just before the start of the Japanese air strike, but he had been unable to retract his landing gear and had therefore dropped out. Weis was not molested as he circled out of range of the fight, and he eventually joined up on the group of Torpedo-3 searchers led by LCdr Charlie Jett. He landed safely aboard *Enterprise* at 1838.

At 1839, Ens John Jorgenson, who had flown wing in his SBD on Ens H. L. Bingaman's TBF during the afternoon search, ran out of fuel in the *Enterprise* landing pattern. He and his radioman-gunner were picked up by a destroyer.

Lt Ray Davis, the Bombing-6 skipper who had found and attacked the Japanese carriers, was forced to buzz around during a very long delay and wound up landing aboard *Enterprise* at 1839 with a mere four gallons of fuel remaining in his reserve supply. Davis was the last of the main group of *Enterprise* searchers to land.

卐

As evening came on and his fuel supply began running low, Ens Bob Disque, of Fighting-6, dropped down into the landing pattern to go aboard *Enterprise*. As he flew alongside his ship, he saw for the first time that she had been heavily damaged. Huge steel plates covered several large holes in the after flight deck; starboard-aft gun positions were twisted and burned; only three of the normal twelve landing wires were deployed. Disque's Wildcat came aboard fast at 1840 with inoperative landing flaps because the stainless steel vacuum tank that controlled them had been holed by the Zero that had gotten 110 rounds into his fighter. In fact, Disque wound up on his back in the barrier. A bit dazed by the unanticipated impact and his sudden inversion, Disque automatically released his safety belt—and dropped to the flight deck, right on his head. Disque was pulled clear and his fighter was pushed aside in time for three Dauntlesses from the antisubmarine patrol to begin landings at 1841—only one minute after the barrier crash.

卐

Immediately upon completing her twenty-fifth recovery at 1843, *Enterprise* sharply veered from her course, far to the left.

213

The astonished helmsman shouted at Capt Arthur Davis, "Lost steering control, Sir."

A returning fighter right over the ramp responded to the LSO's wave-off and roared across the turning deck.

Instantly, the TBS (Talk Between Ships) radio network was filled with dire warnings, and the huge carrier sounded several blasts on her siren. Another siren sounded from far within the bowels of the ship to indicate that the steering control room could not control the huge vessel as it cut a 24-knot swath through Task Force 16.

When the massive rudder had gone as far to the left as it could, it began swinging back to the right. Further and further it went, crazily bending the carrier's wake in a sharp S-turn until the ship's massive bows were bearing directly down upon destroyer *Balch*.

The rudder jammed at 20 degrees right rudder as *Balch*'s stack emitted a puff of black smoke to signify that she was on full emergency power. *Enterprise* missed the tiny plane-guard destroyer by less than 50 yards.

Once *Balch* was clear, all the attention of Captain Davis and the bridge watch could be placed on slowing the runaway carrier and safely guiding her between more-distant obstacles—or, rather, on warning the more-distant obstacles to stand clear—and to finding and correcting the cause of the steering problem.

Captain Davis tried to correct the sharp rightward swing by cutting power to the port engine and increasing power on the starboard engine. But that only endangered the massive engines, so Davis halted the effort. All he could do was cut speed to 10 knots and get the rudder fixed.

As *Enterprise* helplessly circled within a moving stockade of destroyers, cruisers, and a battleship, news arrived from LCdr Bullet Lou Kirn that the Japanese follow-on strike was on the way in. Exceptionally nervous radar operators watched their scopes and called out new readings for the junior FDOs manning Radar Plot. Hurriedly refueled fighters were launched in makeshift divisions from *Saratoga* and stationed in a northerly arc outward from Task Force 61. Soon—miraculously—the large bogey described a 50-mile arc to the south, around the U.S. task force. The fighters were withheld; no one wanted to attract attention while *Enterprise* was helpless. In time, the Japanese bogey disappeared altogether.

卐

Enterprise had lost steering control due to a freak accident in her steering control room, a tiny metal box located hard against the rudder and one deck beneath the waterline. The room contained a control panel and two large electric motors—one in use and one spare—which were used to respond to steering orders automatically signaled from the bridge helm. It was also possible to steer the ship from the steering control room by means of a compass and a wheel and orders passed from the bridge by sound-power phone.

The tiny blind compartment, its two motors, and a complement of three electrician's mates, three machinist's mates, and one quartermaster were cooled by means of a long ventilator shaft that began at the starboard after gun gallery, topside. The ventilation was routinely and briefly shut down—so the fresh air would not feed a fire—during General Quarters. Thus it was not unusual during such periods for the temperature in the room to rise to 120 degrees.

The first bomb to strike *Enterprise* went right through the starboard after gun gallery—Gun Group 3. There it tore apart the ventilation shaft leading to the steering control room. When the 500-kilogram bomb finally detonated three decks down, it did so right above and ahead of the steering control room. Thick black smoke immediately entered the blind compartment by means of the local engine cooling system. At the same time, hot water sprayed out of the starboard engine cooling jacket. The seven-man crew quickly shut off the fans that were pulling in the smoke and sealed their end of the large ventilator shaft. The room was thus effectively proofed against air—fresh and smokey—from outside compartments.

Soon, because compartments all around were on fire, the temperature in the tiny room rose to over 140 degrees and on up as high as 160 degrees. Several of the sailors lost consciousness and the rest were on the verge of doing so.

As firefighters attacked the blazes in adjacent compartments, an automatic safety system reopened the ventilator shaft. Immediately, thick clouds of black smoke again entered the overheated compartment along with a goodly supply of water and fulmite fire retardant that had entered the vent shaft through splinter holes and ruptured seals from as high up as the bomb-damaged gun gallery. The hot water shorted the control panel, and that caused the steering motor to reverse. The ship's huge rudder ran out of control all the way to the left, reversed again, and came to rest at 20 degrees right rudder.

When the steering alarm sounded, only one of the seven steering control room inmates, MM2 William Marcoux, had enough strength left to attempt to switch over to the undamaged port motor. He got partway through the drill just as *Enterprise* knifed past *Balch*. Then he was felled by the 170 degree heat.

There was one man aboard *Enterprise* who could be considered an expert in every aspect of the vast ship's machinery. He was ChMach Bill Smith, a diminutive curly-headed blond man who had set something of a record in putting on rank since he had enlisted in the Navy in 1925. He had become the Navy's youngest chief machinist's mate and had gone on to become its youngest chief warrant machinist. There were a number of officers above Smith in rank, but not one could run the machine that was *Enterprise* the way Bill Smith and his picked team of chief machinist's mates could.

As soon as the emergency siren sounded, Bill Smith dropped whatever he was doing and headed toward the source of the trouble. He placed a call by sound-powered phone to the blind compartment and explained to dopey, overheated CEM Alex Trymofiev how he could draw fresh air into the compartmnt by switching the vent baffles. Trymofiev passed out after removing only the first of a number of screws.

Smith's only alternative was to rush through burning, smoking sectors and enter the vital compartment himself. He buckled on an RBA vest and proceeded forward. This particular vest had been modified by one of Smith's leading acolytes, CMM Murell Twibell, to provide added breathing power. It had a safety line attached to the back in case Smith fell along the way and had to be pulled out in a hurry. Smith also grabbed a number of wrenches he felt he would need once he reached the vital smoke-filled compartment.

Smith made it only halfway to the steering control room on the first try. He fell to the burning deck and had to be pulled clear. Following a quick breather, Smith entered the smokey realm again, this time in the company of MM1 Cecil Robinson.

By the time Smith and Robinson started toward the compartment together, it had already been breeched by F3 Ernest Visto, a huge man quite capable of carrying other men great distances. Visto had left his battle station without permission as soon as he learned there were men trapped below. He joined a rescue party descending by way of a trunk from the chiefs' quarters above. The trunk proved too small for Visto and his RBA, so he traded the breather in for an ordinary gas mask. Visto could do nothing for the steering gear, which was beyond his ken, so he latched onto the nearest fallen body and dragged it up the escape trunk. In the end, he carried or cajoled all seven men—whose condition ranged from groggy to unconscious—to safety from the 180 degree heat. As the last man was lifted from Visto's arms, the big fireman uttered a weak apology and collapsed.

Six of the seven rescued men survived.

Meantime, ChMach Bill Smith and MM1 Cecil Robinson reached the compartment, but both were felled by the heat and had to be hauled to safety for a breather. They went back through the smoke yet again, and this time entered the abandoned compartment after undogging the watertight door.

Smith quickly surveyed the situation and went to work. With Robinson assisting, he completed the transfer of power to the port motor and got the steering system back on line.

High above, the bridge helmsman reported to Captain Davis, "Steering control regained, Sir."

It was 1926. Steering control had been lost for thirty-eight of the longest minutes anyone involved would ever remember.

22

☀

The flight of five Torpedo-8 TBFs commanded by Lt. Swede Larsen, which had launched from *Saratoga* at 1645, succeeded in effecting a rendezvous with the pair of SBDs flown by Bombing-3's Lt(jg) Bob Elder and Ens Bob Gordon at 1725. Though all the *Saratoga* pilots maintained a lookout for the small *Enterprise* strike group, no contact was made during the flight north into darkness.

Larsen's mixed group found a target at 1805, just about dusk. Several ships, 15 miles to the west-northwest were seen as they sailed away to the southeast at a speed of 15–20 knots. Within a minute or two, the U.S. Navy airmen were able to count an estimated four heavy cruisers, six light cruisers, and six or eight destroyers. This was clearly VAdm Nobutake Kondo's Advance Force—combined with RAdm Hiroaki Abe's Vanguard Group—which appeared to be rushing to catch up with the American carrier battle force.

At the time of the sighting, the five TBFs were at 7,000 feet and the two SBDs were at 9,000 feet. Lieutenant Larsen led his bombers in a great circle to the north to set up a torpedo attack. As soon as the TBFs flew within range, the Japanese ships fired heavy concentrations of antiaircraft gunfire at them.

"Get the nearest big one," Swede Larsen ordered. They were the only words anyone said during the entire attack.

The path of the diving torpedo attack carried the TFBs into a cloud. When they emerged into the face of antiaircraft fire, they were coming up on the port quarter and port bow of a clump of cruisers and destroyers. The antiaircraft fire was so heavy that all the torpedo bomber pilots had to take independent evasive action.

The best targets were several cruisers sailing in line abreast and dead ahead of the Avengers. Larsen led his tiny strike group over the tops of the first line of light cruisers, for he was intent upon getting the biggest ship around, a distant heavy cruiser.

Drops were made by all five torpedo bombers at roughly the same moment. Each pilot then pulled away in a gut-wrenching twist and turn, then all five TBFs retired to the west.

At 1820, at more or less the same instant the TBFs were dropping into their attack run, the SBDs piloted by Elder and Gordon were diving from 12,500 feet on what both perceived in the fading light to be a battleship they had discovered by accident seven miles to the north.

The "battleship" was really seaplane tender *Chitose*, which sought the protection of intervening clouds and steamed with its protective ring of destroyers in tight counterclockwise circles to evade the dive-bombers. Very heavy antiaircraft fire from the warships barred the way. Bombs were released at 2,000 feet. During the recovery and retirement, both pilots observed what appeared to be a direct hit on the "battleship." In fact, *Chitose*, which had almost no armored protection, was severely damaged by a pair of near misses, and several search planes she had aboard were set afire. Plates loosened on her port side led to flooding, and her port engine room had to be shut down.

Elder and Gordon ran southward to join on the TBFs. They arrived in time to see what looked in the fading light like a massive explosion beside one of the heavy cruisers. The rendezvous was something of a shock, for only three Avengers and the two Dauntlesses joined up for the flight home.

At a point about 40 miles south of the Vanguard Force, Larsen and the others were overtaken by a Japanese twin-float fighter. The Japanese pilot made a single firing pass at the TBF section and then followed the flight for two or three minutes before flying off into the darkness.

The three TBFs and two SBDs under Lieutenant Larsen's group landed safely aboard *Saratoga* beginning at 2010.

The two missing TBFs, flown by Lt Jack Taurman and Lt(jg) Frenchy Fayle, groped through the lowering darkness near the Japanese surface force for some time before proceeding southward in the hope of reaching Guadalcanal's Henderson Field. Taurman got as far as San Cristobal. He made one low pass across a moonlit beach to see if he could draw fire. The place was deserted, so he completed a superb water landing just off the strand and led his two crewmen ashore. Fayle found a tiny islet in the darkness and dared go no farther. On the last of his nervous energy, he settled his fuel-starved TBF into the water and had to be dragged into the life raft by his equally tired aircrew. Taurman and his crew were rescued on August 28, and Fayle and his crew were picked up on August 30.

卐

Lt Rube Konig was one of the most worried airmen alive by the time he lost sight of Task Force 61 following his late launch as leader of seven Torpedo-3 strike aircraft. After the TBF piloted by RE Werner Weis aborted because of a landing gear problem, Konig missed a rendezvous with an eleven-plane *Enterprise* SBD group led by Lt Turner Caldwell. Fearing an attack by Japanese fighters—the TBFs had already been shot at by a Val—Konig finally severed his ties with Task Force 61 at the height of the Japanese air strike and shaped a course to the north to find *Shokaku* and *Zuikaku*.

The things that really worried Rube Konig were that he had already seen *Enterprise* sustain at least one bomb hit, he had not been given a good fix on his target, he had not been given a good fix on his own task force, he had no charts, no radio call sign, no frequency-change schedule, no way of monitoring news of changing conditions anywhere in the wide Pacific.

After about an hour's flight along the northward track, Ens Ed

Top: A Val dive-bomber bursts into flames over *Enterprise*'s radar mast on August 24, 1942.
(Official USN Photo)

Above: Wreckage from two downed Vals as seen from *Enterprise*'s fantail. *(Official USN Photo)*

Left: *Enterprise*'s Gun Group 3 explodes in flames as it is struck by a Japanese bomb.   *(Official USN Photo by R. Read)*

Top: This low-order bomb detonation on *Enterprise*'s flight deck instantly killed BM2 Art Davis. The ongoing blaze in Gun Group 3 can be seen at upper left.   *(Official USN Photo by R. Read)*

Above: Effects of the bomb that wiped out *Enterprise*'s Gun Group 3.
                    (Official USN Photo)

As *Wasp* burns in the background, destroyer *O'Brien* is struck by a torpedo fired by Japanese submarine *I-19*. *(Official USN Photo)*

VAdm Chuichi Magumo.
(Official USN Photo)

North Carolina. *(Official USN Photo)*

Above left: Lt Birney Strong.
(Compliments of H. L. Buell)

Above right: LCdr Bucky Lee.
(Compliments of J. R. Lee)

Left: Lt(jg) Ralph Hovind.
(Compliments of R. Hovind)

Above: "Proceed Without *Hornet*" is the message flashed to a Torpedo-10 Pilot as he prepared to take off on October 26, 1942.

(Official USN Photo)

Above left: Zuikaku. *(Official USN Photo)*

Left: Chikuma after being struck by bombs on October 26. The hit near the bridge is clearly visible as a light smudge.

(Official USN Photo)

Above: Smoke billows from *Enter prise*'s forward elevator well, follow ing the Japanese strike of October 26 1942. *(Official USN Photo*

Left: F3 Don Morgan.

(Compliments of R. C. Morgan

Holley reported by radio that his engine had developed a major oil leak and that his Avenger's windshield was covered with goo. It was beginning to get dark, so Konig advised Holley to maintain his place in formation for as long as possible; if he had to land in the water, Konig would do his best to get a fix on the spot.

The minuscule strike group was about 250 miles from home when Konig spotted what he thought might have been the moonlit wake of an enemy warship. He immediately gave the signal to attack, and the Avengers split into two groups of three to deliver coordinated attacks on either bow. Each group fanned out in line abreast formation.

Moments before coming upon the release point at a mere 50 feet over the water, one of the pilots exclaimed that the target was a round reef and the "wake" was the surf pounding against it. This was Roncador Reef, 100 miles northwest of Santa Ysabel. The TBFs joined up, climbed, and carried on along their original northward heading.

They were about 300 miles from home when Rube Konig announced that they would fly 30 miles further before heading for what he hoped—but secretly doubted—would be the place the friendly ships were waiting.

The distant point was reached without a sighting, so Konig led the formation to the west for 50 miles. Nothing there. The next turn was for home. They were 50 miles along the return leg when Konig decided to conserve fuel. He ordered everyone to jettison their heavy torpedoes. At that instant, a stream of tracer passed close to Konig's cockpit from the rear. There was moment of stunned silence, then Lt(jg) Fred Herriman's abashed voice came up on the radio: "Sorry, Konig. I pressed the wrong button."

After a little inner battle, Konig announced to the group that he felt they did not have enough fuel to take them to Henderson Field—even if anyone knew where it was. A straw poll revealed that everyone felt they had to find the carriers. Konig told them that if one plane had to ditch they would all ditch together.

The flying was grueling. Ens Ed Holley's oil line had not ruptured, but it was not difficult to imagine the pressure he had felt over the long flight; his engine might freeze on him at any second.

After five hours in the air, Konig felt that his fuel supply was getting dangerously low. Typically, the flight leader used less fuel than following aircraft, which expended a certain extra margin to remain in formation. If Konig's tanks were nearly dry, it was only a matter of time before one of the others completely ran out.

At about 2145, Konig's radioman, ARM2 David Lane, announced on the intercom, "Mr. Konig, I think I hear an 'N.'"

If Lane had indeed heard the single faint Morse code signal— for no one else in the flight did, and Lane did not hear it again— then Lt Rube Konig and the others were back from the dead. It could only have been the carrier homing signal, no doubt received at extreme range.

Konig led the flight 45 degrees to the right, the correct move for the "N" signal. (Other letters would have indicated other headings.) Fifteen minutes after the single faint contact, at precisely 2200, the tiny TBF group found Task Force 61. Konig easily identified the huge moonlit silhouette of *Enterprise*, which was already turning into the wind to recover the Avengers.

Mach John Baker landed first without incident. Next up was Ens Ed Holley. It was a dark night, Holley had oil all over his windshield, and he was physically, mentally, and emotionally drained. He came in way too fast and way too high and did not see the LSO wave him off. He missed all the arresting cables and the barrier, and flew right into the carrier's island. The heavy torpedo bomber flopped straight into the deck on its three wheels and literally fell apart around its three-man crew. Holley suffered a minor laceration on his forehead, but the radioman and bombardier both emerged without a scratch.

The *Enterprise* flight deck was effectively closed down by the stunning crash, so Lieutenant Konig and his fellows were ordered by signal lamp to proceed on to *Saratoga*.

Of the four TBFs that landed aboard the flagship, two completely ran out of fuel as soon as they were down. These had to be pushed out of the way by the plane handlers. When the fuel level in Lt Rube Konig's tanks was measured by dipstick, he learned that he had not had enough fuel aboard to go around again if he had been waved off.

⇄

No one in Lt Rube Konig's TBF group had spotted Lt Turner Caldwell's 11 *Enterprise* SBDs, but they occupied pretty much the same volume of air at least until sunset. Caldwell's Dauntlesses were much higher than Konig's TBFs, and they were no doubt further ahead, but they flew up the same heading as Konig.

The Dauntless group—designated Flight 300—found nothing in the darkness. With far less fuel than the Avengers, and less hope of finding their way home, the SBDs were in serious straits. Several pilots were truly worried about the future by the time Caldwell announced that he was shaping a course for Henderson Field.

The grueling flight into the unknown ended when Caldwell saw in the vague moonlight what he thought was a familiar strand of coastline. He had only seen Guadalcanal during the strikes he had led over Tulagi on August 7 and 8. Neither he nor any of the Scouting-5 and Bombing-6 pilots behind him had ever landed on the crude coral-and-earth strip.

The intruders' identity was established by signal lamp to the satisfaction of Marine antiaircraft gunners manning everything up to 90mm antiaircraft batteries on the beach and around the runway. After Marine ground crew had set out flashlights to mark the extremities of the runway, Caldwell attempted to raise the tower by voice radio. There was no reply; air-ground communications were down.

The Flight 300 pilots were released from the squadron formation and ordered to land, every man for himself. Nine of the eleven, with Caldwell leading, made standard individual approaches from the landward end of the runway, and all safely landed. Two individualists made straight-in approaches from seaward, which began an exciting interlude due to an undisclosed, unperceived high stand of palm trees at the seaward end of the dirt-and-coral strip. Nevertheless, all Flight 300 SBDs landed, precious bombs and all, without damage or injury.

Friendly Marine ground crew helped the Navy pilots and gunners secure the airplanes in tree-lined revetments, after which the twenty-two exhausted Navy airmen were led into the nearby cocunut grove, where they were fed and billetted in tents.

卐

The last airplane to return from the precipitous late strike launches just before the Japanese appeared was piloted by LCdr Max Leslie, the Air Group 6 commander. Leslie had flown off alone in his modified TBF command bomber and had tried— vainly, as it turned out— to catch up with the small Dauntless and Avenger groups that had been sent north only minutes earlier.

When Leslie had flown as far as he dared without once seeing a friendly airplane, he came upon what looked like the wake of a ship. Though he had only two 500-pound bombs aboard, the air group commander—who had been cheated out of an opportunity to hit a Japanese carrier at Midway—reflexively followed the tell-tale marker toward its source.

There was no source. A trick of the waning light had made waves breaking over an isolated submerged reef—Roncador Reef, again—seem to Max Leslie's eager eyes to be an enemy ship. The air group commander broke off his useless attack, took a bearing, and reluctantly headed for Point Option.

The command TBF flew to within radar and radio range of Task Force 16 at 1912, but Leslie was unable to see any ships in the pitch blackness. He transmitted a radio signal he hoped would be answered, but it was not, though it was picked up and an attempt at answering was made by a friendly destroyer. Doggedly, Leslie flew on down the course heading he hoped would carry him over a friendly flight deck or two. All the while, he was wondering if either of the carriers had survived the pounding he had seen in the making as he flew flat-out for the horizon as the first Vals were entering their dives.

By now at extremely low altitude, Leslie thought he saw a small ship—perhaps two small ships—pass beneath his wings. A good sign for a lost aviator. Then it occurred to Max Leslie that they might be Japanese destroyers. He flew on. There was no choice.

Finally, the silence was broken. Leslie's earphones crackled with the sound of a familiar voice: "Max, this is Ham Dow. Keep coming. Get some altitude."

Leslie flew on into the darkness, the icy grip of fear around his heart melting with each passing minute. Several more terse messages arrived from LCdr Ham Dow, who refused to leave *Enterprise's* Radar Plot compartment so long as a friendly airplane was still aloft. Besides, Max Leslie was a Naval Academy classmate, a fellow naval aviator, and a close personal friend.

Leslie had not had much schooling in the use of new-fangled radar in his long flying career. He was aware of its potential, but until that midnight ride he had never considered it to be a life-saving tool.

At long last, a big full moon peeked out from behind dark clouds. The vista below was of many ships trailing silvery wakes. To make matters better, Ham Dow announced that *Saratoga* would flick on her deck lights at the last minute. This was an enormous concession, and Leslie was humbled by the risk his fellow Navy men were taking in his behalf.

Leslie's experience flying the new TBF was minimal, and he had never done so at night. This was also the first time he would be landing a TBF aboard a carrier; until a week or so earlier, he had been flying only SBDs.

The lights went on at just the right moment and Max Leslie completed a perfect landing at 2333.

卐

With the recovery of LCdr Max Leslie's command Avenger, Task Force 61 was free to sail from the scene of the battle. This was indeed VAdm Frank Jack Fletcher's reasonable solution to the facts he had at hand. The two most important facts were that he had a damaged carrier and the Japanese had at least two *un*damaged carriers within range of one another.

At Fletcher's order, Task Force 61 turned south to join *Wasp's* battle group beyond the range of the potentially onrushing Japanese carriers.

֎

For their part, the Japanese were content with honoring reports from returning strike pilots that they had left two U.S. carriers burning and sinking off the Stewart Islands. VAdm Nobutake Kondo's Advance Force joined RAdm Hiroaki Abe's Vanguard Force at 1630 for a dash to engage the U.S. battle fleet. The combined force was attacked at 1805 by Lt Swede Larsen's TBFs and two SBDs, and *Chitose* was damaged. When the small strike had ended, Kondo pressed his ships southward again, but the chase was abandoned at 2330 following a fruitless high-speed search.

After Kondo and Abe turned back north, the only piece remaining on the board was RAdm Raizo Tanaka's Reinforcement Group, which was still charged with delivering 700 Imperial Army infantrymen and 800 Imperial Navy infantry bluejackets to Guadalcanal.

23

The job of getting RAdm Raizo Tanaka's transports fell to the weak air establishment at Guadalcanal, by now dubbed the Cactus Air Force after the Allied code name for the island.

Inasmuch as Tanaka's fleet supports had fled, the Japanese transport chief dispatched his five covering destroyers ahead of the main body of Reinforcement Group to bombard Henderson Field in order to keep the American dive-bombers down. As the Japanese warships were coming on station at 0230, August 25, Maj Dick Mangrum, commander of VMSB-232, led two other Marine SBDs aloft in an effort to get at them. Night-bombing techniques among Navy and Marine squadrons in mid-1942 were rather basic and in no way assisted by such modern conveniences as radar guidance. Thus all three of the extremely brave Marine pilots missed their targets.

A second three-plane strike—this one composed of newly arrived Dauntlesses from Lt Turner Caldwell's *Enterprise* Flight 300—was mounted at 0400. The Navy airmen found the Japanese warships retiring past Savo Island, but again no hit was scored.

Indeed, Ens Walter Brown lost his way in the dark and he had to ditch his precious dive-bomber off Malaita.

卐

Major Mangrum responded to a PBY sighting report at 0600 by leading four Marine SBDs, three *Enterprise* SBDs, and four VMF-223 Wildcats against Tanaka's force of four old destroyers, three slow transports, and light cruiser *Jintsu*.

The takeoff was at first light. No briefing had been given, nor were the pilots given the anticipated position at which the enemy ships were expected to be found. Moreover, the Navy Dauntlesses, which had been rearmed during the night by Marine ground crew, had not been refueled. No one knew how long they would fly.

The entire strike rendezvoused over Lengo Channel and headed over Savo before turning to a north-northwest heading. Hours of boring flight ensued.

Second Lieutenant Hank Hise, flying off Major Mangrum's right wing, was getting a stiff neck from constant craning to watch for trouble and keep station on the flight leader. Endless columns of puffy white clouds could be seen marching across the vast emptiness of sea and green-hued islands. The short-legged Wildcats had long since turned for home. Suddenly, at 0835, as Hise looked off to port from an altitude of 12,000 feet, he spotted three columns of ships sailing in a southerly direction, toward Guadalcanal. The strain of long hours of flying instantly dissipated.

卐

Without prior planning, the Marines broke off to go after the largest warship, light cruiser *Jintsu*. Caldwell chose to lead his wingmen after the largest transport, *Kinryu Maru*.

Mangrum executed a classic dive-bombing attack, approaching from east to west, 90 degrees to the direction in which the ships were traveling. Then he waggled his wings, broke the flight off to the left, and pitched over his right wingman, 2ndLt Larry Baldinus. When Baldinus went, Hise kicked his airplane up and over, dropped flaps, eased back on the throttle, and rolled on the left trim tab to overcome the lack of torque. As the young Marine pilot swung on his seat harness, fighting to keep down the bile rising in his throat, he instinctively looked around for the biggest ship; he was determined to go out in a blaze of glory.

Baldinus and Hise plummeted toward *Jintsu*. It was over within seconds, Hise reached his release point, came back on the stick, and added power. All emotions were overcome by the pull of gravity on the blood supply to his brain. An instantaneous gray mind-numb vaporized.

Unable to bear missing the result of his first combat dive, Hise broke a cardinal rule. While he was closing his dive flaps, he eased off to the right to look back at the target. The anticipated ball of fire did not emerge, but Hise did see his bomb explode into the water beside *Jintsu*'s hull. He advanced his throttle to full power, got his flaps all the way up, and joined on Baldinus, thankful to be with someone he was certain would know the way home. The two were surprised to see Mangrum execute a second dive, which did not score; the major's bomb had not released on his first dive, so he had hauled it back up to 10,000 feet and bravely tried again.

Baldinus's 500-pound bomb, which had been planted between *Jintsu*'s forward gun mounts, knocked RAdm Raizo Tanaka unconscious.

卐

Lt Turner Caldwell led his two wingmen—Ens J. T. Barker and Ens Chris Fink—after *Kinryu Maru*. Fink, who was the last man in the Navy formation, saw Caldwell's 500-pound bomb miss the target, but he did not have time to track Barker's 500-pound bomb—which also missed—because he quickly arrived at his own release point. As Fink was pulling out, he heard his rearseatman shouting over the intercom that his 1,000-pound bomb had hit the transport dead amidships. Fink quickly glanced back and saw smoke rising and debris settling out of the air. He also saw that *Jinstsu* was afire.

All seven American dive-bombers made a running rendezvous as they headed south for home. As soon as the Navy Dauntlesses were clear of the action, Caldwell signaled his wingmen to check their fuel situation. Fink had 40 gallons remaining while Caldwell and Barker each had only 25 gallons aboard. All three—and all the Marine airmen—safely reached Henderson Field and went right to work refueling their airplanes, a job that consisted of straining aviation gasoline from 55-gallon drums through chamois skin into 12-quart buckets that were then emptied into fuel tanks.

When the fueling had been completed, all the Navy SBDs were ordered out to find Tanaka once again. All of the Navy pilots except Ens Chris Fink were able to get airborne.

卐

Meanwhile, RAdm Raizo Tanaka came to after narrowly escaping death in the vortex of 2ndLt Larry Baldinus's 500-pound bomb, transferred his flag to one of the destroyers, and sent the damaged *Jintsu* back toward Truk under her own power. He was going on!

Kinryu Maru, which was carrying most of the rear echelon of an elite Imperial Navy infantry landing battalion, was definitely sinking. Destroyer *Mutsuki* came alongside to begin taking off the crew and the naval infantrymen when eight U.S. Army Air Forces B-17s from the 11th Heavy Bombardment Group arrived from their base at Espiritu Santo. The destroyer captain felt safe where he was; vertical bombing was known by everyone to be highly inaccurate. The man was blown into the water when five of forty-four 500-pound bombs dropped by the heavy bombers blanketed his ship, which immediately sank at 1015. The remaining destroyer stopped at once to pick up survivors. Tough, resolute Raizo Tanaka bore on but was soon recalled by Rabaul, well short of his goal.

卐

The second U.S. air strike—ten Flight 300 Dauntlesses under Lt Turner Caldwell—found just one Japanese destroyer about 150 miles northwest of Henderson Field. Six of the Dauntless pilots were ordered to attack; the rest were held in reserve pending the discovery of the Japanese main force.

Ens Hal Buell, a Scouting-5 veteran of the Coral Sea and Midway, was the third man in the string. He saw the first two bombs miss by a fair margin, and he saw a good deal of antiaircraft gunfire rising to meet him. The lithe destroyer was well into a hard starboard turn when Buell released his 500-pound bomb at what he felt was just the right instant. However, his radioman reported only a near miss to starboard.

The fourth and fifth pilots dropped their bombs close aboard the destroyer's port side, and the last man was not even close. The destroyer appeared to have been amply damaged by the underwater blasts.

After tooling around for a while, using up precious fuel, the Navy pilots returned to Henderson Field.

卐

The last air action of the day was undertaken by seven 11th Heavy Bombardment Group B-17s from Espiritu Santo that found a large unidentified Japanese vessel being towed by a much smaller vessel. The two were presumably a destroyer and seaplane tender *Chitose*, which had been damaged the evening before by Lt(jg) Bob Elder and Ens Bob Gordon, of Scouting-3.

All seven of the heavy bombers made individual runs against the larger vessel, and several hits were claimed. However, *Chitose* did not herself report any new damage.

24

For the most part, Task Force 61 had a busy August 25.

The fleet was steaming due south, away from the battle, when it passed *Wasp's* Task Force 18 at 0300. The fresh warships had completed their refueling and were rushing northward to join the action. Task Force 18 continued on some miles to the north and then swung around to screen the main body of Task Force 61. *Wasp's* Air Group 7 immediately assumed responsibility for guarding the entire assemblage of U.S. warships.

After daylight, *Saratoga's* Task Force 11 began refueling from oilers *Cimarron* and *Platte*.

At 0800, *Enterprise's* Task Force 16 detached battleship *North Carolina*, cruiser *Atlanta*, and destroyer *Monssen* to join Task Force 18. Then, in the company of her remaining guard vessels, the battle-damaged carrier steamed away from Task Force 61, bound for the friendly base at Tongatabu. There her damage would be fully assessed and preliminary repairs would be undertaken.

Soon after *Enterprise* left Task Force 61, LCdr Charlie Jett, commanding Torpedo-3, was ordered to ready himself and several other TBF aircrews to fly to Henderson Field to join the minuscule Cactus Air Force. All the TBFs selected for the flight were loaded down with spare parts and a full load apiece of four 500-pound bombs. High heat and humidity combined with the heavy weight of the airplanes to result in a complete fiasco. Every one of the TBFs that was launched could not quite gain altitude, and every one of them ditched. Several bombs detonated during the tricky ditching operations, and several airmen were injured and killed. The mission was canceled and the few TBFs that were not launched remained aboard *Enterprise* as she sailed from range. (About half of Torpedo-3, under Lt Rube Konig, had remained aboard *Saratoga* following their hairy night landings, and all of those were absorbed directly into Torpedo-8.)

Early that sunny afternoon, *Enterprise* conducted a memorial service for the ship's company and air group killed in the August 24 action. Altogether seventy-four bodies were buried at sea. Several other dead sailors and officers had been blown overboard in the bombing raid, and, of course, several airmen never returned to the ship.

At 0727, toward the end of one of a series of single-plane searches conducted by *Wasp*'s Scouting-71, Lt(jg) Chester Zalewski came upon a Japanese single-engine, twin-float monoplane, which he managed to shoot down on the first pass with his cowl-mounted machine guns. An hour later, and only 30 miles from *Wasp*, Zalewski came upon a second identical Japanese search plane. He executed a perfect stern approach and downed the Japanese snooper with a single burst of .50-caliber bullets from his cowl guns.

In the afternoon, *Wasp* vectored a rather belated twelve-Dauntless strike against the last reported position of RAdm Raizo Tanaka's by then battered and retiring Reinforcement Group. It was discovered on the way out that the Scouting-71 SBDs had attracted the attention of a Japanese four-engine flying boat, which doggedly shadowed the strike group while actually closing the range. After a half hour, Lt M. R. Doughty led his flight of four

SBDs after the approaching flying boat, and the four SBD pilots teamed up to drop the huge airplane into the water.

The *Wasp* attack group searched around north of Malaita until diminishing fuel supplies obliged the Dauntlesses to return to *Wasp*. All hands arrived safely just after sunset.

The very last thread of the Battle of the Eastern Solomons left a three-man Torpedo-3 Avenger crew alone and adrift at the edge of the retiring U.S. carrier fleet.

Ens H. L. Bingaman, AMM3 Calvin Crouch, and ARM3 Paul Knight had safely ditched their disabled TBF and had safely scuttled aboard their life raft. But they had been left behind. Bingaman had suffered a small laceration between his eyes, and Knight had also suffered a throbbing blow to the head as well as a painful, swelling ankle injury.

Fortunately, Ensign Bingaman had spotted a not-too-distant island, and he and Crouch rowed the raft to it over the eight-hour period from 1715, August 24, until sometime after 0100, August 25. Once during the long lonely hours before dawn, the hum of multiple airplane engines passed overhead, but the three marooned airmen were afraid to attract attention to themselves.

At sunrise, August 25, Bingaman and Crouch left the injured Knight in a concealed spot on the beach and went off to explore the island. After an interminable period alone with his worst fears, Knight saw four islanders approaching him. He cocked his heavy .45-caliber automatic pistol, though it was of dubious value after its immersion in salt water. Thankfully, one of the islanders waved and smiled, and all four carried Knight to their village, where he was reunited with Bingaman and Crouch. Over 300 islanders lived in the village, and they had more than ample food to share with the castaways. One islander was permanently assigned to care for Knight's head wound and swollen ankle, which he constantly washed.

Late in the afternoon of the third day, the isolation was shattered by the hum of familiar PBY engines. Ensign Bingaman fired a flare into the sky, and that attracted the attention of the friendly aircrew. The PBY landed in the lagoon, and the entire village transported itself and its guests by outrigger canoe to the amphibian bomber. AMM3 Knight was passed through one of the open waist-gun blisters, and Crouch and Bingaman climbed aboard under their own power. As the canoes pulled away, the PBY aircrew passed out packs of cigarettes to the castaways.

The flight to Espiritu Santo was made without incident, and the three TBF crewmen were treated for their various ills and injuries aboard seaplane tender *Curtiss*.

Everyone who was destined to return alive from the battle had returned.

PART V

Torpedo Junction

25

☀

The big excitement of August 25, 1942, the day after the carrier air battle in the eastern Solomons, was reserved for the crew of destroyer *Grayson*, which had been detached from Task Force 16 late on August 24 to guide stray *Enterprise* and *Saratoga* strike aircraft back to the carriers to pick up downed aviators.

Grayson sighted Task Force 18 at a distance of six miles shortly after 0330, August 25, and exchanged light and radio recognition signals. She then proceeded southward past *Wasp* and her escorts and, at 0625, encountered *Saratoga*'s Task Force 11, which was by then beginning refueling operations. The destroyer joined the *Saratoga* force, which happened to be heading in a southerly direction, toward the retiring and diminished *Enterprise* force. In time, since *Enterprise* was sailing from the scene of any possible action, *Grayson* was officially reassigned to Task Force 11, and she assumed station with the Task Force 11 screen.

At 1143, *Grayson*'s lookouts sighted what appeared to be a carrier's island superstructure far to the west-southwest. The ship's captain, LCdr Frederick Bell, reported the sighting to RAdm Carleton Wright, the Task Force 11 screen commander, and was favored with an order to sail out alone to investigate the sighting. At that moment, the destroyer's lookouts reported seeing what appeared to be smoke rising from right beside the distant object.

Within two minutes of the original sighting, as *Grayson* peeled out of formation, the distant object resolved itself into the less-distant conning tower of a surfaced submarine, hull down on the horizon an estimated 12 miles out. As *Grayson* put on full power to give chase, the target—a Japanese long-range fleet submarine dubbed *I- 9*—disappeared.

Grayson made her approach on the basis of the estimated distance and, upon reaching the 9-mile mark at precisely noon, her sonar operators made a firm sound contact. The destroyer began her first depth-charge drop at 1223. As *Grayson* completed her approach, *I-9* increased speed and turned to starboard, which brought her inside *Grayson*'s own turning circle. The sonar contact was thus lost in the noise of the stalker's own propellers.

Sonar contact ws reestablished at 1244, and *Grayson* dropped the first of her second string of depth charges at 1247, as *I-9* went deep at a speed of 7 knots, about as well as she could do. The American sonar operators reported that the target remained on a steady course until just before the end of the attack, when she turned to starboard.

At 1247, Lieutenant Commander Bell decided to shift tactics in order to conserve his limited supply of depth charges. His ship would launch dummy attacks in order to wear the Japanese down. The game of cat-and-mouse continued on through 1310, when an SBD joined on *Grayson*. At 1312, the destroyer made a normal approach at 12 knots upon the sound-originated target, which was making an estimated 8 knots. At the end of the destroyer's run, *I-9* turned to port and was lost amid the noise of the surface ship's screws.

Contact was again regained at 1329, and the first drop of the third live attack was made. At this point, the sonarmen reported that the target was making only four knots and heading due west. *Grayson*, which was on an intercepting course, dropped the remainder of her third string of depth charges just as destroyer *Patterson* appeared on the horizon.

Sonar contact was lost until 1347, fully two hours since the first sighting. At 1351, *Grayson* began her fourth drop. *I-9* was heading away to the west-northwest at nearly 7 knots, which seemed to the destroyer crew like an extraordinary feat following a lengthy chase that had surely depleted the submarine's electrical storage batteries, her only source of power while running submerged.

Patterson joined *Grayson* at 1402 in order to deliver the next attack. However, *Grayson* regained contact with *I-9* and was directed to proceed with the attack. As *I-9* turned away from south of west to almost due east at 4 knots, *Grayson* opened her fifth attack from the southwest. The submarine turned away to port at the very last moment, but the depth charges appeared to detonate far closer than had any of the earlier spreads.

Grayson stood clear at 1418 to allow *Patterson* to deliver the next attack. However, *Patterson*'s sonarmen were unable to establish sound contact on the first pass, probably because the target had not yet sailed clear of the turbulence created by *Grayson*'s most recent attack.

Destroyer *Monssen* arrived at 1438, as *Grayson* was maneuvering to reestablish sound contact. The sonarmen reported that they had a target at 1440, and the word was passed to *Patterson*, which moved into the attack. At that point, *Patterson* lookouts and *Grayson*'s bridge watch could see clearly the Japanese submarine as it hovered directly beneath the surface at precisely the spot where the *Grayson* sonarmen had said it would be. Undoubtedly, *Grayson*'s last attack had caused some heavy damage and possibly the Japanese found themselves willing to take their chances on or near the surface.

The hovering SBD dropped a smoke pot just as *Patterson* completed her attack, and then *Monssen* launched her first attack.

At that moment, *Grayson*, which had expended all her depth charges and needed to refuel, was ordered to leave the area to find and rejoin Task Force 16. (She arrived safely at 1537 and immediately refueled.)

Though the American destroyers eventually claimed a kill following repeated depth-charge attacks. *I-9* survived the afternoon ordeal, albeit with heavy damage.

Another Japanese submarine, *I-17*, was claimed that day as a sure kill by a carrier-based Dauntless pilot. However, though the aerial bomb fell close aboard, *I-17* was able to limp home for repairs.

卐

Altogether, an even dozen Japanese submarines had participated in the Battle of the Eastern Solomons. Of these, none was sunk and only two were sufficiently rattled by American bombs and depth charges to be withdrawn for repairs. When the carrier battle ended, the remaining ten submarines spread out to cover the Allied supply lines to Guadalcanal as well as to track the *Saratoga* and *Wasp* carrier task forces.

The first post-battle contact came on August 28 in waters southeast of Guadalcanal, when a pair of Dauntlesses from *Wasp's* Scouting-72 drove down a surfaced Japanese submarine within 50 miles of Task Force 18.

The first hard contact between a U.S. Navy warship and a Japanese submarine occurred at 0805, August 29, when lookouts aboard destroyer-minelayer *Gamble* sighted the conning tower of a large submarine at a distance of about 9,000 yards. At that moment, *Gamble*, a World War I–vintage four-stack destroyer that had been downgraded and converted for minelaying operations, was screening a supply convoy bound from the New Hebrides to Guadalcanal. Fortunately, when *Gamble* had been converted, her depth-charge gear had been left intact. The minelayer's crew came to action as their ship chased the submarine, *I-123*, from the surface. The first depth-charge attack was launched at 0844, and *Gamble* made numerous additional attacks until 1147, when a large pool of oil and splintered decking appeared on the surface. *I-123* was no more.

That left nine Japanese submarines prowling the waters—near and far—off Guadalcanal.

⚛

Following the Savo debacle on August 8, the U.S. Navy had been hard-pressed to muster the will or the surface forces required to secure the waters around Lunga and the approaches to them. Indeed, in the immediate aftermath of the epic night surface battle, numerically inferior Japanese surface forces ruled the roost. The U.S. response to the Japanese carrier-borne challenge of August 23–24 was a major attempt to mitigate the moral decline of U.S. naval power in the area. The Japanese had been held from their objectives, but the severe damage suffered by *Enterprise* had put a hold on any designs VAdm Frank Jack Fletcher might have had about seizing the initiative.

In fact, Fletcher was held on a stout string by his superior, VAdm Robert Ghormley, the commander in chief of all U.S. and Allied air, ground, and naval forces in the South Pacific Area. Following Eastern Solomons, Ghormley ordered Fletcher to patrol the area southeast of Guadalcanal but to remain south of the 10th Parallel unless in pursuit of an enemy force. The effect of the order was to restrict Fletcher's two operational carriers to an area only 250 miles long and 60 miles wide east and southeast of San Cristobal Island.

⚛

What, on the face of it, the Japanese failed to accomplish while losing a great many of their best carrier attack pilots on August 24—the landing of infantry reinforcements at Guadalcanal—was attempted at a far more modest and realistic level on August 28. On that date, four troop-carrying destroyers operating under the command of RAdm Raizo Tanaka left the Shortland Islands anchorage with the first contingent of a crack veteran infantry brigade whose mission it was to crush the Lunga Perimeter and recapture Henderson Field.

At 1700 hours, August 28, a pair of VMSB-232 Dauntlesses out of Henderson Field piloted by 1stLt Danny Iverson and 2ndLt

Hank Hise were tooling along at 130 knots on evening patrol over the Russell Islands when Hise spotted the four destroyers silhouetted against the setting sun only 70 miles from Cape Esperance.

Because they both lacked radios, Hise thought Iverson might have failed to see the targets. But Iverson had seen them; he just assumed they were Americans. To Hise's chagrin, the flight leader dropped down so his gunner could flash a recognition signal with his Aldis lantern. The Japanese blinked back with their automatic weapons batteries. Iverson pulled up, with Hise following, to 7,000 feet, where they topped a thin layer of clouds.

Next, without any warning whatsoever, Iverson pitched through a hole in the clouds. Startled, Hise armed his 500-pound bomb and followed. The Japanese were by then maneuvering every which way. Hise selected a target running straight across his flight path and continued to bore in, scared to death as he noted how many guns were firing at him. He cut his bomb loose at 2,500 feet, certain he had missed by a good half mile.

Unable to find Iverson upon recovering from his dive, Hise headed home, where he taxied straight up to the Pagoda—a distinctive Japanese building that housed the Cactus Air Force operations center—to report his find. Soon, Iverson arrived safely home with his bomb still aboard to tell how he had been unable to get lined up on either of two dives.

Hise's report resulted in a late scramble by eleven Marine and Navy Dauntlesses. Lt Turner Caldwell, commander of *Enterprise* Flight 300—by now an important part of the emerging Cactus Air Force—bored through the failing light to score a direct hit on one destroyer. Ens Chris Fink, whose bomb had struck *Kinryu Maru* three days earlier, planted a 500-pound bomb directly amidships on destroyer *Asagiri*, which instantly exploded and sank. A third destroyer was damaged by near misses. A Marine SBD and its crew were lost strafing the last destroyer.

Only one of the four Japanese destroyer-transports emerged from the air strike without damage, and the two damaged vessels were incapable of proceeding. The landing was called off and the three survivors headed back to the Shortlands.

Next day, August 29, five of Admiral Tanaka's troop-carrying destroyers safely landed 450 Japanese soldiers at Taivu Point, well to the east of the Lunga Perimeter.

On August 30, destroyer *Yudachi* left the Shortlands with still another group of fresh Japanese infantrymen bound for Taivu Point. At 1512, a Japanese diversionary air strike caught two U.S. destroyers and an auxiliary cargo vessel in motion as they ran away from Lunga Point. Destroyer *Colhoun* experienced so many near misses by Japanese bombs that she sank within two minutes because of damage she sustained. A total of fifty-one American seamen went down with her.

As if the destruction of *Colhoun* was not sufficient to claim mastery of the waters off Guadalcanal, the Japanese infantry was landed by *Yudachi* at Taivu Point without being discovered or challenged.

On the other hand, August 30 was also marked by the safe arrival at Henderson Field of a fresh squadron each of Marine Wildcat fighters and Dauntless dive-bombers.

As these exchanges were taking place close in to Guadalcanal, VAdm Frank Jack Fletcher's two-carrier Task Force 61 remained locked in its patrol sector southeast of San Cristobal. There had been no hostile sightings since August 27, when the two *Wasp* patrol bombers drove off a Japanese submarine. However, this is not to say that the Japanese submarines had not been at work shadowing and stalking the U.S. carriers.

On August 29, Task Force 61 was joined by RAdm George Murray's fresh Task Force 17, centered around fleet carrier *Hornet*, which had not been in action since Midway and had been held in reserve when the U.S. Navy's other three operational fleet carriers had been sent to support the Guadalcanal invasion. The fresh carrier task force had been dispatched to the Solomons upon the withdrawal of *Enterprise* after she suffered her battle damage during the Eastern Solomons Battle. As soon as Task Force 17 joined, Admiral Fletcher released *Wasp*'s Task Force 18 to revictual at nearby Noumea.

At 0330, August 31, radars aboard both *Saratoga* and *North*

Carolina made contacts with what appeared to be the same small surface target, but which could very well have been a squall. Immediately, destroyer *Farragut* was sent to investigate, but she found no signs of an intruder after combing an ever-widening circle centered on the surface-radar contact.

Task Force 61 continued to sail northwestward.

Dawn General Quarters was routinely sounded at 0600, and all hands went to their battle stations. At 0655, Admiral Fletcher ordered the course reversed to the southeast, initiated a standard zigzag pattern, and brought his vessels up to a speed of 13 knots. All hands except those assigned to the routine morning watch were released from General Quarters at 0706, and breakfast was served aboard *Saratoga* and most of the other warships.

Until 0746, August 31 promised to be another dull day at sea. At that minute, however, destroyer *MacDonough's* sonarmen made a hot contact dead ahead, lookouts saw a submarine periscope only 30 feet from her bows, and the destroyer's hull scraped the submarine's conning tower.

Within that minute—0746—*MacDonough* also hoisted submarine-warning signal flags and so precipitously dropped a pair of depth charges that no one had time to activate the depth-setting device.

And within that very same minute, submarine *I-26* launched a spread of six torpedoes at the biggest target in her periscope sights. One of the deadly cylinders porpoised just astern *MacDonough*, but the remaining five continued on.

Lt(jg) Ivan Swope and Lt(jg) Phil Rusk, both pilots with *Hornet's* Scouting-8, had been idling away the morning in their ship's forecastle watching a pair of dolphins keeping pace with *Hornet* at what, to the pilots, was the incredible rate of 17 knots. Both pilots looked up at once to see distant *Saratoga* veer off the track both carriers had been following. Swope commented aloud, "I wonder where *Sara* is going," for *Hornet* had the air duty and would be the first of the two to turn into the wind if aircraft needed to be launched or recovered.

Quite simply, *Saratoga's* Capt DeWitt Ramsey had seen *Mac-*

Donough's warning flags as they were being hoisted, and he had instantly ordered the helmsman at his elbow to swing the huge carrier's rudder hard right. Immediately upon execution of the precipitous turn, Ramsey ordered all engines to full speed.

Two interminable minutes passed as the five remaining Japanese torpedoes passed through *Saratoga*'s protective ring of surface warships and beat a bubbly path toward the carrier's vast hull.

The two young aviators watching from *Hornet*'s forecastle had a clear view as a single huge plume of water and smoke erupted on *Saratoga*'s starboard beam right abreast the island. Throughout the great ship, hundreds and hundreds of sailors and officers were jarred from their feet.

This was the second time in 1942 that *Saratoga* had been hurt by a submarine's torpedo. The first time had been almost within sight of the West Coast on her first sally from home. She had spent months in port being repaired.

All hands braced for additional impacts, but none came.

As screening vessels surged away from their stations to fight off the attacker—and others, if there were any—electricians and engineers dashed toward the engine rooms to see how their ship's giant electric motors had fared. (An early and aborted experiment in electrical propulsion had been undertaken by *Saratoga* and her dead sister, *Lexington*. The electrical power output of each ship was so great that in 1928 the entire city of Tacoma, Washington, had been bailed out of a power outage for two months by only two of the ten boilers feeding energy to *Lexington*'s huge electrical plant.) As many had feared from the outset, the worst had happened. The detonation jarred a high-tension cable, which momentarily closed an arc, causing an explosion that filled below-decks spaces with fumes, causing automatic emergency devices to shut down the two main electrical power generators, throwing the largest part of the power grid thoroughly out of kilter.

Saratoga's power output fell to negligible levels. After hours of grueling labor, the engineers and electricians would be able to assure Captain Ramsey of, at best, 12 knots of speed.

Even before *Saratoga* was struck her painful blow, *MacDonough* was joined by destroyer *Phelps,* and together they went after *I-26* with a vengeance. Sonarmen achieved repeated contacts, and depth charges were repeatedly unleashed, but *I-26* successfully evaded the two destroyers. At last, destroyer *Monssen* was detached from the screen to merely hold down the intruder until nightfall, by which time it was hoped *Saratoga* could be gotten clear of the ongoing danger—for there was no assurance that *I-26* could not slip away from the destroyers and launch more torpedoes at the crippled carrier, nor that other pigboats were not coming in station to do the same.

Monssen eventually lost contact and put in a claim for a kill, but *I-26* really slipped away.

When it became apparent that *Saratoga* would have to be withdrawn from the battle arena to undergo repairs, heavy cruiser *Minneapolis* passed up a towing cable and, with the aid of a stiff breeze, pulled the carrier along fast enough to launch a total of twenty-one bombers and nine fighters, which flew 347 miles to Espiritu Santo. (Between September 6 and September 13, these and other Air Group 3 veteran aircrews from Fighting-5, Torpedo-8, and the two SBD squadrons would all be committed to the Cactus Air Force. And they would, as much as anything, save Henderson Field.)

Saratoga reached Tongatabu without suffering any additional problems, but she would be out of the war for three crucial months.

Only an even dozen Americans were hurt in the torpedo attack. Eleven of them were *Saratoga* crewmen, who were all treated and returned to duty. The twelfth casualty was the only one who was actually wounded. Though light, the wounds were sufficient to force VAdm Frank Jack Fletcher to stand aside as commander of Task Force 61. That in itself was probably the day's most fateful outcome.

Command of the carrier armada passed temporarily to Task Force 17's RAdm George Murray, who had recently been promoted to flag rank after commanding *Enterprise* with great distinction at the start of the Pacific War. Unless a more senior officer was dispatched from outside the region, Murray would turn Task Force 61 over to Task Force 18's commander—RAdm Leigh Noyes, a senior and seasoned Midway veteran—when *Wasp* returned from her revictualing at Noumea.

That same night, at least seven Japanese troop-carrying destroyers landed fresh veteran Imperial Army infantrymen, engineers, and artillerymen at Guadalcanal's Taivu Point.

26

By September 1, 1942, the American strategic offensive at Guadalcanal had pretty much bogged down. The successes of August 7 and 8, in which all strategic and tactical objectives had clearly been won by 1st Marine Division, had been replaced by the isolation of the Marines after the Savo debacle and a confusion and loss of purpose that were not perceived by the operation's naval commanders based at Noumea.

It quickly became evident that the Marines were not yet capable of mounting large or sustained operations—either because of their training or their horrendous logistical situation. On the one hand, 1st Marine Division literally had to learn to fight as a fully integrated combat division, for Marines had not fought in even battalion strength since 1918. On the other hand, the lack of supplies and ammunition all but precluded any meaningfully sustained operations. The defeatist attitude of the distant naval command also played havoc with the inherently combative spirit of this large body of U.S. Marines.

The fault lay with VAdm Robert Lee Ghormley, the commander in chief of the South Pacific forces. Ghormley and many of his close advisers were so overcome by the Savo defeat that they were unable to conceive of Guadalcanal as anything more than a defensive operation. Having suffered the loss of four first-line heavy cruisers, the Ghormley administration was unwilling to commit vital transports and surface warships to any sort of meaningful logistical support of the Marine enclave. Land-based warplanes, admittedly in short supply, were likewise held back—in premature anticipation by Ghormley himself that they would be needed to defend rear bases once Guadalcanal had fallen! By the same convoluted logic, veteran carrier pilots and aircrews were held in readiness one step removed from the central arena.

Henderson Field was held by the Marines during the first month for only two reasons: The Japanese were unable to mount a meaningful offensive on short notice and, after August 20, a very thin line of American land-based fighters and dive-bombers narrowly achieved air superiority during the day. At night, however, Japanese air and naval forces ruled the air space and sea lanes around Guadalcanal.

卍

The Eastern Solomons Battle had been the second part of a multi-objective Japanese grand plan that had gone awry. On the one hand, RAdm Raizo Tanaka's tiny Reinforcement Group, which had ultimately been turned back on August 25, was intended to provide more infantrymen to a land operation that had already come acropper days before the naval operation began. The Japanese had seriously misjudged the size of the Marine force occupying the Lunga Perimeter, had committed too few soldiers and naval infantrymen to seriously threaten the Marines, had even split both of those tiny forces, and had attempted to commit the second echelons even after learning that the first echelon of the army infantry force had been utterly destroyed in battle. The only support provided by the naval planners for the schizoid land operation was the minuscule August 24 attack by *Ryujo*-based fighters and torpedo bombers and an associated Rabaul-based strike by medium bombers and fighters.

The land phase of the late-August grand strategy was a sham.

The real intent was to bring out the U.S. carriers and defeat them. This plan also failed. While not soundly defeated, the Japanese lost the battle.

It would take time to regroup, but Adm Isoroku Yamamoto and his Combined Fleet would be back, carriers and all. Meantime, except for local air and surface forces based at Rabaul and a changing roster of submarines, the Imperial Navy all but withdrew from the Solomons arena.

⤵

It was a vital characteristic of the Japanese Pacific War effort that the Imperial Army and Imperial Navy failed to achieve operational unity except informally, between individual commanders, at very low operational levels.

At the beginning of the U.S. South Pacific offensive, the Solomons were the exclusive domain of the Imperial Navy. The first responses to the Allied invasion at Guadalcanal were by naval air and surface units, and the first infantry unit sent was one-half of a naval infantry battalion. Shortly, however, the scope of the Marine occupation—dimly perceived as it was—cried for the commitment of Imperial Army forces. This the Army was able to achieve by simply rerouting an independent self-contained infantry force on its way home to Japan—which is to say, without drawing resources away from any ongoing or contemplated operation on its Pacific agenda.

While Imperial Navy warships and land-based warplanes shelled and bombed Henderson Field at will—there were *no* Allied warships or warplanes present for nearly two weeks after August 9—the Army force commander, Col Kiyano Ichiki, struck a personal deal with the Navy transport chief, RAdm Raizo Tanaka, and the first half of *Ichiki Butai* was shipped to a spot east of the Lunga Perimeter to await the balance of the force and the onset of the naval offensive. When the presence of *Ichiki Butai* was prematurely and inadvertently disclosed by a Marine patrol, Colonel Ichiki panicked, precipitously assaulted the Marine line, and was utterly defeated; nearly all his soldiers were killed and he committed ritual suicide.

While the implementation of the naval grand strategy rolled forward days after Ichiki's death, the Imperial Army at last routed an independent infantry brigade—35th Infantry Brigade, commanded by MGen Kiyotake Kawaguchi—from the Palau Islands, through Rabaul, to the Shortland Islands. There, General Kawaguchi struck a personal deal with Admiral Tanaka for the shipment of his brigade to Guadalcanal, partly by slow-moving landing barges and partly by swift destroyers. It was Kawaguchi and several groups of his infantrymen, aboard Tanaka's destroyers, who were landed around Taivu Point beginning August 29, the night after the first group of four troop-carrying destroyers were defeated near the Russell Islands by Cactus dive-bombers.

By August 29, the Cactus Air Force consisted of two Marine fighter squadrons, two Marine dive-bomber squadrons, what amounted to one land-based Navy dive-bomber squadron, and part of one Army fighter squadron. This tiny force was charged with preventing superior Japanese naval air and surface units from molesting Henderson Field or the Lunga Perimeter. Its total support was provided on occasion by one group of Army B-17 heavy bombers based at Espiritu Santo and pilots rotated forward from a Marine fighter squadron also based at Espiritu Santo. No warships were committed to keeping the Japanese at bay; the only warships to reach Guadalcanal were older, ultimately expendable destroyer-transports, minesweepers, and minelayers assigned to guard infrequent and inadequate supply ships that had to sneak into the area between Japanese air raids and be gone by sunset.

The mission was ludicrous for so insignificant an aerial force, but the pilots and aircrews halfway pulled it off. The Japanese were quickly put on notice that the Cactus Air Force ruled the sky and sea approaches to Guadalcanal so long as there was sunlight. The Marine and Navy pilots attempted to extend the hours of their hegemony into the night, but they did not have the numbers, training, or equipment to launch sustained or even successful night operations.

So, while Imperial Navy land-based fighters and bombers tested the mettle of the Cactus Air Force almost every day, Japanese warships and troop-carrying vessels pretty much conceded the day and opted for night landings and night—almost nightly—gunnery passes along the beaches around Lunga Point. The objective of the night naval gunnery—and a stream of individual night bombers— was twofold: the destruction of vital facilities, particularly war-planes and airfield facilities, and the demoralization of Americans on the ground, including pilots and aircrews, whose rest was constantly interrupted. Daylight bombing raids by Zero-escorted Rabaul-based bombers aimed to achieve similar results, along with the direct destruction of Cactus fighters and the deaths of Cactus pilots.

卐

The war at Guadalcanal in late August and early September 1942 was a war of attrition. Each side had precisely the same objectives: to maintain an active presence, to wear down the other side, and to build up ground, air, naval, and logistical assets for the ultimate battle each side knew was inevitable.

Toward those ends, both sides moved to commit far-flung forces of all types to the central struggle. The Imperial Army was pretty much forced by events to halt its New Guinea offensive in order to redirect a complete fresh infantry division to the Solomons operation, and the United States command was forced to move up its schedule to replace a reinforced Marine regiment in American Samoa so that it could be landed at Lunga.

Crucial to these commitments was the difference in attitudes among the men making the decisions.

The senior Japanese Army commander in the region, LtGen Harukichi Hyakutake, considered the commitment of a fresh infantry division necessary only insofar as it helped pull the Imperial Navy's chestnuts from the fire; his mind was firmly set on taking New Guinea, and he would be slow to commit additional Army units if they were requested. Moreover, the Imperial Army would steadfastly refuse to commit even one warplane from its vast strategic reserve to the Solomons campaign.

Most of the U.S. commanders outside of South Pacific Area headquarters *wanted* to commit everything they had to the vortex at Guadalcanal, but prudence dictated the schedule. For the time being, only small ground and air units guarding vital rear bases could be replaced, so only those small units could be committed.

Notwithstanding the prevailing attitudes at high Imperial Army levels, the task of committing fresh resources in the Solomons was easier for the Japanese than it was for the Allies because the Japanese had standing units in or near the Pacific it could withdraw or redirect from ongoing and contemplated offensive operations. The U.S. forces in the Pacific were thinly spread across a defensive barrier that many considered to be the last line of defense. So, while the Japanese had ample resources and controlled their own offensive schedule, the U.S. had inadequate resources that had to be tied down to far-flung island bases because the Japanese had the initiative and the means for striking many of those bases while simultaneously mounting operations at Guadalcanal.

The Japanese commanders expected to win eventually at Guadalcanal while the senior U.S. commander—Ghormley—and many of his chief subordinates pretty much expected to lose eventually.

The respective psychologies, along with the respective availability of resources, would rule the second—tactical—phase of the Guadalcanal campaign, on land, in the air, and at sea.

⚛

The two sides merely sparred during the first dozen days of September 1942.

The Japanese naval air establishment based around Rabaul delivered regular air strikes at the extremity of the 600-mile operational range of their Zero fighters, and Cactus fighters continued to fend off such air strikes, taking losses and inflicting losses. Indeed, the Japanese lost a daily average of about four aircraft and pilots while the Cactus Air Force averaged far fewer losses in airplanes and pilots.

Japanese warships continued to sail into Ironbottom Sound—as the channel fronting Guadalcanal's northern beaches came to be known—and Cactus dive-bombers and fighters continued to harass them for as long as there was sunlight. The Japanese vessels continued to land infantry and support units without great losses and to bombard Henderson Field at night with virtual impunity.

The significant blows and counterblows of the period were minimal, though equally damaging. The Cactus Air Force discovered the whereabouts of General Kawaguchi's 35th Infantry Brigade's barge-borne element as it slowly chugged southward through the Solomons chain. This led to repeated strafing missions that sank many of the troop barges and killed as many as 1,000 of the fresh veteran soldiers. Cactus Air also discovered 35th Infantry Brigade's main base camp at Taivu Point, and daily bombing and strafing raids killed or injured many Japanese soldiers and totally disrupted the brigade's schedule, to say nothing of its morale.

On the other hand, destroyer-transports *Little* and *Gregory* were both sunk in Ironbottom Sound by passing Japanese warships on the night of September 5. This tragedy was just about the last straw for the distant American naval commanders, who ordered all of their vessels of every type to stand clear of the deadly waters by sunset each day.

On September 8, the battalion of Marine Raiders attached to 1st Marine Division struck at the 35th Infantry Brigade's base camp at Taivu Point. The main body of the brigade had already slipped off into the rain forest on its way to assault the Lunga Perimeter, so the battle was brief and anticlimactic. The Raiders hauled off what stores they could carry and destroyed the camp. Then they returned to Lunga to take up a new defensive position on a short stretch of high ground overlooking the back way into the Lunga Perimeter.

On the nights of September 12 and 13, the main body of 35th Infantry Brigade struck the Raider battalion and a minuscule battalion of Marine parachutists that were holding the ridge overlooking Henderson Field. In the end, 35th Infantry Brigade lost more than 600 soldiers killed on or in front of the slopes of what would evermore be called Bloody Ridge. Hundreds of sick and wounded Japanese died along the trail as the defeated main body of the brigade retreated. Two desultory side attacks on the eastern and western flanks of the Lunga Perimeter were also turned back.

Hornet and *Wasp*, the two remaining operational U.S. fleet carriers, had remained distantly active during the seesaw actions leading up to the Bloody Ridge battle at Guadalcanal. The period was not without incident for the sailors and pilots manning Task Force 61, but the overall characteristic of the period was stultifying, boring routine. Frequent submarine sightings—or scares, at any rate—were about the only punctuation, but even they became routine as the memory of *Saratoga's* crippling damage receded amid feelings of good luck and narrow escapes. Until September 6.

Hornet's captain was resting in his sea cabin during the noon hour and, at 1247, the command duty officer was on the signal bridge watching the last of a series of routine launches to replace the antisubmarine and combat air patrol. Ens Earl Zook, a twenty-three-year-old who had graduated from the Naval Academy on December 19, 1941, had the conn. He was the ship's junior assistant navigator and junior officer-of-the-deck.

It was coming up 1250 when Ensign Zook and others were alerted to unusual goings-on by at least one and possibly two loud explosions abaft *Hornet's* port beam.

Ens John Cresto, an absolutely green twenty-three-year-old Avenger pilot attached to *Hornet's* Torpedo-6, thought he had seen a submarine heading right for his ship and had made the only contribution he felt he could reasonably make on extremely short notice by dropping one of two 500-pound depth charges he was carrying in his bomb bay.

When Ensign Zook heard the detonations, his years of training at Annapolis paid off all at once. He instantly took control and, without any sense of his lowly rank, coolly ordered his great ship to come to hard left rudder. As *Hornet* steadied on a course 45 degrees left of the base course, hundreds of her complement, including Ens Earl Zook, saw torpedo wakes pass down either flank.

It is certain that Ensign Zook's quick action saved the carrier.

After Ensign Cresto landed, he was escorted to the cabin of the task force commander, RAdm George Murray, himself a pilot of wide experience. Murray immediately launched into a lengthy address, assuring a group of officers that Cresto's intentional sympathetic detonation of a torpedo with the depth charge had undoubtedly saved the ship. As the admiral spoke, the ensign's expression dimmed. "I didn't know it was a torpedo," Cresto half-complained. "I thought it was a submarine."

卐

The most significant contribution made by carrier air during the period was not administered by the carrier squadrons on duty with Task Force 61. On September 6, LCdr Bullet Lou Kirn's Scouting-3—really an amalgam of Scouting-3 and Bombing-3—joined Cactus Air as a vital addition to the weary force of Marine and *Enterprise* Flight 300 dive-bombers charged with finding, tracking, and hitting Japanese warships and destroyer-transports on the way to Guadalcanal. On September 11, LCdr Roy Simpler's Fighting-5, which by then mustered a large number of pilots transferred from Fighting-6, flew into Henderson Field aboard twenty-four fresh F4F-4 Wildcat fighters. The commitment immediately and significantly turned the tide against burgeoning Japanese air strikes leading up to 35th Infantry Brigade's assault at Bloody Ridge. On September 12, pilots from *Wasp's* Air Group 7 ferried in a number of fresh warplanes to make good some of the losses of the intense air fighting of the period. The *Wasp* pilots did not tarry and ran no operations from Henderson Field, but their brief stay caused morale to soar at the isolated bastion, for it put to rest the reasonable speculation that there were no friendly carriers within supporting range of the island. On September 13, Lt Swede Larsen's Torpedo-8, which by then mustered a large number of pilots and crewmen transferred from Torpedo-3, also flew into Henderson Field, the first torpedo squadron to be committed to Cactus.

The Japanese had again been soundly defeated on land, and the Cactus Air Force was growing. Things around Lunga were beginning to look up.

27

O n September 14, 1942, as Marines around newly named
Bloody Ridge were rooting out Japanese 35th Infantry Brigade stragglers south of Henderson Field, RAdm Richmond
Kelly Turner, the South Pacific transport chief, sailed from Espiritu Santo with a group of six heavily escorted transports carrying
the first large force of Marines to be committed to Guadalcanal in
the aftermath of the Savo debacle. This was one of two reinforced
Marine regiments that had been sent to the Pacific early in the war
to guard Samoa from invasion. Turner, who had been obliged to
order his transports away from Guadalcanal in the immediate aftermath of Savo, determined to make this delivery and thereby keep
the faith with the all-but-castaway Marines holding the Lunga Perimeter and Henderson Field.

In addition to the cruisers and destroyers under his immediate
command, Turner could count upon support from Task Force 61,
which consisted of two fleet carriers, *Wasp* and *Hornet*. In addition,
a fresh surface battle force built around *Washington*, a new fast battleship, had just arrived for duty in the South Pacific Area. *Washington* was a sister of *North Carolina*, which had remained on duty

with the carriers following the dispatch of *Enterprise* for repairs after the Battle of the Eastern Solomons. If needed, the two fast battleships and a significant force of cruisers and destroyers could be dispatched to Turner's aid as, of course, could carrier-borne Air Groups 7 and 8.

⚛

Despite the seeming boldness of Rear Admiral Turner's reinforcement effort, Turner and his colleagues were rightfully fearful that the Japanese would concentrate their strength and muster a major blow. Thus the transports and screening warships took a long loop far from the usual routes between Espiritu Santo and Guadalcanal, well away from the Santa Cruz Islands, which were incorrectly perceived as harboring Japanese tender-based amphibian warplanes and fast destroyers.

At noon on September 15, Turner's force was gathered for the final dash to Lunga when a Japanese four-engine patrol bomber lumbered into sight. Turner thus felt obliged to alter course and sail away from Guadalcanal until a favorable opportunity presented itself.

⚛

At the moment Turner was sighted, Task Force 61—commanded by RAdm Leigh Noyes, flying his flag aboard *Wasp*—was about 100 miles away, just below the 12th Parallel, about 250 miles southeast of Henderson Field. Routine antisubmarine and combat air patrols were aloft. At 1420, *Wasp* turned northeastward into the wind and launched the first of fourteen Scouting-71 SBDs to search 200 miles out in the direction of Guadalcanal. Four additional Scouting-72 Dauntlesses were added to the inner air patrol, and eight Fighting-71 Wildcats were sent up to relieve the combat air patrol. Most of the other strike aircraft aboard *Wasp* and *Hornet* were ready, or being readied, to launch in the event Japanese warships were found.

As soon as the launch was completed, *Wasp* recovered eight fighters and three dive-bombers. In response to the task force commander's order, Capt Ted Sherman ordered his ship to turn to the northwest. The screen vessels instantly responded, as did the entire *Hornet* task force, which was less than two miles away to the northeast.

As soon as *Wasp* came to her new heading, Captain Sherman ordered sixteen Wildcats to be respotted for takeoff and all dive-bombers struck below to the hangar deck. All aircraft were fully armed. Most of Air Group 7's remaining Wildcats and Dauntlesses were fully fueled as well, but the ten torpedo-armed TBF Avengers aboard the smallish fleet carrier still had inert carbon dioxide in their fuel tanks. The dive-bombers and fighters that had just landed were being taken down to the hangar deck on the midships elevator to be refueled, and additional fighters were being brought up to the flight deck on the same elevator.

It was a gorgeous day. The sky was breathtakingly clear, and visibility was unlimited. If there was a worry at all, it was over the condition of the sea. A 20-knot trade wind blowing up from the southeast had covered the surface with whitecaps, which were perfect concealment for the relays of submarines that had been dogging the carriers nearly every day since *Saratoga* had been struck by a torpedo two weeks earlier. But there was nothing that could be done about the threat beyond keeping search pilots, lookouts, and sonarmen at a high state of alert.

卐

At 1444, Cdr Takaichi Kinashi ordered torpedomen aboard *I-19* to fire six of their deadly cylinders.

Kinashi had been tracking a sea full of fat targets—almost too many to comprehend—and had finally fallen heir to a clear shot at one of the two American carriers that were crossing at right angles to his approach track.

When the moment to fire came, Commander Kinashi adhered strictly to his tactical doctrine and fired a fan of six torpedoes along slightly diverging tracks at the nearest target, *Wasp*. As soon as the torpedoes were away, *I-19*'s commander began the arduous task of slinking away as he waited to hear how well he had done. If he was lucky and if his skill was certain, he would hear from one to six detonations. Perhaps some of his torpedoes would overshoot the target, which had been rapidly moving across his line of sight at the moment of firing. In that case, all or several errant torpedoes might strike any number of the screening cruisers and destroyers, which from Kinashi's vantage point had seemed to march in a solid steel wall across the horizon.

⇅

At 1445, only a minute after *I-19* fired the last of six torpedoes, RAdm Leigh Noyes's attention was pulled from whatever it had been focused upon by a lookout's yell, "Torpedo wake!" From his vantage point on *Wasp*'s flag bridge, Noyes saw three torpedo wakes only 300 feet away. He heard a young ensign at his elbow say, "These have got us," but the admiral did not reply as he braced himself for the multiple detonations.

The ship's gunnery officer, LCdr George Knuepfer, was standing his routine afternoon watch in Sky Control, high up in the tripod mast over the bridge, when his assistant, who was standing well to starboard, blurted out, "Torpedoes!" Knuepfer rushed to that side of the platform and was just in time to see two torpedoes closing to within 50 yards of the ship. He yelled down to the bridge, "Torpedoes! Hard left rudder!"

Capt Ted Sherman also saw the approaching torpedoes, and he ordered the rudder changed from right standard to right full— about the only thing he could do on such short notice.

LCdr John Greenslade, the ship's navigator, heard the hail "Torpedoes on the starboard bow" as he sat in the charthouse. He stood up and stepped to the hatchway leading to the starboard catwalk and immediately saw two torpedoes go out of sight beneath the edge of the bridge decking just forward of the bridge and immediately beneath the forward 1.1-inch gun group. The starboard side of the ship was instantly enveloped in smoke and debris, and Greenslade was forced to retreat back into the charthouse, which had become a shambles of broken fixtures.

Lt(jg) T. D. Wells, who was on duty in the starboard forward 5-inch gun group, clearly heard the shouted warning from Lookout-1 and saw one of the gunners point to starboard. Wells had just

enough time to order all hands to stand as far back as possible before the first torpedo struck the 1.1-inch group just to the rear.

LCdr George Knuepfer, in Sky Control, clearly saw the second torpedo slam into the ship forward of the first, directly beneath
Lieutenant (jg) Wells's forward 5-inch gun group. The cumulative
effect of the two blasts threw Knuepfer to his knees. Sky Control
was whipsawed in several directions at once and the foremast tripod on which it was perched seemed about to break up.

On the flag bridge, Rear Admiral Noyes's knees were buckled,
but he remained on his feet. Captain Sherman also remained standing. By and large, throughout the ship, anyone who was on his feet
was knocked down by one or another of the quick succession of
crippling body blows.

Cdr Mike Kernodle, the carrier's air officer, was in Air Plot at
1445. His talker, an enlisted communicator fitted out with sound-
powered battle phones whispered a message from Lookout-1 barely
loud enough for Kernodle to hear: "Torpedo wake on starboard
bow." The words were barely spoken when the first detonation
occurred. The second detonation was almost instantaneous. Air
Plot, which was high up in the island, was severely whipped
around by the force of the first two warheads detonating in quick
succession. All the lightbulbs were blown out, fixtures were blasted
loose, and a great mixed volume of glass, gear, and papers was
thrown to the deck along with every man in the now-darkened
compartment. Compartments throughout the ship suffered similar
damage.

Cdr Fred Dickey, the carrier's executive officer, was sitting in a
closed compartment when the torpedoes struck the starboard side
of the ship. He immediately headed for Battle-II, the secondary
command and control center from which he would conn the ship in
the event Captain Sherman was unable to do so from the primary
control bridge. As Dickey passed an open hatchway leading out to
the flight deck, he saw what seemed to him to be damage from
high-altitude bombs. Debris and spray were flying over the deck,
and a pall of thick smoke was hanging over the forward part of the
flight deck. In fact, he probably witnessed the secondary detona-

tion of ready ammunition and powder among the starboard 1.1-inch guns.

All hands throughout the ship climbed to their feet—just in time to be felled again by yet another violent detonation. The third torpedo had broached in the waves but had plunged on to strike the side of the ship about 60 feet forward of the bridge and quite near the surface. Damage above the waterline, particularly to antiaircraft guns mounted along the starboard catwalks, was considerable.

When everyone in Air Plot had recovered from the triple shock, Cdr Mike Kernodle ordered battle lanterns to be lighted and all hands to remain at their stations. Officers, petty officers, and leading seamen throughout the ship did the same. Long months of training took hold; there seemed to be nothing to do but carry on.

No one in the forward starboard 5-inch gun gallery had been hurt when the second torpedo detonated almost directly beneath their feet, but an ample number of gunners were overcome by noxious fumes thrown off in the wake of the third torpedo detonation. The gun-group commander, Lt(jg) T. D. Wells, ordered the gallery abandoned, and the sickened gunners were carried to the port forward 5-inch gun gallery, where all hands who were able helped dump ready ammunition and powder over the side. Meantime, Wells tried to enter the berthing compartment where most of his gunners lived to try to locate members of the gun group who had been off duty. He was driven out by the extremely thick smoke.

At the instant the first torpedo struck, about sixty plane handlers, armorers, and mechanics were working on the hangar deck forward of Elevator 2, the midships elevator. Lt Raleigh Kirkpatrick was standing by beside the elevator, which had just gone up to the flight deck after an SBD had been rolled off on the hangar deck. Four refueled fighters were waiting to be rolled on for movement to the flight deck, and fueling of the recently recovered patrol bombers was underway.

The hangar deck was made an instant shambles by the sheer force of the first two torpedo detonations. The second blast was accompanied by a sheet of flames, which seemed to Lieutenant Kirkpatrick to engulf the entire starboard side of the forward half of the enclosed cavernous work area. A number of the sailors forward of Kirkpatrick's position had to jump overboard to escape the flames, and at least one aviation metalsmith was blown over the side. Thick, dark smoke instantly permeated the entire work area.

Many of the twelve F4Fs, ten SBDs, ten TBFs, and one observation plane on the hangar deck were lifted up and bounced down with such force as to shatter their landing gear. At least two of the four spare Wildcats lashed to the overhead were jarred loose from their bindings and fell on the planes on the deck. The result was an impenetrable mass of aircraft scrap and armaments that could not be moved from the soup of aviation gasoline leaking from the ruptured aircraft fuel tanks.

Lieutenant Kirkpatrick immediately grasped the extremity of the situation and yelled for the men on the hangar deck to trip all the sprinklers and water curtains. However, it was quickly discovered that the water pressure was nil. The two men who tried to start the water were trapped by the flames and saved themselves only by taking a circuitous and arduous path to the rear of the ship. Kirkpatrick next found ChMach Elmo Runyan, who had just returned from the flight deck after doing all he could to secure the gasoline fuel lines. Kirkpatrick asked Runyan to go below to open the main sprinkler valve by hand, but Runyan was unable to get forward to the valve junction due to the spreading fire on the second deck. He did reach a set of valves on the port side of the second deck, but activating these brought forth no water.

卐

LCdr J. T. Workman was on the flight deck beside Elevator 2 overseeing the respotting of the ready fighters when the first torpedo struck. The flight deck in front of Workman buckled, and he saw flames shoot up from the starboard side. Workman thought the second torpedo blast was from internal sources. The hatch over Elevator 1, the forward elevator, was blown open and flames belched out of the elevator shaft. Elevator 2, which was caught at flight-deck level, was severely buckled.

Behind Lieutenant Commander Workman, several of the Wildcats spotted on the flight deck were blown over the side and others were damaged in place. These had to be jettisoned.

࿕

Even before the effects of the third detonation had dissipated, Captain Sherman ordered the ship slowed to 10 knots and the rudder put over hard to the left. Next, he backed the ship at full right rudder to get the wind to blow the flames and smoke away from the undamaged portion of the ship as well as to stand clear of the volatile fuel oil that had been dumped into the sea when fuel tanks ruptured. Though communications were marginal, the engineers responded without difficulty to all the captain's requests. The bulk of the ship's power plant was intact and available.

࿕

The ship's damage control officer, Cdr John Hume, was in Air Plot when the first two torpedoes struck. As soon as he lifted himself from the floor, he headed for Central Station to orchestrate efforts to save the ship from the deadly serial blows. Before Commander Hume could reach his objective, however, he was informed that it had had to be abandoned.

Eight sailors under Lt(jg) R. D. Taylor were on duty at Central Station at the time of the blasts. It took a few moments for all hands to get untangled and find battle lanterns clipped to the bulkheads, but they soon settled into the earnest workmanlike routine they had trained for years to achieve. Alarms were ringing, but the bank of indicator lights that would have told them where the damage was greatest was out. There was neither AC nor DC power, and a smooth shift to an emergency transformer yielded no results. Central Station was literally in the dark. Worse, the ship had rapidly taken on a 15-degree list, and the vital control center was beginning to take in water and fuel oil through a tear in the forward bulkhead and by way of the trunk leading up through the island.

Since the station was not functioning and in danger of being swamped, Lieutenant (jg) Taylor reasonably decided to evacuate.

He and three sailors made their way up the trunk to the third deck and eventually reached the flight deck, where Taylor reported to Commander Hume.

However, the fifth man to enter the escape trunk from Central Station was driven back by a powerful explosion directly over his head at the level of the third deck. He and the three sailors still remaining in Central Station dogged down all the doors to adjacent spaces and reported by phone to the bridge. They were instructed to leave when they had to, a move that became necessary quite soon as the station continued to flood and as the power remained out. By the time they left, the bubble level in Central Station showed that the ship's list had come back and she was only 5 degrees down by the bows.

The loss of control that might have been afforded through Central Station was not itself catastrophic—there were numerous back-up systems in place—but it would make damage control quite a bit more difficult.

卐

Lt(jg) C. A. Rogers was in the starboard 1.1-inch clipping room when the torpedoes struck. All hands were thrown to the deck, but none was injured. Rogers ran straight to the gun mount through smoke billowing up from below. No one was manning the starboard 1.1-inch guns, so Rogers returned to the clipping room to help break out the nearest fire hose to help combat flames that were about to penetrate from the adjacent hangar deck. Neither the hose nor the clipping room's sprinkler system issued any water, so all hands began throwing ammunition over the side as fast as they could. They were barely started when a huge explosion and ball of flame swept over the entire 1.1-inch mount. Everyone immediately abandoned the area by way of the 20mm catwalk and then struggled toward the stern of the ship, which seemed to be cooler and safer. Rogers was burned about the face and arms while negotiating the catwalk, and several of his gunners were also hurt, but they all safely reached the fantail.

Shortly after Lieutenant (jg) Rogers's gun crew left the area, LCdr George Knuepfer, the ship's gunnery officer, ordered all the starboard clipping rooms cleared and flooded. However, the flooding system was inoperative and the fire was moving in. All hands were ordered away before the 40mm, 1.1-inch, and 20mm ammunition stowed throughout the vicinity began cooking off.

A fire-induced explosion on the powder hoist for one of the starboard 5-inch guns blew the gun mount right up onto the flight deck and the splinter shield into the water. A sailor who failed to heed a last-instant warning before the blast was killed when a powder case he had cradled in his arms was set off by the blast.

At least one other forward powder hoist laden with a lethal cargo was detonated by the encroaching fires.

卐

Below decks, throughout the injured carrier's berthing and working spaces, officers and sailors sorted out their fearful impressions and made their way in the dark by the most direct means to their battle stations or safety, whichever made more sense. All hands throughout the ship had trained rigorously to get to safety from even the least accessible compartments. But so many of the regular passageways in the forward part of the ship were filled with smoke or blocked by damaged fixtures or fires that sheer luck and perseverance alone spelled the difference between danger and safety, between life and death.

Officers' country, well forward, rapidly filled with smoke, and that resulted in the suffocation of a number of ship's officers and pilots in their staterooms or in darkened, smoke-filled passageways as they groped their way toward clear air and cool safety.

The forecastle was completely isolated from the rest of the ship by smoke and flame, and the failure of water mains in the vicinity of the forward detonations made fire control a wishful endeavor. At least one gasoline-filled pipe against the starboard hull was actively spewing burning fuel. Sailors, particularly damage controlmen, in the isolated forecastle area did what they could to mitigate the effects of the blast and fire. Someone tripped the carbon-dioxide system in the volatile paint-storage locker, and all doors and hatchways were closed and dogged to fully compartmentalize that part of the ship (as, indeed, they were throughout the ship).

Lt(jg) J. L. Edwards and his roommate made their way from the stateroom on the third deck through dark, smoke-filled passageways to a ladder leading up to the second deck, which was also filled with smoke. A red glow could be seen up the passageway leading starboard and aft through officers' country. Overhead, Edwards could hear a fellow officer urging men crowded around the foot of the next ladder to safety to "take it easy; you are all okay." Edwards also heard many voices crying for help, but he saw through the smoke that many of the pleaders were moving under their own power. It was impossible to move aft to the hangar deck because the only passageway was filled with flames. Fortunately, the lower part of the ladder leading from the first deck up to the 01 Deck—a space located forward of the high hangar deck between the flight deck overhead and the level of the hangar deck—had been lowered from its usual secured position against the overhead. Thus the passage to the 01 Deck was made with ease. Once on the 01 Deck, which was clear of smoke, Edwards found about 150 sailors milling about in confusion, for the flight deck overhead appeared to be on fire. There was really only one way to go, and that was forward, into the isolated forecastle. There, Edwards and other refugees from berthing spaces below were joined by numerous gunners who were being forced to retreat in the face of spreading flames and exploding ammunition in the starboard gun galleries.

By then, fires were raging virtually out of control in many below-decks spaces along the starboard side of the ship. Many men were simply consumed in leapfrogging flash fires while others succumbed to smoke and liquids as they groped through escape routes that were often cut off by torpedo detonations and numerous secondary blasts. For example, the four sailors who had been left behind in Central Station managed to escape through a fire-control tube to the forward mess compartment, but only one man from the post office, one deck up but otherwise adjacent to Central Station, survived the detonation of what was probably the third torpedo.

卐

The torpedoes had struck the carrier while she was most vulnerable. Returning patrol planes were on the hangar deck being refueled. Thus highly volatile aviation gasoline was flowing freely through a maze of pipes throughout the vicinity of all three torpedo hits. Nothing could have been as catastrophic.

It appears that the first torpedo ruptured an important and quite large set of gasoline lines at the level of the second deck. The fuel thus leaked down to the third deck. The second torpedo, which struck forward of the first, caused at least one direct fire below the second deck, and this fire eventually spread to the leaking fuel. The third torpedo ruptured yet additional fuel lines, possibly including an external fuel line running down the starboard side of the ship well above the waterline.

Nearly everyone who was working or resting below decks at the time of the torpedo hits reported smelling gasoline vapors. The detonation of these volatile vapors caused an extremely violent sympathetic explosion at about 1505, nearly 20 minutes after the third torpedo hit. This blast detonated fuel, torpedoes, and bombs on ready aircraft on the hangar deck, and those blasts certainly ruptured fuel lines passing by on the outside of the hull. The fuel in those lines was instantaneously ignited.

The sympathetic explosion was fatal.

Commander Hume ruefully concluded his damage-control report thus: "Had water pressure been available, the hangar deck fire might have been controlled, but it is extremely doubtful that the fire below, embracing the gasoline tank area, could have been extinguished."

Wasp was thus doomed more by secondary gasoline fires than she was by the considerable direct structural damage caused by the torpedo detonations against her hull. That structural damage was vast: From Elevator 2 forward, the starboard side of the ship was pretty much open to the sea; the bulkheads between officers' country and the well of Elevator 2 were blown open; two forward auxiliary diesel generators were knocked from their foundations; and the entire forward part of the ship was without light or power.

⚙

Within only a minute of the last torpedo blast, the entire forward end of the hangar deck was a raging inferno, and Lt Raleigh

Kirkpatrick and the surviving hangar-deck crew had completely run out of ways to fight the fire. The danger was compounded by thousands of rounds of .30-caliber and .50-caliber machine-gun ammunition that were by then cooking off in the airplanes stowed forward of Elevator 2. Indeed, Kirkpatrick and others were repeatedly struck by tiny fragments of exploding machine-gun rounds, though no one was badly hurt.

Soon, ChMach Elmo Runyan found some active water mains in the after part of the hangar deck, and he oversaw the laying of hoses from them to the fire line. A mere dribble of water arrived through these hoses—about enough to help the deck crew keep the conflagration from spreading aft of Elevator 2.

Exploding bombs and airplane fuel tanks added to the carnage and constantly bowled over the hosemen. While Lieutenant Kirkpatrick oversaw the firefighting, Chief Machinist Runyan saw to running more hoses forward. Spare airplane wings lashed to the overhead began falling one by one, adding considerably to the danger.

Lt(jg) Joseph Bodell, a damage control officer who had been stopped by flames on the hangar deck on his way to assess damage in the forward part of the ship, noticed that the paint on bulkheads and the overhead was adding considerable fuel to the fire. Surprisingly, *Wasp* had not joined other ships of the Fleet in extensively stripping paint, particularly from areas where volatile materials were stored or used. (*Enterprise*, for example, undoubtedly had been spared enormous grief at Eastern Solomons because paint in such areas had been carefully stripped.) Bodell perceived that burning paint carried the flames into uptakes, where it certainly spread further out of sight and beyond the reach of any firefighting tools. Perhaps fire spreading across painted surfaces and through painted air intakes and ventilators carried the flames to magazines and ammunition hoists, for these certainly could be heard detonating from Bodell's place on the hose line.

The magnitude of the great sympathetic blast caused by the detonation of fuel vapors and leaking fuel felled nearly every firefighter on the hangar deck. Lieutenant Kirkpatrick was blown through a fire curtain that had been run out to bifurcate the hangar space, and he came to rest fully 50 feet astern of his last position. Miraculously, no one in the area was burned or severely injured.

By then, the feeble hose pressure had been dropping off a little at a time, and the fires seemed to be gaining. About all Kirkpatrick could think of doing was to head for the aft end of the hangar deck to help push undamaged airplanes into the water so they would not add to the creeping inferno. Unfortunately, a great many of the surviving airplanes were entangled with two spare Wildcats that had been jarred from the overhead. The task seemed as impossible as holding back the fire.

LCdr John Shea, who had come down from his battle station at Primary Flight Control to help fight the fires on the hangar deck, was constantly at the closest point to advancing fires despite the continuous detonation of one ruptured aircraft fuel tank or bomb, depth charge or torpedo, after another. He was killed leading one such foray, one of the few firefighters to succumb to the intense heat and smoke.

The bridge became untenable following the great 1505 secondary explosion, so Captain Sherman made his way aft to Battle-II. He arrived at about 1510, a few minutes ahead of Cdr Mike Kernodle, who had been inspecting the inferno on the hangar deck. Kernodle's report—which indicated that there was no water for fighting the fires on the hangar deck and elsewhere—was so depressing that Captain Sherman told his executive officer, Cdr Fred Dickey, that it was about time to abandon ship. Dickey reluctantly agreed with the pronouncement, and Sherman ordered all engines stopped as a preliminary move to get all the living men safely into the water.

Commander Dickey noted at that moment that flames from the hangar deck had burned through the decking of the forward part of the flight deck.

Leaving the exec in charge for a few moments, Captain Sherman climbed to the flag bridge to apprise Admiral Noyes of his decision. The task force commander returned to Battle-II with

Captain Sherman, who ordered Dickey to pass "Abandon ship" to all hands.

It was then 1520.

The word quickly spread through the viable portions of the ship. As most of the officers and sailors continued to stand off the fires as best they could, individuals and work teams began staging life rafts or deploying lifelines over the side of the ship. The routine had been drilled into all hands during quieter times so, despite the dislocations of large areas and escape routes closed off by fire or damage and debris, and the loss of a number of key players and control systems, the effort to get as many men as possible off the ship alive was smoothly run.

Lt Benedict Semmes, the assistant gunnery officer who had taken charge in the crowded and isolated forecastle, ordered volunteers to cut life rafts from the overhead and place them on the deck. No one had heard of an order from higher authority to abandon ship, but Semmes realized that he was on his own and would have to act on his own authority. As it happened, his decision to order everyone in the forecastle into the water neatly coincided with Captain Sherman's abandon-ship order. Mattresses were brought to the forecastle from nearby berthing spaces and thrown into the water to provide flotation for the many nonswimmers who had arrived without life belts.

Cdr Theo Ascherfeld, the carrier's engineering officer, was extremely surprised to receive the order to abandon ship. He knew that *Wasp* was badly hurt, but he was at work deep in her bowels and could not see or hear any of the firefighting or damage-control action. Until Ascherfeld secured the engineering plant and made his way topside, he thought the order was a temporary one. He had no idea until then that his ship had suffered mortal injuries.

While Admiral Noyes and Captain Sherman remained at Battle-II to oversee the operation, Commander Dickey toured the ship to see that the matter was settled in the briefest possible time and with the lowest possible additional loss of life.

After delivering his sad damage assessment to the captain, Commander Kernodle returned to the hangar deck to help fight fires and oversee the movement of the wounded to the safer, cooler fantail.

Among the first men Kernodle contacted was Lt Raleigh Kirkpatrick, who had lost all communication with the world outside of his focus on the hangar-deck fires. Kirkpatrick had already seen sailors and officers going over the side from the flight deck, but he had no idea that abandonment had been sanctioned until he heard the news from Commander Kernodle. Kirkpatrick moved among his firefighters, giving them the word, until he came upon a seaman with badly burned arms. He retrieved some tannic acid jelly from a nearby compartment and rubbed it over the seaman's burns. Then he ordered the man over the side, and followed a few moments later by way of a lifeline from the fantail. Many of the men who survived the ordeal credit Lt Raleigh Kirkpatrick's stand against the flames at Elevator-2 with preserving viable escape routes and for saving the ship from being consumed even more rapidly than it was.

As relays of firefighters and volunteers held the flames at bay, large groups moved to the extremities of the ship and formed orderly lines to await the opportunity to go into the water. Not everyone left his station, however. LCdr Laurice Tatum, the ship's dentist, was too busy treating wounded in the isolated forecastle to heed an order to go to safety. He breathed in far too much smoke and passed out. Though Dr. Tatum was dragged to safety and eventually taken from the ship, he succumbed to smoke inhalation.

The ship's gunnery officer, LCdr George Knuepfer, reached the fantail from the flight deck and found quiet, orderly lines of sailors waiting their turns to go over the side. Nearly a dozen of them willingly answered Knuepfer's call for help in moving a pair of undamaged airplanes from the path of the fire. Then he oversaw the rigging of many lines over the side of the ship, for the abandonment was proceeding at far too slow a pace given the rate of the advancing flames. When Knuepfer realized there were not enough life jackets, he sent volunteers to the nearby Marine Detachment's living compartment to fetch mattresses and pillows, which were passed out or thrown overboard to swimmers.

Lt Dave McCampbell, a red-hot aviator serving as *Wasp's*

LSO, undertook his only approximation of flying during the entire cruise after he had coaxed upward of 200 other men over the side by means of lifelines. McCampbell escaped from the ship nearly as he had always intended to do if it came to that. He climbed to the LSO's platform and, after abandoning the idea of *diving* overboard—he had been an Annapolis diving champion—held his nose, gripped his family jewels, and stepped into space. He joined Lt Raleigh Kirkpatrick and ChMach Elmo Runyan, of the hangar-deck firefighters, as they clung to a plank bobbing in the swell beside the dying ship.

Capt Ted Sherman saw to the evacuation of all flag and bridge personnel, then left Battle-II to begin a long walk through the viable areas of the ship. He arrived at the after extremity of the flight deck and paused to see the last of the men there and in the after gun galleries go over the side. Then he climbed to the fantail, where he again joined up with Admiral Noyes. Nearby, the ship's chaplain was helping a badly wounded sailor over the side. Cdr John Hume arrived to report that the hangar deck was clear of injured. As the admiral's party swung out onto the lifelines, Captain Sherman put off his departure to walk forward into the huge hangar bay. He found only one man there, Carp Joseph Machinsky, whose enduring contribution to the abandonment had been the orderly movement of buoyant lumber from stowage areas throughout the ship to the men in the water. Machinsky was still singlehandedly collecting lumber and mattresses when the captain arrived and ordered him to leave the ship. Only after Carpenter Machinsky left did Ted Sherman concede the loss of his ship and leave by way of a lifeline from the fantail.

The exec, Cdr Fred Dickey, was the last man off the flight deck; he left the ship at 1556 by means of a lifeline affixed to the starboard catwalk. Cdr Mike Kernodle and LCdr George Knuepfer lowered themselves from the fantail at 1557, among the very last half dozen officers and sailors to leave by that route.

Many of the men in the water were threatened—and some were killed—by burning fuel oil that was blazing forward of the island. The ship was drifting, and even the nonburning oil slick presented a number of navigational and health risks to the hundreds of tired and shocked survivors. Everyone who could pulled for the safety of clear seas and five nearby destroyers, which had lowered whaleboats to help pick up the swimmers and tow life rafts.

The work of war continued. Cdr Mike Kernodle and LCdr George Knuepfer both felt the concussion from a depth charge dropped by a destroyer only 500 yards from the swimmers. The underwater blast squeezed Kernodle's bladder dry and caused him a significant amount of abdominal pain. Knuepfer was merely discomforted. Any number of swimmers might have been severely injured; some no doubt were.

☙

Cdr Fred Dickey eventually wound up aboard destroyer *Lansdowne*, where he learned from the destroyer division commander that orders had been received at 1655 to sink *Wasp*'s fire-gutted hulk with torpedoes. Dickey and other senior officers who had been brought aboard *Lansdowne* watched with great emotion as the first torpedo was launched at *Wasp* from 1,500 yards at 1908. It was set for 30 feet and apparently passed under the keel of the ship without detonating.

The second torpedo was set for 25 feet and launched at the carrier's starboard beam beside the island. It clearly struck the aiming point, but it did not appear to add to *Wasp*'s starboard list.

The third torpedo, set for 20 feet, was also launched at the starboard beam beside the island. It failed to detonate, leaving observers to speculate that it might have entered a hole in the hull and detonated unobserved.

The fourth torpedo, which was set for 15 feet, struck true just abaft the island and caused a large explosion. The list increased quite a bit to starboard, but not enough to carry the hulk under.

Lansdowne had just one torpedo left. This was fired at the port beam at a depth of only 10 feet. It exploded on the exposed bottom of the ship at about 2015.

By the time the last torpedo struck *Wasp*, the carrier was engulfed in flames from forecastle to fantail. As *Lansdowne* passed down the starboard side of the carrier, the hulk's list noticeably increased. Commander Dickey could plainly see that she was going down by the head.

At 2100, September 15, 1942, USS *Wasp*, America's seventh fleet carrier, completed her long roll to starboard and disappeared beneath the Pacific.

Of *Wasp*'s crew of 2,247 officers, 193 were killed outright or succumbed to their wounds. Nearly all of the 366 wounded officers and men were burn cases.

⚛

Wasp was struck by only three of the six torpedoes fired by *I-19*. Two other U.S. Navy warships were also struck by Japanese torpedoes within a matter of minutes.

The first warning *Hornet*'s Task Force 17 had of the tragedy unfolding at the center of its sister task force was a partial voice-radio alarm raised within a minute of the first torpedo impact on *Wasp*. Destroyer *Landsowne*, which was then on station several thousand yards off *Wasp*'s starboard quarter, warned in a garbled and barely audible message: "Torpedo headed for [your] formation, course zero-eight-zero."

Hornet was just then routinely coming around to course 280 degrees when a second partial message reached her from a then-unidentified source: "Torpedo just passed astern of me. Headed for you!" At almost the same moment, the source of the warning, destroyer *Mustin*, a member of the *Hornet* screen, raised emergency flags to her yardarm.

If a torpedo had passed astern of *Mustin*'s position in the screen, it was probably heading for the heart of the *Hornet* formation, which was *Hornet* herself. As all eyes topside on every ship in Task Force 17 went to the water to try to find telltale torpedo wakes, *Hornet*'s officer-of-the-deck ordered "Hard right rudder!" The great carrier heeled over to starboard.

As *Hornet* swung through her emergency turn, battleship *North Carolina*'s captain ordered his great warship to follow suit. Emergency power was laid on, and the modern battleship vibrated from stem to stern as her huge propellers bit deeper into the waves. But it looked to be a little too late. As the battleship began to lean into her hard turn, everyone who could see, and everyone who could not, instinctively tensed as the unseen torpedoes bore down on them.

FC3 Larry Resen had been aft on the boat deck when he heard someone scream, "The *Wasp* is on fire!" After the briefest of looks, Resen had instinctively started for his battle station, Sky Control, at a dead run. The quickest way was up the port side, and he was passing the aft dual-5-inch antiaircraft mount when he saw an enormous explosion several thousand yards off the port beam. There was so much smoke at the point of detonation that Resen could not see what had exploded.

The second U.S. warship to be struck by a torpedo was destroyer *O'Brien*, which was holding station on *Hornet* through the carrier's precipitous turn. At 1452, *O'Brien*'s turn carried her right into the path of one of the three *I-19* torpedoes that apparently passed *Wasp*. The destroyer's bows were utterly blown away in the blast. At the same moment, someone saw a second torpedo pass close astern of *O'Brien*. Given the destroyer's position relative to *Wasp*, these were probably the two rightmost torpedoes fired by *I-19* at the extremity of their range.

Less than a minute later—the chronometers still showed 1452—FC3 Larry Resen was still heading for his battle station at Sky Control when the last remaining *I-19* torpedo detonated at the extremity of its range right on the battleship's thickly armored port bow just abreast the forward 16-inch turret. Given *North Carolina*'s position relative to *Wasp*, this must have been the leftmost of the six torpedoes *I-19* had fired in a standard fanlike spread. If so, it is clear that the battleship unfortunately and inadvertently ran into it while she was following *Hornet*'s precipitous evasion maneuver.

A great column of water and fuel oil boiled up over the main deck and rained down upon the passing superstructure. There was so much smoke that Larry Resen was arrested in his path; it was too dark for him to see the side of the ship a foot or two away. The smoke briefly engulfed the control bridge and reached as high as gunnery-control and lookout stations high up in the main mast. Many tons of seawater fell back upon the superstructure and main deck, and one sailor was washed away.

North Carolina completed her turn—and two more in quick succession—matching those of *Hornet* and the smaller escorts. Indeed, she got up 25 knots of speed and kept station on the last operational U.S. fleet carrier in the Pacific.

࿔

Hornet sent off a number of her ready airplanes to the base at Espiritu Santo to make room for the twenty-six *Wasp* search and patrol planes aloft at the time of the torpedoing. One of the searchers ran out of fuel and ditched beside the rescue destroyers attending *Wasp*, but all the others safely landed aboard *Hornet*. When noses were counted, it was seen that Scouting-71 was a nearly intact squadron; for practical purposes, it was all that remained of Air Group 7, which lost forty-five first-line fighters and bombers aboard *Wasp*—a stupendous loss in light of the Cactus Air Force's urgent needs.

O'Brien reported that she was able to make 15 knots despite the loss of her bows, so she was dispatched alone at 1600 to nearby Espiritu Santo for emergency patching. She left there for a trip to the West Coast sometime later, but came apart in heavy seas, from which her entire crew was rescued.

The blast on *North Carolina*'s port bow killed five sailors and opened a gash 32 feet long by 18 feet high 20 feet below the waterline. A flash in the Turret-1 handling room caused the captain to order the forward magazines to be flooded. However, *North Carolina* easily kept station on *Hornet* throughout the balance of the afternoon. She was dispatched at dusk with two escorting destroyers to Tongatabu. She eventually underwent complete repairs and an upgrading at Pearl Harbor. *North Carolina*'s departure left *Washington* as the U.S. fleet's only modern fast battleship taking part in the Pacific War.

࿔

RAdm Kelly Turner's six heavily escorted transports waited out of range through the night of September 15. Next day, Turner decided to make good his pledge to deliver the reinforced Marine regiment to Lunga, and he pressed on. The entire Marine regiment, an artillery battalion, and their supports, along with plenty of needed supplies, were uneventfully discharged on the beaches around Lunga Point on September 18.

As Turner was landing the Marines and supplies, destroyers *Monssen* and *MacDonough*—two Eastern Solomons battle veterans—became the first U.S. Navy warships to bombard Japanese camps and supply dumps on Guadalcanal.

The landing was flawless and Turner was able to leave with the empty transports at sunset—to make way for that night's run of the Tokyo Express, as the almost nightly Japanese troop-and-supply-carrying bombardment missions had been dubbed.

Now only *Hornet*'s Air Group 8 stood between the might of the Imperial Navy's Combined Fleet and the thin line holding Guadalcanal and nearby South Pacific bastions.

PART VI

October
Offensives

28

Task Force 61—now really only RAdm George Murray's Task Force 17—drew in its horns following the loss of *Wasp*. It had to. If the Japanese mounted a carrier strike in the eastern Solomons, only *Hornet*'s Air Group 8 would stand between it and the Cactus Air Force.

For their part, the Japanese were strangely reticent to press their decided advantage in carrier power. *Shokaku* and *Zuikaku*, the only Japanese fleet carriers that had started the war and survived Midway, were about to be joined in the Combined Fleet by two freshly commissioned fleet carriers and a small number of light carriers. The Japanese advantage in carrier-based air was staggering, but it was not put to the test.

The Guadalcanal campaign had entered a seesaw middle phase. Each side built up its infantry strength on the island, though their nighttime mastery of the seas around Guadalcanal assured the Japanese of a more rapid buildup than the Americans could achieve. Air strengths generally rose but remained relatively about the same, though each side poured in whatever new formations of fighters and bombers it could spare. The Cactus fighters continued to dominate the daytime action, however, and that had a hobbling effect upon Japanese ground operations.

In terms of strategy, the Japanese—on land, in the air, and at sea—were predisposed toward mounting crushing definitive operations. This resulted in the episodic commitment to battle of large forces, and that resulted in a series of sorely needed breathing spaces for the hard-pressed U.S. forces.

For their parts, the U.S. ground and air establishments at Guadalcanal could never muster any meaningful strength to sweep the Japanese from the air or the close environs of Henderson Field. So they contented themselves with chipping away at the Japanese, with keeping the enemy off balance by mounting whatever limited land offensives they could afford.

Once the fresh Marine regiment Kelly Turner delivered on September 18 had gotten its land legs, 1st Marine Division was able to raid the strongly held Japanese side of the Matanikau River, which formed the distant western flank of the Lunga Perimeter— more a psychological dividing line than a real barrier. On the far side of the river from the Marine division, the Imperial Army was able over succeeding nights to bolster the 35th Infantry Brigade— shattered at Bloody Ridge in mid-September—with a complete infantry division, the crack 2nd "Sendai" Division, one of the best the Imperial Army had to offer. Moreover, LtGen Harukichi Hyakutake, the Imperial Army's senior commander in the Solomons and New Guinea, showed his rising interest in winning back Henderson Field by taking steps to personally venture forward to Guadalcanal along with the headquarters of his 17th Army. (Despite this show of interest, Hyakutake's main interest remained New Guinea. He thus held back from Guadalcanal a second fresh infantry division to which he had access but which he hoped to commit whole to the "temporarily delayed" New Guinea offensive. To Hyakutake, Guadalcanal remained an irksome responsibility imposed upon him by headquarters far above his head.)

General Hyakutake's apparently newfound interest in Guadalcanal morally obliged the Imperial Navy to commit itself to mounting a huge killing blow against Henderson Field as soon as 17th Army had been able to concentrate adequate infantry and artillery on Guadalcanal. The deal between the two services was struck between a representative of Imperial General Headquarters seconded to Hyakutake's staff and Adm Isoroku Yamamoto himself.

The Marine spoiling attacks of late September and early October unwittingly went a long way toward destabilizing the Japanese timetable. The Marines were unable to overwhelm the Japanese, but they killed or wounded many of them and even managed to put several crack Japanese infantry battalions out of commission. A number of spoiling attacks launched by Sendai Division came acropper, and that set the planned final blow even farther back.

The air fighting over and around Guadalcanal and extending northwestward along the Slot as far as the Russell Islands and New Georgia remained intense but inconclusive. Sometimes the Cactus Air Force was on top, sometimes the Rabaul-based 11th Air Fleet was on top. Both sides inflicted losses upon the other, but each side had a different stake in the losses.

The Japanese were more easily able to replace airplane losses than they were pilot and aircrew losses. Every Japanese warplane that was severely damaged near Guadalcanal faced a 600-mile flight back to Rabaul or a somewhat shorter flight to one of several crude airstrips recently constructed along the way, but no closer than the southern end of Bougainville Island. If a Japanese warplane had to ditch or crash-land, there was a strong probability that the pilot or aircrew would never return.

On the other hand, the Marine, Navy, and Army pilots operating out of Henderson Field and a new grass satellite strip dubbed Fighter-1 were often close to home if they had to bail out, ditch, or crash-land. Though the scout-bombers often flew out to 150 miles or so, a network of friendly islanders overseen by British, Australian, and New Zealand coastwatchers worked throughout the Solomons providing both an early-warning network and a rescue apparatus. Cactus pilots and aircrew who survived bail-outs, crashes, and ditchings close to home distinctly had the odds on their side. Crash boats were instantly dispatched from the friendly shore whenever any airplane ditched in Ironbottom Sound or adjacent waters, and a small number of two- or three-place observation planes could be sent further afield to pluck downed aviators from the water or island beaches. Many of the small fraternity of top-scoring fighter aces survived multiple ditchings or crash landings only because of the proximity of the fighting to their fought-over base. (However, numerous precious pilots were killed or severely injured in the incessant bombings and shellings unleashed against their fought-over base.)

The thing the Americans had a hard time doing was fixing or replacing damaged or destroyed hardware. Had not the *Saratoga* and *Enterprise* air groups survived the damage done their departed ships, there is no telling where the Cactus Air Force might have found the minimal, overworked resources it employed to fend off the Japanese strikes from land, sea, and air. By September 28—when LCdr John Eldridge's Scouting-71, from *Wasp*, arrived at Cactus—fully half of the warplanes and aviators operating out of Henderson Field and Fighter-1 were from the Navy carrier air groups, and their number was in the decline because of battle losses, illness, and just plain physical and mental exhaustion.

卐

Hornet hid out during the last two weeks of September, though she was incessantly shadowed by Japanese long-range patrol bombers (many of which were shot down) and Japanese submarines. On at least a half dozen occasions after the loss of *Wasp*, alert lookouts and expert ship-handling saved the carrier from oncoming torpedoes. In this hunted manner, *Hornet* hovered at the edge of the action until October 2, when she steamed out of her patrol area to deliver an offensive blow against the Japanese rear. This was the first intentionally offensive action by a U.S. carrier since the start of the Solomons campaign.

The Japanese could not lift or support 17th Army to or at Guadalcanal without amassing sufficient ships in relatively close proximity to the objective. Early in the campaign, RAdm Raizo Tanaka, the Japanese transport chief, had selected the Shortland Islands as his base of operations. Located at the southern cape of Bougainville, the anchorage was ideal. It provided several superb harbors for vulnerable tankers, large supply ships, and transports well beyond the range of U.S. land-based bombers.

The Shortlands anchorages were close enough to Guadalcanal for fast troop-carrying warships to make an overnight dash straight down the Slot to Guadalcanal's Cape Esperance, or even far along the island's northern coast. Timed to perfection, the Japanese warships usually arrived at the extremity of the Cactus bombers' range at about dusk. If the Cactus searchers were alert, one hurried strike could be mounted. In any case, the Japanese warships could steam the rest of the way in relative safety—though several surprise night attacks were attempted by Cactus bombers. By dawn, the Japanese vessels would be long gone, far beyond the range of the frustrated Cactus bomber crews. Most nights, the Japanese warships compounded the frustration by hurling deadly 5-inch, 6-inch, and 8-inch rounds at the air-base complex or Marine infantry positions.

The only danger Admiral Tanaka's ships faced at the Shortlands anchorages was from U.S. submarines or U.S. carrier air. The submarines were Tanaka's headache, and he had to hold back a number of destroyers to counter the threat. The carrier air was beyond Tanaka's ability to counter, except at close range with anti-aircraft fire, so he left that mission to the Combined Fleet at Truk and the 11th Air Fleet units based at nearby Kahili and Kieta airfields.

RAdm George Murray and his superiors up the South Pacific Area chain of command set their sights on the fat targets based at the Shortlands anchorages. *Hornet* departed from a brief revictualing at Noumea on October 2 in the company of four cruisers and six destroyers and sailed into harm's way by a circuitous route well away from the Japanese submarines and scouts that daily patrolled around Torpedo Junction. As soon as she arrived in the Coral Sea after sunset on October 4, *Hornet* turned northwestward in the full of night and bent on all speed toward the objective.

The weather turned foul during the night, but there was nothing to do but keep going and hope that the skies would be clear in the morning. Bad weather the night before a major strike was not, after all, an entirely bad omen for a nation's only operational carrier sailing deep into enemy waters.

But the predawn launch was marred by endless vistas of low clouds and foul air higher up. Cdr Walt Rodee, the Air Group 8 commander, had some second thoughts, but he elected to keep them to himself. LCdr Gus Widhelm, the Scouting-8 squadron commander, gloated a bit, for he had consistently warned against dawn strikes that required predawn launches; the bad weather simply compounded his strongly held beliefs. LCdr Art Cumberledge, *Hornet*'s senior weather forecaster, looked into his crystal ball and told the senior decision makers, "Maybe over Bougainville it will be clear." Admiral Murray told the carrier's air officer to launch the strike.

The entire air group, less a strong combat air patrol, launched into the unlighted sky about 90 minutes before sunrise. The only guideposts the harried pilots had to mark the extremities of the flight deck were the reflection of the airplane exhaust flames off the faces of ship's crewmen watching the launch from the catwalks. The bombers were loaded to capacity, so they fell rather than flew off the end of the flight deck and had to be manhandled to altitude by the straining pilots, who also had to keep station on the plane ahead.

Lt(jg) Ivan Swope, of Scouting-8, was going through the usual mental and physical exertions when he was transfixed by the unexpected sight of a rapidly oncoming red light dead ahead. This was the light atop the mainmast of heavy cruiser *Northampton*, which was just then in the process of changing station from the carrier's starboard beam to dead ahead. Swope found the little something extra in his Dauntless's power plant to belly over the obstruction.

There were no accidents during the launch, an amazing feat.

Once clear of *Northampton*, Ivan Swope had to find the receding white light atop the plane ahead, which was piloted by Lieutenant Commander Widhelm. The only airplane in front of Widhelm's was Cdr Walt Rodee's command TBF. If Swope lost Widhelm, the entire air group of about sixty fighters and bombers would come unglued. Swope joined Widhelm without a problem, and each succeeding warplane did the same.

The *Hornet* strike ran into a giant cloud as it neared Bougainville at 14,000 feet. The only thing to do was forge ahead. Walt

Rodee knew that the formation would naturally spread out in the murk, but he was confident that it would reform on the far side.

It was not to be.

LCdr Gus Widhelm emerged from the murk after flying nearly the entire length of Bougainville. In fact, when he got his bearings, he found that he was nearing Buka Passage—at the far northern end of the island! Worse, only he, Lt(jg) Ivan Swope, and his other wingman were in sight. There was no sign of the rest of the air group.

Widhelm turned down Bougainville's east coast and flew directly to Kieta, where he and his two wingmen cratered the runway with their 1,000-pound bombs and a pair each of small 100-pound wing-mounted bombs. They also destroyed several newly constructed buildings with machine-gun fire.

The rest of Air Group 8 groped into the clear singly and in small packets. Several Torpedo-6 Avengers led by the squadron commander, Lt Iceberg Parker, found the Buin area of the Shortlands anchorages beneath the 700-foot ceiling, and a few of these managed to damage a tanker and two cargo ships among the numerous targets that packed the harbor. Avengers and Dauntlesses caused minor damage to ships anchored off nearby Faisi after executing abbreviated torpedo runs and glide-bombing attacks immediately upon popping out of the low clouds. A Fighting-72 Wildcat accounted for a float Zero there—the squadron's first kill of the war. Other Japanese ships and naval facilities much farther afield were also damaged. A group of Dauntlesses that found the airfield at Kahili had to battle through scrambling float Zeros to crater the runway and shoot up the facilities. Shots were exchanged over Kahili, and mutual damage was done, but neither side sustained any losses. Newly promoted Lt(jg) John Cresto, of Torpedo-6, succeeded in downing a float Zero over the Tonolei anchorage.

Miraculously, every strike aircraft safely returned to *Hornet*, which used the foul weather to help cover her escape. Japanese patrol bombers were sent to find her: A Kawanishi four-engine patrol bomber was downed by a Wildcat at 1005, a Betty medium bomber fell to a full Wildcat division 42 miles due south of the carrier at 1204, and Lt(jg) Henry Carey, of Fighting-72, got another

Betty 42 miles northwest of his flight deck at 1249. No other aircraft sightings were made, and *Hornet* was not directly molested.

Damage to Japanese ships and facilities was minimal. Indeed, the Japanese considered themselves lucky to have been rebuked for their laxity in such a mild way. Admiral Tanaka wound up being the chief benefactor of the raid when he heeded the warning and dispersed his resources over a far wider area of the northern Solomons. So, while American morale was given a boost by the audacity, if not the results, of the Shortlands raid, the Japanese gained the most by the inexpensive warning it afforded.

In the end, the rather bold raid did nothing to delay the Japanese juggernaut that would push the Lunga garrison to the brink of defeat.

卍

Beginning with the Shortlands raid by Air Group 8, events on both sides of the Solomons battle lines moved rapidly forward toward the cataclysmic confrontation the Japanese hoped would rid them once and for all of the American interlopers at Guadalcanal.

On the night of October 9, LtGen Harukichi Hyakutake landed at Cape Esperance with key members of the 17th Army staff and the bulk of Sendai Division's artillery group. He immediately proceeded to the north coast village of Kokumbona to establish his headquarters. As soon as Hyakutake was settled in, he ordered all the senior commanders ashore to his headquarters to plan the crushing land offensive.

Before General Hyakutake had left his rear headquarters in Rabaul, he had revealed some new-found sentiments regarding Guadalcanal: "The operation to surround and recapture Guadalcanal will truly decide the fate of the Pacific War." Perhaps Hyakutake meant what he said, but he still planned to launch the decisive land battle without all but a few detachments of the fresh infantry division he was holding back for the resumption of the New Guinea offensive.

On the other side, replacements had been found to assume rear-defense duties from the U.S. Army's 164th Infantry Regiment, a National Guard unit that had been among the very first

U.S. infantry units to be sent to the South Pacific near the start of the war. Once relieved, 164th Infantry was packed aboard a convoy of three troop transports guarded by three destroyers and three minelayers. As soon as the guardsmen were aboard the ships, the convoy, which was directly commanded by RAdm Kelly Turner, was sent toward Guadalcanal. If successful, the deployment of 164th Infantry would be followed by additional reinforcement efforts built around several more regiments of the Army's Americal Division and 2nd Marine Division.

Guarding the troop convoy from a distance were battle groups built around *Hornet* and battleship *Washington*. Closer in was a force of four cruisers and five destroyers—many of them formerly screening vessels for *Enterprise, Saratoga,* and *Wasp*. This force, commanded by RAdm Norman Scott, who had formerly commanded the *Wasp* screen, was standing by off Rennell Island on the afternoon of October 11 in the event the Japanese dispatched a surface force to strike Kelly Turner's transports.

In fact, a Japanese surface force was located in the Slot by long-range aerial searchers, but it was merely another troop-carrying effort bound for the beaches at Cape Esperance. What the searchers missed was a force of three cruisers and two destroyers that had been dispatched to bombard Henderson Field that night.

In the course of a wild, strange engagement off Cape Esperance the night of October 12–13, Admiral Scott's battle force utterly surprised and defeated the Japanese bombardment group. Scott lost one destroyer sunk, one light cruiser severely damaged, and one heavy cruiser moderately damaged. Against this, the Japanese lost one heavy cruiser and one destroyer sunk by Scott's warships. The Japanese flagship, a heavy cruiser, was damaged and the Japanese admiral commanding the bombardment force was mortally wounded.

Scott's nocturnal victory was considerably enhanced next morning, October 13, when Cactus searchers found two Japanese destroyers running up the Slot, their decks filled to capacity with sailors they had stayed to rescue from the sunken cruiser and destroyer. The two rescue ships were repeatedly bombed and strafed by relays of Cactus fighters and bombers throughout the morning.

One of the destroyers was sunk outright by a bomb dropped by LCdr John Eldridge, the commander of Scouting-71, and the other succumbed to a hammer-and-anvil torpedo attack by Torpedo-8.

The Battle of Cape Esperance was the U.S. Navy's first clear-cut victory since Midway. Occurring as it did within sight of Lunga Point, it was an immediate morale lifter for all the American forces ashore—not to mention all the Allied forces afloat throughout the Pacific. For the first time since the Savo battle, the Imperial Navy was put on notice that the U.S. Fleet was willing to engage in surface actions if doing so would help secure the airfield complex at Lunga.

The message was heard and understood, but then it was Japan's turn to win one.

29

Tuesday, October 13, dawned bright and clear at Guadalcanal. Marines and sailors on the beaches around Lunga Point saw a pair of fat fleet transports drop anchors off Lunga Point and watched incredulously as battle-equipped men streamed down the cargo nets slung over the transports' sides to waiting landing craft. And they stood stupefied as the boats disgorged those men on the beach. Reinforcements—the first U.S. Army regiment to be sent to Guadalcanal—had arrived. The long-promised relief of the beleaguered 1st Marine Division seemed to be underway. Once on the beach, the Dakota and Minnesota National Guardsmen of 164th Infantry Regiment took the inevitable intramural ribbing good-naturedly and marched off to their bivouacs between the beach and Henderson Field.

At just two minutes past noon, twenty-seven Rabaul-based Betty medium bombers, with a heavy Zero escort, dropped in unannounced over Henderson Field. Cactus Air launched all of its forty-two operational Wildcats, which arrived at combat level too late to intercept the bombers. Numerous 250-kilogram bombs dropped from 30,000 feet struck both Henderson Field and

Fighter-1 and destroyed 5,000 gallons of precious aviation gasoline stored in caches around the air-base complex. The Americans claimed a Zero and a Betty destroyed, for one Wildcat downed.

Black Tuesday had begun.

A second strike of eighteen Bettys and eighteen Zeros arrived over the airfield between 1330 and 1400. Unbelievably, the American fighters were again caught on the ground, still refueling after the earlier raid. Marine Capt Joe Foss, the unblooded executive officer of a newly arrived fighter squadron, VMF-121, led a dozen Wildcats after the Zeros, but the Bettys plastered both runways, causing severe damage. Only one American scored, and that was Joe Foss, whose damaged Wildcat piled up at the end of Fighter-1 at the conclusion of the raid. The bombing was a complete success. Both runways, which Seabees had just gotten back into shape, were holed from end to end.

卐

Japanese artillerymen had for days been hauling a freshly committed regiment of 15cm howitzers to fresh emplacements west of the Lunga Perimeter. As the day's second air raid flew from sight to the west, the Japanese gunners registered their artillery pieces on the American enclave with slow, methodical precision. The new hazard, not yet fully perceived, made dead men out of more than one conscientious Seabee or Marine engineer working in the open around the runways. The 15cm rounds were fired into the Lunga Perimeter until nightfall.

卐

A Japanese task force built around battleships *Haruna* and *Kongo* slowly lurked toward Lunga Roads, undetected by American search aircraft grounded as the result of runway damage. Each dreadnought carried 500 36cm high-capacity bombardment shells, a type never before used against land targets.

It began with the *put-put* of an underpowered fabric spotter floatplane arriving over Lunga Point to drop flares for the battleship gunners. Once the target area had been sufficiently lighted, *Kongo*'s captain ordered his gunnery officer to begin registering the new

36cm shells. The first salvoes walked right up the beach toward a Marine regimental command post. There, numerous Marines and Guardsmen who were passing through were killed or wounded or at least scared half to death. After several salvos had been fired, the Japanese task force commander ordered his flotilla gunnery officer to resume firing as soon as the moving warships could turn at the end of their firing leg and beat back up the channel off Lunga Point.

The holocaust was horrible, chaotic, as stunned, waking men burst from their sleeping places and bolted for secure underground shelters. Buildings, huts, and tents were ripped open, spilling their contents onto the trembling earth. Steel splinters, wreckage, purple-dyed 36cm baseplates cut through the air to slice holes in trees, tents, trucks, aircraft, and men. Gasoline—more precious fuel— went up in smoky circles of unbearable heat, casting enormous shadows before the exulting Japanese gunners. In the target area, throughout the Lunga Perimeter, terrified men were beset by tens of thousands of terrified rats, which were shaken from their shelters by the awful shelling and sent in scurrying multitudes into the holes and across the backs of cowering Marines, sailors, and soldiers.

A near miss beside the Marine division's command post lifted the division commander from his perch at the end of a bench and unceremoniously dropped him on the damp earth. Another blast injured men around the Marine artillery regiment's command post. Field telephones whose wire survived the pounding brought steady news of irreparable damage and mounting despair throughout the Lunga Perimeter. Two Marine rifle battalions occupying Bloody Ridge—just south of Henderson Field—took the brunt of the "overs" aimed at the main runway but were spared the worst possible fate by the soft, rain-soaked earth, which absorbed most of the killing effects of the huge rounds and smaller shells from accompanying cruisers and destroyers. A direct hit on the tent housing pilots from a newly arrived Marine Dauntless squadron, VMSB-141, killed the squadron commander and executive and flight officers as well as killing or seriously wounding most of the squadron's senior pilots.

When *Kongo* and *Haruna* and their cruiser and destroyer escorts used the last of their ammunition at 0230, they stood out of the channel, their wakes ineffectually dogged by four newly arrived American motor torpedo (PT) boats. However, before anyone in the Lunga Perimeter could organize damage-control parties, a chain of Japanese night bombers arrived to make matters worse. A direct hit on the garrison's main radio station prevented word of the disaster from going out until nearly dawn. By that time, forty-one Americans were dead, and dozens of others were wounded, some mortally.

⚛

The damage was staggering. Thirty-two of thirty-seven Marine and Navy SBDs were damaged or destroyed, and all of Torpedo-8's remaining TBFs were disabled. Of all the Cactus warplanes dispersed around the bomber strip, only two new Army P-39 and four old Army P-400 fighter-bombers survived the night intact. The Cactus Air Force's offensive capability was nil, though Fighter-1 had only been lightly shelled and bombed, and most of the American Wildcats had escaped serious damage.

On the morning of October 14, Henderson Field was incapable of supporting any sort of flight operations. Nearly every gallon of aviation gasoline had gone up during the night or was burning off in the light of the new day. Air operations had to be switched to Fighter-1.

Among the hostages of the bombardment were the crews of six B-17s under the commander of the Army's 11th Heavy Bombardment Group. The B-17s, which had struck Japanese transports on October 13 in an unprecedentedly long mission to Buka Passage, north of Bougainville, and Buna, in northern New Guinea, had been obliged to stop off at Guadalcanal to refuel. The bombers had been kept aloft by the October 13 noon bombing, then grounded by BGen Roy Geiger, the Marine Cactus Air Force commander, who could not spare the required fuel from his burning stocks. As soon as it was light enough to work, the bomber crews went out onto the main runway to clear a path through the sharp shell splinters that littered the area in thick profusion. (As one of the B-17 crew chiefs prepared his airplane for the journey to Espiritu Santo, he boosted a 17-pound hunk of shrapnel out of the pilot's seat.) Only four of the six B-17s were airworthy, and they barely managed to fly off the abbreviated 2,000-foot patch of steel-mat-covered runway optimistically referred to as "operational." The group commander reluctantly ordered the destruction of the two grounded B-17s, which were crammed with super-secret devices.

With no fuel, there would be no defense. Someone remembered that small caches of fuel had been hidden here and there around the Lunga Perimeter weeks earlier. A search was given top priority and, as the day lengthened, the small hoard was painstakingly assembled. Even the nearly empty tanks of the two scuttled B-17s were sucked dry. But it was not nearly enough.

The fighters were scrambled at 0930, October 14, on the strength of a coastwatcher report, but no Japanese aircraft materialized. Twenty-six Bettys, which had flown far off course to kill time while the American fighters used up their limited fuel, struck Henderson Field while the fighters were refueling on Fighter-1. There was no opposition from the Cactus Air Force.

Thirteen F4Fs and eight Army fighters met an 1130 strike of eighteen Bettys and creamed it. Navy fighter pilots destroyed five of the bombers, and the Marines got four Bettys and three Zeros for one loss of their own. It was a meager salve.

An afternoon search to the north by several repaired Dauntlesses uncovered two separate Japanese convoys. The first consisted of six troop-laden transports and eight destroyer-transports heading for Cape Esperance. Two cruisers and two destroyers were also coming on fast, undoubtedly to bombard the runways.

The plight of the Cactus Air Force was so desperate that General Geiger told his airmen that they would fly to the last, then join ground units to repel land or amphibious assaults.

As 15cm shells burst in and around their repair shops, Marine ground crew wrestled with the damaged aircraft, cutting parts from the wrecks to build flyable bombers and fighters. The first offensive strike of four SBDs and seven P-400s went after the transport convoy at 1445 but scored no hits. A second attack mounted at 1545 by seven Navy SBDs was met by heavy antiaircraft fire over the transports and came up empty; an accompanying P-400 was shot down, and a second was lost in a landing after dark.

The only entry on the plus side of the Cactus Air Force's profit-and-loss statement for October 14 was the arrival of a mixed squadron of former *Enterprise* Dauntlesses brought under the command of LCdr Ray Davis and designated Bombing-6. This was the very last contingent of dive-bombers and dive-bomber crews from the three carriers that had been damaged or lost since August 24.

Japanese cruisers and destroyers struck the Lunga Perimeter that night while the six transports disembarked the infantry and their equipment. The cruisers alone dumped 750 8-inch shells on the Lunga Perimeter.

卐

Thursday's dawn—October 15—was a relief. But the sunlit waters to the west disclosed an act of damning gall. In easy view of Lunga Point, the six Japanese transports were methodically and unhurriedly disembarking troops and supplies at Tassafaronga.

The first American aircraft aloft were a pair of P-400s, each armed with two 100-pound bombs for their routine dawn patrol. No sooner had the pilots gotten their wheels up than the Cactus Air Force operations center announced the arrival of numerous Zeros in the area. Both Army airmen turned inland and followed a line of clouds around toward Cape Esperance, where, the air operations center said, there were ample targets. The two P-400s bombed and strafed the transports under the guns of several Zeros, but the brave Army pilots were forced to retire for lack of fuel. The results of this tiny strike, and several like it launched by Navy and Marine Wildcats, were negligible.

卐

Obsessed with an unquenchable rage, BGen Roy Geiger's air- and ground crews drained the last of the fuel from the tanks of wrecked aircraft and gasoline drums and pieced together more SBDs from the profusion of spare parts that littered the field and its environs. As the morning wore on, aircraft composed largely of other aircraft rolled off the reassembly lines one by one and took off to deliver solo attacks on the transports down the beach, which were protected at all times by shipboard antiaircraft guns and no less than thirty-two long-range Zero fighters. Hits were scored and two of the ships had to be beached, afire, amidst the cheers of the shell-shocked gawkers lining the beaches around Lunga Point. But the toll in airmen and aircraft became prohibitive, so General Geiger ordered the bombers grounded until a reasonable number could be collected for a coordinated strike.

Gasoline continued to be found throughout the Perimeter in 40- and 50-drum lots, each drum representing an hour's flying time for a Cactus Wildcat. And word from rear area headquarters indicated that several large gasoline barges were being towed up, and that several ships were on the way with deck loads of aviation gasoline drums.

General Geiger ordered literally everyone to work. He was out for blood. Those who could fly would fly, those who could not would do what they could; Lt Swede Larsen, whose Torpedo-8 had no aircraft, took his pilots and ground crew out to Bloody Ridge to fight as infantry. And Geiger's personal PBY-5A was pressed into service to deliver a pair of aerial torpedoes against the Japanese transports. The Catalina was severely damaged in an attack loosely coordinated with a strike by seven baled-together Dauntlesses, but one of its torpedoes found a target.

B-17s from Espiritu Santo scored three hits upon the Japanese transports for dozens of bombs dropped from high altitude, and SBDs, P-39s, and P-40os caused additional damage at the cost of three Marine aircraft and crews.

With the Cactus Air Force growing stronger by the hour, the Japanese decided to leave before the remaining three transports were sunk or severely damaged. Despite the very best efforts of the American aircrews, a company of medium tanks and nearly 4,000 crack infantrymen and technicians were landed with many tons of supplies.

⚛

Only one major air strike was launched by 11th Air Fleet on October 15, though harassment continued unabated through the day. At 1245, twenty-seven Bettys and nine Zeros were over Henderson Field without a Cactus fighter anywhere in the vicinity. Several fighters did get aloft, but only one Zero was downed by Fighting-5's only operational Wildcat.

Air strength ebbed and flowed through the afternoon of October 15. Without aircraft to fly, fifteen exhausted Army and Navy fighter pilots and Marine dive-bomber pilots were evacuated by air from Guadalcanal. On the other hand, six pilots from a rear-based Marine fighter squadron, VMF-212, ferried up the last six spare SBDs available in the South Pacific; these pilots were returned to Espiritu Santo by air to rejoin their fighter squadron, which was to move to Cactus the next day.

In all on October 15, one float biplane and six Zeros were downed over Guadalcanal at a cost of three SBDs, two P-39s, and an F4F in which four American pilots and three aerial gunners were killed.

卐

Following the October 15 daytime action, Henderson Field was hit for the third night in a row, this time by a cruiser force sent down from the main Japanese fleet anchorage at Truk. Nearly 1,500 8-inch shells were fired beginning at 0030, but Fighter-1 and the repair shops were spared serious harm. It was by then obvious that the Japanese did not know the importance of the little grass strip, for they invariably fired at the main runway.

At dawn, Friday, October 16, BGen Roy Geiger counted ten SBDs on line with four P-39s and three P-400s, plus a reasonable number of Wildcats. While conferring early that morning with Fighting-5's skipper, LCdr Roy Simpler, Geiger blurted out in frustration, "Roy, I don't believe we have a fucking Navy." Simpler had been through the worst of times with Geiger, but he retained his loyalty to his service. "General, if we have a Navy, I know where to find it." Geiger told Simpler to do that little thing, and Simpler climbed into the cockpit of one of Fighting-5's two remaining Wildcats. As soon as he was aloft, he flew southward, across Guadalcanal, and straight out to sea. He had about reached his point of no return when he spotted an American carrier task force, a sight to take the breath away on the best of days. Aircraft had been launched, so Simpler approached with caution, fighting the impulse to declare an emergency so he could land aboard the carrier and partake of a decent meal. But he could not; he flew to his home away from home and landed at Fighter-1. Once assured that a friendly, intact carrier air group was in the area, General Geiger arranged a little retribution.

First, *Hornet*'s fresh Air Group 8 assumed responsibility for protecting the sky over Henderson Field—a relief of the first magnitude. While the bulk of Air Group 8 protected U.S. holdings on Guadalcanal, Scouting-8 was sent up the Slot to find and sink crippled Japanese warships. When nothing but a huge oil slick was found, LCdr Gus Widhelm led his Dauntlesses across Santa Ysabel's central cordillera and threw in a quick strike against the Japanese seaplane base at Rekata Bay, a source of no end of dismay for the carriers cruising Torpedo Junction as well as for the Lunga garrison.

Lt(jg) Ivan Swope, once again flying on Gus Widhelm's wing, found a float Zero in his gunsight—one of a dozen lined up on the beach. Swope unleashed a stream of rounds from his two cowl-mounted .50-caliber machine guns and clearly saw his bullets knocking chunks off the wings, fuselage, and float, but no fire developed until he was under 300 feet. By that time, Swope was paying more attention to the coconut palms lining the beach than he was to his target. As he pulled out to the left, however, he saw the float Zero had begun to burn. Before Swope completed his turn, he saw a cache of fuel drums hidden beneath camouflage netting. Concerned that another Dauntless pilot would beat him to the target, Lieutenant (jg) Swope climbed to only 1,000 feet, transmitted his intent to the other pilots, and initiated a low-level glide-bombing attack. His 1,000-pound bomb started a magnificent blaze in the middle of the fuel dump.

Scouting-8 departed without incurring any damage following a wild ten-minute spree of destruction. It left twelve wrecked float Zeros and a beach area marked by the thick black smoke of numerous fuel fires. It was an altogether satisfying catharsis.

Other *Hornet* warplanes mounted a succession of strikes at

known Japanese dumps along Guadalcanal's northern coast and troop concentrations wherever they could be found. And all returned safely to their ship.

卐

One Marine SBD was lost to ground fire during October 16, and several P-400s all but fell apart from wear. Late that afternoon, the last pilots and aircrew of Fighting-5 departed Henderson Field with the survivors of a Marine fighter and a Marine scout-bomber squadron aboard Marine transport aircraft, and the staff of the Marine air group that had been running the Cactus Air Force since August 20 was replaced by a fresh Marine air-group staff.

One of the day's most important arrivals was seaplane tender *MacFarland*, a converted four-stack destroyer that brought up over 40,000 gallons of aviation gasoline in 750 deck-loaded drums. The first 400 drums had been unloaded and dispersed when nine *Zuikaku* Val dive-bombers arrived over the area. The Vals, which had been out all day vainly searching for *Hornet*, were on the way home to their temporary base at the Buin emergency air strip.

There were many aircraft aloft as the Vals came up from the usually friendly south, so no alert was issued. LCdr Roy Simpler, who had decided to sail south aboard *MacFarland* when there proved to be one seat less than needed aboard the transport aircraft that had taken out the last of his Fighting-5 pilots, noted the heightened activity over the field and told the ship's captain that he had better get some sea room fast, for Cactus airmen never went aloft for training. Next thing Simpler knew, several Vals were heading right for him. A single bomb hit the barge carrying the last 350 fuel drums, spreading flaming gasoline all over the place. A second bomb detonated on *MacFarland*'s fantail and killed or maimed nearly a dozen departing Fighting-5 ground crew.

LtCol Joe Bauer, who had knocked down four Zeros in one sortie during a familiarization flight about a week earlier, was in the traffic circle over Fighter-1, the last aloft of twenty VMF-212 pilots who had just flown up from Efate by way of Espiritu Santo. He went after the Vals alone as soon as he spotted the pillar of smoke from the burning fuel barge, and caught them as they were recovering from their dives. Down they went: one, two, three, four. Minutes later, Bauer landed at Fighter-1 on the last of his fuel. He had earned a Medal of Honor for his back-to-back four-plane kills.

Half of 40,000 gallons of vitally needed aviation gasoline was lost.

MacFarland, which had shot down one of the Vals herself, limped out of the channel, steering on her engines. She was eventually towed up a river channel in nearby Florida Island and repaired while under a camouflage of jungle greenery. Next day, a minesweeper carried out LCdr Roy Simpler and the 160 used-up Navy and Marine ground crew who had survived the attack on *MacFarland*.

⁂

The night of October 16–17 passed more quietly than previous nights; most of the Japanese warships in the area were out looking for *Hornet*, which was retiring. However, the Cactus Air Force learned that Pacific Fleet Intelligence had tumbled to Japanese plans to launch two massive air strikes the next day.

While on a routine dawn patrol around Cape Esperance in a P-400 fighter-bomber, Army 1stLt Frank Holmes chanced upon a find of incredible importance. Flying nearly at wave-top height, paralleling the beach, Holmes saw odd reddish shapes, the same color as the ground, humped up beneath the trees along the beach. Mindful that untoward curiosity might warn the Japanese, Holmes highballed it for Fighter-1 and commandeered a ride to the air operations center to tell of his find—hundreds of square yards of tarp-covered supplies carried ashore from Japanese transports on October 15. The Cactus Air commanders at first thought to call in a heavy-bomber strike, but a pair of American destroyers anchored off Tulagi were ordered across the channel to walk 5-inch shells from the inland side of the dump toward the beach. They took an enormous and irreplaceable toll of the goods the Japanese had landed at so much cost.

The first Japanese air strike of October 17 arrived early. Eighteen Vals and eighteen Zeros, all from carrier squadrons temporarily based at Buin, were intercepted at 0720 by eight Marine

303

Wildcats as they went after the destroyers that were shelling 17th Army's main forward supply dumps. The destroyers were not hit, but six Vals and four Zeros were downed. One Wildcat was lost, but its pilot was saved.

Following the morning strike, three SBDs spotted targets for the destroyers, which, with a succession by Army fighter-bombers and a flight of six B-17s, blasted the dumps to oblivion.

࿕

Numerous Japanese destroyers and cruisers managed to reach Guadalcanal unnoticed that night, but, while most unloaded troops and supplies at Cape Esperance and Tassafaronga, only five destroyers fired an ineffectual ten-minute barrage at Fighter-1.

After a morning air strike on October 18 was spotted over New Georgia by a coastwatcher, sixteen Wildcats downed three of fifteen Bettys and four of nine Buin-based *Zuikaku* Zeros. The Marines lost one F4F in a takeoff mishap and two in combat, all without pilot loss.

That was the end of it. Eleventh Air Fleet's offensive against Henderson Field had shot its bolt; the Japanese air groups were gutted.

With plenty of gasoline in stock and on the way, and a growing crop of fresh aircrews in operation or coming up, the Cactus Air Force was clearly resurgent.

30

The Japanese were rapidly moving toward what they believed would be the decisive confrontation of the Guadalcanal campaign and, perhaps, the entire Pacific War.

Though weaker in other key necessities, the U.S. combat forces arrayed in the South Pacific Area, or available on short notice, had a distinct advantage over the Japanese in the area of advance information. U.S. Naval Intelligence had long since decrypted the Japanese operational codes, and the U.S. Pacific war effort had been run largely upon the gleanings of that effort. The Midway battle had been planned by the U.S. Navy almost entirely on the basis of information the Japanese unwittingly but quite literally telegraphed ahead.

The combination of the punishing blows administered against Henderson Field in mid-October and decrypted Japanese message traffic pointed to the unmistakable conclusion that the major effort at and around Guadalcanal would begin—and end—on the night of October 21, 1942.

It was just so. The Japanese indeed *planned* to mount and win their three-dimensional—air, land, and naval—offensive on

October 21 and 22, 1942, but last-minute operational glitches prevented them from doing so. The offensive was postponed by means of a rolling delay; when all of its many elements were in place, it would be mounted on short notice. However, profound communications difficulties among and between the Japanese ground-combat elements arrayed at various points around the Lunga Perimeter resulted in a premature feint attack on the American western flank on the evening of October 23. This early attack was beaten back with some difficulty to the Marines and at great expense in manpower and morale to the Japanese.

卐

For its part, the U.S. Pacific command was in something of a state of turmoil arising out of a late-September command inspection by the U.S. Pacific Fleet commander, Adm Chester Nimitz. As a direct result of Nimitz's stopover at Guadalcanal to meet with the Marine commander, MGen Archer Vandegrift, and an overnight stay at Noumea to confer with the South Pacific Area commander, VAdm Bob Ghormley, Nimitz had decided to replace Ghormley with a more aggressive leader. The decision had been an agonizing one for Nimitz, who thought well of his old friend, but who also realized that Ghormley had burned out under the pressures of his onerous job.

It took until October 15 for Nimitz to reach a firm decision— one in which he was substantially assisted by a wide range of subordinates who unabashedly recommended Ghormley's relief. In the end, it was decided to replace Ghormley with VAdm Bill Halsey, who happened to be on an inspection tour of the South Pacific preparatory to replacing the injured VAdm Frank Jack Fletcher as permanent commander of Task Force 61.

Halsey's trip was arrested in mid-flight on October 18, as he was traveling by small boat between his amphibious transport plane and the dock at Noumea. A sealed envelope presented to Halsey by a member of Ghormley's personal staff contained a terse message ordering him to immediately relieve Ghormley and assume command of the South Pacific Area and all Allied forces therein. Both admirals were thunderstruck by what appeared to them to be Nimitz's precipitous decision. In the end, however, Ghormley appeared to be emotionally relieved by the change.

Halsey instantly went to work to clean out the Ghormley people and assemble a new staff from among the many suitable officers with whom he had come in contact over the years. Since the new area commander was a carrier officer, he naturally turned to men on duty with Task Force 61. This led to some dislocations, but none that could not be worked out on the run.

The crisis around Guadalcanal rapidly developed upon the heels of the change of command. It would take Halsey some time to institute many of the changes implicitly required by his elevation, and that prevented him from immediately visiting Guadalcanal, as he would have liked. Thus, when the expected Japanese main offensive was not launched on October 21, Marine General Vandegrift took the opportunity to make a fast trip to Noumea to personally brief the new area commander.

The simmering crisis on land did not await Vandegrift's return to fully burst upon the Lunga defenders. On the evening of October 24, the island commander was conferring with Halsey and other senior officers when the Japanese hurled a magnificent surprise ground assault directly against two thinly spread Marine and Army battalions holding the fought-over ground at Bloody Ridge, just south of Henderson Field. The Japanese were beaten back with grievous losses, but they did not concede the fight.

Throughout October 25, as the Japanse infantry regrouped outside of the range of Marine artillery, Japanese air squadrons kept up an intense pressure and, for the first time in months, Japanese surface warships defied the Cactus Air Force and appeared in waters directly adjacent to the Lunga Perimeter to help support 17th Army's land offensive. U.S. warships in the area came under direct surface attack, and a fleet tug and patrol vessel were sunk within sight of Lunga Point.

The entire Lunga Perimeter was effectively bombarded through most of the day by ships, planes, and land-based artillery. It was a day the Marines and soldiers defending Lunga had ample reason to name Dugout Sunday.

In return, an unchastened Cactus Air Force struck at the brazen—and surprised—Japanese warships through the day. One light cruiser, *Yura*, was disabled and eventually sunk by the Cactus bombers.

On the night of October 25, LtGen Harukichi Hyakutake's 17th Army finally got itself sorted out and launched its planned two-pronged pincers attack upon the southern and western flanks of the Lunga Perimeter. Fortunately for the defenders, both wings of the Japanese land force had been morally defeated and had suffered grievous losses in their uncoordinated, days-apart initial assaults. Thus, against all expectations, October 26 dawned at Guadalcanal as an American dawn.

That dawn, also, awaited the results of history's fourth carrier versus carrier naval and air confrontation.

31

The orders that sent the Imperial Navy's Combined Fleet into action at the end of October 1942 were inextricably linked with the same general directives issued by Imperial General Headquarters in Tokyo that launched 17th Army's abortive land assault on Guadalcanal.

Though the Imperial Army and Imperial Navy had been making some small attempts within the battle arena to arrive at a mutually beneficial working relationship, the long-term effects of a bitter traditional interservice rivalry had proven too strong to overcome by even the realities of the life-and-death Guadalcanal struggle. On the broader plane, both partners were equally at fault. The Army had had to wring personal concessions from Adm Isoroku Yamamoto, the Combined Fleet commander, in order to facilitate its Tokyo-ordained October offensive. However, once the concessions were becoming reality, 17th Army dealt Combined Fleet out of the operational planning. Even more important, 17th Army did not share the details of its final plans—nor even its intelligence estimates—with Combined Fleet. The result was that, except for sharing key dates and making requests of each other, each service went ahead with its own planning without consulting the other. The result was the birth of a pair of nonidentical twins: two separate battles based upon two different strategies that would be undertaken at roughly the same time in two separate but overlaid arenas.

卍

For its part, the Combined Fleet was less interested in helping 17th Army win back Guadalcanal than it was in achieving mastery over the U.S. Navy in the eastern Solomons and, by extension, in all Pacific waters. The Imperial Navy was no longer certain how many operational carriers remained in the U.S. service, but its most senior commanders felt that the number was very low. On the rather broader strategic plane upon which those commanders operated, the objective was the destruction of the *will* of the U.S. Navy to conduct meaningful strategic operations. For, without a viable navy, the United States simply could not conduct an offensive—or much of a defensive—policy in the broad Pacific expanses. Thus the upcoming operation was seen as a global imperative, and the commitment to it was as nearly total as had been the commitment at Midway. But it was also seen as a cleanup operation, which is a role that had never seriously been contemplated for Midway.

The U.S. Navy would certainly be obliged to commit all or nearly all of its few remaining carriers to the showdown, and that could lead to the ultimate victory the flagging Japanese war machine urgently required in mid-1942.

卍

At the local level, Combined Fleet for once did its best to live up to the personal oath Admiral Yamamoto had made to a senior 17th Army representative. Indeed, senior Combined Fleet staffers at Truk had rather naïvely timed their entire operation as if 17th Army would flawlessly live up to its timetable and assurances of ultimate victory.

The naval actions that had been undertaken in daylight on October 25 by the Rabaul-based 8th Fleet in Ironbottom Sound and adjacent waters—actions that resulted in damage to several destroyers and the loss of light cruiser *Yura*—had been an unusual sign of good faith on the part of the Navy. This exhibition of trust—and the movement of vast Combined Fleet battle units from Truk—was met with stony silence from 17th Army. Combined Fleet was not even informed by Army sources that the land assault against the Lunga Perimeter had failed at every point and that 17th Army was withdrawing from the assault.

In support of 17th Army's "victory" at Guadalcanal, the largest force of Japanese carriers since the Midway battle had been assembled in waters between Truk and the eastern Solomons, and Admiral Yamamoto had committed it to another iteration of his final-battle strategy.

᭰

The entire Japanese naval combat force—dubbed the Guadalcanal Support Force and commanded at sea by VAdm Nobutake Kondo—was divided into four forces: Kondo's Advance Force, VAdm Chuichi Nagumo's Striking Force, VAdm Gunichi Mikawa's Outer Seas Force, and VAdm Teruhisa Komatsu's Advanced Expeditionary Force. Admiral Yamamoto, with still other naval units at his immediate disposal, would oversee the operation from his flagship, which would remain at anchor in Truk lagoon.

The Advance Expeditionary Force, an operational component of Vice Admiral Komatsu's 6th Fleet, was composed of eleven fleet submarines strung along a vast screening line. As always, the submarines were to monitor the U.S. Fleet and report sightings, as well as attack Allied ships when possible.

Vice Admiral Mikawa's Outer Seas Force, an operational subsidiary of his 8th Fleet, staged out of Rabaul and the Shortlands anchorages. Its role was to support the 17th Army land offensive, and it suffered for its devotion to the mission when it bore the brunt of U.S. land-based daylight air attacks on October 25.

The Advance Force, which was directly commanded by Vice Admiral Kondo, was divided into the Main Body (five cruisers and six destroyers), the Air Group (one fleet carrier, one light carrier, and four destroyers), and the Support Group (two battleships and six destroyers). It would range ahead of the other major Combined Fleet formation, the Striking Force, by only 60 miles. With any luck, it would both draw off some of the power of the expected U.S. carrier-air attack and be in a position to dash forward to directly engage U.S. warships.

Nagumo's Striking Force was divided into the Carrier Group (two fleet carriers, one light carrier, one cruiser, and eight destroyers) and the Vanguard Group (two battleships, four cruisers, and seven destroyers). As its name implies, this was the force for the U.S. warships to reckon with.

In all, the Advance and Striking forces comprised three fleet carriers, two light carriers, four battleships, eight heavy cruisers, two light cruisers, and thirty-one destroyers.

The Santa Cruz scheme devised by Combined Fleet was quite different from—but also quite the same as—the defeated Coral Sea, Midway, and Eastern Solomons concoctions. For once, no landing force was tied to the naval operation, and no bait was put out. Also, the main Japanese battle formations were within supporting range of one another.

A quite different feature was that a very powerful surface battle force was placed *in front* of the carrier striking force. It is clear that the Japanese planners hoped that the Advance Force would serve as a useful buffer between the expected U.S. retaliatory air strikes and the main body of Japanese carriers. But this is not to say that the planners were using the Advance Force entirely as a means to draw off U.S. air strikes. Unlike the ill-fated Mobile Force built around expendable *Ryujo* at Eastern Solomons, the Advance Force in October was an extraordinarily powerful battle force well able to fend for itself, and it had a meaningful mission that was central to the Japanese master plan. That mission was to track down and destroy the main U.S. battle force operating in support of the Lunga garrison. It was, in every way, a formidable mobile striking force.

Initially, the Guadalcanal Support Force counted three fleet carriers and two light carriers. Two of the fleet carriers—*Shokaku* and *Zuikaku*—and one light carrier—*Zuiho*—comprised the Carrier Group of VAdm Chuichi Nagumo's Striking Force. One new fleet carrier—*Junyo*—and the other light carrier—*Hiyo*—comprised the

Air Group of VAdm Nobutake Kondo's Advance Force. However, on October 22, *Hiyo* was disabled by an engine room fire and had to be dispatched under escort to the Truk anchorage for repairs. It thus *appeared* that *Junyo* might be the bait, for she was one carrier alone with an advance force of surface warships. However, in a radical departure from previously ill-starred plans, *Junyo* was to remain within easy support range of the larger carrier force. Her job was to support the advance surface force and not—specifically not—to act as bait.

Oddly, many senior Japanese officers were not informed that their side was initiating the action, nor even that it was in support of the Army grand assault against the Lunga Perimeter. Cdr Masatake Okumiya, a senior and experienced staff officer embarked in *Junyo*, heard from senior briefers that the foray from Truk was simply in response to a U.S. Navy initiative involving several U.S. carriers.

🔁

Notwithstanding Commander Okumiya's ignorance of his own service's strategic imperatives and initiatives, the essence of his information was correct: The U.S. Pacific Fleet *was* seeking a confrontation with the Combined Fleet. The germ of the bold U.S. plan was conceived by Adm Chester Nimitz during his rather disheartening South Pacific tour of late September and early October. Nimitz's decision to name VAdm Bill Halsey to the South Pacific command was emblematic of his desire to breathe life into the psychologically stalled Solomons offensive. Halsey was known as an aggressive combatant; he had been active in the early part of the war, striking at Japanese bases throughout the Pacific with his limited carrier strength. His chief contribution had been as commander of the two-carrier task force from which LtCol Jimmy Doolittle's small force of Army B-25 medium bombers had been launched against Tokyo in April 1942. Great things had been expected of Halsey until he was laid low by medical problems on the eve of Midway. His reinstatement as Fletcher's replacement, and his ultimate elevation to the area command, had sent gleeful shivers of anticipation right through the heart of the Pacific Fleet.

On October 16, the very day he forwarded Halsey's name to Washington as his choice to replace Ghormley, Nimitz implemented a bold gamble aimed at giving the combative Halsey the means for seizing anew the initiative that had been lost at Savo. Though the wounds *Enterprise* had suffered at the Battle of the Eastern Solomons were by no means fully healed, that ship was precipitously ordered out of the Pearl Harbor repair facilities. The carrier task force of which *Enterprise* was the center made all speed to the south to join *Hornet*. Once Task Force 61 had been reconstituted as a multicarrier battle force, it was to sweep into Japanese-dominated waters to seek out and bring to battle the main elements of the Combined Fleet. Thus the two surviving *Yorktown*-class carriers were to be reunited for the first time since Midway, and they were to operate again under the combative Bill Halsey for the first time since the breathtaking Tokyo raid in April.

32

☀

Wounded *Enterprise* had made her way to friendly Tongatabu immediately after the bloody ordeal of the Battle of the Eastern Solomons. There, her war-weary crew had been allowed to intersperse the hours of grueling repair work with deserved shore leave in a true South Pacific paradise. The damaged carrier was still at Tongatabu when the news reached her that *Saratoga* had been torpedoed.

During the stay at Tongatabu, *Enterprise*'s air group was reduced to a mere dozen warplanes. All the rest that had survived Eastern Solomons were flown off to make good the climbing losses at Guadalcanal or to help bolster the defenses at bases immediately to the rear of the Solomons battle arena. Air Group 6 was disbanded in all but name.

When *Enterprise* was deemed seaworthy for a long journey, she was dispatched to the superb Pearl Harbor Navy Yard—a real disappointment to all hands, who were certain that the only repair facility capable of handling the carrier was at Bremerton, Washington, from which home leave could be taken. Except for a rampant epidemic of dysentery, the long sea journey, undertaken in

315

September, was relaxing for just about everyone aboard the vast carrier. All hands faced a tight, unremitting refitting and training schedule they knew would be leavened by the first decent liberty schedule they had experienced since the previous December.

Enterprise entered the Pearl Harbor Navy Yard on September 10, 1942. Five days later, *Wasp* was destroyed by three Japanese torpedoes. The news electrified the pace of the already frenetic repair work.

The men returned from the war found some strange attitudes among the men supporting the war. LCdr Orlin Livdahl, the carrier's gunnery officer, was greeted upon his arrival at Pearl Harbor by a representative of the Navy's Bureau of Ships who had brought along a comprehensive plan, complete with drawings, for the replacement and bolstering of the inadequate 1.1-inch gun batteries with modern director-guided quadruple 40mm mounts. The new Swedish Bofors guns had a slower rate of fire than the despised Swiss Oerlikons, but they were more reliable, they had a greater range, and they could cause more damage. That was fine with Livdahl, but he was not happy with the planned placement of the 40mm guns. From the standpoint of gunnery alone, the placement of the new mounts would reduce the firing arc that had made the dismal 1.1-inch guns as successful as they had been. Equally important, the ship's executive and air officers determined by means of a scale-model mock-up that the proposed placement of the 40mm guns would reduce the parking of planes on the flight deck by four precious spaces. After detailed consultations with the ship's air officer, Lieutenant Commander Livdahl redrew the plans. However, he ran into an immediate roadblock when the bureaucrats running the Navy Yard told him they were not authorized to change Bureau of Ships plans. So Livdahl went to his ship's outgoing captain, Arthur Davis, who arranged a conference with the yard engineer and the senior officer whose employ he had left months earlier to assume command of the carrier—Adm Chester Nimitz. Next morning, the Pacific Fleet commander patiently listened to both sides of the argument. The yard engineers said that it would take weeks to prepare new plans and have them approved by the Bureau of Ships. The *Enterprise* people said that the 1.1-inch guns had already been removed and that their proposed placement of the new guns and their ammunition stowage had already been marked out on the decks, that work could get immediately underway. Admiral Nimitz asked the yard engineers one question: Could they locate the guns where Livdahl wanted them without interfering with the scheduled date of completion. The engineers allowed as they could, to which Nimitz said, "Do it." And they did.

Other modifications included the installation of a radar direction system for the carrier's 5-inch guns and the addition of super-secret radar-guided proximity shells to the 5-inch magazines. (The radar could "see" targets through cloud cover, and the proximity shells would detonate within 50 yards of an oncoming target, thus throwing a wall of deadly shrapnel into its path.) New men with strange new rates usually arrived with the newfangled gear and, as the modern weapons and machinery were being installed, selected officers and sailors were sent to school to learn how to use and care for it.

All hands who would be sailing back to war in *Enterprise* were supercritical when it came to undertaking, overseeing, or checking repairs to their ship. Every weld was examined and critiqued, every placement was measured and remeasured for accurate dimensions and smooth movement, every yard worker was pushed by the crew to the limits of his ability and endurance. In the words of Lt(jg) Jim Kraker, an Eastern Solomons veteran, "We had to fight this ship, and we wanted a perfect weapon."

The grueling task of repairing and refitting was made yet more grueling by the need to absorb all the new people, familiarize everyone with new equipment and weapons, and generally keep the fine edge of combat readiness honed to perfection. The immediate lessons of Eastern Solomons drove home the need for all hands to be able to function in the dark or in smoke-filled spaces. To the extent possible, drills were realistic. Gunners and others drilled until they dropped, then drilled again, often as not with blindfolds on. Everyone, even the crustiest old sea dog, was eager to practice, and the new kids were eager to learn from the blooded veterans. The time at Pearl was used by many to cram for exams that would win coveted promotions, or even to change specialties within the Navy's dizzying array of ratings.

Every day, old hands were called over the loudspeakers to receive orders to new billets, mainly new carrier constructions in the States. The good-byes were painful, even for the men who were departing for the cherished home leaves that went with the new orders. Daily, new officers and men reported aboard.

During the stay at Pearl Harbor, the nominal Air Group 6 was replaced by Air Group 10, the first reserve carrier air group to report for carrier duty. A small number of Air Group 6 alumni was transferred to the new group—including Lt (jg) Hal Buell, who had not only flown at Coral Sea, Midway, and Eastern Solomons, but had just returned from Guadalcanal, where he had flown for an entire month as a member of Lt Turner Caldwell's Flight 300. For the most part, the new air group was composed of youngsters whose first combat still lay ahead. But many of the new air group's senior officers and flight leaders were combat veterans of the Coral Sea or Midway or both. Many of the green pilots and aircrew had had far more training than many of the veterans of the earlier battles, a definite early payoff of the reserve carrier air group program. With their new home tied up at the Navy Yard, Air Group 10 pilots had to content themselves with ongoing field carrier training at nearby airfields associated with the Pearl Harbor complex.

Also during the refitting the Air Department was expanded to incorporate the ground crews of the air squadrons. Formerly, each squadron had carried its own ground echelon on its rolls. Under the new plan, all ground crews were carried on the rolls of the ship's company, thus reducing paperwork for squadron pilots assigned to secondary administrative duties while streamlining the entire ground crew operation.

When at last *Enterprise* was ordered back to sea on October 16, 1942, she had greater firepower than any carrier afloat, and she was manned by a crew as thoroughly trained and dedicated as there was aboard any warship afloat that day in all the world's waters. If there was one drawback associated with her preparedness on the day of her departure, it was that many of the younger members of Air Group 10 had yet to undertake a landing aboard a real carrier that was underway, a shortcoming that promised to be amply corrected on the dash to the war zone.

The ten-day journey from Pearl Harbor was filled with hard work. Rough edges left from the frantic repair job had to be dealt with, and training continued at maximum levels. Moreover, the wearing routine of watches had to be reinstituted. This meant that, in addition to hard work and hard training, all hands had to learn or relearn the art of getting by on inadequate rest and hurried meals.

At daylight, October 24—the day before the night 17th Army's mainland offensive finally commenced—Task Force 16 rendezvoused with fleet oiler *Sabine*, and all ships topped off their fuel tanks. Later, at 1245, Task Force 61 doubled in size when the *Enterprise* task force joined *Hornet* and her consorts. Command of Task Force 61 passed from RAdm George Murray, aboard *Hornet* (and, incidentally, *Enterprise*'s first wartime captain) to RAdm Thomas Kinkaid, aboard *Enterprise*.

At 1500, October 24, the U.S. Navy's offensive thrust began when Task Force 61 turned northwestward to follow a track beyond the Santa Cruz Islands, out of range of Japanese snoopers and beyond the Japanese submarine patrol line. Kinkaid's mission was to interpose himself between the Truk-based Combined Fleet and Henderson Field. If the Navy's cryptographic extracts were correct, a huge Japanese naval force that had been conducting operations for two weeks just beyond the battle zone would sweep southward sometime during the night or the next night, upon the Imperial Army's announcement that Henderson Field had fallen to 17th Army.

卐

Unbeknown to the Americans serving with Task Force 61, but in complete accord with their expectations, Adm Isoroku Yamamoto had finally grown impatient with 17th Army's slipping timetable. The Combined Fleet commander was understandably nervous. His submarines and reconnaissance aircraft had lost track of the American carrier force on October 16 and, in the ensuing week, had not been able to reestablish even an inferential fix upon it. The only carrier sighting during that week was by a patrol bomber based in the Gilbert Islands, which spotted *Enterprise* far from the battle area as she sped southward from Pearl Harbor. That sighting was not as revealing of American plans as it was worrisome with respect to the ultimate size of the otherwise invisible American force.

The only U.S. naval force of consequence whose position was regularly monitored that week by the Japanese was Task Force 64, a surface battle force built around battleship *Washington* and commanded by RAdm Willis Lee. Task Force 64, primed to guard the carriers from a Japanese surface attack or to rush to the aid of the Lunga defenders, had been sailing for days in the area between Rennell and San Cristobal Islands, frustratingly out of the range of the Japanese strike aircraft.

During that week, Yamamoto's own carriers were at sea and thus vulnerable to an American surprise attack.

The status quo abruptly changed on October 23.

After a quiescent week, U.S. reconnaissance flights throughout the area suddenly picked up. These aggressive searches, combined with the continuing disappearance of the U.S. carrier force, alerted Combined Fleet to a possible renewal of U.S. offensive naval operations in support of the ground forces that, 17th Army still claimed, would be swept from Guadalcanal.

More evidence of aggressive American intentions in connection with the Solomons battle arrived shortly after 0200 on October 23 when three bomb-and-torpedo-armed American PBY Catalina flying boats based at Espiritu Santo mounted a surprise strike in the bright moonlight against Tonolei Harbor, in the Shortlands. This attack severely compounded the discomfort inflicted that same night—and for the next two nights—by small harassing strikes by New Guinea–based U.S. Army bombers against ships anchored off Rabaul.

So, on October 23, Yamamoto's headquarters informed 17th Army that, unless Henderson Field fell that night or the next night, a pending fuel shortage among the warships at sea would oblige Combined Fleet to cancel its part of the overall operation.

Yamamoto's growing concern was heightened considerably when he heard that an American Catalina patrol bomber had been chased off while well within sighting distance of one of his carrier forces. The concern soon turned to outright alarm when one of several American PBYs on the prowl that night launched a torpedo attack against a heavy cruiser on station with the carriers. The attack was unsuccessful, but it left a lot of shaken Japanese in its wake.

On October 24, Japanese units at sea picked up an American commercial radio broadcast that said "a major sea and air battle is expected in the near future in the Solomon Islands area." This went a long way toward bolstering uneasiness as well as reinforcing the belief that the Americans were initiating the apparently upcoming action.

That night, the initial 17th Army main assault south of Henderson Field was beaten back, but 17th Army nevertheless radioed Yamamoto's Truk headquarters in the wee hours of October 25 to announce the fall of the airfield and the ongoing mop-up of shattered U.S. ground forces.

The outright lie—which was amplified and corrected too late, after dawn of October 25—irretrievably set the Combined Fleet in motion. VAdm Gunichi Mikawa's Solomons-based Outer Seas Force mounted its planned daylight surface sally to Guadalcanal, and the carriers of the Advance Force and Carrier Striking Force were released from their tethers to hunt for the lurking American Fleet.

A clash at sea was inevitable.

33

☀

The cat-and-mouse game between the opposing carrier forces
began early on October 25. At the outset, it appeared that
the confrontation both sides desired would take place that
day, too.

The first break of the day came when a PBY-5A piloted by
Lt(jg) Doc Mathews discovered the Support Group of VAdm Nobutake Kondo's Advance Force. While the patrol bomber's radioman reported the position to all friendly bases eavesdropping on
the search frequency, Mathews circled around to get into position
to attack a battleship he correctly identified as *Haruna*. The move
was largely quixotic, for PBYs on daylight searches did not carry
aerial torpedoes, a policy aimed at increasing their productive
search ranges as well, perhaps, as obviating an attack such as the
one Mathews decided to carry out with the only weapons he did
have—a pair of 500-pound depth charges.

The glide-bombing approach was flawlessly executed, though
the projectiles were hurled well short of *Haruna*. As soon as the
depth charges were released from their shackles, Mathews pivoted
his surprisingly nimble parasol-winged patrol bomber into a tight

escape turn and ran from the area. Three float Zeros bounced the Catalina well before it got clear, but they were beaten off by Mathews's gunners, who claimed credit for downing at least one and damaging another.

Other American searchers manning Catalinas out of the Santa Cruz Islands and Espiritu Santo and B-17s out of Espiritu Santo were more circumspect. They found various elements of the steadily advancing Guadalcanal Support Force, but they merely reported positions and progress without resorting to additional heroics.

卐

The Japanese sighted and correctly identified at least two separate American PBYs—at 0907 and 1003. And at 1030 the Japanese fleet commanders received news of a radio intercept indicating that one of the PBYs had correctly reported their position.

At 1315, Admiral Kondo received word that a Rabaul-based patrol plane had found "two battleships, four heavy cruisers, one light cruiser, and twelve destroyers" 170 miles southeast of Tulagi. This was undoubtedly RAdm Willis Lee's Task Force 64, a much smaller force than reported, and not a particularly important one in the day's global scheme.

Still, at 1330, VAdm Nobutake Kondo ordered VAdm Chuichi Nagumo to ready a large air strike to go after Lee. However, Nagumo responded at 1412 that he felt the Americans were in no position to launch an attack of their own. Kondo allowed the attack order to be rescinded.

卐

The big news of the day for the Americans arrived at tender *Curtiss*, anchored off Espiritu Santo, at 1250. According to one of her brood of PBYs, two enemy carriers were sailing southeastward 360 miles from Task Force 61 at a speed of 25 knots. The riveting news was instantly relayed to Task Force 61, which Admiral Kinkaid held steady on a northwesterly course, at a speed of 22 knots, for two hours.

During that time, in which no new information arrived

323

Kinkaid decided to commit only Air Group 10 to searches and an initial strike launch. Air Group 8 would be held in reserve. Kinkaid had studied the results of the three earlier carrier battles and apparently felt that every U.S. offensive strike had lacked the advantage of the follow-up or second-wave strikes the Japanese usually managed to mount.

⚡

Between 1450 and 1510, six U.S. Army B-17 heavy bombers launched bombing runs on battleship *Kirishima*, a member of the Vanguard Group of Nagumo's Striking Force. No damage was inflicted on the ship.

⚡

Twelve Dauntlesses were launched in pairs from *Enterprise* at 1448 to search outward 200 miles along a fan of sectors from due west to north-northeast. Then, beginning at 1520, a strike group from Air Group 10 was launched—twelve Dauntlesses and six Avengers escorted by eleven Fighting-10 Wildcats.

Ens Jeff Carroum, who was flying on the wing of LCdr James Thomas, the Bombing-10 skipper, was in too many ways typical of the young pilots launched on that afternoon search and strike mission. Above all, Carroum was scared to death of what the strike might encounter; he did not truly believe he was quite ready for combat, and he doubted that so small a strike force would have much impact if it did find the Japanese carriers.

The plan was for the strike group to fly out 150 miles along the median line of the search sectors until it received word—or did not receive word—of firm sightings by the scouts. If no word was received, the strike group was to return to the ship followed by the pairs of searchers. There were delays enhanced by everyone's desire to stretch the endurance of the strike bombers in the event a contact was made at or beyond the last minute. This devotion to duty would have a dear cost for Air Group 10.

Cdr Dick Gaines, the Air Group 10 commander, was leading the strike. After going out to 150 miles, Gaines angled the formation toward the right and flew on for another 30 minutes—loitering in the air in the hope of receiving a flash from the searchers. No joy there, either, so Gaines executed another shallow right turn and flew on for another half hour. Nothing. By then, the strike group had flown about 280 miles and was at the extremity of its operational range.

Though the searchers flew well beyond the Santa Cruz Islands, no contacts were made. The Japanese did not have a firm fix on Task Force 61 and thus did not desire to fight. The carriers and many of the surface warships of the Carrier Striking Force and Advance Force had turned north in the afternoon to sail out of range of American carrier-based searchers and strikers. In fact, the turn to the north had been monitored and reported by an American PBY, but Admiral Kinkaid had withheld the news from the searchers and strikers because he feared the consequences of breaking radio silence.

卐

Jeff Carroum was one of many Air Group 10 pilots who was thrilled by the order to turn for home. However, it was quite late and the night sky was closing in. Carroum had made only fifteen actual carrier-deck landings in his life, and none at night, so the darkening sky was ample cause for considerable concern. He had flown a total of ten hours that day, including a fruitless four-and-a-half-hour morning patrol, so he was dog tired. His oxygen system had developed a leak on the outward leg of the search-and-strike mission, so he had flown without oxygen at 19,000 feet for three hours, an extremely dangerous situation. He had a killer headache and could barely keep his eyes open, the inevitable results of oxygen deprivation.

The many inexperienced pilots in the strike formation were having fuel-consumption problems. The junior pilots had been exactingly trained to maintain formation on their leaders, so they tended to waste a lot of fuel keeping station.

The strike group was still in the air after sunset. Scattered cumulonimbus clouds obscured the horizon, adding a sense of vertigo to the fatigue everyone was feeling by then.

As the strike group was nearing the end of the mission, Ensign

Carroum discovered that his YE-ZB homing device had apparently malfunctioned; at any rate, he received no comforting directional signals from *Enterprise*. However, Carroum was not overly concerned; he assumed that Commander Gaines—or someone—would be able to find Point Option without difficulty.

Indeed, Commander Gaines did find Point Option. But there was nothing there. Following one circuit of the area, Gaines led the entire strike formation upwind, a pretty safe bet in that sort of a situation.

At length, Lt Doc Norton, who was leading the second section of Torpedo-10 Avengers, heard the faint homing signal. Norton had by then become separated in the clouds from the leading Avenger flight, so was responsible for navigating on his own. He had not closely followed Gaines's turns during the search phase of the flight, so he was not sure of his position relative to anything. There was not enough light from the cockpit instruments to read the teletyped YE-ZB interpretation code, which was stuck onto a strip of aluminum riveted to the dashboard. Thus Norton had to work the aluminum strip loose from the rivets, a tedious chore that took his attention away from his flying and flight leadership of three other Avengers and a pair of escorting Wildcats. Once the code strip came free, Norton had to slide it around in the glow of the instruments, also at the expense of attention to his flying.

Maintaining the formation in the clouds was extremely difficult and, in Ens Jeff Carroum's case, a matter of life and death because of his Dauntless's malfunctioning YE-ZB receiver. Things got a little better when a bright moon rose an hour after sunset, but Carroum began wondering if there was a carrier on which to land. Maybe the Japanese had struck a deadly blow during the afternoon. Maybe that was why all the flight leaders seemed to be milling around in confusion. Maybe he was not receiving the homing signals because home had been sunk.

All the *Enterprise* warplanes returned to the vicinity of Task Force 61 more than an hour after sunset.

As Lt Doc Norton was leading his flight of four Avengers and two Wildcats down through 4,000 feet and into the clear, the Wildcat flown by Lt Don Miller—a Naval Academy classmate—rolled onto its back and fell away toward the sea. It was thought that Miller, who disappeared in the crash, either ran out of fuel or suffered from oxygen deprivation.

Doc Norton finally thought he saw *Enterprise*'s dim night-recovery illumination and blinked his TBF's blue formation-flying wing lights before breaking out of formation at 500 feet to take advantage of a gap in the ragged recovery formation just below. Though Norton was a 1939 Annapolis graduate, he had only been flying since early in the year. (Annapolis graduates served two years with the Fleet before attending flight school.) He had been accelerated through the latter stages of training due to a command pilot shortage early in the year, though he had had as much finishing as any of the junior pilots. This was Doc Norton's first night landing. He came up the groove okay, and took the "Cut," but his tail hook caught the wire far to the right of center. The heavy TBF was just coming to rest when its right wheel dropped over the edge of the flight deck into the starboard aft 20mm gun gallery. Landing operations were briefly shut down as a deck tractor tugged the damaged Avenger back up on deck by the tail. When Norton was safely parked, he checked the fuel gauges and found that his Avenger had come to rest with only a gallon or two of aviation gasoline aboard.

Ens Jeff Carroum was coming up the groove with all his gas gauges reading empty when he received a "Wave-off" for being a bit too high. There was no way, he knew, to go around again on no fuel, so he gave himself the "Cut," confident that he could mitigate the offense by making a good landing. But the Dauntless kept floating in high, right over the Number-9 arresting wire, right on into the island. The right wing crumpled and fell off, and so did the right wheel. Jeff Carroum and his rearseatman climbed unsteadily from the wreckage and made a sheepish exit from center stage. No one ever mentioned the accident to Carroum.

Lt Scoofer Coffin, the Torpedo-10 exec and torpedo flight leader this day, was just five seconds from touchdown when his Avenger's engine died. He could not even turn aside from *Enterprise*'s wake before sliding into the water, from which he and his crewmen were plucked by one of the plane-guard destroyers.

Of the forty-one search-and-strike warplanes, one fighter

crashed with the loss of the pilot, and one fighter, two dive-bombers, and three torpedo bombers were obliged to land in the water when they ran out of fuel in the traffic pattern.

The seven warplanes lost at night had to be added to a tally of four ready airplanes that had been destroyed on *Enterprise's* flight deck early in the day when a Wildcat pilot attempting a powerless landing bounced over three barriers. So, the score for October 25 was eleven Air Group 10 warplanes and one pilot lost in operational accidents. The only mitigating factor was that *Enterprise* had plenty of spare planes aboard, for she had been carrying a number that were otherwise destined to serve as replacements for the Cactus Air Force. These were broken out of storage and reassembled to make good some—but not all—of the operational losses.

That night, the *Enterprise* air officer, Cdr John Crommelin, gathered the weary Air Group 10 pilots together in the wardroom and gave them an inspiring peptalk in which he revealed his certainty that the next day, October 26, would find them in battle:

"This may be the beginning of a great battle.

"You men do not need to be babied, and I don't intend to hold your hands. We know that the Jap task force we are looking for will have a three-to-one superiority over us. Four of our PBY patrols sighted the Jap task force. . . .

"You men will have the privilege tomorrow of proving the worth of your training, your schooling, our way of life as against the Japs'.

"The offensive strength we have in the Pacific is at this moment in the hands of you men in this room and of those on the *Hornet*.

"On you rests the safety of our Marines at Guadalcanal who have fought magnificently. Last night, they were bombarded again, and the Japs made an assault upon our position, but they held, proving their worth.

"Wherever we have met the Jap at sea with our carriers, despite overwhelming odds, we have stopped them.

"The Japs are determined to drive us out of the South Pacific.

If they get through to Guadalcanal with their carriers tomorrow, the Japs will take it. If Guadalcanal falls, our lifeline to Australia will be menaced.

"To stop them, you must knock out their carrier force.

". . . We are on the right side of this war. God is with us. Let's knock those Jap bastards off the face of the earth."

⚛

The Japanese also received a sort of a peptalk that evening—an operations order from Adm Isoroku Yamamoto that arrived at the Guadalcanal Support Force at 2118:

> 1.   Army units plan to storm Guadalcanal airfield this evening at 2100; accordingly, there is great likelihood that the enemy fleet will appear in the area northeast of the Solomons.
>
> 2.   The Combined Fleet will seek to destroy the enemy fleet on October 26.
>
> 3.   All forces will take appropriate action to above.
>
> 4.   [Guadalcanal] Support Force will operate as designated by Commander-in-Chief.

Yamamoto's order was rewritten and transmitted by Admiral Kondo to all ships of the Guadalcanal Support Force at 2240: "Commander-in-Chief, Combined Fleet, orders that since there is a great possibility that we will engage in a decisive action, aircraft of all units continue searching and tracking operations regardless of weather and enemy planes, in an attempt to discover the size and nature of the enemy forces."

⚛

At about 0015, October 26, the operator of a new radar set aboard the Catalina piloted by LCdr Jim Cobb, commander of Patrol Squadron 91, found destroyer *Isokaze* among the anthill of warships comprising the Carrier Striking Force's surface Vanguard Group. Beginning 12 miles out, Cobb allowed himself to be coached to the release point for his torpedoes by the radar operator—the first time this had ever been attempted on an operational mission. At an altitude of under 100 feet, Cobb conducted a straight-in approach until he visually acquired *Isokaze* dead ahead. He released both of the aerial torpedoes slung under the Catalina's parasol wing. But it was not to be. In his excitement, Cobb had flown too close to the target for the torpedoes to arm themselves, and *Isokaze*, which had spotted the PBY at a distance of six miles, took nimble evasive action. Cobb and *Isokaze* both ran from the spectral confrontation.

卐

At 0250, October 26, the main strength of the Guadalcanal Support Force was sailing southward again. It had run northward, out of range, until sunset, then had turned again to race through the night to within range of the American carrier task force.

Suddenly, the drone of aircraft engines intruded above the noise of machinery and ships' engines. They were coming closer. They passed overhead. Then they seemed to begin to recede. Suddenly, the darkness was pierced by two white flashes and the stillness was shattered by two ear-splitting explosions of a pair of 500-pound bombs. Debris and seawater washed over the superstructure of fleet carrier *Zuikaku* while, high above and farther out, the racing engines of a lone U.S. Navy Catalina patrol bomber carried a brave pilot and crew toward safety.

Capt Toshitane Takata, the senior staff officer serving with VAdm Chuichi Nagumo's Carrier Striking Force, made his way from fleet carrier *Shokaku*'s bridge to report details of the attack to Nagumo and his chief of staff, RAdm Ryunosuke Kusaka. Nagumo had not yet arrived at a decision when he also learned of the torpedo attack on *Isokaze*.

The Carrier Striking Force commander concluded that he was sailing into the teeth of an American trap. Immediately, his chief of staff shot off a message to all ships of the Carrier Striking Force: "Emergency turn, together, 180 degrees to starboard." Then, "All ships, execute turn. Speed 24 knots."

Another American PBY accurately reported light carrier *Zuiho*'s position at 0410. However, the news—which did not include the Japanese course or speed—took two hours to get from tender *Curtiss*, based at Espiritu Santo, to Task Force 61 because someone in the communications chain incorrectly assumed that Admiral Kinkaid's staff would be monitoring the original sighting broadcasts. Thus when the PBY that made the sighting report left station because it was running low of fuel, the most important element of the Guadalcanal Striking Force slipped from American view. The delay was decisive.

卐

Cdr Masatake Okumiya was the senior staff officer on watch aboard fleet carrier *Junyo*, which was part of VAdm Nobutake Kondo's Advance Force, which was 60 to 80 miles south of the Carrier Striking Force before Nagumo's turn. Okumiya was thus one of the first of Kondo's officers to learn of Nagumo's turn. He informed his RAdm Kakuji Kakuta, commander of the Advance Force's Air Group, and Kakuta transmitted the news to Kondo's chief of staff, who was with Kondo aboard heavy cruiser *Atago*. Kondo took only a few moments to reach his decision, an order for the Advance Force to turn northward and follow the Carrier Striking Force out of the area at high speed. Kondo's Advance Force executed its turn at 0400. Like Nagumo's Carrier Striking Force, Kondo's Advance Force—including carrier *Junyo*—was lost to view by the American commanders and planners.

卐

Nagumo's turnabout at 0300 had been made as the Carrier Striking Force was coming to within 250 miles of Henderson Field. Nagumo had been planning a night launch at full strength. Now Nagumo would have to settle for a daylight battle, for if there was no battle on October 26, the Guadalcanal Support Force would have to break contact and refuel.

PART VII

The Battle of the Santa Cruz Island

34

The American and Japanese carrier forces north of the Santa Cruz Islands had avoided a confrontation on October 25 only because the Japanese had been unable to pinpoint precisely the position of the American carriers and had thus sailed back and forth just outside of the operational range of the American carrier-based bombers. However, both sides fundamentally desired a clash, and both sides were determined that it would take place on October 26. Toward that end, the Japanese had been resolutely steaming southward through the early morning hours preparatory to launching a skyful of search planes from land bases, the carriers, and many of the large surface warships that carried reconnaissance and observation airplanes. Even a specially equipped fleet submarine or two were to launch reconnaissance planes before dawn.

Task Force 61 had also been resolutely steaming forward to join battle with the Japanese. Except to turn southward into the prevailing wind to launch and recover airplanes, the American carriers had been heading north for two days. Through the night, in clear weather, beneath scattered clouds, in bright moonlight with visibility of 15 miles, Task Force 61 had been zigzagging northward at a speed of 23 knots.

During the night, VAdm Thomas Kinkaid and his staff reviewed everything they had learned about the Japanese fleet dispositions: Two separate battle groups had been reported by land-based search planes. One, portions of Kondo's Advance Force, was reported to have been 80 miles south of the other, two of Nagumo's three carriers.

It was incorrectly assumed by the Americans that the two Japanese battle groups were positioning themselves to support a thus far undiscovered reinforcement group. The incorrect surmise was understandable; the Japanese had dispatched ground elements or reinforcements in all of the three previous carrier confrontations. In fact, the mid-October crisis at Guadalcanal had arisen out of the early dispatch of the reinforcements; all the ground troops that were going to be sent for the time being had been sent.

In anticipation of news that far-ranging night patrols would be able to reestablish contact with the Japanese carrier force—no one dreamed that there might be *two* Japanese carrier forces—Admiral Kinkaid had ordered *Hornet*'s rested Air Group 8 to stand ready to launch an immediate strike mission, even at night.

卐

In a rather harebrained variation on Kinkaid's order, someone specifically ordered four Fighting-72 Wildcats to prepare to undertake a presumably one-way mission to try to damage the Japanese flight decks in advance of the arrival of the main attack group. The first volunteer was LCdr Mike Sanchez, the Fighting-72 skipper, who also volunteered his entire division for the mission. The scheme was to load the four Wildcats with .50-caliber tracer rounds to be fired off at the flight decks of the Japanese carriers. Ens Phil Souza, who was facing his first live combat hop, was surprised after deep reflection at how sane the plan seemed: Position reports from hovering patrol bombers were said to be absolutely accurate; the moon would light the sky and sea fairly well, so the pilots would be able to see the carriers; and presumably, the enemy flight decks would be crammed with highly flammable fuel- and munitions-laden attack aircraft, which the .50-caliber tracer rounds would certainly ignite. Realistic as the plan seemed to Souza following hours of endless rationalizations in the squadron's dimly lighted ready room, an order to stand down was registered with relief.

卐

As the search planes on *Enterprise*'s flight deck were going through their final checks just before dawn, Task Force 61 received its order of the day from the South Pacific Area commander. Characteristically, VAdm Bill Halsey had honed his message to the absolute essential. The entire message read: "ATTACK. REPEAT, ATTACK!"

卐

To the west, VAdm Chuichi Nagumo's Carrier Striking Force, once again preceded by VAdm Nobutake Kondo's Advance Force, was sailing directly at the American carrier task force.

The only news of note following the night's final turnabout to the south was a report to Combined Fleet from Guadalcanal indicating that 17th Army's assault on the Lunga Perimeter had been unsuccessful. By then, 17th Army's failure was beside the point for the Guadalcanal Support Force. The American carriers seemed to be closing to within range, and that was all the reason Kondo and Nagumo needed to be there.

Just before dawn, Nagumo's Carrier Striking Force launched sixteen reconnaissance planes from battleships and cruisers and eight Kate torpedo bombers from *Shokaku*. Their mission was to undertake extended sweeps across sectors centering on due south, to find the American carriers no matter what stood in their way.

卐

Enterprise came about into the wind at 0512 and began launching her first search mission of the day, sixteen Bombing-10 and Scouting-10 Dauntlesses, each armed with a 500-pound bomb. Each pair of searchers was assigned a 15-degree sector out to 200 miles. The area covered was from due north to west-southwest. Right behind the searchers were eight Fighting-10 Wildcats for the

337

day's first combat air patrol and six Dauntlesses for the antisubmarine patrol.

Minutes after the last of the searchers was away, a messenger arrived at Admiral Kinkaid's side and handed the task force commander the delayed sighting report from the PBY based at Espiritu Santo that had found light carrier *Zuiho* at 0410 at a spot just 200 miles west of Task Force 61's present position.

Without a doubt, an earlier reading of the sighting report would have caused Kinkaid to cancel the search mission, incorporate the searchers into a strike group, and get the bulk of Air Group 10 into the air and on the way to hit *Zuiho*. But the news was now two hours old and the *Enterprise* searchers were gone and could not be recalled because of the fear of breaking radio silence.

At about the time *Enterprise* was turning into the wind to launch her search teams, Lt(jg) George Poulos, of Patrol-11, was 500 miles down his outward search leg from Espiritu Santo. Poulos and other Patrol-11 pilots and crewmen had been fully briefed about the probability of a carrier battle taking place that day, and he and the others had been exhorted by their superiors to turn in a maximum performance.

The sun had barely begun to rise when one of Poulos's crewmen reported a submerging submarine about five miles ahead. He also said he saw a float biplane taking off near the swirl created by the submerging pigboat. Poulos realized that he was too far away to make a useful attack on the submarine, and he did not want to take on the biplane, which seemed insignificant in view of what might be sailing just over the horizon. So, to the utter disappointment of his crew, the pilot flew on. As he did, he thought about the position of the biplane, which was in a direct line between his base at Espiritu Santo and the probable location of the Japanese carriers. PBYs out of Espiritu Santo would be flying into the sun on the outward leg, so the biplane fighter would be able to approach them before he could be seen. If that was the case, the only thing that saved Poulos's PBY from being attacked was its launch two hours before PBYs were usually launched. The Catalina had just been passing up-sun of the submarine when the biplane had been sighted.

All of the little decisions made that morning by George Poulos and his superiors paid off at 0630, when one of the lookouts called out that he had spotted many vessels. The cruising warships far ahead slowly resolved themselves into what appeared to be four carriers and their escorts. The nearer carriers, at least, seemed to have launched their attack planes, for their decks were clear.

George Poulos's entire purpose in life came down to evading the Zeros guarding the Japanese fleet and gaining some altitude so his sighting report would be heard at distant bases. As Poulos climbed, amid the bursts of the nearest Japanese antiaircraft guns, he ordered his crewmen to count the ships below, identify them by type, and report to the radioman. There was some disagreement about the number and types, but all agreed that there were four carriers. When the best count the crew could get was in, the radioman trailed a long antenna designed for long-range transmissions and sent the first of many repeats of the size, position, and heading of the carriers.

As soon as the first message had been sent, Poulos turned back toward the Japanese fleet for a better count. This time the crew came to quick agreement about the size and types of the ships, so Poulos decided to leave the area. He was just turning away when four Zeros detached themselves from the combat air patrol. This frankly surprised the American pilot; he had been within sight of the Japanese for an hour by then, and he had been shot at early on by several ships. The Zeros had had plenty of time to mount an attack. Moreover, Poulos was surprised that the combat air patrol—the only line of defense against a possible American air strike—was being compromised for the sake of harassing a patrol bomber that had certainly already reported its findings to its base.

Poulos took his slow amphibian bomber as low as he dared, right over the 15-foot swells on the surface of the ocean. At least the Zeros would not be able to launch attacks on his PBY's vulnerable belly, and they would have to pull out of their firing passes early to avoid plunging into the sea.

As Poulos maneuvered from side to side, from swell to swell, the Zeros came on. As each fighter began its firing run, Poulos flicked the patrol bomber to the right and left, into the line of flight of the approaching fighter. This forced the Japanese pilots to tighten their own turns and reduced the amount of time they had to spray bullets at their huge target. The nearest any of the Japanese were able to get their bullets to the Catalina was 20 feet. After several passes each, the four Zeros departed.

Later, Poulos's PBY encountered a Japanese four-engine patrol bomber on a reciprocal course. The pilot gave in to the loud pleas of his crew and gave chase, but the Japanese eventually drew ahead and escaped into thick cloud cover. With that, Poulos called it a day and shaped a course directly for his base at Espiritu Santo.

Lt(jg) George Poulos's sighting report was picked up by friendly bases, but it was not immediately transmitted to Task Force 61, yet another decisive omission.

卐

The two fleets were very close to each other; the Japanese were less than 200 miles due west of Task Force 61.

Lt Vivian Welch and Lt(jg) Bruce McGraw, of Bombing-10, had the 266–282-degree search sector. They were outward-bound at 1,200 feet and only 85 miles from *Enterprise* when they both spotted a *Shokaku* Kate heading past them 3 miles to starboard and on a precise reciprocal course. Both pilots instantly surmised that the carrier attack bomber would be heading straight out from a carrier, so they flew on with mounting excitement.

Welch and McGraw flew for only another 20 minutes before they saw the shapes of vessels on the distant surface at 0717. Welch led McGraw up to 2,000 feet to take advantage of the scattered clouds at that altitude and then headed around to a spot about ten miles east of the Japanese ships.

Except for a few fast-moving squalls, Welch and McGraw enjoyed unlimited visibility. The sun was behind them and the Japanese lookouts would certainly be concentrating their energies to the west. Both pilots and radioman-gunners began counting and identifying the array of warships below. They checked and re-checked, but it was clear that there were no carriers in sight. At

0730, Welch ordered his radioman, ARM1 H. C. Ansley, to key a sighting report on the Morse transmitter: "Two BB [battleships], one CA [heavy cruiser], seven DD [destroyers]. Lat[itude] 08-10S, Lon[gitude] 163-55E. [Course] north. [Speed] 20 [knots]."

Welch and McGraw had found RAdm Hiroaki Abe's Vanguard Group of VAdm Chuichi Nagumo's Carrier Striking Force.

Still intent upon finding the Japanese carriers, Welch and McGraw headed north to the extremity of their 200-mile search, but they found nothing. At about 0800, they again passed over Abe's Vanguard Group on the return leg. This time, as a second contact report was being transmitted, Welch and McGraw were spotted and fired on by the nearest surface warships. The gunfire was heavy but it fell well short of the Dauntlesses. With that, since they were nearing the extremity of their search sector, Welch led McGraw back toward *Enterprise*. On the way back, about 100 miles from home, another *Shokaku* Kate passed them one mile away on a reciprocal course, but, as before, none of the warplanes opened fire.

Welch's position reports were only a little bit off. Rear Admiral Abe's two battleships, four cruisers, and seven destroyers were actually 25 miles south of the reported position.

For once, the sighting message was directly picked up by *Enterprise* and rushed to the flag bridge to be placed in Admiral Kinkaid's hands.

That firmly fixed one piece to the puzzle.

卐

Rank hath its privileges.

LCdr Bucky Lee, the Scouting-10 commander, was the senior searcher sent aloft on the morning of October 26, so he selected the center search sector—298–314 degrees—the one in which everyone thought the Japanese carriers would be found.

Lee and his wingman, Ens William Johnson, were at 1,200 feet at 0750 when they approached the end of their 200-mile search leg. No enemy carriers had been sighted. Were they up ahead, or somewhere else in the sector?

Just as the two Scouting-10 Dauntlesses reached the end of the outward leg, Lee saw vessels dead ahead—he reckoned 35 miles away. The squadron commander adjusted his course, and Johnson followed. They were 15 miles from the enemy force when both pilots and rearseatmen definitely identified at least two carriers busily launching airplanes.

Lee's radioman, ACRM Irby Sanders, keyed the transmitter: "Two CV [fleet carriers] and accompanying vessels at Lat[itude] 07-06S, Long[itude] 163-38E." The message was sent four times in as many minutes.

Lee was only 10 miles off in his fix on *Shokaku* and *Zuikaku*. *Zuiho* was also in the area, but she was not sighted.

Lee and Johnson were climbing through 3,000 feet to get into position for a bombing attack when Johnson reported that seven Zeros were overtaking the Dauntlesses from the starboard beam. Lee assumed the Zeros would try for a head-on attack before he and Johnson could reach some nearby clouds, and that is exactly what happened. As a Japanese 7.7mm bullet starred his windscreen, Lee fired his cowl-mounted machine guns and sent the leading Zero diving away in flames. Ensign Johnson accounted for two more Zeros with his fixed guns. A moment later, the Dauntlesses reached the clouds, which were disintegrating in the heat of the rising sun.

When Lee and Johnson flew out of the cloud, the Zeros were waiting. They ducked back in, but almost immediately flew into the clear. A three-dimensional guessing game ensued as the Dauntless pilots tried to stay in the disappearing clouds and the Zero pilots tried to find the spot where they would inevitably leave the cover. At length, the Americans became separated during one wild maneuver, and they were unable to reestablish contact. Lee thought of making a try at the carriers, but the game became futile and he eventually was able to get clear and head for home—hopefully to refuel in time to join the strike he knew his contact report message would generate. He arrived safely and found that Ensign Johnson had arrived minutes earlier.

卐

The immediate consequence of Welch's and Lee's separate sighting reports was the spontaneous rerouting of search teams in the adjacent sectors.

Lt(jg) Howard Burnett, an Eastern Solomons veteran now serving with Scouting-10, was leading Lt(jg) Kenneth Miller in the 272–298-degree sector—between Welch and Lee—when he heard Welch's sighting report on RAdm Hiroaki Abe's Vanguard Group. Burnett immediately turned toward the reported coordinates and led Miller up to 14,000 feet in preparation of launching a dive-bombing attack on one of the large targets.

The two Scouting-10 pilots easily found Abe's group. Burnett reported the sighting and then quickly led Miller in an attack against *Tone*, the heavy cruiser that had accompanied *Ryujo* on the day of her death. The antiaircraft fire put up by *Tone* and nearby vessels was intense and accurate. As Miller's Dauntless passed below 10,000 feet, a near miss by a large-caliber shell sent it spinning out of control. Miller was below 6,000 feet when he regained control of his airplane and resumed his attack. Though neither Dauntless was shot down or seriously damaged, the intense antiaircraft fire had the next best effect—it threw off the pilots' aims. Both 500-pound bombs narrowly missed *Tone*, which was shaken but unscathed. Both Dauntlesses emerged from the maelstrom in flyable condition, joined up, and headed for home.

卐

The search team immediately to the north of LCdr Bucky Lee's sector was composed of two more Scouting-10 Dauntlesses flown by Lt(jg) Les Ward and Lt(jg) Martin Carmody.

Carmody was particularly tense this day; he was sure he would find Japanese ships. After about two hours in the air, he kept seeing what he thought was black smoke on the horizon. However, closer inspection invariably revealed that the "smoke" was merely the reflection of clouds on the surface of the ocean.

Ward and Carmody were nearing the end of their outward leg when both of them heard Bucky Lee's sighting report. Both pilots leaned over their chartboards and came up with identical solutions: The Japanese carriers were 80 to 100 miles to the west of their position, well within range. Ward led Carmody around to the new heading and began a slow fuel-conserving climb to attack altitude. The pair flew on for 30 minutes and was just topping 8,000 feet when Carmody saw black smoke—*real* black smoke—on the horizon about 50 or 60 miles dead ahead. The two pilots, conversing by means of well-rehearsed hand signals, agreed to stay close to the fluffy clouds in order to cover their approach. If all went well, their attack would come as a complete surprise to the Japanese.

Minutes later, and quite far from the carriers, both Dauntlesses temporarily ran out of cloud cover. They were only partway across the large gap on the way to the next nearest cloud when they were spotted and attacked by at least six Zeros. As Ward and Carmody jerked their SBDs around in radical and unorthodox evasive maneuvers—they nearly collided several times—the two American rear gunners—ARM3 Nick Baumgartner with Ward and ARM2 John Liska with Carmody—each shot down one Zero.

The wild melee lasted only a few minutes, the time it took Ward and Carmody to reach the nearest clouds and sneak away from the area. But it was a crucial few minutes, for another American search team was permitted to sneak in while the Japanese fighters were busy with Ward and Carmody.

⇵

No one ever said much about it, but Lt Birney Strong had been under something of a cloud since August 24, the day he had found *Ryujo* but had stood off monitoring her position while other searchers had launched attacks. When Strong had returned to *Enterprise* with his bomb to file his formal report, the ship's air boss, Cdr John Crommelin, had flown into a rage, had questioned Birney Strong's nerve, and had thrown Strong into "hack"—confinement to quarters—until he, Crommelin, calmed down a few days later.

No one quite knows what occurred when *Enterprise* returned to Pearl Harbor. Strong was still aboard as acting skipper of the small remnant of Scouting-5, and he stayed aboard when Air Group 10 arrived to replace Air Group 6. Many thought that Birney Strong, newly married just before he shipped out at the start of the war, should have gotten some good home leave after a long combat tour beginning in February 1942, on a raid against Japanese bases in New Guinea, through an attack on the Japanese carriers during the Coral Sea Battle and the loss of his carrier, *Yorktown*, at Midway, then on to the invasion of Guadalcanal, and culminating in his ill-received judgment call at Eastern Solomons. Moreover, Strong's reassignment to Scouting-10 placed him in a subordinate roll to two or three more senior lieutenants, something of a blow to a man who had commanded a squadron, even on a temporary basis. Some pilots saw this as a punitive measure.

A 1937 Annapolis graduate and a superb flyer, Birney Strong was "Old Navy" all the way. His first and middle names—Stockton Birney—were the names of early American naval heroes. He was a quiet, serious young man, known by all as an unremitting perfectionist who set the highest personal standard imaginable.

Whatever the reasons or reasoning, Lt Birney Strong had sailed to the war once again when *Enterprise* left Pearl Harbor on October 16. So far as anyone was concerned, the August 24 question was past history.

When LCdr Bucky Lee assigned himself the choice search sector, Lt Birney Strong drew him aside and said, "I think you'll find the yellowbellies are in your sector. When you discover them, give us the word, loud and clear."

Before the flight, Strong gave his radioman, ARM1 Clarence Garlow, a cheerful "Good morning!" and admonished him to keep the radio carefully tuned to the radio search frequency.

On October 26, Lt Birney Strong was flying into the prevailing wind in the 330–335-degree search sector with Ens Chuck Irvine when he heard Lt Vivian Welch's sighting report on Rear Admiral Abe's surface Vanguard Group. Though he and Irvine were only five minutes from the end of their 200-mile outward leg, Strong turned his Dauntless southward at 0740. He was determined to fly nearly 150 miles to drop his 500-pound bomb on one of the Japanese battleships. If his estimates were correct, a long climbing approach would leave him with just enough fuel to reach home after throwing in a quick dive-bombing attack—but only if the battleships were where Welch said they were, and only if his navigation was perfect.

Strong and Irvine were 30 minutes along the down-leg when their earphones crackled with another sighting report. As promised, Bucky Lee's radioman was filling the air waves with the loud and clear news that the carriers had been spotted. A quick navigation check revealed that Nagumo's carriers were about 50 miles closer than Abe's battleships. But it was no conflict in any case; Strong wanted a carrier if he could get one.

The two Dauntlesses altered course slightly to chase down Lee's contact report. They flew for only another 20 minutes and arrived dead on. Ahead, filling a break in the intermittent cloud cover, were two carriers—*Shokaku* and *Zuiho*. *Zuikaku* was nearby, but she was obscured by the clouds.

Irvine drew up as close to Strong's Dauntless as he dared and followed the section leader from cloud to cloud as Strong sought the best way to sneak up on either of the carrier flight decks. At that moment, out of sight behind other clouds, the entire Japanese combat air patrol was going after Lt(jg) Les Ward and Lt(jg) Martin Carmody.

At almost precisely 0830, Birney Strong signaled Chuck Irvine that he was set to commence the attack. Irvine slowed down a bit as Strong tilted his Dauntless's nose up just a hair, began slowing down, and plunged away from 13,000 feet toward the nearest orange-painted flight deck. Irvine waited for just a moment before following Strong after the same carrier.

The Japanese were totally surprised and utterly unable to counter the Dauntlesses's swift descents with more than a desultory burst or two of small-caliber antiaircraft gunfire.

As Strong dived through a last layer of cloud and went through all the ingrained motions on the way down, he tried to identify the carrier from his odd angle of approach. He thought it was *Shokaku* or, perhaps, *Zuikaku*. In fact, his target was *Zuiho*, a light carrier commissioned at the end of 1940.

Strong was pulled back to the job at hand as he dived clear of the obscuring cloud layer when ARM1 Garlow called out the altitude readings. Strong knew that the altimeter was unwinding far behind the actual altitude, so he checked his aim one last time and immediately released his 500-pound bomb. Garlow's last call was at less than 1,500 feet. Next, Strong closed his dive flaps, flattened out the dive, and ran for safety at full throttle just above the waves. An instant later, Chuck Irvine exactly repeated Strong's actions.

"Your bomb was a hit, Mr. Strong," Garlow intoned. "Mr. Irvine got one, too."

Both 500-pound bombs had driven into *Zuiho*'s flight deck between the island and the stern.

During their recovery to the west, Strong and Irvine received all the gunfire they had avoided during the approach and attack. But they flew through the instantaneous eruption without ill effect and swiftly got beyond the range of most of the gunfire. There, at the edge of the ring of fire, they were met by the surviving Zeros.

The two Dauntlesses executed a close approximation of the Thach Weave, the weaving scissors pattern designed to draw attackers intent upon one airplane into the fire of another airplane. Designed for fighters with forward-firing wing guns, the weave was superb under these conditions for a pair of warplanes equipped to fire to the rear as well as forward. The rearseatmen did their share, and more. When one Zero misjudged and swung too wide on a firing pass, ARM1 Garlow got his twin .30-caliber free guns to bear before the Zero could whip from range and nailed him; the Zero's belly bore the brunt of Garlow's fire, and the plane burst into flames as it skidded all the way into the sea. ARM3 Williams smoked another Zero and watched it fall into the sea.

When Garlow found a moment that was not filled with oncoming Zeros, he reached for his voice-radio transmission key and passed the vital news that a Japanese carrier had been hit, along with position and course information. Then he went back to keeping the Zeros away.

During a 45-mile tail chase, the Japanese shot up Irvine's tail and holed his starboard main fuel tank. Of equal importance was the amount of fuel both Dauntlesses sacrificed during the full-power chase. When the surviving Zeros finally withdrew at about 0900 after chasing the Dauntlesses into a large cloud, Strong and Irvine both chopped back to minimum power and leaned out their fuel mixtures as much as they dared. It was by no means certain that they would reach a friendly flight deck.

Later, Cdr John Crommelin was instrumental in writing a recommendation to award Lt Birney Strong a Medal of Honor. In the end, Strong received a Navy Cross, which was nothing compared to the unyielding respect he earned this day.

35

At 0730, the moment ARM1 H. C. Ansley was transmitting the Welch-McGraw sighting report to Task Force 61, a Japanese cruiser-launched reconnaissance pilot peeked over the horizon and saw *Hornet*'s Task Force 17. Twenty minutes later, at 0750, he reported, "Large enemy unit sighted. One carrier, five other vessels."

At the time of the sighting report, Task Force 61 was just 185 miles east of VAdm Chuichi Nagumo's Carrier Striking Force.

The Japanese did not waste a moment pondering the implications of the reconnaissance report. As soon as Admiral Nagumo heard of the sighting—at 0758—he ordered his force's first strike group to be launched.

Within minutes, LCdr Mamoru Seki led twenty-two Val dive-bombers off *Shokaku*. Seki would be the *hikotaicho*, the strike commander, of a group consisting of his own Vals, eighteen *Zuikaku* Kates under Lt Jiichiro Imajuku, and twenty-seven *Shokaku* Zeros under LCdr Hideki Shingo.

348

Task Force 17 maneuvers at high speed moments before the first Japanese bomber wave begins its attack on *Hornet*.   *(Official USN Photo)*

Top: LCdr Mamoru Seki's Val plummets toward *Hornet*'s superstructure. The carrier is already burning from several bomb hits. A departing Kate torpedo bomber can be seen on the background. *(Official USN Photo)*

Above: Seki's Val at the moment of impact. *(Official USN Photo)*

Hornet's shattered signal bridge.   *(Official USN Photo)*

Above: *Hornet* fire fighters move to extinguish the fires ignited by flaming gasoline from Seki's wrecked Val, parts of which are strewn across the flight deck.   *(Official USN Photo)*

Above right: WT1 Lyle Skinner.   *(Compliments of Mrs. L. M. Skinner)*

Right: *Northampton* preparing to pass a tow to *Hornet*. A pair of destroyers are close aboard the carrier so their crews can help fight fires.

(Official USN Photo)

Above: Lt Robin Lindsey.   *(Official USN Photo)*

Right: Porter.   *(Official USN Photo)*

Smith's main deck forward was a charre‹ ruin after the ship was struck by a Kat torpedo bomber.   *(Official USN Photo*

Lt Swede Vejtasa.   *(Official USN Photo*

All of the Japanese warplanes were aloft and forming up within twelve minutes of Nagumo's order, by 0810. And, as soon as they had been launched, a second strike of twelve *Shokaku* Kates under LCdr Shigeharu Murata, twenty *Zuikaku* Vals under Lt Sadamu Takahashi, and sixteen *Zuikaku* Zeros commanded by Lt Kenjiro Nohtomi was readied for launch. The *hikotaicho* was Lieutenant Commander Murata.

Neither *Junyo's* nor *Zuiho's* air groups were included in the first two strikes; they would be used for follow-on missions, a luxury of the first magnitude. However, *Zuiho* was struck by bombs dropped by Lt Birney Strong and Ens Chuck Irvine before she could launch, but *Junyo*, which was far from the eyes of American snoopers, readied a twenty-nine-plane strike. Even as she did, *Zuiho's* engineering officer informed her captain that he would soon be able to launch warplanes, though recovery on the damaged after flight deck would be out of the question until the light carrier had undergone major repairs at a naval shipyard in Japan.

卍

The first American strike bombers, seven Scouting-8 and eight Bombing-8 Dauntlesses under Scouting-8's LCdr Gus Widhelm, did not begin launching until 0830, a full 20 minutes behind the first Japanese launch. Following Scouting-8 were six Avengers under the Torpedo-6 commander, Lt Iceberg Parker. Last aloft were eight Wildcats, two divisions of Fighting-72 under the squadron commander, LCdr Mike Sanchez. This strike, under the overall command of Lieutenant Commander Widhelm, was vectored directly against the last reported position of the Japanese carriers.

The next strike group began launching from *Enterprise* at 0900, 30 minutes after Widhelm's strike began launching. This force was led by Cdr Dick Gaines, the Air Group 10 commander, who was flying his own command Avenger. It consisted of just three Bombing-10 Dauntlesses flown by Scouting-10 pilots; seven Avengers under the Torpedo-10 commander, LCdr Jack Collett; and eight Wildcats under the Fighting-10 skipper, LCdr Jimmy Flatley.

Several Avengers available aboard *Enterprise* could not be launched on this mission because three Avenger aircrews were stuck aboard the plane-guard destroyers that had fished them out of the water during the night landing fiasco. In addition, two Torpedo-10 crews were temporarily marooned aboard *Hornet*, having been obliged to stay overnight after ferrying two replacement TBFs over late the previous afternoon. The minuscule showing by *Enterprise* dive-bombers was the result of the requirements of both providing the morning search and maintaining antisubmarine patrols for the entire task force.

The *Enterprise* strike group, such as it was, took an extremely long time getting airborne. Torpedo-10's Lt Doc Norton, who was one of the last in line, saw that each pilot ahead of him was stopping to read from a chalkboard held up by one of the flight-deck crewmen. When Norton's turn came, he read, "Proceed without *Hornet*." Norton, who took off a few minutes later, did not even see any *Hornet* aircraft, though that ship was starkly visible on the horizon.

Beginning at 0915, 45 minutes after Widhelm's strike commenced launching, the Air Group 8 commander, Cdr Walt Rodee, led off the second *Hornet* strike aboard his command Avenger: nine Dauntlesses under Lt John Lynch, the Bombing-8 exec; eight Avengers under Lt Ward Powell, the Torpedo-6 exec; and seven Fighting-72 Wildcats under Lt Warren Ford. This was the clean-up formation; it would strike what there was left to strike, carriers or surface warships.

The problem with the cobbled-together attack plan was that it was not cohesive. Both carriers initially launched the bombers and fighters it had available on the flight deck or at the ready and within easy reach on the hangar deck. Because each strike group was obliged to fly up to 200 miles to reach the Japanese—a condition aggravated by the need of the U.S. carriers to sail *away* from the Japanese during launches into the prevailing wind—forming the first *Hornet* and *Enterprise* groups into a single unit was deemed too demanding on fuel supplies. Moreover, there was no U.S. doctrine allowing the subordination of one air-group commander to another, nor the meshing of squadrons of one air group with like squadrons of another.

So the U.S. strike groups went off as a stream of separate

mixed units, each one composed of whatever aircraft happened to be available at the time of launch. Indeed, each of the three strike groups lacked internal cohesion; each was itself strung out over distances of several miles. The U.S. Navy had been developing types of formations that would cluster the bombers in such a way as to make them mutually supporting and to take full advantage of the forward- and rear-firing machine guns, but there was no doctrine for mixing dive-bombers and torpedo bombers in the same formation. Fighter-escort procedures were also relatively crude, but even these methods were defeated by the distance that had to be covered between each strike group's lead and rear bombers. The Wildcat divisions—two to each strike group—tended to stay high because the Wildcats needed an initial altitude advantage to effectively combat faster-climbing Zeros. In the case of the two fighter divisions escorting the lead *Hornet* strike, one division was obliged to fly cover with the higher Dauntlesses while the other was obliged to fly at 2,000 feet with the Avengers. The mixed *Enterprise* strike planes all flew at roughly the same altitude, with the two fighter divisions split up to guard either flank just ahead of the bombers.

卐

The opposing strike formations began passing one another when LCdr Gus Widhelm's lead strike group was only 60 miles out from *Hornet*. The low group of Wildcat-escorted Avengers actually passed directly beneath the larger Japanese formation. Widhelm and his pilots warily eyed LCdr Mamoru Seki's strike group, and Seki and his pilots reciprocated. Many individual gunners in both forces trained out their machine guns, but no one opened fire and none of the fighters broke formation to molest the enemy. Within minutes, each group had passed from sight of the other. Assuming the Japanese had warned their ships of his presence, and thus feeling no need to maintain radio silence, Lieutenant Commander Widhelm notified Task Force 61 that a large Japanese strike was inbound.

卐

Next up—about ten miles behind Widhelm and 5,000 feet lower to starboard—was Cdr Dick Gaines's smaller *Enterprise* strike

351

group, which had been launched only 20 minutes earlier and was only 45 miles from the ship. The *Enterprise* group was still low and climbing very slowly to conserve fuel—except for Commander Gaines, who had more fuel aboard than the other pilots and who rapidly climbed far ahead and higher than anyone else.

The Dauntlesses, which were the slowest of the three aircraft types, had the lead so that the swifter Avengers could hold station on them. This required the Avengers to weave a little in order to keep from overrunning the straining SBDs in the long, slow climb. The two fighter divisions—LCdr Jimmy Flatley's on the right and Lt(jg) John Leppla's on the left—were weaving back and forth 1,000 feet above and just ahead of the bombers in an effort to match speed with the much slower Dauntlesses.

Flatley and Leppla were both former *Lexington* pilots, veterans of the Coral Sea. Indeed, both had won Navy Crosses in history's first carrier versus carrier battle—Flatley for his superb fighter leadership and Leppla for being the most aggressive Dauntless pilot anyone could remember. Leppla's radioman-gunner at Coral Sea, also a Navy Cross holder, was ARM2 John Liska, who was returning home to *Enterprise* at that very moment with Scouting-10's Lt(jg) Martin Carmody.

About half the twenty-seven accompanying Zeros broke away from the Japanese formation and launched a vicious, scything attack from up-sun directly at the Torpedo-10 Avengers that made up the bulk of the *Enterprise* strike. Neither they nor the rest of Lieutenant Commander Seki's strike group had yet been seen by anyone in Gaines's group. For some reason, LCdr Gus Widhelm's warning message to Task Force 61 had not been monitored by anyone in the *Enterprise* strike group. Thus the attack came as a complete surprise. Ironically, only moments before the Japanese struck, LCdr Jack Collett, in the lead Avenger, had wondered aloud about the total absence of chatter on the radio—radio silence was seldom perfectly maintained—and had asked ARM1 Tom Nelson if the radio was okay. Nelson indeed found that someone had turned the frequency selector from the torpedo channel, and he made the necessary change. But it was too late.

The first Americans into the fray were Lt(jg) John Leppla and his division—Ens Al Mead, Ens Dusty Rhodes, and Ens Chip Reding, all novices except for Leppla, who flew directly into the oncoming Zeros. The four Wildcats instantly received hammer blows from hundreds of 20mm and 7.7mm rounds.

Ensign Reding, Leppla's second-section leader, saw the Zeros as they closed on the Avengers and immediately charged his guns and dropped his wing fuel tank. However, the transition from the drop tank to the main tank did not go well and Reding temporarily lost air speed. In a second or two, the fuel-starved engine sputtered and died, and the Wildcat spiraled toward the ocean as Reding desperately tried to restart the engine.

Ens Dusty Rhodes, Reding's wingman and the division's tail-end Charlie, also had a problem with his wing tank. It stuck in place when he tried to jettison it, and a Japanese incendiary or tracer round set it aflame. Rhodes nevertheless stayed on station above Reding while the latter fluttered toward the sea and until he got his engine restarted. During those few bleak moments, oncoming Zeros riddled Rhodes's canopy, shot out most of his instruments, and clipped his pushed-up goggles from his forehead—all without injuring him. Meanwhile, the wing tank continued to spew dangerous flames.

As his engine restarted, Chip Reding distinctly saw two Avengers struck by at least eight Zeros diving from above and both sides, from directly out of the sun. He led Rhodes right at the attackers, but other Japanese fighters intervened and pressed home their own attacks at such steep angles and at such quick intervals that neither Reding nor Rhodes was able to get any of the Zeros in his reflector gunsight. Somewhere in the swirling fight, however, the fire in Rhodes's wing tank abated, by then a small consolation.

Lt(jg) John Leppla was gone. The last person to see him was Dusty Rhodes, who had looked back just once to see Leppla making a head-on run at one Zero while a second Zero doggedly clung to his tail. A few moments later, Rhodes saw a parachute streaming toward the water and thought it might be Leppla, but there was no way to be sure because by then several Avengers had been culled from the formation.

Long before Rhodes's last sighting, Leppla's wingman, Ens Al Mead, had evacuated his disabled Wildcat—only an instant after the action got underway. He safely parachuted into the water.

After a while—it could only have been a minute or two—Reding and Rhodes became separated. Each of their fighters had suffered massive damage. Rhodes had no instruments and Reding's electrical system was gone, which meant he could not use his radio or fire his wing guns. Each pilot instinctively looked around for the other, and they managed to get back together. They had been flying as a team for months and simply fell into a smoothly executed Thach Weave, less as a means of suckering in Zeros—for neither Wildcat was able to fire its guns—than as a way of evading Zeros. Slowly, the two Wilcats were being pulverized. But neither pilot had yet been injured.

Then Rhodes's engine burned out and froze. He was at 2,500 feet when he put the nose down for speed and turned upwind preparatory to ditching. A Zero dead astern opened fire, and the 7.7mm bullets severed the rudder-control cable. By then, Rhodes was approaching 1,000 feet. It was time to leave. He threw back the remains of the Wildcat's canopy, stood up, kicked the stick right into the instrument panel, and yanked the D-ring on his parachute. The unfurling silk canopy neatly plucked Dusty Rhodes from his dead fighter and carried him gently to the sea, where he made a hard landing. When Rhodes next looked up, Chip Reding was zooming away with three Zeros glued to his tail.

Reding tried to stay over Rhodes, but the Zeros on his tail quickly drove him away. He dived toward the water and was beneath 100 feet before he was able to break away from the attackers. The strike group was long gone, and the Japanese seemed to be gone, too. Chip Reding turned the nose of his scrap-heap fighter toward *Enterprise*'s last known position.

卐

LCdr Jimmy Flatley's division did not initially see the Zero attack nor Leppla's response because it happened to be weaving away from the main formation when the attack was sprung. By the time Flatley realized that his group was under attack, the relative position of Leppla's division had shifted from the formation's port vanguard to well astern. At the same moment, Flatley saw one Zero take position below and ahead of the TBFs.

As soon as Flatley saw the attack on the Avengers get under way, he turned into the main formation to harass the lead Zero, which was by then well along in its approach from beneath the Avengers. Flatley executed a diving turn, came up with a full-deflection shot, and unleashed a stream of .50- caliber bullets. The Zero pulled up and turned away from the Avenger as Flatley recovered above and to the side to begin a second run. Flatley again got the Zero in his sights and flicked his trigger while still at extreme range; a Zero hardly ever stayed put long enough for a perfect set-up. The instinctive gamble paid off when the Zero began smoking. A third, high-side attack sent the Japanese fighter hurtling into the waves.

When Jimmy Flatley looked up for more targets, he saw that the Zeros were gone and that the group of Torpedo-10 Avengers had been reduced from eight to six. Moments later, two of the six Avengers turned back toward *Enterprise*, apparently with engine trouble or severe battle damage. Leppla's Wildcat division had vanished.

卍

The first American warplane to be struck by the Japanese fighters was the lead Avenger, piloted by the Torpedo-10 skipper, LCdr Jack Collett. ARM1 Tom Nelson had just heard a bleat of "Bogies!" over the radio and was cranking back his tunnel-mounted .30-caliber machine gun when he heard the throaty voice of the .50-caliber turret gun overhead. An instant later, the lead Avenger shivered right down her air frame and involuntarily fishtailed. Then the starboard wing went down a bit. ARM1 Nelson realized that the torpedo bomber was gliding toward the ocean. A quick peek out the starboard porthole revealed a sick look on the face of Lt(jg) Robert Oscar, the pilot of the TBF stepped off Collett's starboard wing.

Oscar's expression told Nelson that it was time to go. He was just beginning to move when he realized that smoke was pouring into the fuselage. Nelson grabbed the interphone mike and yelled into it to get Lieutenant Commander Collett's attention, but there was no answer. It looked more and more like the engine had been damaged or destroyed and the pilot had been injured or killed.

Nelson crawled into the radio compartment and pulled the locking pins on the hatch, which he kicked out into space. AM1 Steve Nadison was still in the turret, so Nelson had to get his attention and hand him his parachute. As he did, he realized that Nadison had balked at wearing even his parachute harness in the cramped turret. So, while all Nelson had to do was clip his emergency parachute to his harness, Nadison had to climb into his harness and then clip on the 'chute. It was a life and death difference.

Nelson tarried for a moment to help Nadison into the harness, but it was too cramped in the radio compartment for so much frantic movement. When it became clear that the struggle was getting nowhere, Nadison looked right into Nelson's eyes and cocked his head, a signal for Nelson to give him room by bailing out. With that, Nelson clipped on his 'chute and stood in the hatchway. The slipstream was powerful and the airplane was still accelerating as it dived toward the ocean. It took a real concentration of energy for Nelson to dive through the tiny hatchway, but he did. The last thing he saw in the Avenger was the altimeter, which showed a reading of 2,000 feet.

Tom Nelson instantly yanked the D-ring on his parachute pack, far too soon for inertia to overcome his momentum, which was the same as the falling airplane's. The force of the pilot 'chute's impact with the rushing air tore it away from the main 'chute and knocked Nelson out. When the radioman came to, he was floating beneath a beautiful white silk canopy. He saw a large burning fuel slick on the surface of the ocean about a quarter mile away. This was certainly his airplane. He quickly looked around for more parachutes, but there was none. At that moment, a Zero made a firing pass on Nelson, and the 'chute was badly riddled. However, Nelson slipped into the water a moment later and ducked beneath the surface. The respite was short-lived; he had bluffed the Japanese pilot, but one of the parachute shroud lines had become entangled with the buckle of his flight suit. He was being dragged down by the sodden, heavy parachute when he found the tangle and pulled it free. He yanked the twin D-rings on his Mae West life jacket, but only one side automatically inflated. He blew the other side up by the mouth tube and discovered that it had a hole in it, which gave him something upon which he could focus his attention. He had no idea what to do next.

⌗

AMM3 Tom Powell, the turret gunner aboard Lt(jg) Robert Oscar's TBF, located on the right wing of LCdr Jack Collett's lead Avenger, was concentrating on the right side of the formation when the Zeros hit. This was his role in a new method of formation defense known as "concentrated cone fire." All the turret gunners on the right watched and fired to the right, and all the turret gunners on the left watched and fired to the left. The area overhead and between the right and left airplanes was a free-fire zone. The tunnel gunners similarly directed their attention and fire by the same method. From the first moment the Zeros broke out of the sun firing all their weapons, Powell was engaged up to his eyeballs in returning the fire. He never even noticed that the lead Avenger had fallen out of the formation.

During one sweeping firing pass by a Zero *shotai*, Powell thought he saw one of the enemy fighters explode in midair, but his attention was instantly diverted elsewhere. A few moments later, during a fast peek over the side of the airplane, he definitely saw another Zero smoking as tracers from another Avenger passed all the way through it. The ensuing kill was credited to ARM3 Charles Shinneman, the turret gunner aboard Lt Tommy Thompson's TBF, the lead plane in the stepped-down second torpedo element. Powell had no fewer than three Zeros in view at all times throughout the brief engagement.

⌗

The tail-end Avenger in the first section, piloted by Ens John Reed, was mortally hit by the second Zero *shotai* passing from ahead to astern. AMM3 Murray Glasser, the turret gunner, barely had time to fire a few spurts of .50-caliber at the passing Zeros when the intercom crackled with Ensign Reed's screams, "Bail out! Bail out!" At precisely that moment, Glasser realized that pieces of the airplane were flying back past the turret, and he thought he saw the ends of some flames licking around his post. He instantly locked the turret and dropped into the large radio compartment.

The gunners' chest parachutes, which were too large to wear in the confined turret and tunnel, were secured by large bungee strips to the bulkhead right over the starboard hatch. Glasser was the first to get to them, and he threw one to the radioman-bombardier, RM3 Grant Harrison, who was sitting in the jump seat in front of the bombsight. It took Glasser another instant to realize that Harrison was already pushing the hatch open against the slipstream, though he did not have his parachute on. Glasser was about to say something to Harrison, but he saw that the radioman was glassy-eyed and realized that he was in a catatonic state.

Glasser dived through the open hatchway and pulled his parachute's D-ring. As the 'chute billowed above him, he saw a Zero knife straight into the water. Minutes later—he lost track of time—he gently entered the water and climbed out of the encumbering parachute harness without any difficulty. When next he looked, the sky was empty and eerily quiet.

It took several seconds after the initial attack on the lead Avengers for the Japanese fighters to work their way back to Lt Doc Norton's airplane, which was next to last in the formation. Both Norton's plane and the rearmost, piloted by Lt(jg) Dick Batten, were instantly riddled by accurate, heavy 20mm cannon and 7.7mm machine gun fire. However, both of the turret gunners got rounds into one of the Zeros as it flashed on by from astern to ahead, and the Zero ignited like a torch just before it grazed Norton's right wingtip. Though all the gunners probably got a piece of the destroyed Zero, the entire kill was credited to Batten's tunnel gunner, AM2 Rex Holgrin.

When the Zeros were gone—they made only the one sweeping pass—Doc Norton checked his riddled TBF for damage and discovered that he had no hydraulic power. This meant that the bomb bay and .50-caliber turret were inoperable. The Avenger's right aileron was flapping in the slipstream, its control cable severed, and there was a large hole in the right wing disturbingly close to the locking mechanism. A closer check of the right wing revealed that the red warning tab was projecting, a pretty fair indicator that the locking pin was not properly seated. No one aboard Norton's plane had been injured.

Norton conducted a brief internal argument with himself. It was almost certain that Japanese carriers lay ahead, and getting Japanese carriers was what he was drawing pay to do. But the fact that the bomb bay doors were locked tight by the disabled hydraulic system, and that the rear turret could not be worked at optimum performance for the same reason militated against continuing. The clincher was that projecting wing-lock warning tab. There was a better than even chance that the right wing would fold back if Norton pulled too many negative gees, and doing so was a virtual certainty in a combat torpedo approach. So Norton gave the section leader, Lt Tommy Thompson, the hand signal for "sick airplane" and gingerly peeled into a turn for home. Lt(jg) Dick Batten, whose TBF was in similarly bad condition, took Norton's lead and joined him for the trip back to *Enterprise*.

It naturally occurred to many of the six airmen aboard the returning Avengers that they were behind the Japanese strike group; all of them had an uneasy feeling about what they might find.

36

The lead American attack formation—seven Scouting-8 Dauntlesses, eight Bombing-8 Dauntlesses, six Torpedo-6 Avengers, and eight Fighting-72 Wildcats—found Japanese ships at 1025. A pair of Japanese cruisers escorted by at least two destroyers were sighted first, off to the right, only 150 miles from the American warplanes' launch point. Twenty miles farther on, someone reported what appeared to be a pair of battleships to port; closer inspection revealed what appeared to be the two battleships plus two cruisers and as many as seven destroyers.

As soon as the battleships were spotted, nine carrier Zeros reached out at the Air Group 8 formation from almost dead ahead. For some reason, the four Wildcats escorting the Dauntlesses had fallen far behind the dive-bombers and were level with them, hardly the best spot from which to parry a challenge from the lithe Zeros. Nevertheless, the four Wildcat pilots, led by LCdr Mike Sanchez, turned to meet them.

Instantly, the second element of Sanchez's Wildcat division—Lt(jg) Thomas Johnson leading Ens Phil Souza—was separated from Sanchez's element. The Zero that pounced on Johnson and

360

Souza came across from the left, over the top of both F4Fs. Ensign Souza, who had shared credit for a Japanese four-engine patrol bomber on October 16, was spellbound by the enemy carrier fighter's quick passage until it occurred to him that the man flying the gorgeous fighter out there was trying to kill him. He began weaving to throw off the Japanese pilot's aim, but too late. About seventy-five 7.7mm rounds struck Souza's Wildcat.

The Wildcat's slow speed, Souza's heightened adrenalin-induced strength, and the impact of so many bullets caused the Wildcat to snap-roll several times. Souza's erratic flying undoubtedly caused the Japanese pilot to assume that Souza was dead, so he eased off to work on Johnson. Souza recovered to find that his right aileron was about shot off and that the Wildcat was extremely difficult to maneuver. However, the Zero was dead ahead, a perfect target. Souza quickly checked his reflector gunsight and applied pressure to the trigger. The Zero staggered and began throwing large chunks into the air as it rolled away. An instant later, the sky in front of Souza's fighter was empty; both the Zero and Johnson's Wildcat were gone.

As Souza looked for other airplanes, he noticed that another Zero, which was nearly obscured by his wings, was working over the Wildcat piloted by Lt(jg) Willie Roberts, LCdr Mike Sanchez's wingman. Souza fired a burst at long range, which scared the Zero off. As Souza flew beside Roberts's Wildcat, he saw that its fuel tanks were pouring fuel into the air and that the other pilot was bathed in blood. Souza's earphones came alive: "We better go home." There was no sign of Sanchez or Johnson, so Souza and Roberts turned their damaged Wildcats for home. As Phil Souza had initially feared, Lt(jg) Thomas Johnson had been shot down.

After losing track of Lt(jg) Willie Roberts, LCdr Mike Sanchez outmaneuvered one of the attacking Zeros; he was given credit for a probable. At the same time, Lt Jack Bower's Wildcat division, which had been escorting the first group of *Hornet* Avengers, went after several Zeros hovering at the fringes of the action. Two of the Zeros were knocked down, one by Bower's wingman, Lt(jg) Robert Jennings, and the other by the second-element leader, Lt(jg) Robert Sorenson. In the general melee, however, Bower was shot down.

After emerging from the melee, Sanchez took over the lead of Bower's division and bored on ahead to try to overtake the receding friendly strike group. He eventually joined on the Avengers Bower's division had earlier been escorting, but that still left the first wave of *Hornet* Dauntlesses unescorted.

⇄

After flying on for many minutes past the battleships, one of LCdr Gus Widhelm's Dauntless pilots radioed the attack-group leader with some helpful advice: "There's no carriers in sight here; let's return."

Widhelm briefly considered turning back to comb the vicinity of the battleships, but his instincts pointed ahead. Five minutes later, an eagle-eyed pilot reported seeing two carriers, a light cruiser, and four destroyers. Closer attention revealed that one of the carriers—*Zuiho*—was smoking. The other, larger, carrier was *Shokaku*. The third carrier, *Zuikaku*, was safely beneath a rain squall when *Zuiho* and *Shokaku* were spotted by the American carrier bombers. Without a flicker of hesitation, Widhelm had his radio-man broadcast a sighting report while he selected the larger of the two visible carriers, undamaged *Shokaku*.

The dive-bombing attack was to have been coordinated with an attack by the six Torpedo-6 Avengers, but the Avengers had never climbed beyond 800 feet and their pilots had entirely missed the carrier formation. As the fifteen SBDs, each carrying a 1,000-pound bomb, moved to find the optimum attack position, several Zeros from the carriers' combat air patrol flew out to investigate the incoming carrier bombers.

A moment after the first Zeros turned to meet the Americans, two bursting antiaircraft rounds marked the Dauntless formation for yet more Zeros. The Dauntlesses were then at 12,000 feet and still many minutes from the point at which they could begin their dives. At the approach of the first Zero, Widhelm patted the side of his airplane: "Close up."

The American pilots tightened their defensive formation and coolly plowed on. Gus Widhelm lifted his dive-bomber's nose and drew a bead on the lead Zero. When the sight reticle fell on the

Zero's engine cowling, Widhelm squeezed the trigger and unleashed his machine guns. He had a fleeting sensation of flame as he flew past the oncoming fighter.

The pilots following Widhelm had all they could handle just trying to maintain formation on the weaving, bucking, bobbing flight leader. The Zeros appeared to Lt(jg) Ralph Hovind, the next man behind Widhelm, to be coming directly out of the sun. As each one came into view, Gus Widhelm violently turned in toward it, and the entire Dauntless formation followed, guns blazing as the Zero passed above it from ahead to astern. About all Hovind took time out to do was keep an eye on Widhelm, whose moves would be exactly echoed by the entire formation. Hovind had enormous confidence in the flight leader; he was placing his life entirely in Widhelm's hands. Indeed, his major concern was that he would be catching the 7.7mm and 20mm rounds meant for the leader.

Each attacking Zero ran into the concentrated fire of as many of the guns as the Dauntless defensive formation could bring to bear. No amount of gunfire, no amount of diving and twisting and weaving by the Japanese fighter pilots could break the integrity of the American formation.

As Ralph Hovind followed the progress of yet another approaching Zero, he distinctly saw a pattern of 7.7mm bullets strike the cowling of the flight leader's bomber. Oil immediately began leaking, soon followed by thin wisps of smoke. It would be just a matter of time before Widhelm's engine suffered a complete failure. For the time being, however, Widhelm doggedly held his place at the head of the formation, still plainly visible as the flight leader.

The pace of the action was unremitting. Far back in the formation, Lt Fred Bates, the Bombing-8 flight officer, glanced over at Lt(jg) Phil Grant's Dauntless just in time to see a fresh belt of .30-caliber ammunition ripped from the gunner's hands by the slipstream and lost over the side. A moment later, Bates's attention was redirected at a Zero making a steep diving run on his element. As all the nearby gunners trained out their free guns on the intruder, the Zero came on so fast that his wingtips were pulling white vortices. Suddenly, the fighter's right wingtip flipped off, and the fuselage and remaining wing spun awkwardly toward the sea.

Following a continuum of attacks—too many firing passes for the beleaguered Dauntless pilots or gunners to count—the first victim fell away; Lt(jg) Phil Grant and his radioman-gunner rode their mortally damaged SBD all the way into the sea. A minute later, Lt(jg) Clay Fisher's Dauntless rolled away from the formation and glided toward the waves. Several concerned friends saw Fisher land his Dauntless on the water, but neither Fisher nor his rearseatman was ever seen again. Lt(jg) Ken White, who was shot in the left hand and shoulder, had to abort when his Dauntless's port aileron was shot away in the same burst; though the Dauntless was virtually uncontrollable, White managed to head out of the battle area without ditching or being downed. All of the other Dauntlesses had been damaged to one degree or another. Lt(jg) Ralph Hovind was certain his airplane had over a hundred bullet holes in it; all the wing tanks had been holed, and a 7.7mm bullet from a Zero Hovind never saw entered the cockpit and shattered a plastic control knob, which sent slivers of the bullet and the plastic into Hovind's right leg.

The loss of Grant, Fisher, and White left an even dozen Dauntlesses, which closed ranks behind Gus Widhelm as each new loss was counted. The running fight had carrried the evading Dauntlesses too low for an optimum dive-bombing attack. But there was no way to regain altitude in the little distance remaining; to do so would mean going around in the face of the unremitting Zero attacks.

Finally, as the reduced bombing formation was swinging into its final approach, the last of the oil drained from Gus Widhelm's SBD, and the engine immediately overheated. Widhelm held position through another set of gunnery runs by the Zeros, but the engine froze as overheated bearings visibly began burning. The flight leader patted the top of his head—"Take over"—and pointed his right forefinger at a thoroughly startled Lt(jg) Ralph Hovind, who had begun the mission as a stand-in for Widhelm's ailing regular number-two pilot.

The bomber formation passed just overhead as Widhelm jettisoned his 1,000-pound bomb and began his long glide toward the sea. As soon as the Scouting-8 skipper was clear of the formation, the Bombing-8 skipper, Lt Moe Vose, surged ahead with all his Bombing-8 Dauntlesses. As Vose passed Ralph Hovind's lead Scouting-8 Dauntless, he gave Hovind a broad grin and signed that he was to relinquish the lead. Thoroughly thankful, Hovind nodded his assent and eased off the throttle a little so that he could drop back with the surviving Scouting-8 Dauntlesses.

Gus Widhelm's Dauntless must have seemed like buzzard meat to the only Zero pilot who bothered to follow it as it corkscrewed away from the main dive-bomber formation. But as Widhelm tried to find a small patch of unoccupied ocean in the midst of the surging, circling Japanese battle formation, ARM2 George Stokely dueled the Zero to a standstill. Widhelm was flying at extremely low altitude, nearly ready to pancake into the water, before the Zero finally broke off. At the last moment, Widhelm popped his dying airplane's landing flaps and dropped the tailhook—to warn him that he was about to enter the water as well as to slow the Dauntless when it did connect with the waves. The riddled Dauntless came to a smooth stop and Widhelm and Stokely instantly climbed onto a wing and deployed the life raft.

The Zeros kept hammering away at the eleven remaining Dauntlesses throughout the final approach. Two American gunners were severely wounded, and all the Dauntlesses were damaged by the time they arrived over *Shokaku*'s flight deck. Up to that point, the excited American pilots and gunners had counted fifteen Zeros downed, though the Japanese counted only five. Conversely, the Japanese pilots claimed fifteen Dauntlesses.

At nearly the last moment, Lt(jg) Joe Auman saw a Zero streak by his Bombing-8 Dauntless from high right to low left, firing all the way. Shrapnel from a 20mm cannon round stung Auman in the back of the head and riddled the radio set between the cockpit and the gunner. As Auman reflexively wiped blood from the back of his flight helmet, he instinctively banked his Dauntless around to the left in the slim hope of hitting the departing Zero with his forward machine guns. The Zero pulled up and away, and Auman tried to follow the maneuver, which nearly stalled the Dauntless. The abrupt maneuvers and near stall caused Auman to miss the final group maneuver before the dive. When Auman finally looked up, he was alone.

Lt Moe Vose armed his 1,000-pound bomb and pitched his Dauntless into the nose-down diving attitude. Then the others followed at regular intervals. Thousands of feet below, *Shokaku* used all her formidable maneuvering power to try to slip from beneath the American bombsights.

Midway back in the bomber stream, Lt Fred Bates's gunner warned Bates of a Zero approaching from dead astern as Bates was trying to concentrate on following the SBD dead ahead into the dive. Bates shrugged off the news, spread his dive flaps, and pushed over.

Lt(jg) Ralph Hovind's Dauntless, which was leading the Scouting-8 group, was struck by a Zero just as Hovind executed his dive. A stream of bullets carried away the rear canopy and blew the guns from the hands of Hovind's radioman-gunner.

Lieutenant Vose dropped his bomb at low altitude and zoomed down to hug the waves. Each of nine remaining Dauntless pilots did the same. Vose got a confirmed hit; the detonation of Vose's bomb blew a large splinter from one of the two remaining flight decks to launch warplanes against Pearl Harbor into the open cockpit of Lt Fred Bates's Dauntless just as Bates was pressing his own release. As Bates pulled away just off the surface, he looked back in time to see *Shokaku*'s after elevator heaved high above the flight deck in a cloud of flames and smoke.

Lt(jg) Ralph Hovind was unable to reach his radioman on the intercom, and assumed the gunner had been killed or injured. He had no idea how badly his Dauntless had been damaged. The Zeros were gone, but the antiaircraft fire rising from the carrier and her consorts was extremely intense. By the time the remaining Scouting-8 SBDs began their dives, the Japanese gunners had the range and deflection all worked out. The oncoming rounds looked to Hovind like Roman candles. He was certain that each new burst was going to strike his dive-bomber, but each blob of rising red light fell away at the last moment. Hovind decided that if he was badly injured before he reached his bomb-release point, he would dive straight into the carrier's flight deck, bomb and all. As it was, his bomb narrowly missed the carrier's island.

Lt(jg) Joe Auman, who had become detached from the Bombing-8 group, entered his dive alone a few moments after he saw the tail of the last Scouting-8 Dauntless pitch up and over. He was able to follow the plane ahead to the bomb-release point by keeping his dive brakes closed and flattening out his dive to only 60 degrees, as opposed to the usual 70–75-degree dive. Doing so also meant he would have to find an aiming point fast and get his bomb detached at fairly high altitude if he was to have a chance to recover over the water. Auman's concentration was perfect; nothing else in the world mattered as much as that onrushing flight deck. As Auman angled across the carrier from the starboard bow to the port quarter, a detached part of his mind saw that the flight deck was already burning, that smoke was spreading back from about midships, abreast the island. The rest of Auman's mind was scrolling through an endless set of barely perceived mental calculations aimed precisely at matching his dive, the pitch of the bomb, and the momentum of the carrier. The bomb was released well below 2,000 feet. As Auman used the speed of his no-brakes dive to get away, his gunner sang out with the news that their bomb had solidly struck *Shokaku*'s flight deck.

The American pilots and gunners counted three hits, the Japanese reported as many as six, and Gus Widhelm, who was bobbing nearby in his raft, counted six. Whatever the actual number of hits, *Shokaku*'s flight deck was riddled and had to be shut down, and her innards suffered grievous harm. Neither she nor *Zuiho* would be lost, but both would be in repair yards for very long refittings.

The retirement was nearly as exciting as the approach. Lt Fred Bates saw large-caliber shells detonating on the water dead ahead and on both sides of his recovering Dauntless. Lt(jg) Joe Auman pulled out of his no-brakes dive to the northeast, so had to turn back and pass around the edge of the Japanese task force. He was so low over the water that he had to dart between rather than over the screening warships. As Auman turned left just outside the screen, he finally met up with a half dozen friendly bombers and joined on them as he chomped into a candy bar he had brought along for some quick energy. He was amazed at how much saliva his overexcited system was producing as he ate.

彡

The six Torpedo-6 Avengers that had been accompanying Widhelm's SBDs entirely missed seeing the carriers and did not pick up Widhelm's sighting broadcast. The torpedo squadron commander, Lt Iceberg Parker, doggedly led his flight to the appointed 210-mile extremity of the outbound search leg, then turned northwest to scout another 50 miles out. Nothing was seen during the extended search, so Parker led his torpedo bombers around to try to relocate the cruisers and destroyers they had seen earlier. The carriers were again obscured by intervening rain squalls, so Parker decided to go after the surface targets. At no time during the long search was he or any of his pilots in radio contact with any of the other American attack elements.

Parker selected for his target heavy cruiser *Suzuya*, a part of RAdm Hiroaki Abe's Vanguard Group. Attacking through extremely dense antiaircraft fire from an assortment of cruisers and destroyers, Parker's six *Hornet* Avengers spread out across *Suzuya*'s bows and delivered a classic hammer-and-anvil attack. Theoretically, the cruiser should have been hit by torpedoes on one side or the other, no matter which way she turned to evade the onrushing fish. Two of the American aerial torpedoes were seen by American airmen to run erratically, and one torpedo hung in its bomb bay. Of the remaining three, American airmen counted three hits: two on the cruiser's port side and one on her starboard side. In reality, *Suzuya* combed the wakes of the three American torpedoes and sailed on without an iota of damage.

The six Avengers recovered without loss or damage and headed for Point Option in the company of the four remaining Fighting-72 Wildcats led by LCdr Mike Sanchez.

彡

The battle-depleted *Enterprise* strike group of, now, three Dauntlesses and four Avengers heard Gus Widhelm's initial report pinpointing the carriers and was rushing to catch up at 1030 when, during a course correction, several of the bomber pilots and crewmen spotted the two Japanese battleships and their consorts. At 1030, Lt Tommy Thompson, who had taken command of the Avenger flight following the loss of LCdr Jack Collett, radioed LCdr Jimmy Flatley, the fighter leader, to see if the Wildcats had enough fuel to fly on another 90 miles to the location of the carriers reported at 1025 by Gus Widhelm. Flatley's four remaining fighters were about wrung out; they had dropped their auxiliary tanks before plowing into the Zeros during the earlier ambush, and high-speed maneuvering had used up a great deal of the fuel in their main tanks. Flatley replied that he was sure the fighters could not fly the full distance. The decision was Thompson's, and he decided to briefly search in the immediate area for other carriers.

During the 10-minute search, the three *Enterprise* Dauntlesses —three Bombing-10 airplanes flown by three Scouting-10 pilots— flew off on their own to take up attack positions over battlecruiser *Kirishima*. The three dived from 12,000 feet. The element leader, Lt(jg) John Richey, a former Scouting-5 veteran now flying with Scouting-10, claimed a near miss. Lt(jg) Skip Ervin, a 1940 Harvard graduate on his first mission, claimed a solid hit on Turret-2, forward, which housed three huge 14-inch guns. Lt(jg) Glenn Estes, another Scouting-5 alumnus, claimed that his bomb struck the starboard deck amidships. A number of American pilots, including LCdr Jimmy Flatley, saw smoke issuing from the huge ship. However, the 30-year-old battlecruiser was well protected by her thick armor and suffered negligible material damage, if any. The three Dauntlesses rendezvoused at wave-top height and fled for home. As they ran, the three Scouting-10 gunners shared a kill by converging the fire of their six .30-caliber free guns on a lone stalker.

The four remaining *Enterprise* Avengers descended to wave-top height in a series of skid turns and there found heavy cruiser *Chikuma* crossing their path. As antiaircraft fire—estimated by the harried pilots to be up to 3-inch—burst well behind the tiny torpedo formation, Lieutenant Thompson dropped his fish at a 45-degree angle off the cruiser's port bow, and his wingman, Ens

Robert Oscar, dropped his off the cruiser's port beam. The other element—Lt Jim McConnaughhay leading Lt(jg) Raymond Wyllie—followed Thompson and Oscar toward the cruiser's port side, but McConnaughhay's torpedo hung in the bomb bay. Wyllie dropped without effect as McConnaughhay swung around for another try. The errant torpedo left McConnaughhay's TBF on the second try, but the cruiser veered away at the last moment and the fish went on by. Five tries, four drops, four misses.

The four accompanying Fighting-10 Wildcats strafed *Chikuma* while the torpedo bombers were boring in. Undoubtedly, the many half-inch machine-gun rounds caused some damage and might have caused some deaths or injuries aboard the cruiser but had negligible lasting effect. As soon as Lieutenant McConnaughhay completed his second torpedo run, the Wildcats joined on the Avengers and headed for home.

⚛

Lt John Lynch, the Bombing-8 exec, unwittingly led nine of his squadron's Dauntlesses around the edge of the ambush of the *Enterprise* Avengers. The action itself was too far away to be seen, but Lynch saw three airplanes crash into the water as well as four parachutes descending. He had no idea whose planes or parachutes they were.

Lynch's group was joined at 1000 by ten *Hornet* Avengers—nine from Torpedo-6 and one piloted by Cdr Walt Rodee, the Air Group 8 commander. At about that time, a transmission from LCdr Gus Widhelm, in the lead attack formation, pinpointed the Japanese surface warships but indicated that Widhelm was boring ahead to try to locate the carriers. Lynch's group reached the Japanese surface force just as one of Widhelm's pilots advised Widhelm, "There's no carriers in sight here; let's return." There was absolutely no way for Lynch to know that he was monitoring an unwanted suggestion and not a relayed proclamation from the leader of the vanguard attack group. Lynch knew that Widhelm was a half hour ahead of him and he could see that visibility ahead was unlimited, so he reasonably deduced that there were no carriers within effective range. Accordingly, he radioed Commander

Rodee with news of his decision to immediately attack a heavy cruiser that was just then passing beneath his wings and which was firing its antiaircraft batteries at his formation. Rodee did not protest—he never heard Lynch's transmission—so Lynch proceeded with the attack.

The attack against heavy cruiser *Chikuma* commenced at 1040 from 11,500 feet. The target and four accompanying destroyers put out an extremely large volume of antiaircraft gunfire during the entire approach and on into the Dauntlesses' dives. Lieutenant Lynch, in the lead, and Lt(jg) J. C. Barrett, in the third SBD, each claimed a solid hit. Indeed, one of the two 1,000-pound bombs detonated on the heavy crusier's bridge, injuring her captain, Capt Keizo Komura, and killing or maiming all but a dozen of the numerous Japanese officers and sailors around him. A second 1,000-pound bomb ripped apart the cruiser's main battery control station, damaged torpedo tubes, and started several small fires. And a third 1,000-pound bomb penetrated *Chikuma*'s deck and detonated within the ship's engineering spaces, flooding a boiler room and putting an engine out of commission. Two near misses amidships caused underwater damage while piercing the cruiser's upperworks with numerous splinters.

As Lieutenant Lynch led his unscathed flight away to the east at 500 feet, many jubilant pilots and all the radioman-gunners saw that the cruiser was barely limping along through pillars of flame and oily smoke. Just as the American warplanes flew from sight, the severely injured cruiser was rocked by a secondary detonation that belched a great cloud of smoke high enough to be seen by the Dauntless crewmen.

卐

Nine bomb-armed Torpedo-6 Avengers and four escorting Fighting-72 Wildcats commanded by the Torpedo-6 exec, Lt Ward Powell, were approached by four Zeros as they neared the end of their outbound leg, but the Zeros turned away without attacking. As the Zeros passed from sight, Lt(jg) Jerry Rapp, a Torpedo-10 pilot who had been temporarily dragooned into Torpedo-6 after ferrying a TBF from *Enterprise* to *Hornet* the evening before, saw a large formation of Japanese bombers high overhead on a reciprocal course.

As the Avengers were nearing the end of their search leg about 180 miles from *Hornet*, Lieutenant Powell saw Japanese cruisers and destroyers a little further on. This was Admiral Abe's Vanguard Group. At an altitude of 10,000 feet, Powell led the Avengers to the northwest, around the curtain of antiaircraft gunfire. In the near distance, he was able to see a number of Dauntlesses—Lynch's flight—diving on one of the cruisers.

It took ten minutes for the TBFs to clear the antiaircraft fire, at which point a knot of Zeros made a head-on approach. The Avengers closed up and flew straight at the Zeros. The Fighting-72 division commanded by Lt John Sutherland left the clustered torpedo bombers to strike at the main body of the Zero squadron. Sutherland claimed one Zero destroyed, as did his second-element leader, Lt(jg)Henry Carey.

Only one of the Zero pilots followed through with an attack on the TBFs; he made an opposite-course firing run straight through the Avenger formation. The bombers obligingly spread out to give the Zero pilot some room. The combined speed of the Zero and the oncoming TBFs was so great that turret gunners traversing to follow the Zero had time to get off only a few rounds apiece before the fighter had zoomed out of range. The Zero fired countless rounds without apparent effect, and the American pilots and gunners did the same. The action was repeated in all its details when the Zero made a second firing pass.

As soon as the Zeros left, the Avengers closed formation again, continued northward for ten minutes, then turned northwestward for yet another ten minutes. The weather was generally clear, but towering cumulus clouds obscured the view in some sectors. No carriers could be seen, so Lieutenant Powell decided to go after Abe's force.

Powell selected heavy cruiser *Tone*, which had been with *Ryujo* at Eastern Solomons. The approach was made from astern, using as much cloud cover as there was. Only a relatively small amount of antiaircraft fire rose to greet the Avengers as the pilots dropped their landing gear to help slow the 45-degree dives.

Lieutenant Powell's glide-bombing attack was marred by an electrical failure that both knocked his radio off the air and obliged him to drop all four of his 500-pound bombs in one salvo. At least two of the following Avengers suffered similar failures, with the same results.

Lt(jg) Jerry Rapp found that he had to steepen his dive angle to keep his bombsight on the rapidly oncoming target, which was well into a series of precipitous evasive maneuvers. Because of the tremendous pressure on his stick and rudder, Rapp was only able to make minor corrections after that. Rapp elected to pass through 1,500 feet, at which point he was supposed to have released his bombs. He kept diving through 1,200 and pickled the bombs one at a time with both the electrical and manual bomb releases. The TBF was diving at a 55-degree angle by then, and was too close to the water for a comfortable recovery. As soon as the bombs were away, Rapp retracted his landing gear and closed the bomb-bay doors to reduce drag. Then he leveled off and advanced the throttle to maintain the high speed he had accumulated in the dive. His next hurdle was an enemy ship, dead ahead. He finally came straight and level at about 300 feet and instantly began jinking maneuvers to throw off the aim of gunners ahead, abeam, and astern. He passed directly over the bow of a destroyer and finally broke free from the worst of the gunfire.

None of Lt Ward Powell's TBFs scored any hits on *Tone*.

Lt(jg) Humphrey Tallman, a veteran fighter pilot who had been transferred into torpedo bombers to help make good losses at Midway, executed a glide-bombing attack on *Tone* and released one bomb, went after a destroyer with one bomb, and finally attacked a light cruiser with his last two bombs. However, none of Tallman's bombs found a target.

Lt(jg) Jerry Rapp had become separated from the other Avengers during the recovery from his over-steep glide-bombing attack. He was able to pick up some chatter on the radio, but nothing helpful. Remaining close to the bases of the cumulus clouds so he would have a safe haven in the event he was found by prowling Zeros, the lone Torpedo-10 pilot shaped a course for where he hoped home would be.

The rest of the Avengers flew northeastward through heavy antiaircraft fire until they were out of visual range of the Japanese, then they rendezvoused and turned for home. None received any important damage, and none caused any damage.

࿕

So far, losses among the various attack groups amounted to three *Enterprise* Wildcats, two *Hornet* Wildcats, two *Enterprise* Avengers, and two *Hornet* Dauntlesses downed.

Four of the six crewmen aboard the downed Avengers died inside their airplanes and two—ARM1 Tom Nelson and AMM3 Murray Glasser—were eventually rescued by Japanese warships, as were Fighting-10 pilots Ens Dusty Rhodes and Ens Al Mead. Lt Johnny Leppla, of Fighting-10, Lt Jack Bower, of Fighting-72, and Lt(jg) Thomas Johnson, of Fighting-72, were all lost with their Wildcats. Lt(jg) Clay Fisher, of Scouting-8, and his radioman-gunner presumably survived the ditching of their Dauntless, but neither was found by either side. Lt(jg) Phil Grant and his rearseat-man, also of Scouting-8, were killed when their Dauntless crashed. LCdr Gus Widhelm and ARM2 George Stokely were rescued by a Catalina patrol bomber on October 29.

No Japanese ship was sunk, but, counting damage inflicted by the scouts, two carrier flight decks were down, and one heavy cruiser was out of action.

37

The first news Task Force 61 had of the approaching Japanese air strike was at 0930, when LCdr Gus Widhelm's outbound *Hornet* strike group reported that a large Japanese strike group was passing it. At 0942, *Hornet*'s crude CXAM radar—which had been salvaged from battleship *California* after she was sunk at Pearl Harbor—locked onto a large formation of bogies approaching from the known direction of the Japanese carriers. The Japanese were then only 55 miles away.

At that moment, Task Force 61 was deployed in two separate carrier groups, each ten miles from the other. Only thirty-eight Fighting-10 and Fighting-72 Wildcats were aloft or ready to be launched as part of the combat air patrol. Few of them were in an ideal position to defend the carriers. By prior agreement, all the fighters were to be guided by the *Enterprise* FDO, LCdr Jack Griffin.

Griffin was on loan to the Task Force 16 staff from his regular job as director of the Navy's Radar School, which had recently been moved from San Diego to Hawaii. Like Lt Hank Rowe, who had filled in on the *Enterprise* fighter-direction staff at Eastern Solomons, Griffin had studied under Royal Air Force radar officers during the late stages of the Battle of Britain. His job aboard *Enterprise* was both to round out the training of her complement of FDOs and to be in a position to apply and assess the solutions to lessons gleaned from early defensive battles over U.S. carriers, to work toward a standard fighter-direction doctrine. As it turned out, Griffin's task was a long way from accomplishment. As of October 26, 1942, the standard was well beyond the fledgling system's grasp.

The first of many tactical errors this day was Griffin's placement of at least one fighter division well to the south of the carrier. This division, commanded by the Fighting-10 exec, LCdr William Kane, was vectored south to look for incoming Japanese warplanes *after* the *Hornet* radar contact placed the incoming strike farther to the west. One of Kane's pilots was the first defender to make visual contact with incoming warplanes. Ens Maurice Wickendoll, Kane's second-element leader, saw two unidentified warplanes as the division orbited at 6,000 feet well south of the friendly carriers. When Wickendoll rocked his wings to let Kane know that targets were close by, Kane led the division down. Moments later, the distant targets resolved themselves into a pair of *Enterprise* Dauntlesses returning from their search hop.

At 0957, with the Japanese only 34 miles away, *Enterprise's* Task Force 16 slid directly beneath a rain squall. A minute later, Japanese pilots were able to see *Hornet's* Task Force 17, which would thus bear the brunt of the first wave of twenty-two Vals and eighteen Kates. As the American fighter pilots fought their slow-climbing Wildcats—all of which had been posted at 12,000 feet or lower—LCdr Mamoru Seki angled his lead Val toward *Hornet's* flight deck.

🎏

The connection between the *Enterprise* FDO and his own and *Hornet's* Wildcats was substantially below par. It was true that the best solution to the problem of controlling the two fighter squadrons was through the controller closest to the approaching enemy, but the entire system lacked integration—even in standard terminology. It had been determined in earlier studies that the integration of separate squadrons under one FDO should not be undertaken if the carriers were more than 10 miles apart. When fresh combat air patrols were launched from both carriers beginning at 0900, the carriers were well within this optimum range, but *Hornet* slipped farther behind *Enterprise* during the approach of the Japanese strike group. From the start, all of Griffin's vectoring instructions to divisions of both squadrons referenced the position of *Enterprise*. This was fine so long as both carriers were in plain sight and no more than 10 miles apart, but the system continued while the carriers began undertaking evasive maneuvers, even after *Enterprise* became hidden from the view of all the friendly and enemy pilots by the rain squall it had entered at 0957. The factors of maneuver and the rain squall rendered Griffin's references useless for all the Fighting-72 and Fighting-10 Wildcat divisions.

Another of Griffin's options that went awry was the decision to send fighter divisions out only as far as 15 miles from the carriers to investigate contact reports. Griffin's thinking was based on errors made at Eastern Solomons, where fighter divisions vectored too far out had not been able to get back in time to have an impact on the real defense of the carriers. The down side of the decision, however, was that the divisions held back in this manner would inevitably join the action too close to the friendly flight decks to be able to adequately defend them. In order for a balance to be struck between the options, the entire combat air patrol would have to have been much larger. However, the departing strike groups had included nearly one-third of the available fighters. Virtually every fighter left in Task Force 61—a total of thirty-eight Wildcats—was aloft or ready to be launched when the first radar contact was made.

Another option that went awry was Griffin's decision to keep the bulk of the available fighters at or below 12,000 feet. Again, the reasoning was sound. Flight at lower altitudes burns up less fuel, and pilots do not normally need oxygen below 12,000 feet. Again, the large fighter force accompanying the outbound strike groups lay at the heart of this defensive decision. If Griffin had had more fighters available, the criticality of fuel supplies—of flight duration—and turnaround time aboard the carriers would have had very little impact on Griffin's ability to marshall his forces. As it was, Griffin had to stretch his limited resources. He intentionally sacrificed an early altitude advantage for flight duration and numbers. At Eastern Solomons, CXAM radar had picked up the approaching Japanese strike group at over 80 miles, so Griffin fully anticipated receiving adequate advance notice of the approach of the Japanese strike, either from the departing strike aircraft or by means of the CXAM radar sets aboard the two carriers. He received notice at only 55 miles, and it was mixed with warnings of enemy squadrons coming in low and from well to the south. These reports forced him to keep a number of his divisions low and flying in what would prove to be the wrong direction.

Finally, as the pressure mounted, as the radar plot became increasingly confused, as excited pilots began filling the air waves with chatter, and as the fighter-net transmitter interfered with the FDO transmissions, Griffin broadcast what amounted to a verbal shrug of desperation: "Look south for bandits." The immediate result of that broadcast was the intervention of *Hornet*'s frustrated FDO, Lt Al Fleming, who probably should have begun contacting the Fighting-72 divisions earlier.

So for all the intelligent and well-intentioned application of theory and lessons from the past, the fighter-direction system broke down on October 26 as completely as it had on August 24. Only eight Wildcats—all from Fighting-72—met the Japanese strike formation before it broke up into smaller elements. The point of contact was only 15 miles from *Hornet*'s outer ring of screening warships.

卐

Following the initial confusion, Lt Ed Hessel led his Fighting-72 division and Lt Bob Rynd's out on the vector provided by *Hornet*'s Lieutenant Fleming. The result was a head-on confrontation by the eight Wildcats with the Japanese main strike group moments before the Val and Kate formations split off to launch their attacks.

When first seen, the Japanese were at the same altitude and between ten and eleven o'clock. All Lieutenant Hessel could do was

378

lead his two divisions in a sweeping left turn. Lt Claude Phillips, Hessel's second-element leader, lost track of Hessel and his wingman during the turn, as he eased out to Hessel's right to concentrate on the second *shotai* of the second Val *chutai*. Phillips was able to set up a flat 45-degree deflection shot and open fire at extremely close range. The target, which was raked from nose to tail, made an immediate downward turn to the left to evade Phillips's guns. Rather than follow, Phillips got another Val *shotai* in his sights and raked another Val from nose to tail. It, too, dived away from the formation to evade Phillips's fire. By the time Lieutenant Phillips had forced two Vals from the Japanese formation, he had swept wide to the right of the remaining Vals, a good time and place to begin looking for his lost wingman to join up.

Suddenly, Phillips's attention was arrested by the loud explosion of a 20mm round somewhere behind his armored seat back. The Wildcat's cockpit immediately filled with black smoke, obscuring the pilot's forward vision. Though Phillips knew his Wildcat was on fire, his reaction was so cool it surprised him. He opened the Plexiglas canopy hood and dived to facilitate his departure, but the smoke was sucked out of the cockpit. Able to see again, Phillips decided to stay with the fighter, which seemed flyable.

A quick look around revealed that his wingman, Lt(jg) John Franklin, was under attack, so Phillips hauled back on his stick and maneuvered into a head-on run at the Zero on Franklin's tail. The force of the turn was so great that the Wildcat shuddered in a high-speed stall. Unable to get a good shot at the Zero, Phillips nevertheless fired in the hope of rattling the Japanese pilot. The ploy worked and the Zero ran.

Franklin's fighter was in bad shape; the fabric-covered rudder was shredded and the Wildcat was rapidly losing altitude. Phillips tried to get closer to see if his wingman had been wounded, but, before he could, the damaged fighter flew straight into the water. John Franklin did not escape.

⚛

Lt Bob Rynd's Fighting-72 division came apart as it swept in on the Japanese vee-of-vees right behind Hessel's division. Rynd's wingman, Lt(jg) Ken Kiekhoefer, split off to the right as Rynd and Hessel's division swept left into the Japanese formation. Rynd downed two Vals back to back while Kiekhoefer and the second-element leader, Lt(jg) Paul Landry, tore into the Japanese with all their guns blazing. Landry's wingman, Ens George Wrenn, lost Kiekhoefer and Landry in the swift turn and wound up alone, well behind Rynd and Hessel's divisions.

Kiekhoefer scored a probable kill over the fourth Val in line, which began smoking and fell back in the formation; it was scored a probable. The next Val at which Kiekhoefer fired also dropped back, but it did not smoke; no score. Next, Kiekhoefer saw the Kates accompanying the Vals break for the water. He was about to chase them when Zeros flying top cover pounced on the fragmented Fighting-72 formations.

Kiekhoefer initially missed the approach on his tail by the Zeros, but Landry fired a burst over his wing to draw his attention rearward. The two entered a Thach Weave; Landry swung left while Kickhoefer swung out beneath a Val that was crowding his air space. Next, Kiekhoefer swung back in and came straight up on the belly of the Zero that had followed Landry. The quick burst from all six guns sent the Japanese fighter plunging into the waves. Before Kiekhoefer could gloat, however, he was jumped by another Zero. As he pulled into the tightest turn he could manage, he heard what sounded like solid rhythmic hits on his fighter, but he quickly realized that he was breathing so hard that his oxygen hose was banging against the side of the cockpit. Relieved, Kiekhoefer reflexively laughed and inadvertently kicked his rudder over, which sent the Wildcat into an involuntary outside snap roll. This brought him in right behind the Zero. A quick burst sent the Japanese fighter rolling away toward the ocean.

Landry was long gone in his initial dive away from the first Zero, but Kiekhoefer swung around to try to find him. Suddenly, large red popcorn balls—20mm rounds—passed his Wildcat. He had been jumped by a Zero with a broad red stripe around its fuselage, no doubt the Zero *buntaicho*, LCdr Hideki Shingo. Kiekhoefer hunkered down behind his armored seat back and slowed his fighter. Sure enough, the Zero passed overhead. As quickly as he could get his sight pipper on the target, Kiekhoefer fired. Only one thin stream of bullets emerged from the left outboard gun as the Zero swung back to initiate a head-on run. The Zero did not fire, and Kiekhoefer was out of ammunition. Desperate, Kiekhoefer suddenly dropped his Wildcat's left wing in an attitude that must have appeared like an intentional effort to ram the oncoming Zero. The Japanese fighter leader swung out and ran from sight. Kiekhoefer had had enough, too. He ran for the protection of battleship *South Dakota*, whose many guns trained on his fighter and opened fire. He finally ducked into a nearby cloud and broadly cursed battleship sailors on the open fighter circuit.

卐

Ens George Wrenn had become separated from Rynd's division during the first wrenching turns at the point of encountering the Japanese vee-of-vees. He dived through the Val formation without doing any damage and was planning to recover for another firing pass at the Vals when he saw below him Lt Jiichiro Imajuku's eighteen *Zuikaku* Kates as they began descending for their low-level torpedo attack. Wrenn followed through on his dive and sailed right up on the Kates' tails. As he did, two other Fighting-72 Wildcats closed in and followed him into the attack. The Kates were just spreading out into their final attack formation when Wrenn raced into range from behind. He shot the nearest Kate out of the sky with only four guns, then nudged his reflector sight over and dropped the next nearest Kate with four guns. Wrenn was preparing to adjust his sights on a third Kate when Lieutenant Imajuku led the survivors into the wall of gunfire put out by *Hornet* and her screen. The three American fighters turned away.

卐

Lt Louis Bliss's Fighting-72 division had been on the morning combat air patrol and had only just refueled when the incoming Japanese first appeared on radar. Bliss's four Wildcats immediately launched and climbed directly toward the Japanese, which they first saw 35 miles from *Hornet* as the F4Fs passed through 12,000 feet. By then, the large vee-of-vees formation met by Hessel's and

Rynd's divisions had broken down into smaller formations maneuvering to attack *Hornet* from a variety of angles. Bliss went straight at a Val, which evaded by dropping into an immediate dive. Bliss followed and was passing back through 10,000 feet firing all six wing guns. It was an easy zero-deflection shot right up the Val's tail. There was no question in Bliss's mind that he was scoring hits, but he saw no direct evidence of this until he was passing through 5,000 feet. At that point, thick black smoke began pouring from the Val, which jettisoned its bomb as it plunged straight into the water. As the Val began its final plunge, Bliss had to deal with a Zero that had joined on his tail near the end of this firing run on the Val. Many 7.7mm bullets were passing the Wildcat, and one had already penetrated halfway into Bliss's instrument panel. Suddenly, the lighter Zero passed the heavier Wildcat up the right side in a vertical dive, then made a shallow pull-through without taking evasive action. Bliss later learned that the rubber life raft he was carrying in a compartment behind the cockpit had been released by 7.7mm hits. The Zero pilot probably mistook the departing raft for a departing Wildcat pilot and had passed the Wildcat simply to gawk at it. Bliss only needed to fire a very short burst to blow the curious Zero pilot out of the air.

卐

Several Fighting-10 divisions got within range of the Japanese bombers only a moment or two before they entered the curtain of antiaircraft fire put out by *Hornet*, heavy crusiers *Northampton* and *Pensacola*, light antiaircraft cruisers *San Diego* and *Juneau*, and six destroyers.

Lt Dave Pollock's three-plane Fighting-10 division (short one Wildcat because of an engine malfunction) was at 10,000 feet and between the two carrier task forces at 1050, when the first news of the incoming strike was broadcast to the combat air patrol. Pollock was given a heading to the southwest and told to climb, but was called back to orbit the carriers after only four minutes. At 1003, Pollock was again vectored to the southeast to look for bogies. He was 10 miles from *Hornet* and had climbed to 22,000 feet when Lieutenant Commander Griffin radioed, "Bogey. Angels seven.

Look south." Pollock turned as directed and saw distant smudges in the air—burning airplanes at 7,000 to 10,000 feet. This was evidence of Hessel's and Rynd's attack. Pollock asked for permission to get into the fight, received no response, and went ahead on his own.

Pollock's division arrived after the first of the Vals had already begun their dives. To conserve precious ammunition, Pollock fired only his two outboard guns from 500 yards at a receding Val. The burst missed the target. At 350 yards, Pollock fired the two outboard guns again and saw the Val's rear gunner slump in his seat. As he continued to close on the target, Pollock switched on all six .50-caliber wing guns. Momentarily, a long stream of smoke and flame burst from the Val's belly as it dived away from more punishing blows. An instant later, Pollock had to pull away to avoid the streaming wreckage.

Ens Steve Kona, Pollock's second-element leader, was unable to release his empty wing tank a moment before Pollock committed to the attack on the diving Vals, so he hauled it along for the ride. He gave his wingman, Ens Lyman Fulton, the attack signal and commenced a high-side run on the second Val in the *shotai* Pollock had selected as the Vals pushed over at 15,000 feet. As Kona swung into his dive, the errant wing tank was torn away. Kona and Fulton followed their target all the way to 7,000 feet, where they were chased off by intense friendly antiaircraft fire.

卐

Like Lt Dave Pollock, Lt Swede Vejtasa, a veteran dive-bomber pilot, was initially ordered by Lieutenant Commander Griffin to lead his Fighting-10 division to the southwest to look for bogies. He was at 12,000 feet and climbing when he looked up in time to see as many as nine Vals in a loose column glide to their pushover point above *Hornet*. One last look around revealed that the carrier was already under attack by at least one other Val *chutai*, which had approached from a different angle. Next, Vejtasa picked up a diving Val as it passed through the bottom of a cloud exactly at his altitude. He flipped the Wildcat into a sudden wingover, executed a high-side run, and opened fire. The Val faltered in its dive and fell away in flames. By then, there were no more Vals preparing to dive on *Hornet*.

Ens Don Gordon and Ens Gerald Davis were vectored out to the southwest at 7,000 feet to find the incoming Kate torpedo bombers. Gordon chanced to spot a lone Kate well to the south as he looked down from 15,000 feet. He led Davis after the solitary torpedo bomber, but was so close to the friendly antiaircraft belt that he had to flatten the dive and attack level with the unknowing quarry. The Kate made a turn to starboard an instant before Gordon planned to open fire, but the turn took it directly into the line of fire of Davis's Wildcat, which was tucked in under Gordon's starboard wing. Davis opened fire and Gordon pulled away to get into a better firing position. Davis's guns caused the Kate to smoke and turn away from Task Force 61. As Gordon turned and rejoined Davis, another solitary Kate appeared, and the two Fighting-10 pilots turned their full attention to it. The first pass produced no observable results, so the Americans turned back. Having observed no fire from the rear gun during the first pass, Gordon risked a firing run from dead astern. The payoff was that the Kate disintegrated under his guns only 10 feet above the water. As Gordon pulled out, he saw black smoke rising from the spot at which he and Davis had left the first Kate, a good sign that Davis had also scored a kill.

That was virtually all the ready Wildcats could do to forestall the Japanese strike aircraft and fend off the accompanying Zeros—a good last-minute showing, but not nearly enough.

38

From the moment the first news of the Japanese approach was sounded at 0940, the atmosphere aboard *Hornet* had been one of undisguised excitement. Most of the men aboard the carrier were veterans, had been nearly to the gates of Tokyo in April, had had a grueling but ultimately bloodless wait at Midway in June. Now they awaited the inevitable, as had fellow sailors aboard *Lexington* at the Coral Sea, *Yorktown* at Midway, and *Enterprise* and *Saratoga* at Eastern Solomons. The Japanese Vals and Kates were on the way, and the ultimate test of their ship's fighters and gunners was at hand.

RAdm George Murray had commanded *Enterprise* at the start of the war, through early raids on Japanese-held islands and during the Tokyo raid, when his ship had escorted *Hornet* to the gates of the enemy capital. When sailors came to his flag bridge aboard *Hornet* to seal him in with steel shutters, he protested, "Leave them open. I want to see the show, too." In this simple request, Admiral Murray expressed a desire common to all his shipmates that hour, for seeing the show was far better than enduring it in blind compartments throughout the vast ship.

As the last ready fighters were launched, as inert carbon dioxide was pumped into the aviation-gasoline fueling system, as a Marine chaser ran to the ship's brig to free the prisoners in the event the ship was set aflame or sunk, as 3,000 sailors and Marines went to the highest stage of alert, as *Hornet's* own fighters pitched into the oncoming waves of Vals and Kates, Capt Perry Mason passed the word to his senior gunnery officer, "Commence firing at any target in sight." Then to his ship's senior engineer, "Make full speed and maintain it until further orders."

AMM3 Chuck Beck, a Fighting-72 plane captain attached to a damage-control hose team on the flight deck forward of the island, heard nearby Marine antiaircraft gunners talk about the incoming bombers and left his station to retrieve the blue denim flash jacket he had stashed in the forward end of the island. When Beck stepped back onto the flight deck after putting on the jacket, pulling its sleeves and hood tight around his wrists and face, and pushing his trousers into his socks, he found that the fifteen-man hose team he had left moments earlier had disappeared. A quick look around revealed that every gun was pointed skyward. Before Beck could react, the most distant screen destroyer opened fire, and the entire screen—and *Hornet*—followed suit. Beck began running straight down the middle of the flight deck, chided himself for not having the equipment to get airborne, and veered off toward the opening of a bomb shelter, a covered section of the catwalk rimming the flight deck. He tumbled in among at least a dozen other sailors who were all tucked up to prevent concussion damage to their innards.

At the last moment, *Hornet's* loudspeakers advised all the men who could not see, but to all who could hear the pounding of her guns, "Stand by to repel attack." LCdr Oscar Dodson, *Hornet's* and Task Force 17's communications officer, bounded up to the signal bridge from the flag bridge to check on the eighteen signalmen manning battle stations there. Dodson knew that nearly all of them and their young signal officer were facing first combat; he thought his presence would help settle them. He found that many of the enlisted signalmen had neglected to clap on helmets or pull on their protective flashproof jackets.

As soon as the signalmen were properly rigged out, Dodson

trained his binoculars outboard and picked up the incoming Kates at maximum range. When the surviving *Zuikaku* Kates were about five miles from *Hornet*, the two *chutai* split up and began circling the ship to find the best attack angles. The Japanese torpedo leader, presumably Lieutenant Imajuku, if he had survived to that point, fired a large smoke bomb over the tail of his dark green airplane. On that signal, the dozen remaining Kates turned toward *Hornet* from as many directions.

卍

The lead Val, flown by *Shokaku*'s LCdr Mamoru Seki, began its dive at *Hornet*'s port quarter at 1010. Captain Mason at first thought he could evade the diving Vals by precipitous maneuvering, but he quickly noticed that the Japanese had obviated neat solutions by commencing their squadron attacks from at least four directions, all more or less off the port quarter, but spread over enough of an arc to confound any simple scheme.

As Mason looked on in frustration, the pilot of the second Val, Lt Kazuo Yakushiji, looked on in terror as Lieutenant Commander Seki's lead Val staggered under the impact of a direct hit from one of the surface antiaircraft guns and rolled over onto its back while maintaining its lead position. Yakushiji saw Seki's burning dive-bomber reach the release point and dive on through with its 250-kilogram centerline armor-piercing bomb and two wing-mounted 60-kilogram antipersonnel bombs still aboard. Then Yakushiji and the third Val released their bombs and twisted to evade the funnel of gunfire rising from the carrier. Seki maintained his inverted dive, but did not release his bombs.

At 1012, the first and second 250-kilogram bombs splashed into the water off *Hornet*'s starboard beam, in line with Captain Mason's bridge. The third bomb smashed into the flight deck forward, near the centerline, and penetrated to the third deck before detonating.

EM1 Tom Kuykendall was prone on the deck in the forward crew messing compartment, one of sixty-five members of the forward repair party. The repair officer, who was wearing headphones, had been keeping the sailors abreast of events as they occurred, and the loud detonations of the antiaircraft guns easily penetrated to the compartment, though it was insulated on all sides and above by other compartments and decks. Suddenly, the deck beneath Kuykendall's body quivered as though an earthquake had struck. Kuykendall heard a huge muffled explosion and saw the lights go out; all he could sense were expanding points of red-hot metal and the smell of burning explosives. A searing heat passed over Kuykendall, who knew right away that he had been severely burned, though his nerves had not yet fully responded to the trauma. As soon as the first shock dissipated, Kuykendall felt around in the dark to locate the men who had been lying near him. He was unable to find a soul, but he was able to crawl to a ladder he knew was only three feet away. The metal rungs seared Kuykendall's palms, but he pulled himself upward toward the hangar deck.

In all, at least sixty of the sixty-five members of the forward repair party were killed outright in the bomb blast.

卐

Pfc Vic Kelber, one of sixteen Marines and two sailors manning the five quad 40mm gun tubs directly abaft the island, picked up several Vals as they followed through past their bomb-release points. Two or three of the Vals were clearly burning and about to fall into the sea. One of the dive-bombers was firing its cowl-mounted 7.7mm machine guns. As Kelber was about to unleash a curse at the strafer, a single 7.7mm round entered his mouth and exited his cheek. He did not know he was injured until someone yelled, "Kelber, you're bleeding." The thoroughly engrossed gunner raised his hand to his cheek, felt that it was wet, and spit out a mouthful of blood and teeth. Then he dopily pressed his eye to the gunsight to track yet another Val.

The Val that had hit Private First Class Kelber, or perhaps another that was firing its guns as it traversed the flight deck from ahead to aft, bracketed S1 Ed Knobel, the plane captain of the Air Group 8 command TBF, as he was boosting a 40mm magazine from the catwalk into one of the gun tubs. An indistinct peripheral view of the approaching stream of bullets impacting on the flight deck caused Knobel to fall to the deck. Two rounds clipped the legs of his trousers.

Seconds later, within the same minute as the first 250-kilogram detonation forward, a second 250-kilogram bomb struck the flight deck aft. It detonated on impact and blew out an 11-foot hole about 20 feet in from the starboard edge. Pfc Vic Kelber was plucked from his seat and wrapped around the gun like a wet rag. The three Marines manning the quad 40mm gun tub to Kelber's right were all killed in the blast, and the three Marines manning the gun tub to Kelber's left were all wounded, as were several Marines and a sailor manning several of the three remaining guns. Though wounded and paralyzed, GySgt Eugene O'Connor, the gun-group chief, continued to issue orders to the surviving gunners by means of his sound-powered battle phones as he lay supine on the catwalk behind the gun tubs.

Though S1 Ed Knobel was only clipped on the back of his left knee by a tiny pinpoint of shrapnel, the blast in front of his eyes was so bright that he found his vision totally impaired. It would be three days before Knobel could see much more than a red film before his eyes.

The third 250-kilogram armor-piercing bomb to strike *Hornet* fell from a Val approaching from dead ahead. It punched a 12-inch hole in the flight deck and angled forward about 53 feet while penetrating two steel barriers on its way to the third deck. Though the blast breached the overhead and several bulkheads of the chief petty officers' messing compartment, penetrated to adjacent compartments, knocked out a 5-inch ammunition hoist, and set fire to upholstered furniture and other combustibles, it resulted in no direct loss of life. However, the force of the blast was felt by all hands in the forward part of the ship. It added to Pfc Vic Kelber's problems by lifting him from his gun tub and dropping him into a ready room beneath the flight deck.

⚛

At 1013, LCdr Mamoru Seki intentionally crashed his disabled Val straight into the forward port corner of *Hornet's* stack. The Val glanced off the stack and fell into the flight deck at the base of the island. One of the 60-kilogram bombs detonated upon impacting with the stack; it killed seven signalmen manning the carrier's signal bridge, destroyed all the signaling apparatus, and burned all the flags in the flag bags. A moment after the bomb detonated, flaming aviation gasoline poured directly down on the survivors on the signal bridge. Most of the signalmen were instantly bathed in the burning fuel, and many were instantly killed. By sheer luck, LCdr Oscar Dodson happened to be shielded from the bomb and burning fuel by one of the steel legs of the ship's huge tripod signal mast. He waded right into the circle of burning men and tried to beat out the flames, but his own gloves caught fire; he was helpless as soon as he pulled them from his hands, and he had to watch his subordinates writhe in agony and succumb to the intense heat and trauma. One terrible sight that Dodson missed was a rush by one uninjured signalman into the arms of his twin brother, who was in the center of a large pool of burning gasoline. The twins died together, locked in a final embrace.

Seki's unarmed 250-kilogram bomb passed through the wooden flight deck and a steel bulkhead and came to rest on a catwalk beside the island. It did not explode. The second 60-kilogram bomb passed through the flight deck and three steel bulkheads before coming to rest beneath a table in one of the squadron ready rooms. It, too, proved to be a dud, though flight personnel in that ready room nimbly stepped into the nearest companionway as the steel projectile rolled from beneath the table to block the only available hatchway.

After falling away from the stack, the hulk of Seki's Val—minus one wing, which stuck in the funnel—cracked open on the flight deck and burning aviation gasoline flooded down into the companionway in front of the Scouting-8 ready room, where about fifteen unengaged pilots and crewmen had been listening in total silence to the hammering of 20mm and 40mm antiaircraft guns right outside. The flaming fuel quickly spread into the ready room. Already shaken by the impact of the three 250-kilogram bombs, the squadron flight officer, Lt Ben Tappan, lurched to the rear of the compartment and began undogging the emergency hatchway. An immediate scramble ensued.

CY Ralph Cotton, the Bombing-8 chief yeoman, was one of the last to leave the adjacent Bombing-8 ready room. As Cotton was moving toward the hatchway, he saw a large object fall from the overhead and felt a warm sensation across his belly. Sure he had been hit, Chief Cotton reached down and pressed his hand against a thick greasy substance, no doubt a dollop of hot oil from Seki's Val. Behind Cotton, a pool of burning aviation gasoline was spreading into the Scouting-8 ready room.

Scouting-8's Lt(jg) Ivan Swope, who had been blown out of the leather-upholstered high-back seat nearest the companionway, came to on his back to find flaming fuel within inches of his face. The entire Scouting-8 ready room seemed to be engulfed in flames. Before Swope's head quite cleared, someone reached in from the adjacent Bombing-8 ready room, grabbed him under the shoulders, pulled him to safety, and helped him toward the flight deck.

⚛

EM1 Samuel Blumer, operator of the midships crane, left his station to watch the show from the port side of the hangar deck. He arrived just as the Kates were turning toward the ship, and he picked out a torpedo bomber that was heading right at him. When the Kate finally dropped its fish and banked to the left, Blumer saw its pilot turn his head and stare at the ship. He also distinctly saw the foamy wake of the oncoming torpedo, so went back to the crane room to await the inevitable detonation.

On the starboard side of the ship, in a bomb shelter built into the flight-deck catwalk, AMM3 Chuck Beck saw another Kate release its fish as it was heading straight at him. Beck began to crawl forward along the catwalk, which had large perforations that protruded upward to assist sailors in keeping their footing. Though Beck's hands and knees ached beyond description, he continued forward as far as he could, until stopped by the emergency LSO platform affixed to the starboard forward corner of the flight deck in the event the ship had to back down to recover airplanes. He tucked himself into a ball and waited.

Almost as soon as Capt Perry Mason recovered his stance following the impact of three 250-kilogram bombs and Seki's Val, he saw two torpedo wakes heading straight for the starboard side of his ship. "Right full rudder," Mason brayed in the hope he could throw the carrier's stern around in time to evade the fish.

The two torpedoes passed from the captain's view beneath the overhang of the flight deck. Several long seconds passed before LCdr Harry Holmshaw, the command duty officer, spoke up from Captain Mason's elbow. "I guess they missed us, sir."

"Well," Mason ventured, "it seems as though there's been enough time."

卐

WT1 Lyle Skinner was in the compartment just abaft the one occupied by the gutted forward repair party when the first bomb detonated. After a moment in which he lost all his senses, Skinner saw sparks flying through the darkness that had instantly engulfed his space, he heard groans and shrieks, and he smelled the strong odor of the vaporized explosives. As his senses fully returned, Skinner found that he was lying atop and beneath twisted rubble. He was afraid to move at first because he knew that the deck on which he lay was directly above a fuel-oil tank; if the tank had ruptured, he feared he might fall in. He had lost all sense of direction except up and down and had no idea which way to go when he finally began easing out of the rubble. The fumes seemed to be growing stronger, and breathing became increasingly difficult. Skinner groped for his handkerchief and placed it over his nose and mouth, but it did not help. As he lay in the dark feeling the successive bomb detonations reverberate through the steel deck, he calmly reached the conclusion that he would eventually die in that compartment. His only question at that point was whether he would succumb to fire, suffocation, or drowning. He lay back to await the inevitable conclusion of his life.

Then fate intervened. An unknown crewman who was probably trying to find a way topside momentarily opened the hatch at the after end of the dark compartment and shined in a battle lantern. Apparently convinced that there was no escape by that route, the man closed the hatch and departed. The briefly shining light was Lyle Skinner's beacon to life, for it gave him back his sense of direction and showed him that he could safely make his way across the debris-strewn deck. Skinner wriggled out from the confining rubble and pushed the hatch, which had mercifully been left un-dogged by his departing shipmate. He took only two or three steps before the ship was rocked by a vast explosion.

⚛

At that moment, the deck beneath Capt Perry Mason's feet jarred, and a great geyser of water rose into view.

AMM3 Chuck Beck was bounced violently up and down between the perforated steel catwalk and the forward emergency LSO platform, his ears ringing from the nearby concussion. Beneath Beck, the entire ship lifted out of the water and jumped to the left.

Thirty seconds after Seki's burning Val came to rest on the flight deck, the first shallow-running aerial torpedo detonated against *Hornet*'s starboard hull in line with the forward engine room. Lights throughout the ship flickered and fuel oil bunkered in a breached cell beside the engine room poured in atop the engineers and electricians manning the vast engineering compartment.

ARM1 Billy Cottrell, of Bombing-8, was just stepping from the squadron ready room, over Lieutenant Commander Seki's un-exploded 60-kilogram bomb, when he was staggered by the impact of the first torpedo. Someone yelled, "Look out!" and Cottrell reflexively reached up to help several pilots and gunners hold up a spare 5-inch gun barrel that had been jarred from its lashings against the overhead.

Within seconds of the first torpedo blast, *Hornet* had taken on a list to starboard just under 11 degrees and had lost her primary electrical circuits.

Twenty seconds later, the second shallow-running aerial torpedo struck the starboard hull abreast several magazines filled with antiaircraft rounds and powder. Once again, AMM3 Chuck Beck was violently bounced between the catwalk and the forward LSO platform as the ship twisted up and away from the force of the blast.

Closed off from any view of the action, the sailors manning the engineering spaces and all below-decks compartments had to ride out the twisting shudders of each successive body blow. They had heard the loudspeaker messages announcing that the strike was imminent, and they had heard the guns firing—5-inchers at maximum range, and the 40mm guns, then the 20mm guns, which sort of marked the progress of the Japanese warplanes. They knew the ship had been struck, but they had no idea what had hit it or what the damage was. Only the officers and sailors who were topside and had a clear view, or those in damaged compartments, had a sense of the battle or any of its parts.

彡

Seconds after the torpedoes struck, at 1017, a fiercely burning, bombless Val arrived from off the port quarter and attempted to fly into *Hornet's* flight deck. Every gun that could bear poured bullets and explosive rounds into the tattered Val. The pilot misjudged or was jarred from his course by the repeated hammerblows of anti-aircraft gunfire, and the Val overshot the mark. But the nerveless, doomed pilot swung around the carrier's bow and, with his forward machine guns blazing, flew straight into the port side just below the leading edge of the flight deck. Both wings sheared off on impact, but the fuselage penetrated 120 feet through the forecastle and officers' staterooms and came to rest in the forward elevator shaft, directly over the ship's main supply of aviation gasoline. The fuel supply thrown from the Val ignited and, as the dying pilot and gunner writhed in the wreck, the fuel spread over the steel deck around the elevator shaft. By the time the last of the machine gun ammunition aboard the Val finished cooking off, the steel deck was glowing cherry red.

Less than a minute after the Val crashed into the forecastle, the pilot of a torpedoless Kate tried his luck from dead ahead, but his shattered airplane fell into the sea off the carrier's port bow.

The effects of the multiple bomb blasts and crashed Vals were devastating but by no means mortal. But the first torpedo hit abreast the forward engine room could prove fatal, for it deprived the great ship of electrical power needed to run her propellers and, worse, essential to maintaining water pressure at the firefighting mains.

A moment after the Val crashed into the forecastle, Captain Mason noticed that his ship was losing way. "Does she respond to helm?"

"No, sir," the helmsman responded. "The rudder is jammed hard right."

It was 1020. The Japanese had departed. The guns of the fleet were silent. *Hornet* was dead in the water. All power and communications aboard the carrier were out.

卐

On the wreckage of the signal bridge, LCdr Oscar Dodson, the carrier's communications officer, heard a query from one of the screening warships: "Is [*Hornet*] hurt?" Dodson got on the task force radio net and replied, "Affirmative." A moment later, a bleeding signalman raised his semaphore flags and wigwagged to the nearest ship, "We are ready to receive messages."

卐

RAdm George Murray looked down from the flag bridge and saw several gray forms emerge from the smokey pall covering the signal bridge. Four of the sailors were carrying two other sailors. A seventh man, a chief signalman, was in the lead, groping for a route to safety. Murray saw that all seven men were wearing the charred remnants of their work clothes, and all the bare skin the admiral could see was glowing red through a layer of what looked like black grease.

"Where are you taking those men?" the admiral called down to the man in the lead.

The chief signalman straightened up to attention, "To the dressing station, sir."

The admiral told him that the access was barred. "Bring them in here, man," he called, pointing to his small flag bridge.

The two sailors with the worst burns were helped to the deck while the two with the least severe burns ran to fetch a doctor or corpsman. Admiral Murray stood over the chief, who was on his knees over the two recumbent signalmen. "Go below to the dressing station," the admiral ordered the chief.

"Sir, must I? I'd rather . . ."

"Yes, you must."

As the tearful chief left, Admiral Murray knelt beside the two burned bodies. One, the younger, looked up and apparently recognized the task force commander. "Sir," he breathed, "am I being brave enough?"

The admiral nodded, which was all he could do for a choked second, then answered in a cracked voice, "Yes, son. Just take it easy." The youngster, who was seventeen years old, eventually died on the deck of the flag bridge.

Meanwhile Lt Robert Noone, the signal officer, refused treatment for his burned and shattered leg until every one of the surviving signalmen had been treated. As he waited, Noone wondered aloud to LCdr Oscar Dodson if the leg injuries would prevent him from qualifying for flight training.

⁂

At 1025, there were major fires burning out of control on the signal bridge, flight deck, ready rooms, chiefs' quarters, forward messing compartment, storerooms, Number 1 elevator pit, hangar deck amidships and aft, and along the forecastle deck.

AMM3 Chuck Beck was just pulling himself together from the torpedo and bomb concussions in the catwalk space beneath the forward LSO platform when he heard the Air Group 8 line chief yell, "Fire crew! Fire crew! Get your asses out here!" Beck instantly responded to the call, peeled a hose off its drum, and headed for a fire amidships on the flight deck, next to the island—Lieutenant Commander Seki's Val. As Beck aimed the nozzle, several other fireman arrived to help steady it against the water pressure. "Turn it on," Beck yelled as he braced himself for the onset of the pressure. A sickly *pshshshshoo* emanated from the limp hose. Then nothing. The lack of electrical power throughout the ship had disabled the water mains.

The air group line chief improvised a team to break out large cans of dry fulmite, a fire retardant usually mixed with water in high-pressure hose lines. Other sailors were sent to break out buckets and lines, and they began dipping the buckets into the ocean and painstakingly hauling seawater up to the flight deck. Then, as the line chief and Chuck Beck threw the dry fulmite into the fire, other sailors threw buckets of water in after it. The results were slow in coming, but the tide was turned as scores of men—officers, sailors, Marines—converged on the Val to help. For all the effort, however, Beck was not sure if his efforts had helped retard the fire or if the fire around and within the Val simply burned itself out.

Word of the flight-deck improvisation spread to fire-ravaged areas below decks, and those fires were also slowly fought by hand to uncertain standstills. However, most of the effective firefighting was performed by destroyers *Morris, Russell,* and *Mustin.* Under the direction of the carrier's air boss, Cdr Marcel Gouin, the three warships gingerly came alongside the carrier, close enough for sailors on their decks to play streams of water on all the fires they could reach.

At length, *Morris* was ordered alongside to starboard, and she passed three hoses directly to sailors aboard *Hornet.* That act, incredibly brave because of the danger from submarines and the swell, turned the tide. One of *Morris's* hoses was used to beat down the persistent main fire on the signal bridge, and the last of the major fires in the forecastle area was contained by *Hornet* firefighters using *Morris's* other two hoses.

Russell came alongside next, off the port bow, to help with the forecastle and elevator pit fires. She was only just getting into position when a large swell pushed her right up against the carrier's side. The shock of the contact released a lever controlling one of the destroyer's depth-charge racks, and a 600-pound depth charge dropped off the fantail. When the captain, LCdr Glenn Hartwig, heard the news, he just started counting. Then, after enough time had passed without the feared detonation, he passed the word to forget about the depth charge; it apparently had remained locked on "safe."

Finally, *Mustin* came alongside *Hornet's* port quarter so her hoses could be used by *Hornet* firefighters against the blazes in the chiefs' quarters and the storeroom.

All major fires were under control by 1100, though a great deal of work still needed to be done to finally quell several of them. The most persistent fire was in the chiefs' quarters; it was fed by mattresses and upholstered chairs. Though contained by hoses passed from *Mustin*, this series of smoldering blazes was finally extinguished altogether by seawater supplied by a portable handy-billy water pump set up on the carrier's own main deck. Another persistent fire was in the Scouting-8 ready room; it too was fed by upholstered chairs, and it was eventually quenched by a hose from *Morris* and a 200-man bucket brigade using water and dry fulmite.

While being rocked by the swell, *Russell* had her starboard anchor knocked off in a particularly violent collision with the carrier, and a good part of her starboard hull and bridge and every gun-director were dished in by repeated shocks. *Morris*, a destroyer leader, suffered major damage to her superstructure and antenna system; the damage eventually obliged the commodore of Destroyer Squadron 2 to transfer his flag to *Mustin*. (Coincidentally, *Morris* had suffered similar damage conducting a similar task alongside *Lexington* during the Coral Sea battle.)

Hornet was saved for the moment largely because, unlike *Wasp*, her gasoline handlers had flooded her aviation fuel lines prior to the attack with inert carbon dioxide gas. The potential for disaster was great, and the fear was palpable, for *Hornet*'s crew had witnessed the death by burning of *Wasp* a month earlier. However, the huge fireball everyone expected to erupt did not engulf them.

卐

Doctors, dentists, and corpsmen from the medical department—M Division—manning seven medical battle stations throughout the ship swung into action at the instant burning fuel from Seki's Val cascaded onto the signal bridge. While the carnage there at first appeared absolute, survivors were plucked from the flames, and their burns and other injuries were quickly and expertly treated.

The first bomb, which gutted the forward repair party, also killed Dr. John Johnson and several of his corpsmen. Thus, in addition to severe casualties among the nearest firefighters, treatment of the wounded in the immediate area of the detonation was severely limited. The Val that drove itself through the forecastle into the forward elevator pit severely wounded Dr. Gerald McAteer and killed or wounded several corpsmen at his medical battle station. Though Dr. McAteer could not participate directly in the treatment of the wounded, he issued a steady stream of directions to his surviving corpsmen and volunteers, who constantly got in over their heads as they treated the casualties.

PhM1 Floyd Arnold, who stopped to help pull a hose to the vicinity of the ready-room fires from the deck below, made his way to the midships area of the hangar deck and began treating several sailors who had sustained burns on exposed areas of their skin, particularly hands and faces. The treatment consisted mainly of cleaning the burned areas with gentian violet and larding on a thick dollop of burn ointment. The wounded were bandaged, tagged, and ordered to casualty clearing stations on the flight deck and fantail, but a number of them undoubtedly ignored the order and returned to work to help save the ship.

After being pulled from the path of burning aviation gasoline spreading across the Scouting-8 ready room, Lt(jg) Ivan Swope was assisted to the flight deck. He was groggy and unable to focus on his plight because of a mild concussion he had suffered when he was thrown from his seat to the steel deck of the ready room. He aimlessly wandered around on the flight deck for a few minutes before the haze in his head cleared enough for him to realize that he had suffered burns on his face, left hand, both legs below the knees, and both feet. Oddly, his pants legs and shoes were not even scorched. He found the tiny dressing station in the after part of the island. There, gentian violet, burn ointment, and gauze bandages were applied to his burns and he was placed in one of the tiny compartment's six narrow bunks.

S1 Ed Knobel, who had been temporarily blinded by the flash of one of the flight-deck detonations, lay still while corpsmen moved to succor the Navy and Marine gun crewmen around him who had caught the full force of the blast. Knobel spent the time trying to fix in his mind what had been hit and who might have been injured. After a few minutes, he was handed up to the flight deck and stretched out beside other wounded men on the after edge of Number 3 elevator. Unable to see and with ears still ringing, all Knobel had to do was fight against his worst fears taking hold.

EM1 Tom Kuykendall, who had barely survived the conflagration that destroyed the forward repair party at the site of the first bomb detonation, reached the flight deck and went right to work helping beat back the flames from what at first seemed like windrows of dead and wounded sailors. Only as Kuykendall confronted the flames did he realize that he had been badly burned himself. Indeed, he was covered with blood. The skin on his face, legs, and arms looked like loose strips of torn cloth. As the pain and shock began taking hold, a doctor grabbed him, helped him lie down on a litter, and injected a stiff dose of morphine. Then litter bearers carried him to the open fantail, where other wounded men had already been assembled. By the time Kuykendall's litter was set down, the pain and shock were virtually unbearable.

WT1 Lyle Skinner, who had escaped from the compartment directly abaft Kuykendall's obliterated battle station, nearly went into shock when he reached the hangar deck and saw the vast scene of destruction and suffering. Thankful for his own salvation, Skinner went to work with another watertender sorting the living from the dead.

Pfc Vic Kelber, who had been shot through the cheek and blown from his 40mm gun tub, was ordered to the hangar deck to have his face treated. Though blood was pouring from the hole in his cheek, Kelber made his way below under his own power and reached an emergency operating room adjacent to the burned-out ready rooms. The scene that greeted the Marine was right from the depths of hell. The narrow compartment was packed with sailors—sitting, standing, lying, wounded, dying, and dead. The doctors and corpsmen were working with machinelike precision, totally immersed in their jobs. A Marine sergeant had both legs mangled and was bleeding profusely despite the two tourniquets that had been applied above his wounds. He nodded a greeting to Kelber, who immediately left. Later, Kelber learned that the sergeant bled to death where he lay. After leaving the operating room, Kelber entered an adjacent compartment that had three empty cots and a dark ball on the deck. A closer look revealed that the ball was in fact a human head. At last, Kelber was ordered to report to the fantail sick bay for treatment. On the way, he passed a body that had been burned totally beyond recognition. On reaching the fantail, Kelber's facial wounds were tightly patched, the free flow of blood finally staunched.

卐

Lt(jg) Earl Zook was the only officer on duty this day in Central Station—the damage-control center located in a vertical steel tube two decks beneath the hangar deck. When the first torpedo detonated 70 feet away from Central Station, the concussion traveling through the confined space buckled Zook's knees, severely jarred his body, and left him confused, without any direct memory of the moment of impact. Within seconds, gasses released by the bomb that had detonated in the forward messing compartment leaked into Central Station and further impaired Zook's ability to control the fight to save *Hornet*.

Cdr Henry Moran, the ship's first lieutenant and damage control officer, was at a conference of officers in the wardroom when the guns started firing, and he did not reach Central Station until the action had nearly abated. Within a minute, the ship had taken on an 11-degree list to starboard, which Commander Moran began working to correct with a set of valves controlling the flow of seawater into trimming tanks in the hull of the ship. The best Moran could accomplish was a reduction of the list to 7 degrees. As he worked, crewmen who had been manning the compartments adjacent to Central Station entered the crowded space to get away from the effects of a bomb blast. A warrant officer who had been standing directly beneath a ventilation duct was blackened with soot from the blast and had to be treated with salve for flash burns.

Faulty communications throughout the ship prevented the Central Station crew from accomplishing much more than the correction of the list, which they could monitor themselves with the aid of an inclinometer. Thus the firefighting and other repair efforts were conducted locally, without central control.

After leaving the burning ready rooms, ARM1 Billy Cottrell, of Bombing-8, made his way up to the flight deck to see what was going on. By the time he arrived, other air-group enlisted men were breaking out spare .30-caliber airplane machine guns and setting them up on improvised sandbags around the edge of the useless flight deck. Cottrell, who was drawing pay as a Dauntless rear gunner, joined one of the guncrews and waited for the next Japanese strike to appear over his ship. Most of the men streaming up to the flight deck, however, worked at fighting fires or treating the wounded, or did nothing at all but mill around in stunned confusion.

⇄

EM1 Samuel Blumer, who had left his post in the hangar-deck crane room to see what was going on, saw F1 Harold Blanco burst out onto the hangar deck from a ladder leading from below. "Blanco," Blumer called, "what are you doing up here?" Blanco looked at Blumer and blurted out, "Abandon ship!" At that instant, many other sailors from below began streaming up to the hangar deck in nearly uncountable numbers. Blumer instantly grasped that something was amiss; it seemed as though the incessantly practiced lessons of *Hornet*'s year afloat had been lost in a universal wave of panic undoubtedly brought on by the loss of viable communications throughout the great ship. Blumer sensed that the refugees from below were on the brink of panic, but there was nothing he could do to set things right, so he joined the exodus to the flight deck.

Unbeknown to EM1 Blumer, officers and sailors manning many compartments and work areas below the waterline had indeed been ordered by the captain to make their way topside. For example, electrician's mates manning the blind after generator room received the word to abandon their station without having, to that point, a clear idea of the damage that had befallen their ship. EM1 Leroy Butts got all the way up to the hangar deck before he saw any clear evidence of damage. There, spread out on the steel deck, were many wounded sailors. Stunned, Butts wandered over to the 12-inch hole that had been punched by the first bomb in the forward section of the vast space. Beneath his feet, officers' state-rooms had been destroyed in the conflagration that gutted the forward repair party. Further forward, smoke was still rising out of the forward elevator pit.

While twenty-nine other officers and ratings left the forward engine room due to flooding by bunker oil from a torpedo-breached fuel tank, the ship's chief engineer, Cdr Pat Creehan, stood by his post with a chief machinist, a chief machinist's mate, and EM3 Tom Reese. It was Reese's job to try to get the electrical pumps going in order to clear the deck of the sloshing oil, but there was no way to stem the flow of the thick, gooey fuel from the adjacent tank. After only a few minutes of frenetic, prayerful activity, Commander Creehan had to tell the captain that his was a losing fight. He was ordered to clear out of the compartment.

卐

Once Lieutenant Commander Seki's Val had stopped burning, AMM3 Chuck Beck got a grappling hook from an emergency locker and went fishing in the smoldering wreckage for souvenirs. He pulled out several instruments, from which he pried metal tags with Japanese characters on them, then got the tail wheel, and finally snagged a large book. The book was of definite interest and, on inspection, appeared to be filled with recognition silhouettes of Allied aircraft and a great many notes. Beck was just shoving the book into the front of his shirt when a voice from the island called down and ordered him to bring it topside. Grudgingly, the plane captain handed the book over to the officer and went back to fishing in the wreckage. His next catch was a charred corpse, Lieutenant Commander Seki or the Val's gunner. After only a moment's hesitation, Beck dragged the body up the canted flight deck with the intention of dropping it over the side of the ship. He was again stopped by an officer, who asked if he was sure it was not an American body. Beck answered that he was not sure. As the two spoke, a wild-eyed sailor ran up and began plunging a knife into the corpse. The man told Beck, "I want some Jap blood on my knife." When the deranged sailor had had his gruesome revenge, the officer ordered Beck to leave the body where it was and get back to work.

After his ship had been drifting aimlessly for about a half hour, Cdr Henry Moran, the damage control officer, decided that there was no point in his staying below in Central Station. He checked with the bridge to see if there was anything else he could do from that post—there was not—and ordered all hands to clear the compartment and climb over 100 feet to the bridge-level deck of the island.

Counting engineering personnel from adjacent spaces, over 100 officers and men had to evacuate the lower decks through the 3-foot-wide escape trunk. One, a chief machinist's mate whose palms had been severely burned, had to drag himself up the entire ladder without assistance, for there was no room for anyone to lend a hand. An officer from a nearby compartment began screaming at the top of his lungs while ship's cooks who had been manning an ammunition-handling room preceded his group with a bit less alacrity than he thought was warranted. The going was tedious because everyone insisted upon wearing his life vest in the confined tube. Lt(jg) Earl Zook, who was third from last to leave, was nearly overcome by fumes by the time he reached the exit, which was located in Radar Plot, high up in the island. The next to last man asked Commander Moran for the honor of being the last to leave the compartment, but Moran turned him down; it was the senior's duty to be the last man out.

Once Commander Moran was clear of the tube, he walked forward to the bridge to confer with Capt Perry Mason, the exec, and others. The senior group determined that *Hornet* was in no immediate danger of sinking and that she could be saved, but she might also be lost in the event more Japanese bombs or torpedoes—including submarine torpedoes—struck her. In that case, it was decided to evacuate the wounded and nonessential personnel to destroyers and to attempt to take aboard a towing cable from heavy cruiser *Northampton*, for it was clear that it would take hours of frantic activity for the electrical department to get *Hornet*'s vital electrical power back on line.

39

As *Hornet* was twisting under the impact of Japanese bombs, torpedoes, and dive-bombers, Ens Maurice Wickendoll, of Fighting-10, was recovering from his dive on what turned out to be friendly Dauntlesses when he first noticed that his division leader, LCdr William Kane, and the division leader's wingman had disappeared. Well to the south of the carriers and without a clue about the battle raging over *Hornet*, Wickendoll led his wingman back up to 12,000 feet to look for approaching enemy bombers. As soon as the two Wildcats reached 12,000 feet, Wickendoll saw two bombless Vals enter a shallow dive right over his head. Wickendoll made a low-side firing run, but each of his guns fired only two rounds before freezing. Repeated efforts to recharge the guns finally produced a dribble from the left outboard gun. By then, the Vals were gone, but two Zeros, also at 12,000 feet, looped in to get at the two Wildcats, which were by then cruising at slow speed. Wickendoll decided to evade the challenge in favor of picking up more speed, so he led his wingman away from the Zeros. At length, the Wildcats entered a head-on run at the Zeros, but the Japanese broke away and ran.

As Ens Steve Kona, also of Fighting-10, recovered from a long dive in pursuit of the first wave of attacking Vals, he spotted three bombless Vals as they passed through 3,000 feet to recover from their dives on *Hornet*. Kona attacked the first Japanese dive-bomber as it leveled off at 50 feet. A high-side run and recovery produced no discernible results because the body of Kona's Wildcat cut off Kona's view. Kona recovered in time to slip into attack position on the third Val. Again, no results were observed because the body of his Wildcat got in the way. Kona was recovering from the attack when a Zero attacked from dead astern. Kona and his wingman, Ens Lyman Fulton, instantly entered a Thach Weave, but ran into a cloud before the Zero pilot could be suckered into committing himself.

Once Lt Swede Vejtasa, of Fighting-10, recovered from his one quick attack on the diving Vals, and without any new instructions from the FDO, he led his Wildcat division toward the surface and picked up two retiring Vals. Vejtasa smoothly dispatched one of the Japanese dive-bombers before it could even begin defensive maneuvering, and his wingman, Lt Leroy Harris, got the other.

Ens George Wrenn, of Fighting-72, also recovered at low altitude from his fleeting double-kill attack on the inbound Kates. He found another pair of Kates as they ran from antiaircraft fire after releasing their torpedoes. Both Japanese inadvertently turned toward Wrenn, who dispatched them with light, easy bursts from only four of his wing guns. However, Wrenn's firing pass carried him too close to Task Force 16 and he ran afoul of *South Dakota's* jumpy 5-inch and 40mm gunners. It was all Ensign Wrenn could do to escape. In so doing, he passed a Val that was running away from the fleet at wave-top height. Almost without thinking, the young pilot got the Val in his gunsight and let loose with virtually all the ammunition remaining in the four wing guns with which he had already destroyed four Kates. The Val flew into the water, giving Ens George Wrenn five kills for five tries. He was an ace.

The first of *Enterprise's* morning scouts began returning to the vicinity of Task Force 61 shortly before the arrival of Lieutenant Commander Seki's leading strike group.

When Lt(jg) Hal Buell, of Bombing 10, and his wingman arrived from their fruitless search mission, they saw that *Hornet* was burning. Buell made a long orbit well away from the carriers to make sure it was safe to proceed. As he did, other search elements appeared and joined on him. Suddenly, at 1026, *Enterprise* turned into the wind and signaled all returning planes to land. Buell led the way up the groove, from which he could see that the flight deck was clear; everything had been launched or stowed on the hangar deck. The landing was routine and Buell's SBD was spotted in the forwardmost position on the flight deck. Behind it, numerous scouts and fighter pilots responded to the crisp signals Lt Robin Lindsey signed with his LSO paddles. After jumping from the wing of his Dauntless, Hal Buell walked over to a 40mm gun tub on the starboard bow, just below the level of the flight deck. It was then that he learned that a follow-on strike had been picked up on *Enterprise's* radar.

Ens Martin Carmody and Ens Les Ward, of Scouting 10, returned from their confrontation with the Japanese carriers, but could not immediately locate any friendly vessels at the appointed place. Finally, smoke from *Hornet* appeared on the horizon and served as a grim beacon for the two searchers at the end of a mission filled with altogether too much adventure. It was clear to Carmody that he could not land aboard *Hornet*, and he did not at first see *Enterprise*, which had not yet emerged from its concealing rain squall. Fuel was nil aboard the two Dauntlesses and Carmody was just resigning himself to a water landing when *Enterprise* sailed into view. The two joined up on the gathering behind Lt(jg) Hal Buell and made safe landings on the very last of their fuel. Carmody and Ward had been airborne for nearly five boring hours and more than a dozen exciting minutes.

Ens Steve Kona had only about one-fourth of his starting ammunition supply left when the sky was finally clear of Japanese. He lost track of his wingman while scuttling to and fro between *Enterprise* and *Hornet* in response to radar contacts erroneously showing a follow-on strike coming in from the south. At length, Kona was joined by another Fighting-10 pilot who had also been shaken loose from his parent formation. The two heard orders from *Enterprise* to "pancake"—to land as quickly as possible—and they instantly joined the line in the carrier's traffic circle. Kona was certain his fighter would be quickly serviced and relaunched, but he was sent below to the ready room without an explanation.

Lt Claude Phillips, of Fighting-72, only wanted to land his damaged Wildcat. He knew he needed ammunition for his wing guns, and he did not know the extent of the damage the Wildcat had suffered from a 20mm round fired into the fuselage by a Zero; the airplane had already been burning once. Phillips saw that *Hornet* was throwing up a huge pillar of black smoke, so he headed for *Enterprise*, which looked okay. Enroute, Phillips saw a retiring Kate that was still very low on the water. The Japanese warplane was dead ahead and coming head-on, so Phillips fired his guns as they passed but kept on his course steady toward *Enterprise*, which was sailing into the wind. Phillips passed along the carrier's starboard side with his wheels down. When he attempted to lower flaps, however, he discovered that the 20mm round had holed the vacuum tank through which the flaps were controlled. Only the protection of the armored seat back and self-sealing tanks had saved Phillips from a fiery death, for the vulnerable vacuum tank was directly behind the cockpit. Having committed himself to flying up the groove, Phillips watched for the LSO's fine-tuning signals. He got a "Come ahead" followed by a "Too fast," followed by a last-instant "Wave-off." As Phillips passed right over the LSO platform, he signed that he had no flaps. He came around again, hoping his message had been clear, and was allowed to come ahead and execute a hot landing. In fact, Robin Lindsey had disobeyed a direct order to keep damaged airplanes from landing aboard the only operational American flight deck left in the Pacific. If Phillips had piled up, many other warplanes might have been lost. As it was, he was the last pilot allowed to land aboard *Enterprise*.

Lt Louis Bliss, of Fighting-72, needed more ammunition. He started back toward *Hornet* minutes behind his squadron mate, Lieutenant Phillips, but saw for the first time that she was burning, so he also headed toward *Enterprise*. Before flying into the groove, Bliss took the precaution of clearing his presumably empty machine guns and found that the right outboard gun was still operating;

clearly, it had jammed earlier and still had an unknown number of rounds left in its magazine. As Bliss flew up *Enterprise*'s wake, he received a curt "Wave-off." He had no idea why the signal was passed, but the rule was that he had to clear out. Presumably, another Japanese strike was inbound. Lacking options, Bliss nudged his Wildcat over toward a cloud bank 2,000 feet up and virtually beside battleship *South Dakota*. As soon as he arrived, the jumpy battleship gunners fired a pattern of 5-inch rounds all around the orbiting Wildcat. Bliss radioed the battleship to remind its crew that all the midwing monoplanes in the sky were friendlies. The firing abruptly ceased and Bliss maintained his station around the dreadnought, ready for anything.

Among the many fighter pilots turned away by *Enterprise* was Ens Chip Reding, the only survivor of Lt(jg) John Leppla's Fighting-10 division, which had been ambushed along with the outbound Torpedo-10 Avengers. Reding had made it back home after the survivors of the first Japanese strike had left, and he joined right up at the end of the traffic circle. When Lt Robin Lindsey finally had to shut down landing operations in deference to the oncoming second strike, Reding obligingly flew to the nearest cloud and hid out.

As *Enterprise*'s flight-deck and hangar-deck crews worked furiously to refuel and respot the mixed bag of Wildcats and Dauntlesses Lt Robin Lindsey had guided in, everyone in the know turned his attention to the first radar contact with the approaching Japanese follow-on strike. In so doing, everyone missed seeing an old nemesis enter Task Force 61's tight protective circle.

40

☀

The first American strike aircraft to return to Task Force 61 were the two damaged Avengers that had survived the ambush of the outbound Torpedo-10 strike group. Lt Doc Norton, in the lead TBF, saw that *Hornet* was burning on the horizon so continued on to find his own ship, *Enterprise*. Rather unwisely, in view of the terrible condition of his Avenger, Norton made a pass at the carrier's LSO platform. Rather than a comradely offer to guide the Avenger down, Lt Robin Lindsey vigorously waved Norton away. Norton was put off by the rejection, for he had no way of knowing that another Japanese strike group had been picked up on the ship's radar. There being no alternative, Norton raised his Avenger's wheels, remained low and slow, and looked for a place to land amidst the Task Force 16 screening vessels.

The landing was shaky. Too low for Norton to back out, the damaged right wing seemed about to buckle, and a shudder passed through the Avenger's abused frame. Then the torpedo bomber settled in. Immediately, Norton and his crewmen deployed their life raft and furiously paddled away from the sinking wreck. But the Avenger did not sink. Its nose disappeared into the water, and then most of the fuselage. What remained was a section of the tail, which looked exactly like a small replica of a submarine conning tower.

Lt Louis Bliss, of Fighting-72, was still orbiting his Wildcat over battleship *South Dakota* when the 5-inch guns that had earlier menaced him opened on what appeared to be a submarine conning tower but which Bliss correctly identified as the tail of a bilged airplane.

Five miles from the battleship, the 5-inch rounds were splashing into the water all around the submerged TBF and its thoroughly shaken crew. Without a word, the three airmen dived overboard and flipped the yellow life raft over to show its muted blue underside. As visions of their lives passed before the three airmen, LCdr Max Stormes saw what was happening and conned his ship, destroyer *Preston*, to a position between the bilged airmen and the nervous gunners. At the same time, Lieutenant Bliss again admonished the battleship gunners for firing on a friendly airplane. Though Japanese bombers were virtually overhead, Lieutenant Commander Stormes ordered his vessel stopped so that Doc Norton and his crewmen could be safely hauled aboard. As soon as the mission was accomplished, *Preston* resumed full speed and caught up with the *Enterprise* screen.

⁂

Doc Norton's wingman, Lt(jg) Dick Batten, followed Norton away from *Enterprise* and landed his virtually fuelless, badly damaged TBF at about 1100, only 200 yards off destroyer *Porter*'s port beam. While Norton's crew was menaced by *South Dakota*, *Porter* was ordered to leave the *Enterprise* screen and pick up Batten and his crewmen.

Porter was an 1,850-ton destroyer leader, flagship of Capt Charles Cecil's Destroyer Squadron 5 and thus larger than the *Mahan*-class destroyers under Cecil's command. Though *Porter* was outfitted with four dual 5-inch gun mounts, she was not of much use in defending *Enterprise* against Japanese warplanes because none of the 5-inch guns could be raised far enough to provide antiaircraft fire. This, along with the spot in which Dick Batten chose to ditch, was undoubtedly behind the decision to send *Porter* to the aid of the downed TBF crew.

The sinking TBF was to port when *Porter* began slowing for the pickup. To avoid bilging the three aviators in the life raft, the destroyer's skipper, LCdr David Roberts, ordered the ship to come dead in the water a short way from the raft and to wait while Batten and his crewmen paddled to the leeward side of the ship, which happened to be to starboard. Thus the attention of Commander Roberts and most of the topside crewmen was directed toward the airmen as they clambered up the starboard side of the ship.

S2 Ross Pollock's attention was fleetingly diverted from the clambering airmen to a diving fighter to port. A 1.1-inch loader with a clear view all around the ship, Pollock realized that the fighter was friendly and that it was strafing an unseen object in the water off the port side of the ship.

By odd coincidence, the Wildcat pilot was also named Pollock, Lt Dave Pollock, of Fighting-10. He had seen several torpedo wakes rushing toward *Porter* and had dived in the slim hope of detonating one with his machine guns. The torpedo upon which Lieutenant Pollock could lay his guns was curving toward the destroyer. He fired two long bursts without results, pulled up, and dived again. During those two dives, Lieutenant Pollock became increasingly aware of the fire *Porter* was putting out in his direction. Since he could not hit the torpedo and was in danger of being downed by the ship he was trying to save, he zoomed from range under the prodding of the friendly guns.

Only as Lieutenant Pollock flew from range did it dawn on Seaman Pollock—a veteran of only three months in the Navy—that the fighter's unseen target might be a torpedo.

As Ensign Batten and his crewmen climbed aboard *Porter*, Lt(jg) Bill Wood, the officer-of-the-deck, glanced to port and saw a torpedo wake heading right at him from a relative bearing of 270 degrees. At the same instant, S1 Don Beane, a signalman striker manning a lookout station on the port wing of the bridge, also saw the oncoming torpedo. He yelled "Fish!" as loud as he could. The captain and executive officer turned toward Beane.

In Control-II, one deck above the main deck and abaft the

bridge, SM2 Al Muccitelli, saw three torpedo wakes to port. One was clearly going to pass ahead, and one was clearly going to pass astern. The center wake was heading for the ship. Y2 Francois Ogden, Destroyer Squadron 5's staff yeoman, saw only two torpedoes. When he realized that one would pass ahead and the other would pass astern, he relaxed. A messman who had just brought coffee to the bridge stopped in his tracks beside Ogden and became so agitated that Ogden thought he was going to jump overboard. "Take it easy," Ogden said in his most soothing voice, "they missed us." That said, he finally spotted the center torpedo heading right at him. Instantly, he dived into the corner furthest from the presumed point of impact.

RM3 R. C. Tannatt was leaning out of the radio shack to watch the rescue when he glanced to port in time to see Lt Dave Pollock's diving Wildcat veer away from the ship. Tannatt clearly saw the center torpedo coming right at him. A sailor on the main deck, just below the radio shack, was leaning against the railing, his back to the oncoming torpedo. Tannatt and a fellow radioman bellowed a warning.

As the center torpedo—one of at least three fired minutes earlier by submarine *I-21* from the midst of the Task Force 16 screen—raced toward *Porter*, Lt(jg) Bill Wood dived into the pilot house from the port wing of the bridge and rang up emergency flank speed on the repeater to the engine room. It was 1002.

卐

MM1 Al Anundsen, in the after engine room, instantly responded to Wood's signal from the bridge. The throttle was thrown forward as the chilling call "Torpedo wake" sounded over the intercom. But it was too late. Before the destroyer could move, SM2 Al Muccitelli helplessly watched as the torpedo passed from view beneath *Porter's* whaleboat, almost directly between her two firerooms—dead on the transverse bulkhead between the two compartments. The blast instantly deprived *Porter* of all her power. MM1 Al Anundsen, one compartment behind the point of impact, heard what sounded to him like the vastly amplified sharp *crack* of

413

two stones being thrown together. The ship went dead still and seemed to settle.

F1 Thomas Anderson was standing in the after fireroom right beside the point of impact and was blown out into the water. A radioman saw Anderson almost as soon as he emerged from the hole in the side of the ship, and he dived into the water to rescue the dazed fireman. Clad only in a skivvy shirt and shorts, Anderson's only apparent injury was an instant reddening of his exposed skin from exposure to steam escaping from ruptured steampipes. The burns would prove fatal within several days.

The sailor below the radio shack did not have time to react to RM3 R. C. Tannatt's shouted warning. The detonation lifted him high into the air and 20 feet out from the ship. He was pulling for the stricken warship almost as soon as he plunged into the water. He later told Tannatt that he had found himself looking down on the ship from midair without any idea about how he got there. He was one of the lucky ones. The full force of the blast erupted upward and engulfed the midships repair party, located on the main deck just abaft the bridge. One officer and one sailor were blown overboard, or perhaps vaporized; neither was ever seen again.

S2 Ross Pollock was knocked back against his 1.1-inch gun shield as the entire ship seemed to rise out of the water within a funnel of smoke, flame, and debris. Shrapnel and flying metal impacted all around and within Pollock's gun tub, denting the fixtures but sparing the guncrew from serious injury.

CWT Robert Baner and WT1 Charles McCarthy were on the starboard side of the after fireroom—away from the blast—when the torpedo detonated. Neither was hurt, though nine other members of the "black gang"—watertenders and machinist's mates—were killed in the blast. Baner thought he heard someone shout that the airlock exit was blocked, so he decided to lead McCarthy to the escape hatch on the port side. There was absolutely no light, so Baner ordered McCarthy to hang on to his shirt while he felt his way over the catwalks. Three more sailors found them on the port side of the fireroom, and Baner ordered them to fall in behind McCarthy while he, Baner, led the way up the escape trunk—a metal tube with a ladder—to the escape hatch. The five men were only halfway up the ladder when they entered a cloud of superheated steam that had become trapped against the overhead. Though Chief Baner could feel the flesh melting from his hands, he reflexively scuttled to the top of the ladder and used his belt knife to cut through a rope securing the hatch. McCarthy and WT2 Chester Schirmer were also scalded as they followed Baner to the top of the ladder. When the hatch flew open, the hot steam dissipated into the air outside.

RM3 R. C. Tannatt was one of the men who had gathered outside the escape hatch to help Chief Baner and the other men to the main deck. He grabbed one of the emerging sailors by a wrist and placed his other hand beneath one of the man's armpits. Only after the man was safely supine on the deck did Tannatt notice the victim looked like stewed beef. Indeed, he had been literally cooked to the bone. Only the last two of the five emerged without injury. Baner, McCarthy, and Schirmer had all received fatal doses of the superheated steam.

卍

Lt Harold Wells, the damage-control officer, arrived on the bridge and requested permission to jettison all the ready torpedoes in order to reduce topside weight. Lt(jg) Bill Wood, who was the ship's torpedo officer as well as officer-of-the-deck, had to refuse Wells's request on several counts. In the first place, two of the four fish in the forward mount had been triggered by the detonation of *I-21*'s torpedo and had become embedded in the forward stack; they were running hot in their tubes. Also, Wood thought he had seen a submarine periscope feather off the port bow, and he wanted to hold torpedoes in the aft mount in case there occurred a chance to launch them at the Japanese submarine.

Nine burned and scalded firemen and watertenders provided a gruesome sight for many members of the topside crew as they were treated by corpsmen on the main deck. Nearly all of the injured were a deep red color, and one had long strips of cooked flesh hanging from his arms and legs.

The carrier battle force had long since passed from sight and sound over the horizon. As the stricken destroyer's entire crew assembled topside, the odd quiet moment brought forth a ponderous creaking from below as bulkheads gave way under the unremitting pressure of the water entering through the gash in *Porter*'s side. The ship settled slowly but remained on an even keel. No one quite knew if she might simply break up, or how much time there would be to abandon her if she did. Once, when the ship settled with a particularly nasty jolt, a group of rattled sailors sitting on the fantail jumped over the side. Nearby, destroyer *Shaw* was circling the cripple in search of a submarine, and she released a spread of eight depth charges as the group of sailors stepped into the water from *Porter*'s fantail. The detonations washed the swimmers back aboard *Porter*, where they nursed bloody noses and ears inflicted by the pressure of the underwater blasts.

S2 Ross Pollock passed the time carrying on a semaphore conversation with a signalman on the bridge. In due course, the vital matter of where the nearest land lay came up. The crew was forbidden to go below in the event the ship suddenly sank. Pollock was chagrined by this order because he had had to leave behind a carefully hoarded stash of candy, cookies, and twenty-dollar bills.

Porter's fate was sealed by the condition of her firerooms, which were dead. Though the crew was well in hand, without a trace of panic, and the damage was limited to the area of the initial detonation, *Porter* could not sail under her own power. The decision, a difficult one, was made to scuttle her rather than risk more precious warships in a towing operation through submarine-infested waters. At 1055, *Shaw* was ordered to close on *Porter* and take on survivors.

As soon as the order to abandon ship was passed, Y2 Francois Ogden, the destroyer-squadron yeoman, went to his office to begin disposing of secret documents and codes. There was a delay in getting the safe opened in the dark, and the staff communicator, a young ensign, began needling Ogden about hurrying up. Ogden had had earlier run-ins with the abrasive young officer and simply told him to "Shut up," which sufficed. The codes and documents were tossed into a canvas bag, which Ogden weighted with a typewriter, and then thrown over the side. However, the weighted bag did not sink. Ogden removed his shoes and jumped overboard to cut holes in the tough material with a belt knife. As he climbed back aboard the doomed destroyer, Ogden realized that all the secret materials could have been left in the safe to be scuttled with the ship.

Shaw closed on Porter's undamaged starboard side and began taking the wounded first. The entire evacuation was calm and orderly, entirely without untoward incident. Before leaving the ship, the two bridge signalmen, S1 Don Beane and SM3 Dave Meredith, ran up flags meaning "good luck" on the port and starboard yardarms. Y2 Francois Ogden was so rattled that the only possession he took aboard Shaw was a little sign that read, SMILE, DAMNIT, SMILE!

As Shaw held her position after taking off the bulk of the survivors, LCdr David Roberts headed forward to make sure everyone was off while Lt(jg) Bill Wood headed aft to do the same. They and the commodore, Capt Charles Cecil, were the last survivors to leave the ship.

When all the living, and most of the dead, had been removed from Porter, Shaw circled around and fired two torpedoes at point-blank range. Both fish struck Porter, but they failed to detonate. With gunners and loaders from Porter helping out to speed the action, Shaw fired fifty 5-inch rounds into the destroyer leader. A short time after Porter rolled over to starboard and sank stern-first, Bill Wood spotted a submarine periscope from his place on Shaw's bridge. But Shaw was by then bending on all speed to rejoin Task Force 16, and no effort was made to confront the submerged raider.

The carrier battle force was still over the horizon when a mishap in the engineering department caused Shaw to slink to a halt with black smoke pouring from her stacks. It took a half hour for the black gang to correct the problem and get her under way again.

The British Broadcasting Corporation announced the loss of Porter less than a day after the event, a distressing bit of news for next of kin who would not hear from their loved ones for nearly two weeks.

Ten sailors and one officer were killed or disappeared at the time of the blast. Three of the nine sailors injured in the blast succumbed to their grievous burns aboard Shaw and one died later aboard South Dakota.

41

ask Force 17 was still reeling from the effects of the first Japanese air strike when, at 1105, heavy cruiser *Northampton* arrived off *Hornet*'s bows, in position to pass over a tow line. The work had not yet begun at 1109 when a single Val plunged through the bottom of the cloud cover dead ahead of the wounded carrier.

Onlookers on the carrier's bridge were certain the Val was heading straight for them, and many feared a crash to outdo LCdr Mamoru Seki's spectacular suicide. Lt(jg) Bob Brown, destroyer *Russell*'s gunnery officer, was on the deck of his ship, having been forced from his gun director by repeated collisions with the carrier. Brown was both certain that the Val was going to hit *Russell* and totally frustrated because he had been caught out of position to direct his guns.

There was almost an audible sigh of relief aboard the carrier and the three destroyers nuzzling at her flank as the 250-kilogram bomb detached itself from the Val, which recovered and ran. The bomb sailed into the water outboard of destroyer *Morris* and detonated 60 yards from the carrier and only 25 yards astern of the destroyer—without doing any damage. Nevertheless, all the destroyers around *Hornet* stood away from the target and prepared to repel another Japanese air strike.

Northampton also ran from her vulnerable position ahead of *Hornet*, thus further delaying the vital towing operation.

卐

The lone Val was the only warplane from the second Japanese strike force—twelve *Shokaku* Kates and twenty *Zuikaku* Vals escorted by sixteen *Zuikaku* Zeros—to launch against *Hornet*. The entire balance of the force, which had taken off at 0922, went after *Enterprise*. It was greeted by fewer fighters and more clouds covering its approach than had been the first strike, but it came through in two distinct waves rather than the coordinated mass of Vals and Kates that had struck *Hornet*.

The first wave of the second strike was composed entirely of nineteen *Zuikaku* Vals commanded by Lt Sadamu Takahashi, who opted to deliver his strike without waiting for the arrival of the Kates, which were commanded by the *Shokaku hikotaicho*, LCdr Shigeharu Murata, a torpedo pilot of legendary skill who had been the first Japanese pilot to launch a torpedo at Pearl Harbor.

卐

At virtually the last moment, Cdr John Crommelin, the *Enterprise* air boss, noticed that one Wildcat was still on deck, in position to be launched. He sent word down to the Fighting-10 ready room, and Lt Macgregor Kilpatrick was dispatched to take the fighter aloft. It was Kilpatrick's distinct impression that his job was more to clear a space on the flight deck than to actually engage the incoming strike.

The state of the American combat air patrol was deplorable. A number of Wildcats had had to land because of damage or the depletion of ammunition or fuel supplies, and, except for the one Lieutenant Kilpatrick was flying, not one had been replaced. Only two organized fighter divisions remained, and many fighter elements had been broken up by the action over *Hornet*. The depleted fighter units had not even begun reorganizing themselves when the second strike was first picked up by *South Dakota*'s radar while it was still 55 miles out between due north and northwest. The *Enterprise* FDOs had no opportunity to organize or vector their slim resources before the first Val *chutai* began its 45-degree glide-bombing attack on their hitherto undamaged carrier.

卐

Minutes before the Vals flew into view, Lt Dave Pollock was ordered to race to a position east of the *Enterprise* battle group and orbit at 12,000 feet. He arrived on station just in time to watch the first Val *chutai* commence its dive from the opposite side of Task Force 16.

As Pollock looked on in helpless frustration, he thought he saw two Wildcats in among the diving Vals. If he did, one was certainly flown by Fighting-10's Ens Don Gordon, who had been turned away from the landing circle as he waited with his wheels down to go aboard *Enterprise* to rearm and refuel. As Gordon rolled up his wheels and clambered back up to 10,000 feet alone, he saw two Vals go by right in front of him. He fired bursts at both dive-bombers, but missed each time. He met another Val as he continued to climb out of the rising antiaircraft gunfire. After setting up the best shot he could manage, Gordon squeezed the trigger. He felt the heavy recoil of his F4F's six wing guns for only a second, until the last of his ammunition was suddenly gone. Gordon watched the diving Val long after it passed his climbing Wildcat and was rewarded for his diligence when the Val suddenly pulled out of its dive at about 4,000 feet and exploded in midair. Gordon had no idea if the kill was his or the result of the antiaircraft gunfire.

The other Wildcat Pollock saw could well have been flown by Lt Macgregor Kilpatrick. As the Japanese were coming down, Kilpatrick was climbing through 8,000 feet. Before he quite knew what was happening, a Val appeared from out of the murk, well into its dive. Kilpatrick had time for only one quick firing pass, saw the Val begin to smoke, and lost sight of the quarry as they both bored on into the clouds.

卐

For all practical purposes, the fighter response was nil. Thus the carrier's last line of defense—its antiaircraft batteries—became her first line of defense.

Enterprise sported a new array of modern quadruple 40mm guns in place of all but one of the 1.1-inch gun stations that had performed so marginally at Eastern Solomons. Though the larger caliber 40mm guns fired at a slower rate than the 1.1-inch guns, they automatically ejected spent magazines, which saved time for the loaders. Also, the 40mm antiaircraft rounds were fused to automatically detonate at 4,000 feet if the round did not connect with a target before that. Thus unlike the 1.1-inch point-contact rounds they replaced, the 40mm rounds built a curtain of flak at intermediate ranges that oncoming bombers had to fly through. This allowed for the possibility of more damage even if the gunners were less than perfectly accurate. Unlike the 1.1-inchers, the new guns were controlled automatically from a gun director but could be fired manually. The tracker in the gun director had only to hold his target in a light-reflected cross-shaped reticle. The 40mm battery officer, also manning the gun director, watched the fall of tracer and could adjust vertically or horizontally while the tracker traversed the guns. The system seemed perfect, but the gunners were concerned because practice had pointed out that the guns could fall behind sudden swerving motions by the ship—exactly the sort of problem that was bound to crop up in combat while the ship was evading incoming Vals and Kates. Still, on balance, the former 1.1-inch gunners found little to complain about when making comparisons.

In addition to the quad-40s and a beefed up complement of 20mm cannon, *Enterprise* was about to use radar-guided proximity-fused 5-inch antiaircraft rounds for the first time anywhere. This thoroughly modern invention was ideal for the battle unfolding directly over the carrier's decks. The radar could "see" through the thick cloud cover that otherwise obscured the approach of the Vals, and the proximity-fused shells would self-detonate within 50 yards of the incoming cloud-obscured Vals, close enough to inflict mortal damage. The technological combination—a total surprise to the oncoming Japanese—was expected to be awesome and deadly.

In addition to *Enterprise*'s many modern antiaircraft guns, the screen included *South Dakota*'s numerous 5-inchers and lighter weapons, and light antiaircraft cruiser *San Juan*, which sported sixteen rapid-fire 5-inch guns in eight mounts and a large array of 1.1-inch and lighter antiaircraft guns. Batteries aboard heavy cruiser *Portland* and the five highly maneuverable destroyers remaining in the *Enterprise* screen were also trained out to meet the oncoming Vals.

When the radarmen reported that the Vals were getting close, Capt Osborne Hardison, *Enterprise*'s new skipper, ordered the ship to begin a tight skidding turn to the right. While this maneuver was well known to carrier captains, it had not been rehearsed with the screening warships. The result was confusion in the screen, where, in the best of circumstances, the lighter vessels had to race to keep station on the ship at the center of the formation; the carrier's tight right turn forced the screening vessels further out into much wider turns, and the carrier's great speed all but outdistanced the other warships.

卍

All the modern marvels in the world are of no use if someone in authority will not allow them to be used. Lt(jg) Art Burke, who had overseen *Enterprise*'s starboard 20mm guns during Eastern Solomons, was back as the gunnery fire-control radar officer in charge of the forward 5-inch radar gun director. The new gear was working perfectly, and Burke's radarmen had acquired an excellent track as the lead Val *chutai* ducked into the 40-percent cloud cover at 15,000 feet during its final approach on the carrier. The fire-control solution was perfect, and the forward 5-inch battery was dead on target. Burke was about to request permission to open fire when the officer in charge of the director pulled it off the oncoming planes. That officer, who had made his negative feelings about the newfangled radar well known to the young radar enthusiasts serving under his command, began sweeping the horizon in search of nonexistent torpedo bombers with the old optical range-finding equipment. By the time it became clear that there were no torpedo bombers, it was too late to reacquire the high targets with the radar and lay on the forward 5-inch guns.

The remaining Task Force 16 5-inch antiaircraft batteries opened almost in unison at 1115. Antiaircraft cruiser *San Juan*'s 5-inch guns belched so much smoke at the outset that the pilot of an orbiting Wildcat was certain she had suffered a catastrophic internal explosion. Officers and sailors topside aboard *Enterprise* and several other vessels were certain that *South Dakota* had also blown up, so thick was the smoke around her main deck and upper works.

LCdr Orlin Livdahl, *Enterprise*'s gunnery officer, was in Sky Control, high up on the main mast over the bridge, when the attack commenced. He was certain that the amount of gunfire put out by the fleet far surpassed the prodigious volume put up at Eastern Solomons, but he was not sure it would be enough to finish the huge job the fighters had barely started. Livdahl's worst moment came early, when a smoking Val carried its bomb all the way down toward the island and seemed about to crash. At the last moment, the ship heeled over and threw the pilot's aim off. The Val flew straight into the water, the bomb exploded, and debris and water fell across the flight deck and as high as Livdahl's perch in Sky Control.

卐

The first bomb struck *Enterprise* at 1117. It was a 250-kilogram armor-piercing projectile that passed through the forward lip of the flight deck 20 feet from the leading edge and just to port of the centerline. It penetrated 50 feet through the forecastle, passed through the outer hull, and exploded in midair in front of the carrier's bows, just above the water. The upward force of the blast blew Lt(jg) Marshall Field, scion of the Chicago newspaper and department-store family, out of the 1.1-inch gun director and up onto the flight deck, where he lay unconscious with shrapnel in his neck, an arm, and a leg. Bomb fragments pierced the 5-inch radar gun-director compartment in the bow, where one sailor was killed and several were wounded, and the radar-control equipment was destroyed. The blast also blew the forwardmost Dauntless right over the side. The airplane carried AMM1 Sam Davis Presley to his death moments after he had jumped into the rear compartment to fire the twin .30-caliber machine guns at the incoming Vals.

There was so much noise going on around the 40mm gun tub in which the lost SBD's pilot, Lt(jg) Hal Buell, had taken refuge that Buell, who weathered innumerable bombing raids while flying with Flight 300 on Guadalcanal, did not hear the bomb that destroyed his Dauntless.

As the ship settled back on course, Mach Bill Fluitt, the carrier's gasoline officer, saw that the fuel tank of a parked SBD had been ruptured by the blast and that leaking aviation gasoline was fueling a spot blaze near the point of impact. Fluitt yelled for volunteers and raced down the exposed flight deck under the guns of incoming Vals to oversee the jettisoning of the burning scout-bomber before its 500-pound bomb cooked off.

卐

Pfc George Lanvermeier, who was serving as loader on one of the Marine-manned starboard 20mm guns forward of the island, was lying back on the flight deck, looking straight up, when he saw a bomb detach itself from the underside of a Val and begin the long fall toward *Enterprise*. So keenly was Lanvermeier staring that he saw the finned after end of the projectile swing through several brief arcs before settling on its plummeting course. For a heartstopping moment, the Marine was certain the bomb would hit him. It didn't miss by much.

The ship had not yet settled down from the first blast when Ens Ross Glasmann, who was in charge of Sky Lookout Forward, high up in the mainmast, also became convinced that the second bomb was going to hit him. Just after it passed close by his perch, he saw a hole suddenly appear in the flight deck just abaft the forward elevator.

The second 250-kilogram bomb, which struck *Enterprise* within less than a minute of the first, fell through the flight deck, struck a girder, and broke in two. One half of this bomb blew up right on the hangar deck while the other half penetrated to the third deck, where it blew up in a warren of officers' staterooms.

The hangar-deck detonation destroyed two warplanes lashed to the overhead and scorched the fabric off the control surfaces of five SBDs. The concussion killed several sailors, but it was of relatively low order and, on the day's scale of terror, was relatively minor. Firefighters moved straight into the eye of the storm and overwhelmed any nascent conflagrations before they quite took hold.

卐

Repair Party II—one officer and thirty-five enlisted sailors—was located on the third deck just aft of the forward elevator. Nearby, an emergency medical team was manning a battle dressing station. The core of the repair party had been together since the start of the war, had been through Eastern Solomons, knew what could happen if a torpedo or bomb detonated anywhere near its position; they called their station "torpedo junction" because it was located right at the waterline on the level at which most armor-piercing bombs seemed to detonate. The job was nerve-racking be-cause it involved a long wait without anything to do or see; the only useful sensation was hearing the progression of antiaircraft gunfire from the long-range 5-inch batteries to the light 20mm guns, and that only added to the anxiety.

Repair Party II had been at General Quarters for what seemed like days, and the sailors had heard loudspeaker announcements about the incoming strikes—the first strike, which hit *Hornet*, and the second strike, which might hit anywhere. Then there was the chilling announcement, "Stand by for air attack."

At that, all hands lay prone in the narrow steel passageway outside a suite of officers' staterooms. They were well protected, dressed in flashproof jackets with the hoods and cuffs secured and wearing steel helmets with clear pull-down face shields. Everyone had a gas mask near at hand and a large flashlight. All the firefight-ing and lifesaving equipment was neatly laid out within reach. As the crescendo of outgoing gunfire rose, each man supported the weight of his torso and abdomen on his forearms and elbows; if there was a hit, the deck would be likely to bounce hard enough to knock the wind out of someone whose chest and abdomen were all the way down. Breathing through open mouths was mandatory to overcome the effects of concussion. All the ship's ventilators had been secured, the air tasted really foul from body odor, and that discomfort was heightened by the strong odor of camphor from the denim flashproof jackets.

F3 Don Morgan, who had on a set of battle phones, heard "They're going after the *Hornet.*" He repeated the announcement aloud and relaxed. Experience had shown that the Japanese invariably concentrated their strength on one carrier. No doubt the message was germinated by the attack on *Hornet* by the lone Val from the second strike group. Though the *Enterprise* antiaircraft batteries were still firing all out, all hands in the repair party relaxed. F3 Morgan first sat up and leaned against a six-inch steel stanchion welded to the deck and the overhead, then he stood up, removed his helmet, and bent his head to take off the earphones.

At that precise instant, the half bomb that had punched through the hangar deck detonated in the cramped passageway. F3 Morgan was engulfed in a great orange flash and the loudest noise he had ever heard. Then there was total silence. Somewhere in his head, Morgan saw his whole family gathered around a Christmas tree. Then he spluttered as the piercing odor of sulfur dioxide assaulted his sense of smell. He was fully alert, lying on his back, unable to get up. There was the taste of blood in his mouth and a loud ringing in his ears. His nose was bleeding and clogged. He groped for his flashlight and turned it on, but the strong beam penetrated all of about 6 inches; the area was completely filled with thick, black smoke. Morgan could see and smell fires breaking out, so he wiggled out from beneath a steel ladder that had fallen across his legs and felt his way through the murk. He found a hatchway and crawled through—and by feel and memory alone kept right on going through six more compartments, all plunged in total darkness. On the way, he found a gas mask, which relieved him of a great deal of his anxiety. There was light behind the eighth door, and people, all balanced on their forearms and elbows. In a great catharsis of words and emotion, Morgan tried to explain that there were fires breaking out forward, that help was needed. But no one listened. The ship was still twisting and the guns were still firing; everyone seemed to be mesmerized by some inner vision of doom. Finally, there was a lull. Someone yelled an order for firefighters to head forward to fight the fires.

Don Morgan grabbed a firehose while someone else turned on the water. As Morgan was clearing the first hatchway, the hose in his hands went stiff and then burst; he had neglected to turn on the nozzle. He grabbed a fire extinguisher and rushed back to his original station, where he fought down several small blazes. Within minutes, all the small fires in Repair Party II's passageway were doused. By then, dozens of firefighters had converged on the area to fight fires in adjacent staterooms, in which bedding and clothing were feeding the flames.

The confined bomb blast had killed the repair-party officer, Lt John Acree, and killed or mortally wounded nearly every other member of Repair Party II. Fragments that penetrated into the nearby emergency medical compartment killed several corpsmen and wounded most of the others. And three of five sailors in an adjacent ammunition handling room were killed. Power cables to the stricken area were out, so lighting and communications were out.

F3 Don Morgan's hair, eyebrows, and eyelashes had been burned off in the fireball, and his face and hands were red from burns. After the fires had been doused and the smoke cleared, Morgan saw that the 6-inch steel stanchion he had been standing next to had been ripped out of the deck and bent into a U shape. There were shrapnel holes everywhere.

On balance, despite the catastrophic loss of life from the blast, the worst blow to the ship's capacity to operate was the jamming of the forward elevator in the up position.

卐

The third—and last—250-kilogram bomb to get within hurting distance of *Enterprise* detonated at 1119 right next to the carrier's hull on the starboard side aft. It threw seawater up over gunners manning the starboard catwalks and the 40mm gun tubs abaft the island, ruptured numerous hull-plate welds below the waterline, tore a 50-foot-long, 3-inch-wide gash in the side of the ship, and damaged the main turbine bearing. In addition to other serious damage caused by the severe shock of this detonation, the foremast rotated a half inch, throwing a complex of antennas mounted on it out of line. Also, two empty fuel tanks and a full one were opened to the sea. So, to add to her troubles, *Enterprise* was trailing a broad patch of fuel oil to help guide additional Japanese warplanes up her wake.

卐

One of the recovering Vals passed right over destroyer *Cushing*'s bows, a perfect set-up for the forward 20mm gun. However, the gun jammed. Instantly, a signalman standing on the bridge yanked out his .45-caliber pistol and emptied all seven rounds into the departing dive-bomber. At the last second, the Japanese rear gunner thumbed his nose at the destroyer.

All guns in Task Force 16 ceased firing at 1120. The dive-bombing attack lasted just four minutes. One of the relatively few survivors was Lt Sadamu Takahashi, the Val commander. His airplane suffered severe damage to its rudder and was capable of flying only in huge circles. It would take Takahashi over four hours to return to *Zuikaku.*

卐

The second wave of the second strike was composed entirely of the twelve *Zuikaku* Kates led by Lieutenant Commander Murata. Japanese officers aboard their carriers monitored Murata's order— "All planes go in"—and then lost contact with the flight leader.

Lt Dave Pollock was sent to the northwest and ordered to orbit just 15 miles from *Enterprise.* When he reported himself on station, the FDO told him to look down to see if he could spot any incoming torpedo bombers. Moments later, Pollock was ordered to search above a cloud bank, but he opted to remain at 12,000 feet. The FDO radioed again to warn Pollock that the incoming airplanes might be friendly, but Pollock told the FDO that he could see nothing. An instant later, Pollock sighted the Kates to the northwest and only 15 miles out. Immediately, with an ammunitionless Fighting-72 F4F in tow, Lieutenant Pollock started an overhead firing run on the first Kate on the port side of the Japanese formation. A last-minute glance to starboard revealed that two more Wildcats were boring in on the Kates from that flank. Pollock opened fire as he was passing through 4,000 feet and used up the last of his ammunition as close in as he could get. The Kate began smoking just as it disappeared from view into the base of a large cloud. Pollock followed the Kate into the cloud, more for the sake of protecting his unarmed fighter from Zeros he knew were in the area than to chase the Kate. However, as the Fighting-10 division leader broke out of the cloud at low altitude, he saw a burning Kate he presumed to be his former target plunge into the sea. Pollock turned toward the remaining Kates in time to see a last-minute attack by the only fully staffed Wildcat division in the sky over Task Force 16.

⚛

Lt Swede Vejtasa had only been able to nip around the edges of the Japanese strike against *Hornet*, but he had nevertheless succeeded in dumping two recovering Vals into the water.

At 1135, as his second element was diving on two Zeros, and just after listening to the *Enterprise* FDO warn Lt Dave Pollock that the incoming aircraft might be friendly, Vejtasa heard Ens Hank Leder sing out, "Tallyho! Nine o'clock, down." From his vantage point at 13,000 feet, the division leader clearly saw eleven dark-green Kates arrayed in a stepped-up vee of three three-plane *shotai* followed by a single two-plane element. By that time, Vejtasa's second element—Lt Stan Ruehlow and Ens Hank Leder—were already well into their attack on the Kates after aborting their run on the Zeros.

Vejtasa and his wingman, Lt Leroy Harris, picked up over 350 knots of speed in their dive toward the Kates and set up high-side runs on each of two of the Kates in the nearest *shotai*. Each of them set his target afire and broke away as the tight torpedo formation broke up so that individual *shotai* could deliver their attacks from numerous points around *Enterprise*. As the Kates flew into a large cloud—instead of beneath it, as expected—Vejtasa latched on behind a *shotai*. Two short bursts blew the number two Kate out of the formation from dead astern, and a third burst shot the rudder off the lead bomber, which began burning. The last Kate in the *shotai* began a shallow turn as Vejtasa adjusted his aim on it. A rather long burst set this Kate on fire.

As Vejtasa pulled up after swatting his fourth Kate in a row, he saw yet another dark-green torpedo bomber sailing by overhead. He tried a low-side firing run, but missed, then followed the straggler out of the clouds. At this point, the Kate pilot must have realized that he was too high and coming on too fast to make an effective torpedo run on *Enterprise*, which was coming up fast, so he continued on through the heavy antiaircraft fire and dived into the bow of destroyer *Smith* as she guarded the carrier's far flank. Swede Vejtasa, who had pulled up just before entering the curtain of friendly fire, saw the Kate erupt in a great ball of flame.

卐

During the lull between the attacks, immediately after the last of the Vals had flown from sight, Pfc George Lanvermeier had taken the opportunity to change barrels on his 20mm guns. He had extracted a new magazine and stepped in front of the gun to twist the barrel off when a round he had inadvertently left in the chamber cooked off from the heat of the recent firing. The round passed right in front of Lanvermeier at shoulder height, and he would have been burned if he had not been wearing a flashproof coat. Now, still a little shaken by the near miss, Lanvermeier looked out and saw several Kates dodging in toward the carrier.

Suddenly, one of the torpedo bombers made a pass right down the starboard side of the ship from ahead to astern. Every gun that could bear depressed to follow the attacker, but none could reach him. Many of the gunners thought they saw the rear gunner raise his hand and offer a middle-finger salute as the plane flew from sight. Even if it had been hit, its job was done; its torpedo had been launched and was following the Kate toward the carrier.

Though observers counted nine Kates, no more than seven could have succeeded in dropping their fish from as low as 75 feet and at ranges of 1,000 to 2,000 yards.

卐

When Captain Hardison counted three torpedo wakes coming in forward of his starboard beam—along parallel tracks, a small blessing—he wrenched the huge ship into a hard right turn to comb their wakes. Pfc George Lanvermeier, manning a starboard 20mm gun, saw only two fish pass from view beneath his position on the catwalk, but neither of them—nor the third torpedo, if there was one—struck the vessel's side.

Captain Hardison had straightened *Enterprise* from her tight evading turn when lookouts announced the approach of another torpedo, also from the starboard bow. Once again, Hardison ordered his helmsman to bring the rudder all the way over to the right. Once again, the great ship swung toward the oncoming torpedo. Once again, she slid by the danger, this time with 100 feet to spare. The Kate that dropped that fish was shot down close aboard *Enterprise* as it followed through its release. The pilot and gunner were climbing out of the bilged wreckage when *Enterprise* passed so close that 20mm gunners on the catwalk could distinctly see their upturned faces.

While the first group of Kates bored in from starboard, a group said to number five came straight up *Enterprise*'s wake to evade the worst of the antiaircraft gunfire. While the carrier was evading the last torpedo to starboard, the Kates astern swung wide to port to set up their drops against the carrier's port side. Two torpedoes definitely missed following a long chase up the carrier's wake after she had turned to evade the starboard fish. Three torpedoes—perhaps dropped by Kates but more likely fired by a close-in submarine— clanged into the side of heavy cruiser *Portland* as she doggedly stuck with the carrier through the tight right turns. Fortunately for the crew of the relatively thin-skinned cruiser, none of the torpedoes detonated.

卐

The retiring Kates—numbering no more than five—were not quite out of danger.

Ens Don Gordon, who had been joined minutes earlier by Ens Chip Reding, the only survivor of Lt(jg) Johnny Leppla's escort division, saw a Fighting-72 Wildcat make a mock firing pass at one of a pair of the recovering Kates, and he decided to do the same despite the knowledge that he had no ammunition left aboard his Wildcat. Hoping against hope that his guns would resume firing,

Gordon bored in at the Kate from dead ahead. The Japanese pilot flinched when he became aware of Gordon's close approach, and he dropped one of his wings. The lowered wingtip bit into the surface of the water, not 10 feet below, and the entire torpedo bomber cartwheeled into the water, where it was consumed in a violent explosion.

Lt Macgregor Kilpatrick also picked up a recovering Kate as it passed beneath and in the same direction as his diving Wildcat. He pulled up behind the torpedo bomber, which was at about 100 feet, and chased it, getting in an occasional burst while the rear gunner pecked away at his Wildcat. The fight was a complete standoff. Suddenly, another Wildcat rocketed past from overhead and began firing at the stubborn Kate.

Lt Swede Vejtasa had been circling around the antiaircraft curtain after dropping four inbound Kates when he spotted two outbound Kates as they flew close to the water. Though he knew he was about out of ammunition, Vejtasa selected the nearer Kate—which was being chased fruitlessly by Lieutenant Kilpatrick—and dived on it. As Vejtasa fired his last bullets, the Kate violently skidded to evade. It began burning, but would not fall until it had flown 5 miles further. This was Swede Vejtasa's seventh confirmed kill of the day. Quite possibly, Vejtasa ended the life of LCdr Shigeharu Murata, for *Zuikaku's hikotaicho* did not make it home.

If indeed only twelve Kates began the attack, and if all the claims were accurate, no more than three survived—a fantastic ratio, but not enough to get Task Force 61 out of the woods. *Junyo's* fresh, untried *hikokitai* had not yet been heard from.

42

L Cdr Hunter Wood's destroyer, *Smith*, commenced firing all guns at 1115 as Task Force 16 came under attack by steeply gliding Vals. Five minutes later, after *Enterprise* was struck on the forward edge of her flight deck, the survivors of the second group of Japanese dive-bombers left the area and Lieutenant Commander Wood ordered powder and shell brought up from the magazines to replenish the ready ammunition boxes. It was known that another attack group, presumably torpedo bombers, was on the way in.

When Lieutenant Commander Murata's torpedo attack commenced, *Smith* opened with 20mm and 5-inch batteries as soon as targets were visible. At 1148, Ens Herb Damon, *Smith*'s machine-gun officer, saw a burning Kate torpedo bomber—one of Lt Swede Vejtasa's victims—closing on the starboard side of the ship. The Kate was so close that Damon could hear the crackling noise of the flames that were enveloping the fuselage and could clearly see the pilot and rear gunner. The Kate briefly paralleled *Smith*'s course 20 yards to starboard and 50 feet off the water, then it abruptly swung left, toward the destroyer.

Ens Phil Souza, of Fighting-72, arrived over Task Force 16 during the last moments of the Japanese attack in the company of a fellow Fighting-72 pilot, Lt(jg) Willie Roberts, whose Wildcat was leaking fuel from many holes in its gas tanks. As the two Wildcats prepared to make an emergency approach on *Enterprise*, several screening destroyers reflexively opened fire on them. Souza screamed into his microphone, "For Christ's sake, we're trying to get back in with damaged airplanes! Cease firing!" At that moment, Roberts's engine died from lack of fuel and his Wildcat tipped over and flew straight into the sea. Severely shaken by the sudden demise of his comrade, Souza flew on past the outer ring of screening warships. He saw a flaming Kate deliberately turn toward destroyer *Smith*—and crash into the forward gun mount.

Smith's exec, LCdr Bob Theobold, was preparing to return to the secondary conn from the bridge following his examination of a false sonar contact, when he happened to glance forward in time to see the Kate dive on *Smith* from slightly abaft the starboard beam. The burning torpedo bomber hit the shield of Number 2 5-inch gun, and crashed into the forecastle deck on the port side, abreast Number 1 5-inch gun.

Observers throughout the task force and topside aboard the stricken destroyer saw a bright flash as the entire forward part of the ship was enveloped in a sheet of flame and a pillar of smoke, undoubtedly caused by the Kate's bursting gasoline tanks. Most of the wrecked Kate tumbled over the side and sank astern the swiftly passing vessel.

BM1 Lee English, a member of the after damage-control party, was on the main deck between the aft torpedo tubes when the Kate struck. He felt the shock of the impact and looked up in time to see smoke and debris passing over the mainmast. Muttering imprecations, English ran to the starboard rail and peered forward. The entire forward section of the ship was engulfed in smoke and flame. Streaming out from the smoke was a ragged line of sailors. Many of the survivors of the forward gun crews were grotesquely burned, with strips of skin hanging from their bodies, hair burned off their scalps, and clothing still smoldering. English saw that a cord dangling from the earphones of one survivor was slowly burning.

MoMM2 Pat Cosgrove, who was manning a 20mm gun on the well deck, abaft the bridge, reflexively ducked as the first sheet of burning aviation gasoline passed right over his head. When Cosgrove stood tall again, he immediately saw that another sailor was leaning back over the rail. Cosgrove asked the man how he was, but he received no response. Slowly, the other man leaned overboard and fell into the water. At that moment, an officer standing near Cosgrove screamed "Abandon ship!" and led a dozen panicked sailors into the water. Horrified, Cosgrove nevertheless remained aboard *Smith* and watched as the next destroyer in the screen passed right over the swimmers, none of whom was saved.

Ens Herb Damon was scared witless by the clear view he had of the Kate's intentional dive on *Smith*, but he clung to his post while all around him sailors abandoned their battle stations. Within a few seconds, Damon realized that he was alone. Though he felt he had his fear under control, Damon angrily tried to pull apart the cord of his headset rather than simply remove his earphones. Then, cursing the human race, he grabbed the nearest machine gun and began hammering away at every airplane—friend or foe, it did not matter which—that flew into his sights.

BM1 Lee English looked aft from his position beside the aft torpedo mounts in time to see a knife-wielding sailor preparing to cut loose a pair of life rafts. English ordered the sailor to get down and leave the rafts alone. He looked up from the panicked man in time to see another sailor standing on the propeller guards, getting set to jump. English cursed at the sailor and pointed out that the ship was still making better than 30 knots.

卐

At 1149, the intense heat being swept from the forecastle back along the ship forced Lieutenant Commander Wood to order the bridge and gun director cleared. The captain made his way back to the secondary conn with CQM Frank Riduka, who had been at the helm when the Kate struck the ship. Communications with the steering-engine room had by then been disrupted by the damage and excitement, so Chief Riduka proceeded to that compartment, where he took the conn and controlled the ship until, after several

435

unsuccessful attempts, control could be shifted to the secondary conn. As soon as that was accomplished, Chief Quartermaster Riduka was able to guide the ship by means of phoned directions from Lieutenant Commander Wood. With Wood guiding him, Riduka nudged the stricken warship beside battleship *South Dakota*'s wake, the spume from which helped smother several of the smaller forecastle fires. Shortly thereafter, Wood guided Riduka to *Smith*'s former position in the screen around *Enterprise* and together they maintained that position through numerous tight maneuvers.

卐

While Chief Quartermaster Riduka and Lieutenant Commander Wood were fighting to regain control of the ship, *Smith*'s exec, LCdr Bob Theobold, ran forward to direct the firefighting effort. The forward repair party was already leading out hoses, and the destroyer's torpedo, engineering, and damage-control officers arrived on Theobold's heels with reinforcements to help quell the intense flames that were sweeping back from the bows. As the repair parties began dumping accessible ready ammunition over the sides to prevent its cooking off in the advancing flames, Theobold dispatched one sailor down through the mess-hall hatch to check the status of a key fire main and to ascertain the situation in the forwardmost part of the hull. Then Theobold struck out alone to assess damage in the wardroom spaces, which were located on the main deck.

The exec found that the entire forward deck was burning, and the entire upper deck forward of Number 1 stack was made untenable by flames, smoke, or intense heat. The wardroom was filling with smoke. Though no flames were yet visible, the ship's surgeon had to shift his main battle-dressing station from there to the sick bay. Theobold continued forward and found that the next compartment was just beginning to burn. He then returned to the forward repair party, where he learned that the forward fire main was unaffected by the crash and fires.

A second large detonation—probably the warhead of the Kate's torpedo—was felt throughout the ship at 1153. Sparks and burning debris from the center of the blast showered the upper works and started several new fires among the flag bags and on the bridge. These small blazes were immediately extinguished by alert firefighting teams. Several smaller explosions—ready ammunition cooking off around Number 1 5-inch gun—were also distinctly felt and heard.

About then, Lieutenant Commander Theobold grabbed a carbon dioxide fire extinguisher and returned to the smoke-filled wardroom just as a powder case that had fallen into the space from Number 2 5-inch gun ignited. Flames drove the exec back to the main deck, where he turned on the fire extinguisher in his hands and blindly tossed it into the compartment. At that moment, 1154, the leading hose team caught up with Theobold and turned the stream on the advancing flames. The fires never got beyond that point.

Smith's remaining guns ceased firing at 1154.

֎

When Ens Herb Damon, the ship's machine-gun officer, came to his senses and realized that the Japanese were gone and the sky was clear of targets, he let go of his machine gun and looked around to see that several sailors were preparing to cut loose several life rafts already manned by other sailors. Damon was instantly gripped by the shared sense that the ship might blow up at the next instant. Still he tried to dissuade the nearest sailors from abandoning ship. His intense anger, which had not nearly been quenched by the cathartic release of bullets at every warplane in sight, took the form of curses at the sailors about to leave the ship. Damon called them fools and cowards, and managed to dissuade a few. But others left the ship and were never seen again.

BM1 Lee English, who had run forward with most of the after repair party, was leading a hose team up the starboard side of the forecastle deck at 1158 when the captain ordered the forward magazine flooded to prevent a fatal detonation. The pressure to all firefighting hoses immediately dropped as seawater was diverted to the magazine.

At 1159, a minute after the magazine was flooded, smoke and flame being sucked down to the forward fire room by forced-draft blowers resulted in the securing and abandonment of that space by the black gang.

BM1 Lee English's hose team reached the Number 1 5-inch crew shelter and put out the gasoline fires there, but residual fires threatened to set off ready ammunition and powder in the hoists. English shot a stream of water down the hoist and then dogged down the cover. The shells and power cans were still intact in the mount's stowage racks, but very hot. English turned to Lt George McDaniel, the ship's engineering officer, and said, "Let's get this stuff out of here." He handed McDaniel the hose nozzle and asked him to cool ammunition and powder while he and MM1 Red Cottrell threw it over the sides. English had earlier taken off his work gloves to help load 20mm ammunition clips and had forgotten to put them back on when he ran forward to help fight the fires. Thus his hands were instantly burned by the first round Cottrell passed to him as he stood at the mount hatch, six feet from the rail. English got the first two shells safely over the side, but the third was too hot to hold on to, and he dropped it on the main deck halfway to the rail. There was nothing to do then but gingerly kick the volatile refuse overboard. English held on to all the rest of the hot shells to avoid the trauma of dropping another one. The powder cases were not as hot, and all were efficiently dumped into the water.

卐

Though the firefighting crews were making steady progress, as a precaution the four torpedoes in the forward mount were jettisoned at 1212. The forward fire room was reoccupied; the boilers there were relighted at 1240 and put on line again at 1245.

The scene around the smoldering gun mounts was ghastly. Bodies lay everywhere, dismembered and burned in the explosion and flames. Several were charred beyond recognition. BM1 English only saw one dead man who was not burned; he was stretched out on the forecastle, his intestines and blood trailing back to the gun shield. As soon as order was restored, officers ordered dogtags removed from the charred corpses around the forward guns. BM1 English was rolling over one body to get at the dogtag when the man's charred arm came off in his hands. Ens Herb Damon, who had come forward to help, wordlessly watched as sailors removed dogtags from bare bones from which the flesh had sloughed off. The living then rolled the diminished, disintegrating charred corpses right into the water.

All fires aboard *Smith* were declared secure at 1335. Losses amounted to two officers and twenty-six men killed in action, two officers and twenty-seven men missing in action, and twelve men wounded in action. Major awards to *Smith*'s crew amounted to nine Navy Crosses, thirteen Silver Stars, and two Bronze Stars.

43

☀

Following the American air strikes on his battle formations and the launching of the first follow-on strikes, VAdm Chuichi Nagumo turned his Carrier Striking Force northwest, away from Task Force 61. Of the three carriers directly under Nagumo's control, only *Zuikaku* could support flight operations. Moreover, Nagumo's flagship, *Shokaku*, had suffered the loss of most of her communications and the fleet communications duty eventually had to be handed off to a destroyer.

As Nagumo steamed away from Task Force 61, VAdm Nobutake Kondo's Advance Force—Kondo's own Main Body of five cruisers and six destroyers, VAdm Takeo Kurita's Support Group of two battleships and two destroyers, and RAdm Kakuji Kakuta's Air Group of fleet carrier *Junyo* and two destroyers—maintained a southeasterly heading, toward Task Force 61. It was Kondo's hope to continue conducting air operations against the American carriers exclusively from *Junyo*'s flight deck and, if necessary, engage the carriers and their escorts with his formidable surface battle forces. *Junyo* had already launched two strikes—eighteen Vals escorted by a dozen Zeros followed by nine Kates escorted by five Zeros—beginning at about 1000, and these groups were well on their way toward finding the two halves of Task Force 61. The new carrier was also prepared to recover survivors of the earlier strikes, and to launch them again if necessary.

Though two of their flight decks were down, the Japanese were in far better shape than the Americans. *Junyo* had not been found by any American search or strike aircraft, her air group was boring in against two damaged carriers, which had virtually been stripped of their fighter protection, and *Zuikaku* could be turned back toward Task Force 61 if the use of her undamaged flight deck became necessary. And those were just the options they knew about. They did not yet know that *Hornet* was dead in the water, a fantastic target if she could be found by the *Junyo* strike.

⌘

At noon, just five minutes after the last second-strike Kates flew from the area, *Enterprise* was making 27 knots into the wind, streaming a great plume of black smoke through holes in her flight deck. She had been brutally damaged, but she appeared to be in no danger of sinking. The greatest danger was from fires that could spread to volatile fuel-storage and ammunition-storage areas, from undetected submarines known to be lurking in the area, or from an accident closing down her flight deck.

Dozens of American strike aircraft were due to arrive back at Task Force 61 anytime, and fuel-depleted combat air patrol fighters were forming in the landing circle. However, Cdr John Crommelin, the carrier's air boss, decided to shut down the flight deck until the damage-control parties had fought the potentially explosive fires to a standstill.

The worst fires were forward, on two decks of living areas directly over magazines packed with 5-inch projectiles and powder cans. As was the case aboard *Hornet*, where living areas were also ablaze, the fires were being fed by mattresses, clothing, upholstered furniture, and similarly flammable material. In addition, fires on the hangar deck were being fed by aviation gasoline from ruptured fuel tanks aboard shattered warplanes; this firefighting problem was exacerbated by burning fuel leaking into the forward elevator pit.

Though the hangar deck was burning at its forward end, plane handlers began bringing down fighters and bombers by way of the midships and after elevators; the flight deck had to be cleared if the returning strike planes and remaining combat air patrol fighters were to be safely landed. It was a calculated risk, but there was absolutely no sense in avoiding it; if the ship blew up, all would be lost anyway, and if the ship did not blow up, much could be gained by jumping the gun a bit.

⁂

At 1155, one of the departing Kates got off a broadcast pinpointing the positions of both American carriers for the incoming *Junyo* strike waves. At 1201, *South Dakota's* CXAM radar picked up the *Junyo* attack formation 45 miles out to the northwest.

At 1210, *South Dakota's* trigger-happy antiaircraft gunners opened fired on six returning Dauntlesses that were trying to find a way into the *Enterprise* landing circle. All of the targets escaped without damage.

At 1215, Commander Crommelin reopened the newly cleared flight deck in the hope of recovering the *Hornet* and *Enterprise* Wildcats, Dauntlesses, and Avengers with the most serious battle damage or most critical fuel shortages. All the American fighters that could still fly and fight were given a general heading and ordered to altitude to try to blunt the oncoming attackers. In fact, there were no such birds in the sky.

As it was, the *Enterprise* FDOs had no means for controlling another air battle. The violent jolts from the bomb hits had thrown the CXAM antenna out of line, and the entire radar complex was down. The ship's radar officer, Lt Brad Williams, had climbed the mast with a toolbox in hand and had lashed himself to the radar dish to free both hands for work. He was frantically attempting to repair the antenna and its hobbled drive motor when news of the incoming strike arrived from *South Dakota*. There was no way Williams was going to get the job done in time.

Two hundred feet below Lieutenant Williams's perch, Lt Robin Lindsey stood out on his tiny LSO platform and held his paddles straight out from the shoulders as the first returning fighter swung into the groove directly astern the carrier. At that moment, news arrived that the midships elevator was temporarily stuck in the down position. Lindsey shrugged off the bad news; there was room enough for at least the first few returning warplanes. Out behind the carrier, the first fighter was on its final approach. Behind it, a mixed bag of broken airplanes flown by desperate men was wobbling in the landing circle.

Nearly out of gas and flying a rickety wreck of an F4F, Ens Phil Souza, of Fighting-72, passed the "Prep Charlie" emergency signal to Lieutenant Lindsey and rocketed toward the ramp for his landing. When Souza was in the groove, he took his final adjustment signals from Lindsey, received his "Cut," and fell heavily to the deck. Supercharged plane handlers released the Wildcat's tail hook and Lindsey's assistant told him the barrier was clear. The Fighting-72 Wildcat was in such poor shape that it was peremptorily jettisoned over the side—before Souza had a chance to retrieve his expensive sunglasses from the cockpit. By then, the second warplane, a Dauntless, was already well up the groove, and the third, another Dauntless, was swinging up the wake right behind it. "Cut." And "Cut" again. Two more birds were home, and more were swinging into the groove.

Then the word arrived from Commander Crommelin: Secure landing operations; the approaching gaggle of bogies was coming within range of the 5-inch guns. All the circling warplanes scattered to avoid the friendly fire that was about to erupt.

卐

In gun positions ringing the U.S. Pacific Fleet's last operational flight deck, tense gunners and pointers peered into the murky sky and tried to divine the location of the incoming strike. In the bomb-damaged bow 1.1-inch gun director, Lt(jg) Marshall Field continued to shrug off the numerous shrapnel wounds he had suffered when blown out of the position by the bomb that had passed through the forward lip of the flight deck during the first strike. Like everyone else aboard the damaged carrier, Field well knew that the ship might evade destruction, but only by the slimmest of margins. When Lt(jg) Ken Kiekhoefer, of Fighting-72, heard about the incoming strike, he purposefully strode out onto the flight deck with a group of fellow pilots, ready to do battle with the best weapons they had at their disposal, their .45-caliber automatic pistols. Lt Robin Lindsey and his assistant LSO, Lt Jim Daniels, climbed into the gunners' compartments of the last two SBDs to have landed. They armed the twin .30-caliber machine guns and began scanning the low clouds.

卐

The *Junyo* pilots were having problems of their own. The cloud cover was down to 500 feet along the line of approach, and *Enterprise* herself was partially obscured by a passing rain squall. Unable to dive from great height, the two Val *chutai* split up to find whatever targets they could; the flight leaders were by then willing to launch attacks against any surface target. So the dive-bombing attacks were initiated piecemeal against secondary targets.

At 1220, *Enterprise* reported "no bogies." At 1221, the squall line passed, the ceiling abruptly rose to 1,500 feet, and *Enterprise* appeared in the sights of the lead *chutai*. By then, however, the nine Vals were all committed to shallow glide attacks. The lifting cloud cover revealed their positions as much as it revealed the American warships. Instantly, the carrier's 5-inch batteries opened fire, but the Vals were too low for effective radar control, and the automatic fuses were set for many thousands of feet higher than the Vals. On the other hand, the shallow-diving Vals were perfect targets for *Enterprise*'s 40mm and 20mm guns and every gun that could bear from aboard all the screening warships.

Lt Louis Bliss, of Fighting-72, had been orbiting at about 2,000 feet over *South Dakota* and two or three miles to one side for nearly two hours. In that time, he had nearly been a victim of the battleship's gunners, and he had seen other friendly warplanes menaced by them. A 1938 Annapolis graduate who had served aboard a battleship for two years as an antiaircraft gunnery officer, Bliss had been mildly contemptuous of the battleship's accuracy. As the Val *chutai* dived past *South Dakota* on its way toward *Enterprise*, Bliss was gratified to see the ship's gunners finally find their stride. The Vals were massacred. Most of them fell into the sea.

The Japanese attackers were also met by fire from burning, battered destroyer *Smith*. However, *Smith* claimed no kills.

In under two minutes, seven of the nine Vals were destroyed in the air by 40mm and lighter automatic weapons. In that time, the Japanese scored only one near miss, which caused minor damage to the carrier's starboard hull about 15 feet below the waterline. The closest brush with disaster came when a Val streaming flame turned back on *Enterprise* with the apparent intention of ramming her. CTC Ralph Willson instantly directed his 5-inch mount against the dive-bomber, and the Val was vaporized by a direct hit—a miraculous shot by any standard.

Lieutenant Bliss saw only the lead Val escape the carnage and followed it down at the end of its recovery. To evade Bliss, the pilot swooped all the way to the surface and stayed there, running at full power. Bliss followed at a very close distance, but withheld fire until he was sure of scoring; he had no idea how much ammunition he had left and was sure that only his right outboard gun was operable. The Val had been badly damaged by antiaircraft fire, and the rear gunner never fired; perhaps he had been killed. At last, Bliss felt he had to fire a burst. As expected, only the one gun worked, and its heavy lopsided recoil caused the Wildcat's nose to kick strongly to the right. He fired several bursts, violently correcting each time, but he was unable to down the fleeing Val before he exhausted his ammunition.

Some observers reported that up to twenty Japanese attacked *Enterprise* from a variety of directions. If the reports are even remotely accurate, they might account for the nine Kates that followed the eighteen Vals from *Junyo*'s flight deck. The precise fates of most of the Kates is a mystery; several returned with a fanciful tale of three torpedo hits on an American carrier, but most of the torpedo bombers were simply swallowed up in the fog of war. It is certain that only one *chutai* of nine *Junyo* Vals struck at *Enterprise*, for the second Val *chutai* was about to be heard from.

卐

There was a brief lull over Task Force 16 while the remaining Val *chutai* groped through the clouds and came into the clear only 1,000 feet above the screen. It was nearly 1227.

445

At the last possible moment, a power failure left *Enterprise's* forward 5-inch gun director inoperable. Thus the radar-director officer, Lt(jg) Jim Kraker, was left with nothing to do except watch; it would be his first direct view of an air strike, though he had been through Eastern Solomons and had directed his 5-inchers only minutes earlier. The first and biggest thing Kraker saw was *South Dakota*, which was steaming close in to the carrier's starboard beam when she opened fire with everything she had. The great fast battleship was instantly wreathed in billows of smoke. Kraker was aghast; he turned to the battery officer, Lt Joe Roper, and yelled in his ear, "Oh, God, Joe, the *South Dakota* is burning from stem to stern!" Roper could not see the battleship from where he was sitting, so he slowly lifted himself from his seat and peered over the side of the roofless director station. "Hell no," he drawled in his good-old-boy drawl, "that's muzzle blast!"

No sooner said than a Val planted its 250-kilogram bomb directly atop the battleship's Number 1 main turret. There was a large explosion and a great deal of smoke. Lieutenant Roper watched for a second, deep in thought, and drawled to Kraker, "Look. The sonsabitches can' even sink 'er." In fact, the turret's crew was unaware that the bomb had detonated right over their heads.

What neither Kraker nor Roper could see was the bomb fragments that peppered the battleship's bridge and laid open the throat of her skipper, Capt Thomas Gatch, as he stood erect on the walkway in front of the armored bridge. Only the quick thinking of the helmsman saved the captain; the sailor closed off the open artery with his fingers until corpsmen arrived. In that moment, control of the battleship passed to Battle-II, but the phone lines also went dead, so the great ship was running out of control. For a heartstopping moment, she veered directly at *Enterprise*, then she veered away. Fifty battleship officers and sailors were injured either by fragments or the concussion, and one sailor was killed.

卐

Six *Junyo* Vals picked on light antiaircraft cruiser *San Juan* just as she was turning at maximum speed with full right rudder. GM2 Jim O'Neill, a 20mm gunner, saw a silver streak low in the sky, then made out the entire string of Vals. He got a good burst into the second silver streak just as a bomb detonated in the water 100 yards off the port beam. A second later, a second bomb detonated only 15 yards off the port beam and threw up enough water to drench everyone on that side of the ship. The concussion lifted O'Neill from the deck, but he was saved from a nasty tumble by the harness with which he was attached to his gun. The blast knocked down everyone who was not strapped in and severely jolted everyone who was.

Almost instantaneously, a third bomb struck the water 25 yards away, just to starboard and well forward, and a fourth bomb fell 50 yards to port and wound up detonating only 25 yards from the port quarter. A second later, the fifth bomb struck *San Juan* a glancing blow on the starboard side at the level of the second deck; a delayed-action bomb, it fell into the water before exploding.

At almost the same instant the fifth bomb detonated, another 250-kilogram armor-piercing bomb plummeted through *San Juan*'s fantail deck. Its shallow trajectory carried it forward through the chiefs' quarters and a storeroom, and it emerged through the bottom of the ship and exploded beneath her keel. The entire stern of the ship was lifted out of the water and wrenched sideways. Sailors who were just recovering from the string of near misses tumbled to the steel decks again. The smoke generator, located on the fantail, was jarred into action; a great plume of black smoke trailed from the ship, and everyone aboard it and the other screening vessels were certain that *San Juan* was afire. As it was, the rudder was jammed hard right and the cruiser veered sharply clockwise, away from its position in the screen. She nearly ran down several smaller vessels as they raced to get out of her path.

Thirteen men aboard *San Juan* were injured, and it was ten minutes before steering control could be regained. As it turned out, the rudder suffered no material damage; the concussion of one of the bombs had jarred loose the circuit breakers in the steering-control system.

࿊

A mixed flight of nine Scouting-8 and Bombing-8 Dauntlesses led by Lt John Lynch had been in the *Enterprise* landing circle at the start of the action and had swung far to the north to get out of the way as the antiaircraft curtain was put up around Task Force 16. Lynch led the SBDs around to a spot he thought might intersect the route of retirement of the *Junyo* raiders, and he was rewarded when someone spotted a small disorganized gaggle far below. In a running fight that broke up most of the Dauntless formation, Lt(jg) Tommy Wood and his rearseatman combined the firepower of their twin .50-caliber and .30-caliber guns to share kills on two Vals. And a mixed three-plane section led by Lt Ed Stebbins worked together to down one Val and one Kate, the only Kate actually claimed from the *Junyo* strike.

Lt(jg) Joe Auman, of Bombing-8, was beset by a Zero about ten miles from *Enterprise*. As the Japanese fighter ran straight up on Auman's tail, Auman's radioman-gunner did the best he could to parry the aggressive fighter pilot, but repeated hits by 7.7mm bullets were holing the Dauntless's wings and fuselage. The only way out was a tight left turn. The Zero got off one burst before losing Auman, and the bullets riddled the already damaged right wing. At the precise moment Auman turned, his gunner sharply pivoted his guns to get the Zero and wound up putting a solid burst into the SBD's tail, disabling the rudder. Thoroughly chastened, Auman headed for the nearest cloud to sit things out.

卍

The departing *Junyo* strikers were the last Japanese to find and attack Task Force 16. As they left, the first of the circling American fighters, dive-bombers, and torpedo bombers made a beeline for *Enterprise*'s flight deck. In a way, what followed was the most important contribution the Pacific Fleet's last marginally operational fleet carrier made that day.

44

Lt Robin Lindsey, the senior *Enterprise* LSO, and his assistant, Lt Jim Daniels, emerged from the rear cockpits of a pair of Dauntless dive-bombers, from which they had been firing .30-caliber machine guns at the incoming Vals and, Lindsey was sure, Kates. As soon as plane handlers cleared the Dauntless from the barrier, Lindsey assumed his stance on the tiny steel LSO platform at the aft port corner of the flight deck, flexed his paddles, and locked his attention on the wake of the ship. Higher up, in the island, the air department signalman broke out the flags required to indicate that flight recovery operations were resuming. Though Lindsey did not know it, and the order did not stick, someone radioed the returning warplanes that Wildcats would be taken aboard first, then Dauntlesses, then Avengers.

All around the carrier, damaged and fuel-depleted *Hornet* and *Enterprise* fighters, dive-bombers, and torpedo bombers vied for position in the constantly widening landing-traffic circle around the carrier, which was steaming at full speed into the wind. It was clear from the outset that the recovery operation would be limited by the absolute storage capacity on the flight deck itself; the forward elevator was jammed in the up position and the midships elevator would eventually be overwhelmed by the influx of airplanes. Since most of the returning fighters and bombers were signaling one sort of emergency or another, Robin Lindsey was determined to take them aboard without much let-up between landings; he would stop only when he ran out of room, but he would not pause in what appeared to be an endless series of life-or-death decisions. Lindsey's only criterion in turning away incoming aircraft would be their apparent ability to get aboard without crashing and thus closing down the flight deck to other planes. The fate of U.S. carrier air operations in the Pacific for the next several months literally hung upon Robin Lindsey's decision-making powers.

The screen was warned that many warplanes would be ditching, a situation made more onerous by the confirmed presence of lurking Japanese submarines and the searing memory of *Porter's* fate during just such a water rescue.

Lt(jg) Joe Auman, whose gunner had inadvertently shot the rudder off their Dauntless, made it aboard on the first try, though the airplane had a marked tendency during the final approach to sideslip to the left. The harried plane handlers took one look at the riddled dive-bomber and pushed it straight over the side as soon as Auman and the gunner jumped to the flight deck. Auman's was one of many such sacrificed warbirds; the air department had decreed that it wanted to keep only those airplanes that were fit to fly or required only minimal repairs.

In they came, one after another, practically nose-to-tail— *Hornet* and *Enterprise* warplanes all mixed together. Frantic though they were, the plane handlers and flight-deck crewmen worked with a coldly rational precision, never faltering and never causing Robin Lindsey to falter.

Inevitably, inexorably, the ranks of parked planes reached the forward edge of the midships elevator. Word came down from Air Operations to stop recovery operations.

🎏

Lt(jg) Jerry Rapp, a Torpedo-10 pilot flying a Torpedo-6 Avenger, circled well away from the main landing pattern because he had decided to obey the instruction that Avengers land last. At length, however, Rapp's fuel supply appeared to be about gone, so he joined the traffic circle and eventually found himself next in line to go aboard. Rapp was passing down the carrier's starboard side when he received a "Roger" from Robin Lindsey; it was okay to keep coming. He then proceeded upwind, lowered his wheels and flaps, and turned into his downwind leg. Everything was looking great going in, but Rapp saw a great deal of activity on the fantail around the Dauntless that had just landed. He received another "Roger," followed by a "Wave-off," followed by a "Bye-bye." The *Enterprise* flight deck had been shut down due to overcrowding.

Rapp figured that he had only 25 gallons of fuel aboard, and no place to land. He dodged around the task force for a few minutes in search of a flat stretch of clear ocean near a destroyer; he found what he was looking for with only 15 gallons of fuel remaining. He alerted the destroyer crew of his intention to ditch and flew up-wind, turned back into the wind, and began letting down. Above all, Rapp wanted to get down with his engine still turning over so he could better control the airplane. He got his wish, but barely. The landing about 1,000 yards ahead of the destroyer was uneventful, the Avenger remained afloat, and Rapp and his crewmen waited on the wing as the destroyer made a beeline in their direction.

As the warship was slowing, a man on the bridge raised a bull-horn and asked if there was any live ordnance aboard the Avenger. When Rapp candidly admitted that there were two 500-pound bombs hung up in the bomb bay, the destroyer neatly sidestepped while a second, perhaps unapprised, destroyer came up in its wake and slowed.

By that time, the airplane had begun to sink and the three bilged airmen had climbed into their rubber life raft. As the second destroyer, *Cushing*, gingerly crawled forward, someone yelled for the airmen to grab hold of a cargo net that had been rigged over the side. All hands aboard the life raft made quick grabs and hung on for dear life. The destroyer never came to a complete stop—a legacy of the *Porter* tragedy—and the life raft was dragged along. At length, Rapp and his crewmen inflated their life vests and stepped out of the tossing raft. By that time, *Cushing* was making about 15 knots. A large group of sailors that had gathered at the top of the cargo net reached over and heaved the three aviators to the deck.

Rapp's airplane was one of five Torpedo-6 Avengers to make water landings, and he and his crewmen were three of about twenty pilots and air crewmen from all squadrons rescued by *Cushing*.

⁂

When a number of *Hornet* pilots saw the endless traffic pattern around *Enterprise*, they chanced flying on to *Hornet* in the hope she would be able to recover their damaged and fuel-depleted airplanes. At one point, the *Hornet* air-department signalman flashed "Go to *Enterprise*" with his Aldis lantern. The warplanes turned away, and so did light antiaircraft cruiser *Juneau*, which thought the signal was meant for her.

⁂

Shortly after Lt(jg) Jerry Rapp and other pilots were waved off, thirteen early arriving Dauntlesses that had been refueled on the hangar deck were brought topside and launched—even while other warplanes were being struck below by way of the midships elevator. Once aloft, the Dauntlesses were vectored out toward Espiritu Santo. That ensured the survival of nearly a squadron of the precious scout-bombers and provided space for thirteen more lucky orbiting *Hornet* and *Enterprise* warplanes. At that point, Lt Jim Daniels spelled Lt Robin Lindsey on the LSO platform. However, when the space left by the departing SBDs had been filled, Air Operations again ordered flight operations secured. For all that, however, the air boss, Cdr John Crommelin, decreed that *Enterprise* would continue to head into the wind at full speed.

Lieutenant Lindsey decided that he simply *had* to continue to land the circling warbirds. Though the red flag was up, indicating that flight operations had been terminated, Lindsey guided in the next six warplanes. The midships elevator was again overrun by parked warbirds. Someone on the island screamed down, "That's all. Knock it off, brother." But Robin Lindsey played deaf and continued to bring them in, even when the midships elevator was lowered in a gamble to clear some more space. Though he was determined to answer every call, Lindsey knew that they had passed into the realm of pure luck; under these crowded conditions, a flight-deck crash by a damaged plane flown by a nervous, frantic, possibly injured pilot was all but inevitable. If a plane missed the arresting wires while the elevator was down, lives would certainly be lost and the ship might suffer fatal damage.

At this point, Lindsey bet Lt Jim Daniels that he could land the entire next batch of planes on the Number 1 arresting wire. Daniels agreed to the sum of ten cents a plane.

The officers manning Air Operations were having apoplexy and were recommending that Commander Crommelin come down hard on the rogue LSO, who appeared to them to be endangering the lives and fortunes of everyone aboard *Enterprise*. But Crommelin parried the advice and finally said in a dead-calm tone, "Leave the kid alone; he's hot."

卐

Lt Fred Bates, the Bombing-8 flight officer, was one of the *Hornet* pilots who thought there was a chance that *Hornet* might take him aboard, but he never got the opportunity to really find out. Two approaches were met by a hail of gunfire from the Task Force 17 screen, so Bates cautiously approached *Enterprise*. By the time his turn came to fly up the carrier's wake, he was in a do-or-die situation; he did not have enough fuel to go around again. Bates had half-convinced himself that he would land no matter what the LSO had to say about it. But the test of wills never came; Robin Lindsey gave him the "Cut." His was the next to last warplane to be recovered.

Bates's hook snagged on the Number 1 wire, as had the two planes ahead of him and as would the plane behind him. When the last plane was down, *Enterprise* precipitously veered from her course, away from her track into the wind. The flight deck was definitely closed. Lt Jim Daniels handed Robin Lindsey the payoff on their bet, four dimes, and took over on the LSO platform to ensure that no one else tried to land.

卐

A minute later, Lt Louis Bliss guided his fuel-depleted Fighting-72 Wildcat up *Enterprise*'s wake. He could see that planes were parked well aft of the barrier. Though Bliss's approach was superb, he was waved off and ordered to land in the water. He found destroyer *Mahan* and made an approach close by the ship's starboard side at an altitude calculated to bring him down about 200 yards ahead of the ship. As he passed the bridge, Bliss gave the standard emergency arm signal to let the captain know that he was in trouble and needed help. Then he made a normal water landing. The tired Wildcat slowed without coming to an overly abrupt stop, then the nose cowling dug in and all forward motion ceased. As the tail swung up through 45 degrees, Bliss climbed out onto the canted wing and reached for the rubber-boat stowage compartment right behind the cockpit. The space was open and empty. (The raft had apparently flown free hours before, fooling the pilot of a pursuing Zero into believing that Bliss had bailed out.) With that, the F4F sank from beneath Bliss's feet.

Bliss began pulling for *Mahan* with long, strong strokes and was about abreast of the bows and less than 20 feet away when he saw a big, strong-looking sailor just forward of the bridge swing a heaving line far out over the side. Bliss swam right to the life ring at the end of the line and then to a cargo net that had been rigged over the side. When Bliss was led to the bridge to pay his respects to the destroyer's captain, the senior officer asked why he had been waving his arm, then listened with great interest as Bliss explained the procedure for hailing a ship from an airplane in trouble. A bit shaken by the need to explain his action, Bliss was nearly decked by the captain's bland announcement that he was glad Bliss had come aboard on the first try because he was not going to be given a second chance in these submarine-infested waters.

卐

Once she had recovered all the warplanes that could be fit aboard her hangar and flight decks, *Enterprise* turned away from the oncoming Japanese surface forces and beat a rapid withdrawal she hoped would take her beyond the range of any possible Japanese follow-on air strikes and beyond the line of Japanese submarines infesting the battle area. *Hornet* was left to her fate, totally in the care of her screen, which had been diminished by the mistaken departure of light antiaircraft cruiser *Juneau* and the dispatch of heavy cruiser *Northampton* to rig a tow for the powerless carrier.

45

ollowing a pensive wait and word that *Enterprise* was the target of the first Japanese follow-on strikes, *Northampton* again approached *Hornet* and arrived in position to pass up the tow at 1134. It was decided that the tow line would be passed from the cruiser to the carrier and made fast to *Hornet*'s port anchor chain. Before the towing operation could commence, the port anchor had to be detached from the chain, after which a heaving line was thrown from the cruiser and a 1¾-inch steel wire was hauled up by hand, there being no power aboard *Hornet* for running the winches. The cable was attached with a shackle to the port anchor chain, 60 fathoms—360 feet—of cable were veered, *Northampton* began taking up the slack at 1230, and speed was gradually built up to just under 4 knots.

So far, so good.

Then *Northampton* inadvertently tugged too hard and the steel hook at her end of the cable parted. The *Northampton* end of the cable fell into the water. Since the break was not aboard powerless *Hornet*, the entire length had to be jettisoned because there were no winches to haul it aboard the carrier.

The only cable that could begin to do the job was a 200-fathom length of 2-inch steel cable stowed at the bottom of *Hornet*'s midships elevator pit. The greased cable weighed many tons and had to be moved nearly 800 feet from its stowage space to the forecastle. There being no power winches operating aboard the carrier, the vast reservoir of manpower that was available was pressed into service. Hundreds of sailors eagerly—thankfully—responded to the call.

One end of the great cable was secured to the starboard anchor chain and the other end was passed to *Northampton*, which gingerly reeled it in to take up the slack and then began easing forward. *Hornet* began to move at about 1345, and the tandem soon built its speed back up to nearly 4 knots.

Everything looked good.

⁂

Several important details and decisions were worked out during the long interval between *Northampton*'s arrival on towing station and the rigging out of the second cable.

First, at about noon, RAdm George Murray decided with great reluctance that he would have to transfer his flag from *Hornet* to heavy cruiser *Pensacola*. Together with his staff, the former captain of *Enterprise* transferred to one of the screen destroyers at 1245, and then onto his new flagship. Sailors who greeted him as he arrived aboard *Pensacola* thought he looked tired and despondent.

Next, all of *Hornet*'s serious casualties—about seventy-five in all—were gathered on the flight deck for transfer to one of the screen destroyers. While the casualties were waiting, cooks and bakers passed through the crowd with vanilla ice cream and fresh doughnuts. Lt(jg) Ivan Swope, who had been painfully burned in the Scouting-8 ready room, received a dish of the ice cream laced with bourbon from two of his fellow SBD pilots, and it really hit the spot.

AMM3 Lamar Cotton had been wounded by shrapnel from one of the torpedoes as he was working in the propeller shop during the raids. Only a few tiny fragments had entered the lower portion of his left leg, and they did not even hurt much, but the blood soon filled his left shoe. The leg was bandaged and he was placed on the fantail to await evacuation. During the wait, he was visited by his brother, CY Ralph Cotton, of Bombing-8. Ralph remained until Lamar was lifted away by highline to destroyer *Mustin* on a wire litter.

The burn cases were the hardest to transport and deal with. They came from all parts of the carrier, but most of them were survivors of the two fiery crashes by Japanese warplanes. The survivors of Lieutenant Commander Seki's death crash had all been brought to the after end of the flight deck and laid out in rows for tending by the corpsmen. After a brief time in the sun, someone thought to build a sun shelter to protect them. Many were beyond pain, and the unavoidable bumpy move certainly exacerbated their suffering. Some, who might have succumbed anyway, were helped along to their deaths by the renewed trauma.

EM1 Tom Kuykendall, who had been grievously burned as a member of the bomb-gutted forward repair party, was also transferred to *Mustin* in a wire litter. The destroyer sailors had a difficult time getting him below through narrow hatchways to the sick bay, but he hurt so much already that he barely noticed the added discomfort. The last thing Kuykendall was aware of that day was the ship's doctor working over him.

On the other hand, Pfc Vic Kelber, whose facial wounds had been securely bandaged aboard *Hornet* and who arrived aboard *Russell* by highline in a bos'n's chair, was not treated at all that day by the destroyer's instantly overworked corpsmen. S1 Ed Knobel, who had been temporarily blinded by one of the torpedo blasts, was also transferred by highline. Since, like Kelber, he had no apparent life-threatening injuries, he was led to an out-of-the-way corner of the destroyer's machine shop.

As soon as the casualty-evacuation operation was completed at 1540, the evacuation of all ambulatory wounded and all personnel not essential to running or salvaging the ship began. The word was put out that the partial evacuation of able-bodied officers and men was by no means an indication that the ship was in danger of sinking; rather, the men were told, the danger lay in Japanese sub-

458

marine attacks and follow-on air strikes against their virtually defenseless ship.

When destroyer *Russell* came alongside, sailors on the flight deck dropped cargo nets to her main deck, and the air group personnel, who were first to go, climbed with great alacrity from their ship directly to the other—all without getting their feet wet. For the second time that day, *Russell's* upper works were severely damaged as she sideswiped the higher side of the carrier.

In all, 800 air group, flag, and other personnel transferred to the destroyers by about 1615.

⤵

Hornet's only serious hope of salvation lay in restoring power and moving from the battle arena under her own power. Thus began an heroic effort by her engineers and electricians to restart the engines and provide power for essential systems.

EM1 Samuel Blumer was one of seven electrician's mates ordered to the auxiliary generator room. Next to last in the single column at the start of the hot, smokey trek along dark lantern-lighted passageways, Blumer found himself in last place by the time he reached the auxiliary generator room. Once there, the six remaining electrician's mates disconnected the lines from the controls and hooked them directly into the power source. Eight more electrician's mates arrived before the job was half finished, and that resulted in the ability to work in teams so that relays could leave the hot, airless space for some fresh air topside. The work was going very well there and in the fire room, where the black gang was trying to get up steam to run the electric generators.

ChElec David Sword rounded up a bunch of his electrician's mates and organized them to bypass water- and fuel-filled engineering spaces with jumper cables from the after emergency diesel-generator room. The problem with Sword's plan was that numerous watertight doors had to be left open to allow for the passage of the cable through scores of compartments and along numerous passageways. The threat to watertight integrity was overlooked in the face of the greater threat brought on by the ship's total lack of viable motion-generating power sources. The work began in the bowels of the ship, on the seventh deck. The cable was manhandled up to the third deck, then forward past the galley, and then back down to the seventh deck to one of the after fire rooms. Each length of cable had to be connected to the next length with U-bolts, and each connection had to be carefully wrapped in protective rubber sheets to prevent accidental electrocution of anyone nearby in the steel passageways when the juice was turned on.

When an engineering officer called for volunteers to reman the fire rooms and engine rooms, WT1 Lyle Skinner was one of the first to sign on. He was sent to one of the fire rooms and began working on a system to shunt all the available power to the undamaged after engine room—assuming a usable supply of power could be restored in the ship. The boilers had to be fueled by means of a hand pump, which was worse than exhausting in the hot, airless space. Still, the firemen and watertenders did get a fire going in one of the boilers, and they eventually got pressure up to 150 pounds.

EM1 Samuel Blumer was taking a break from his work in the auxiliary generator room when a machinist's mate he knew asked him for help in the steering-engine room. The ship's rudder had been hard to port when the ship lost power, and the hydraulic ram piping had to be opened to relieve pressure in the hope the rudder could be brought back to 0 degrees, a maneuver that would greatly affect the success of the towing operation. The first effort failed, and the ram piping had to be reconnected. Then Blumer and the machinist's mate begged some emergency power from the diesel-generator room. Meanwhile, a volunteer crawled to the very bottom of *Hornet*'s hull and all the way astern—including 70 feet through a dark, water-filled tunnel—to free the rudder. Power from the briefly redirected diesel motor did the trick. *Hornet* could at least be towed straight ahead.

While the electrician's and machinist's mates were working on getting up some power, Cdr Henry Moran, the ship's first lieutenant and damage-control officer, conducted a thorough investigation of all the major damage, particularly the hull damage that had caused the list he had mostly straightened earlier. Moran had no trouble persuading himself that the damage was not life threatening and that the ship was seaworthy. However, it was too extensive to be reckoned with outside of a major navy yard.

⇄

The Japanese had by no means been idle during the early afternoon. *Zuikaku* had turned back toward the American task force after escorting damaged *Zuiho* and *Shokaku* safely beyond the range of possible American follow-on air strikes. Though *Zuikaku* was beyond operational strike range, about 280 miles northwest of the action, the remainder of her air group could make use of *Junyo's* nearer flight deck.

Adm Isoroku Yamamoto, at Truk, messaged VAdm Nobutake Kondo at 1400 with explicit instructions: "The [Guadalcanal] Support Force will pursue and attack the enemy." Fifteen minutes later, *Junyo* began launching a scraped-together and rather strung-out second strike of her own, *Shokaku's*, and *Zuikaku's* surviving airworthy Kates, Vals, and Zeros.

⇄

At 1555, word arrived aboard *Hornet* by means of battery-powered radio sets and flag signals from the screen that unidentified aircraft were approaching. Admiral Murray radioed *Enterprise* from *Pensacola* to request air cover, but the departing carrier had not had an opportunity to sort out the mess on her flight and hangar decks or to refuel and rearm any of the fighters she had taken aboard. RAdm Thomas Kinkaid reluctantly turned down the request.

When the air-raid warning arrived, firemen and watertenders manning *Hornet's* only operating fire room were ordered to bank the fire and evacuate. Most of the black gang reluctantly climbed toward the hangar deck, but several fanned out on the lower decks to evade possible injury from falling bombs.

During the lull between the warning and the strike, EM1 Samuel Blumer, who had remained on duty in the steering engine room following the release of the locked rudder, climbed up to the hangar deck for a breath of fresh, cool air. When he arrived, the ship's chaplain was officiating at the burial of a number of dead shipmates. Blumer was sickened but not particularly surprised to see large fish, presumably sharks, attacking the bodies as quickly as they were tilted from boards into the water aft of the fantail. The ongoing service was interrupted by the air-raid alarm.

At 1620, six *Junyo* Kates weaved in from starboard at 6,000 feet and commenced their attack on the carrier. Several of the Kates used destroyer *Russell* to cover the last part of their approaches; *Hornet* pilots and aircrew on the destroyer's main deck were certain they were going to be rammed, but each Kate pulled up and over at the last instant despite the heavy fire *Russell's* guns were putting out. The rear gunner of one of the Kates strafed *Russell's* full deckload of Air Group 8 pilots and crewmen, killing and injuring several evacuees and destroyer crewmen. Another Kate gunner strafed heavy cruiser *Pensacola*, now the Task Force 17 flagship; he killed three sailors and wounded sixteen others.

At the last second, *Northampton* severed her end of the tow and turned sharply to port, narrowly evading a torpedo dropped by one of the Kates.

Hornet and the screen warships put up all the antiaircraft gunfire they could manage, but it was not enough. The accidental dispatch of light antiaircraft cruiser *Juneau*—and her sixteen 5-inch rapid-fire antiaircraft guns—to Task Force 16 a few hours earlier was about to become a deadly blunder.

The carrier's antiaircraft batteries were fully manned, but they were severely hobbled by the lack of electrical power, both for training the guns and for operating ammunition and powder hoists. FC3 Richard Cartwright, who had been helping to run the ship's central fire-control system until power was lost, was helping to operate a handy-billy portable pump to bring up water to cool a pair of quad 1.1-inch gun mounts. As Cartwright ran the pump, other volunteers helped the gunners push the guns around by hand, and many others manned an ammunition-passing line from the magazines. All training and traversing had to be done by hand, which badly slowed the aiming.

EM3 Tom Reese watched the Kates from his place midway back on the starboard side of the hangar deck. One *shotai* popped up over *Russell* and fanned out. One Kate went forward, one went aft, and one came straight on. When Reese saw the one coming straight on drop its torpedo, he grabbed a lifeline and held on for dear life.

At 1623, one aerial torpedo detonated on *Hornet*'s starboard hull athwart the midships elevator, just aft of and above one of the earlier torpedo hits. A torrent of seawater rose 50 or 60 feet in front of EM3 Tom Reese's place on the starboard hangar deck, and most of it seemed to fall on Reese, who was desperately clinging to a lifeline. When the water subsided, Reese turned and saw the ship's engineering officer, Cdr Pat Creehan, leaning dazedly against a stanchion, covered from head to foot in thick fuel oil. He had been blown up the last few feet of an escape trunk by the force of the blast.

Survivors on the third deck reported a "sickly green flash" and were able to determine that the blast ruptured the forward bulkhead of the forward engine room and damaged equipment in the after engine room and after generator room. Electrical cables were severed and a fire started, though it was quickly extinguished by a nearby repair party. The after engine room and fourth deck near the explosion began flooding right away, and the great ship slowly began rolling into a progressive list that would eventually reach over 14 degrees.

That was nearly enough for Capt Perry Mason and his senior staff. The prodigious efforts of many hours had been wiped out in an instant. The only towing cable capable of moving the ship hung limply from her forecastle, utterly irrecoverable. The electrical system, so laboriously built up by the tireless electrician's mates, was again a shambles. The engineering plant was damaged anew, and there was no viable potential major source of power left aboard the ship. New fires had broken out, the ship was again filling with water, and there was no power aboard to pump out the heavy burden.

�⚛

As the dust from the new torpedo hit settled, EM3 Tom Reese heard shouts for help as he stood in a daze on the hangar deck right above the point of impact. He looked down two nearby ladders and saw a dazed, bloody man clinging to each of them. Reese slid down one ladder, grabbed one of the men by his belt, and pulled him up to the hangar deck. Then he did the same for the other blast survivor.

WT1 Lyle Skinner was pulling himself up the steeply inclined hangar deck by means of a lifeline when he heard a plea for help rise out of the midships elevator pit. Earlier, Skinner had seen sailors take cover from bombs on the lowest decks. One of them had apparently found a good spot in which to evade bombs, but he had run afoul of the torpedo. EM3 Tom Reese also heard the plaints and joined Skinner at the edge of the dark pit. Putting two and two together, Skinner, Reese, and others who joined them speculated that the cries were actually coming from the upper portion of the already flooded forward engine room. If that was the case, all agreed, the crier was a dead man, for the ship was rolling despite her list, and each dip to starboard brought in a great rush of seawater.

The onlookers remained at the lip of the elevator pit. WT1 Skinner secretly hoped that the next rush of water would still the pathetic screams, but it did not. Skinner finally knew at the core of his soul that he would hear those screams every dark night of his life if he failed to at least try to save the trapped shipmate. There were lifelines all around. Skinner secured one to the guard rail around the elevator pit and tied the other end firmly around his waist. Then he lowered himself into the black pit, climbed over a low bulkhead, and felt his way toward the wounded starboard side of the ship, clearly the direction from which the cries were emanating. It was absolutely black in the confined spaces, and Skinner's eyes barely had enough light to which to adapt. But he could see a large jagged hole at the top of one of the fuel-oil tanks and, atop the hole in the far side of the tank, the two eyes of an oil-covered man who was suspended by his clothing from the torn metal. The man was as frightened as a man can be. There was nothing Skinner could do without another line. He felt silly telling the man to "remain calm" while he went to fetch another line, but he said the words. Strangely, the man seemed to calm down immediately.

Skinner retraced his steps, pulled himself to the hangar deck, got the other line, and went back to the wide-eyed victim. The great fear now was that the man's clothing might give way as he tried to secure the thrown line around his waist. If that happened, he was a dead man. Gingerly, the needed act was completed. Then WT1 Skinner gently pulled up the slack, braced himself to take the man's weight, and pulled him free. Quickly, Skinner pulled the man across the top of the fuel oil and then hand over hand to the top of the tank. They were as good as safe, though the man had a great deal of difficulty scaling the little bulkhead to get into the elevator pit; he had put all his strength into the screaming that had drawn Skinner, and he had nothing left. Once over the bulkhead, Skinner and the man were hauled up to the hangar deck by EM3 Tom Reese and a great number of curious, helpful passersby.

࿊

Moments after the torpedo hit, Captain Mason ordered all hands except several key officers and gunnery-control personnel to evacuate the island. Next, orders were passed throughout the ship for all hands to *prepare* to abandon ship—but not to cast loose any rafts or go over the side. This carefully worded order was garbled along the way and about 100 officers and sailors took to the lifelines after freeing several nests of rafts.

One of the men to leave the ship at this time was PhM1 Floyd Arnold. He joined the small rush to leave the hangar deck and swung overboard by means of one of the many ropes by then hanging off the fantail. Arnold dropped into the water and swam about 25 yards to a life raft already occupied by the ship's chaplain and three other men.

At the order to prepare to abandon *Hornet*, LCdr Oscar Dodson, the communications officer, rounded up three communicators and led them below to the coding room to gather up all the codes, secret messages, and confidential communications materials stored there. The trip was dark and dangerous, and Dodson was particularly consternated when he saw LCdr Mamoru Seki's unexploded 250-kilogram bomb secured to a bulkhead only 10 feet from his objective. Dodson turned back to the flight deck and sought the advice of an ordnanceman, who told him, "Go right up to the bomb and check it. If it's not smoking and not ticking, then it's probably a dud and will not suddenly explode." Thus reassured, the communicators went back to the coding room and filled weighted canvas pouches with the materials they felt they had to destroy. The heavy list nearly bilged the effort; there were ten heavy bags to be moved, and the deck was slippery from oils and slimy fulmite.

⁂

Five *Junyo* Vals commanded by that ship's youngest flight officer—her only dive-bomber leader alive at the time of the launch—arrived at 1640 and dived through relatively sparse antiaircraft fire.

When the Vals arrived, WT1 Lyle Skinner was climbing the slippery deck toward the high port side of the ship, gently pushing the exhausted man he had just rescued in front of him. The two never even paused to brace themselves against possible bomb detonations; they seemed to know they would survive.

By then, though no orders had been issued, sailors were leaving the ship again, mainly by way of the fantail. FM1 Samuel Blumer was only halfway down a fantail rope when he heard someone overhead yell "Let go!" Blumer unquestioningly dropped into the water, and was nearly brained by a nest of life rafts that had been cut away directly over his head. He swam to the nearest raft and pulled himself in along with another sailor. The two grabbed paddles and pulled away from the ship as quickly as they could. The first antiaircraft guns were just opening fire again.

No dive-bombers were destroyed and no bomb hits were scored, though one near miss violently shook the entire ship. As the Vals left, all gunnery personnel were ordered to abandon their stations and prepare to abandon ship. Until that moment, all guns had been fully manned and, indeed, had fired at the Vals.

At 1650, Captain Mason and his staff left the bridge and proceeded directly to the flight deck.

⁂

During the brief inevitable post-strike rush to abandon ship, EM1 Leroy Butts, who had spent the afternoon helping to rig the jumper cable from the diesel-engine room to the after fire room, left by way of a line that, unbeknown to him, had been used earlier by the firefighting bucket brigades. When the sailor on the line ahead of Butts jumped from about halfway up the rope, Butts lost his firm grip on the oily line and went down like a shot. When he reached the bottom, he jammed a foot in the unseen bucket. While Butts was trying to free his foot, another sailor lost control at the top of the line and fell on top of him.

TM1 Jim Goldner left his station at *Mustin*'s torpedo director to help haul swimmers aboard his ship. When Goldner saw one man begin to flounder some distance from the destroyer, he stripped down to his shorts and dived into the water to assist him to the side of the ship. Though anxious about being in the water without a life jacket or life belt, Goldner repeatedly swam out to tired swimmers with buoys and lines and returned time and again to assist other tired *Hornet* swimmers toward the nets rigged out over the destroyer's side. Suddenly, *Mustin*'s General Quarters alarm sounded. Before Goldner could climb back aboard, the ship began moving slowly through the swimmers in a bid to pick up some maneuvering room.

At 1655, six *Junyo*-launched *Shokaku* and *Zuikaku* Kates equipped with one 250-kilogram armor-piercing bomb apiece arrived overhead in a perfect stepped-up vee formation. Two of *Hornet*'s own 1.1-inch guns and one of the sandbagged .30-caliber flight-deck machine guns manned by a radioman on his way down to the hangar deck fired at the approaching bombers along with a moderate number of guns aboard the screening warships.

When destroyer *Russell*'s gunnery officer, Lt(jg) Bob Brown, saw the Kates overhead, he also saw that his ship's forward 5-inch gun was pointed directly at *Hornet*'s side. Brown was frankly afraid to order his batteries into action against the Kates when there was a chance that a round from the forward gun would hit the ship he was trying to protect. It took a precious minute for Brown to learn that the gun had a shell casing jammed in its breech and could not fire. Only then did *Russell* add her voice to the antiaircraft barrage.

The precipitous approach of the Kates caught heavy cruiser

Pensacola's gunners completely by surprise. Most were at ease, eating or making head calls. When one 5-inch loader who had fallen asleep on his feet was jarred awake by his gun captain, the man looked up at the level bombers, muttered, "Aw, they can't hit anything," and promptly fell asleep again.

EM3 Tom Reese, who had gone over the side in the latest premature rush from the hangar deck, was floating on his back when he saw the six silvery enemy warplanes slip behind a cloud directly over the ship.

The Kates made their simultaneous drops while flying through or above the cloud. One bomb plunged on into the water after piercing the after starboard corner of the flight deck, and the other five narrowly missed the ship to leeward, away from where most of the ship's company and swimmers had gathered.

Lt(jg) Earl Zook, who had assumed a fetal position at his abandon-ship station on the port side of the hangar deck, was nearly done in when an airplane lashed to the overhead was jarred loose by all the near misses. It fell right next to Zook, who decided it was time to leave the ship.

As soon as the Kates turned away, Captain Mason passed the inevitable order: "Abandon ship."

46

FC3 Richard Cartwright, who was helping to man *Hornet*'s
1.1-inch gun battery, heard the battery officer call down
from the powerless gun director, "Okay boys, let's go." Cartwright climbed down to the hangar deck from the starboard catwalk and there was shocked to find that he virtually had to crawl on
his hands and knees to get across to the large gathering on the port
catwalk. He grabbed a thick knotted hawser that was dangling over
the side and slid down to the armored torpedo belt, which the ship's
heavy list had brought above the water. There he waited for the
chop to carry him away from the ship. However, his timing was off
and the next incoming wave slapped him back into the ship. A bit
stunned, Cartwright pulled away with all his strength and headed
for a pair of destroyers. Fuel mixed with saltwater kept getting in
the fire controlman's mouth and nose, and the chop of the waves
had a nauseating effect. To make matters worse, the nearer destroyer slid off at slow speed just as Cartwright was about to hail
the sailors on her deck. It was only a matter of moments before a
second destroyer—*Mustin*—slowly arrived on station. A life ring
was heaved over the side and Cartwright used the last of his

strength to shoot forward the last few yards and wrap his arms around it. He was reeled in like a prize game fish, but still had a bad time getting his weakened body up a rope dangling over the destroyer's low side. Once on deck, he collapsed against a bulkhead and puked up oil and seawater until he had nothing left inside. Soon he was sent below, where he was treated to a shower and clean clothes.

LCdr Oscar Dodson, the carrier's communications officer, was wrestling heavy bags of classified materials up the slippery canted flight deck when the abandon-ship order was passed. By the time he and three helpers reached the edge of the flight deck, the water was filled with swimmers, making it impossible to throw the heavy sacks overboard. It took about a half hour of waiting for little lulls to jettison all ten bags. When done, Dodson climbed back up to the flight deck and reported to Captain Mason. As soon as the skipper saw the communicator emerge at the top of the ladder, he called, "Damn it, Dodson, what are you doing still aboard. Get off the ship so I can!" Dodson reported that the codes and ciphers in his care were "secure" and wished the captain good luck. But Dodson was not quite ready to leave. A lifelong collector of ancient and rare coins, the communicator still had hopes of rescuing his priceless collection. The leather briefcase in which the coins were stored had been roasted on the signal bridge, but the coins had come through unscathed, and Dodson had stowed them in a corner of the bridge. That was his objective when he left Captain Mason. The briefcase was where he left it, the collection intact. He carried it to the hangar deck, his mind racing for a solution to an obvious problem: How in the world was he going to be able to swim with the bulky, heavy briefcase in tow? The answer was painfully implicit in the question; no way. Dodson removed his shoes, which he placed in line with countless others, and set beside them a fortune that included a small part of the wealth of Rome, of the Kingdom of Lydia, of Athens, of Macedon, and of Carthage. He climbed down to the water and swam for his life. In time, he was rescued by destroyer *Morris*.

Hornet's first lieutenant, Cdr Henry Moran, was one of the last to leave. After waiting for a time with Captain Mason, he made a trip to his stateroom to collect a framed painted miniature of his wife and son. This he placed in his shirt as he climbed back to the hangar deck. Moran went over the side by rope and quickly swam to *Russell*, which was holding steady nearly alongside the carrier. On the way, he saw that the carrier's supply officer, Cdr R. H. Sullivan, was angling in from another direction. "Are you enjoying your swim, Sully?" he called as he reached the destroyer's side just ahead of his colleague. The two senior officers climbed aboard together and joined the crowd of wet, oil-covered refugees.

EM3 Tom Reese, who had gone over the side following the fateful torpedo attack, had long since made his way to a large life raft. When the bulk of the carrier's crew began streaming into the water, Reese helped at least fifteen of them aboard or with hand-holds around the edge. One sailor had swallowed more than his share of oil-fouled seawater, and he had to be hauled bodily aboard to recuperate. At about that point, several of the men aboard and around the raft lost their demeanor. EM3 Reese had been in the water for a while and had become resigned to his plight; he was past the point of panic, so he leaned heavily on several fellow electrician's mates in the group and got them organized to paddle the overfilled raft toward *Mustin*, which was hundreds of yards away. That seemed to snap everyone out of the group funk, and all hands pitched in. On the way, another electrician's mate swam past the raft with a strong, purposeful stroke. "Hey," Reese called, "where do you think you're going?" "Why"—the man called back over his shoulder—"to San Francisco!"—as if that were the obvious answer.

WT1 Lyle Skinner and the man he had rescued from the damaged starboard fuel tank entered the water together and swam toward a crowded life raft about 50 yards from the side of the ship. As they approached, the two were violently cursed by the occupants of the raft, who threatened to harm them if they got too close. This threat of violence seemed absurd, but there was no way Skinner was going to test it. The two veered away and looked for another raft, but they could not find one nearby. They idled away the time, floating on their backs, taking intermittent peeks to check on the progress of a pair of destroyers in among the swimmers. At last, *Mustin* approached to within hailing distance, and Skinner and his comrade were pulled aboard. As soon as Skinner was safely on deck, a sailor in dry clothes handed him a lighted cigarette. Later in the afternoon, one of the destroyer crewmen offered Skinner his bunk. Skinner, who was black with oil, was reluctant to take him up on the offer, but the man insisted.

PhM1 Floyd Arnold, who had been afloat in a life raft with *Hornet's* chaplain since mistakenly abandoning ship early in the afternoon, was finally lifted from the sea by destroyer *Anderson*. It took Arnold three tries to stand up just to get aboard the destroyer because his knees had locked after many hours aboard the cramped raft. Once aboard, he found he could not walk, so he crawled to the bridge and pulled himself up a ladder to report his identity. Next Arnold slid back down the ladder and made his way aft, where he promptly fell into an exhausted sleep. He had not had a bite of food or a sip of water all day.

Many of *Hornet's* Marines went over the side in a group and were picked up in a group by *Mustin*. There the detachment executive officer, 1stLt Leo Dulacki, requested permission to have his troops spell the destroyer's exhausted gunners on the antiaircraft guns. The destroyer's gunnery officer cheerfully obliged, though a number of Marines soon regretted the favor. Unused to the heavy pitch of the small ship's topside gunnery positions, Marines were soon puking the sandwiches and coffee the ship's cooks had so thoughtfully provided as fair compensation.

TM1 Jim Goldner had been left in the water following the rescue of *Hornet* sailors when his ship, *Mustin*, got underway before the last air attack. Goldner found a place aboard a life raft and helped other swimmers out of the oily water. As more swimmers were attracted, Goldner finally had to tell those who seemed able to get back into the water to give weaker survivors a place. All the while, half believing it himself, Goldner assured everyone that *Mustin* would be back to rescue them. At long last, Goldner's ship did come in. A whaleboat was lowered and it came straight to Goldner's raft, which had two dozen tired, filthy men clinging to it. His reward was a hot shower and a fresh change of clothes—his own clothes.

EM1 Samuel Blumer wound up aboard *Anderson*. He was

given dry socks, a shirt, and trousers by one of the destroyer crewmen before being sent to the after deckhouse to join uncountable shipmates.

One of the last members of *Hornet*'s crew to be rescued was Lt(jg) Earl Zook. A recent Annapolis graduate, Zook got the silly notion into his head that he would like to spend some time aboard a cruiser. Thus he passed up an early opportunity to board a destroyer and swam on toward the larger warship. It took a very long time for the young officer to realize that he was in over his head— thousands of fathoms, at least—so he finally pulled for a life raft. When he got there, he saw three very grim-faced occupants, so called out, "Anyone need a fourth for bridge?" The three smiled faintly and moved to make room for the overly chipper jay-gee. They were a little stunned to see that Zook still had on his shoes and, of all things, his heavy .45-caliber pistol. Zook and the others were soon rescued by *Anderson*.

After completing a tour of the silent vessel with his navigator and tactical officer, Capt Perry Mason came up to an abandon-ship station. Beckoning out toward the waves, *Hornet*'s last captain said, "If you please, gentlemen." The two understood perfectly; they selected lines and swung out over the water. Captain Mason followed. It was 1727. No living men remained aboard the ship.

The ship was listing so badly that the three officers were obliged to stop on the ledge of antitorpedo armor. There, Captain Mason paused to smoke a cigarette and, no doubt, ruminate about the terrible day he was having. However, he no sooner lit up than he realized that he was surrounded by a sea of volatile fuel oil, so he immediately crushed out the burning tip on the steel hull of his ship. The two junior officers were sure the captain was simply adjusting to the need to finally give her up. They were about to go when they heard voices from around the curve of the hull. The three climbed along the armored ledge and found twenty sailors working up the courage to enter the water. At once, it dawned on the two junior officers that Captain Mason had no intention of entering the water ahead of these stay-behinds. Indeed. The captain ordered the sailors into the water, and coaxed several who really were too afraid of sharks to proceed. It took a direct order to get the last two sailors overboard. Then, only after his two officer companions, did Captain Mason slip into the water, where he helped the weak swimmers with gentle prodding and words of encouragement.

At length, a motor whaleboat approached the knot of swimmers. Someone called out that Admiral Mason—for his elevation to flag rank had been approved—should be taken aboard first. Mason loudly protested, but the two sailors manning the whaleboat leaned over the older man and dragged him aboard by the collar of his shirt and the seat of his pants. Then, after one more stop to help bilged *Hornet* sailors aboard, the whaleboat made for *Mustin*.

47

The last air strike of four *Junyo* Vals found *Hornet* at 1802. Though there was absolutely no fire from the carrier to throw off their aim, the exhausted pilots, each on his second long combat hop of the day, managed only one hit for the four bombs. That missile was clearly seen by hundreds of former *Hornet* crewmen to explode on the empty hangar deck. Fires burned out of control around the point of impact for about 15 minutes, then abated.

As soon as Capt Perry Mason arrived aboard *Mustin* he was greeted by her captain, LCdr Wallis Peterson, who offered the fuel-begrimed near-admiral his stateroom, a shower, and a fresh uniform. Mason gratefully accepted and was given over to the care of one of the destroyer's junior officers. As Mason was dressing after his shower, he began dictating his after-action report to the young destroyer officer. At length, he began going on about his plans to put a salvage party back aboard his crippled carrier in the morning.

The young officer put down his pen and stared at Mason with a pained expression on his face.

"Yes," Mason snapped, "what is it?"

"Sir, excuse me, but didn't you know the Flag had ordered us to sink the *Hornet* tonight?"

࿕

The last puny Val strike had been the last straw. Though *Hornet* might still have been salvageable, it seemed certain that the Japanese submarines encountered during the day were still stalking the area, and that they would certainly be joined by others of their kind. Japanese surface forces could well be on the way; they had last been seen during the afternoon by retiring American warplanes as they sailed steadily toward Task Force 61. The damaged American flight deck could not be allowed to fall into Japanese hands. Moreover, though the Japanese afternoon air strikes were weak, there was no doubt but that there was at least one Japanese flight deck in operation. Saving *Hornet* would mean conducting a slow recovery operation in submarine-infested waters beyond the effective range of ground-based or carrier-based air cover. In the final analysis, *Hornet* was not worth the possible cost in additional precious American warships.

With great emotion, RAdm George Murray had sealed *Hornet*'s fate with a message from the bridge of his new flagship, heavy cruiser *Pensacola:* Destroyer *Mustin* was to administer the *coup de grace* with torpedoes.

As *Mustin* came on station one mile off the carrier's starboard beam, TM1 Jim Goldner, who had spent most of the afternoon with *Hornet* survivors in the water, made his way to the ship's torpedo director. It would be his job to line up the sights for *Mustin*'s two quadruple torpedo mounts. When Goldner was set, *Mustin* launched all eight of her ready fish in slow succession. As had occurred during the scuttling of *Wasp* in these waters a month earlier, the results were humiliating: Two of the torpedoes ran erratically and never came near the stationary target; three fish ran true but did not detonate; the other three hit *Hornet* and did detonate. However, *Hornet* was made of stout stuff, and she did not sink.

At 2020, destroyer *Anderson* took station off the carrier and loosed all eight of her torpedoes. One veered sharply to the right, one detonated prematurely, and six struck the carrier. Though the damage to the carrier's hull was enormous, she still would not sink.

Mustin and *Anderson*, both filled to brimming with *Hornet* survivors, were left alone by the remainder of Task Force 17, now a surface battle force. As the rest of the ships chased Task Force 16 toward Noumea, the two destroyers began pumping 5-inch rounds into the carrier's vulnerable hull, trying to penetrate weak spots in the magazines and fuel tanks in order to blow her out of the water. Though there was a great deal lacking in the design of *Hornet*'s back-up power system and antitorpedo belt, there was nothing wrong with the integrity of her basic nautical traits. She remained afloat, though the destroyer rounds did indeed start raging fires throughout the hulk.

⁂

The Japanese Vanguard Group of two battleships, four cruisers, and seven destroyers was only 60 miles from *Hornet*'s position at 1900, minutes before *Mustin* began firing her torpedoes, and it was coming on fast. Cruiser-launched scout planes buzzed over the burning carrier just after sundown and lighted her with parachute flares. The Japanese reconnaissance pilots reported the departure of the bulk of Task Force 17 and informed the Vanguard Group commander, RAdm Hiroaki Abe, that a pair of destroyers was shelling the burning carrier.

At 2005, Abe heard direct from Adm Isoroku Yamamoto. The message was essentially a victory exhortation:

> The largest part of the enemy forces north of Santa Cruz has been destroyed. It is quite likely that units composed of capital ships will attempt to rescue survivors.
>
> The Combined Fleet will attempt to destroy these forces.
>
> The [Guadalcanal] Support Force will destroy the enemy forces in a night, or as circumstances dictate, in a dawn engagement.

By the time *Mustin* and *Anderson* had expended a total of 5-inch rounds exceeding 350, the Japanese could see the glow of *Hornet's* fires over the dark horizon. The two destroyers rushed away at 2140, virtually the last moment, with a division of Japanese destroyers in hot but ultimately vain pursuit.

The main body of Abe's battle force arrived at *Hornet's* location at 2220, and Abe sent a message of his find to his chief, VAdm Nobutake Kondo. Then Abe's staff went straight to work trying to figure out a way to get the burning prize under tow. However, an acknowledgment message from Kondo included orders to sink her.

Destroyers *Makigumo* and *Akigumo* closed on the hulk, which was glowing cherry-red in spots, and each fired two of Japan's superb, reliable 24-inch Long Lance torpedoes at her. All four Long Lances struck the carrier and detonated.

USS *Hornet*, the eighth and newest of America's fleet carriers, slipped beneath the waves at 0235, October 27, 1942, and plunged 2,700 fathoms to her final resting place.

As soon as the carrier was gone, the Japanese departed on a northerly heading. Kondo planned to find and reengage the American survivors beginning at dawn, but the plans were scrapped when, at 0300, an Espiritu Santo–based PBY found *Zuikaku* and delivered a torpedo attack that narrowly missed the undamaged fleet carrier. Ten minutes later, a second PBY attacked one of *Zuikaku's* escorts, destroyer *Teruzuki*, with a pair of 500-pound bombs. One of the bombs severely damaged the destroyer, killed two sailors, and wounded forty-seven.

Those, for all practical purposes, were the last shots of the Battle of the Santa Cruz Islands. The remnants of RAdm Thomas Kinkaid's Task Force 61 continued on toward Noumea. And, at 1000, October 27, all the Japanese warships shaped courses for Truk.

Epilogue

Though technically a Japanese victory, the Battle of Santa Cruz—the fourth carrier versus carrier battle in history—was Japan's last serious attempt to win the Pacific War by means of a carrier confrontation. Only one other carrier battle occurred in the Pacific War, in June 1944, in the Philippine Sea. By then, however, the U.S. Navy's Fast Carrier Task Force was operational and Japan's dwindling fleet of carriers was utterly outnumbered and outclassed. Though hundreds of Japanese naval aviators perished in the great Marianas Turkey Shoot of June 1944, it was during the first four carrier battles—in the six-month period from early May through late October 1942—that the fate of Japan's small, elite naval air arm was decided. It was at Eastern Solomons and Santa Cruz that the last best air groups Japan would ever send to battle were ground to dust. After their technical victory at Santa Cruz, the Japanese were never able to use their carriers as a vital strategic weapon again.

Of the Japanese carriers that survived Eastern Solomons and Santa Cruz, only *Junyo* survived the war; she was surrendered to U.S. forces on September 2, 1945. *Shokaku* was sunk by a U.S.

submarine on June 19, 1944, during the Battle of the Philippine Sea, and *Zuikaku* and *Zuiho* were sunk in battle off Cape Engaño on October 25, 1944, as was *Chitose*, which was converted to light carrier (CVL) status from her role as a seaplane tender.

Saratoga, which was damaged in Torpedo Junction, was repaired and returned to duty early in 1943. She survived the war, as did *Enterprise*, the last of the *Yorktown*-class carriers. Indeed, the severe damage *Enterprise* sustained at Santa Cruz was largely repaired in time for her to fulfill a vital support mission only two weeks later, when a Japanese surface force built around two battleships attempted to wage what might have been the decisive surface engagement of the Pacific War.

After Santa Cruz and the series of air and surface engagements known as the Naval Battle of Guadalcanal, the Imperial Navy's Combined Fleet never again attempted a decisive strategic showdown with the U.S. Pacific Fleet that it could win. Though several subsequent surface actions in the Solomons were clearly Japanese victories, their results were short lived. After November 1942, Japan never again mustered the staying power—or the will power—to wage a strategic war afloat or from her carriers. Once the veteran carrier air groups had been shredded at Eastern Solomons and Santa Cruz, Japanese carriers ceased to be a decisive strategic weapon.

Japan's technical victory at Santa Cruz arose from the withdrawal of U.S. naval forces from the battle. That is how "victory" and "defeat" are strictly determined. But on the broader strategic level, the U.S. Navy won at Santa Cruz because it was able to achieve its strategic goal—simply holding the line and winning time—while Japan was unable to achieve its strategic goal—drawing the U.S. Pacific Fleet into a final, decisive battle. The technical victory cost Japan any serious hope she had of winning the Pacific naval war.

Here's why: In the two Solomons carrier battles, only three U.S. carrier strike bombers were shot down over the Japanese carriers, and not one of them succumbed to fire from any of the Japanese warships involved. Conversely, the cream of the Japanese bomber crews in both battles was downed over the U.S. carriers, and many of them fell to the guns of U.S. warships, primarily the U.S. carriers that were the targets of the Japanese strikes. In the long run, the U.S. Navy could replace all the warplanes, pilots, and aircrew lost in battle or in operational accidents. In the same long term, Japan could never hope to make good her pilot and aircrew losses. In those grievous, irreplaceable losses sustained by the Imperial Navy's air arm between May and October 1942—a blow from which Japan was never able to recover—lay the ultimate defeat of the Imperial Navy in the Pacific War.

Eastern Solomons was a draw, and Santa Cruz was a Japanese victory. That victory cost Japan her last best hope to win the war.

APPENDIX A

BATTLE OF THE EASTERN SOLOMONS

August 23–25, 1942

U.S. FORCES

Task Force 61	VAdm Frank Jack Fletcher
Task Force 11	VAdm Frank Jack Fletcher
Saratoga (CV) (FF)	Capt DeWitt C. Ramsey
Air Group 3	Cdr Harry D. Felt
VF-5	LCdr Leroy C. Simpler
VB-3	LCdr DeWitt C. Shumway
VS-3	LCdr Louis J. Kirn
VT-8	Lt Harold H. Larsen
TF 11 Screen	RAdm Carleton H. Wright
Minneapolis (CA) (F)	Capt Frank J. Lowry
New Orleans (CA)	Capt Walter S. DeLaney
Destroyer Squadron 1	Capt Samuel B. Brewer
Phelps (DD)	LCdr Edward L. Beck
Destroyer Division 2	Cdr Francis X. McInerney

Farragut (DD)	Cdr George P. Hunter
Worden (DD)	LCdr William G. Pogue
MacDonough (DD)	LCdr Eric V. Dennet
Dale (DD)	LCdr Anthony L. Rorschach
Task Force 16	RAdm Thomas C. Kinkaid
Enterprise (CV) (F)	Capt Arthur C. Davis
Air Group 6	LCdr Maxwell F. Leslie
VF-6	Lt Louis H. Bauer
VB-6	Lt Ray Davis
VS-5	Lt Turner F. Caldwell
VT-3	LCdr Charles M. Jett
TF 16 Screen	RAdm Mahlon S. Tisdale
North Carolina (BB)	Capt George H. Fort
Portland (CA) (F)	Capt Laurance T. DuBose
Atlanta (CLAA)	Capt Samuel P. Jenkins
Destroyer Squadron 6	Capt Edward P. Sauer
Balch (DD)	LCdr Harold H. Tiemroth
Maury (DD)	LCdr Gelzer E. Sims
Ellett (DD)	LCdr Francis H. Gardner
Benham (DD)	LCdr Joseph M. Worthington
Destroyer Division 22	Cdr Harold R. Holcomb
Grayson (DD)	LCdr Frederick J. Bell
Monssen (DD)	Cdr Roland N. Smoot
Task Force 18	RAdm Leigh Noyes
Wasp (CV) (F)	Capt Forrest P. Sherman
Air Group 7	LCdr Wallace M. Beakley
VF-71	LCdr Courtney M. Shands
VS-71	LCdr John Eldridge, Jr.
VS-72	LCdr Ernest M. Snowden
VT-7	Lt Harry A. Romberg
TF 18 Screen	RAdm Norman Scott
San Francisco (CA) (F)	Capt Charles H. McMorris
San Juan (CLAA)	Capt James E. Maher

Salt Lake City (CL)	Capt Ernest G. Small
Destroyer Squadron 12	Capt Robert G. Tobin
Farenholt (DD)	LCdr Eugene T. Seaward
Aaron Ward (DD)	LCdr Orville F. Gregor
Buchanan (DD)	Cdr Ralph E. Wilson
Destroyer Division 14	Capt William W. Warlick
Lang (DD)	LCdr John Wilfong
Stack (DD)	LCdr Alvord J. Greenacre
Sterett (DD)	Cdr Jesse G. Coward
Destroyer Squadron 4	Capt Cornelius W. Flynn
Selfridge (DD)	Cdr Carroll D. Reynolds

Land-Based Aircraft

Task Force 63	RAdm John S. McCain
Marine Air Group 23	
(at Guadalcanal)	Col William J. Wallace, USMC
VMF-223	Capt John L. Smith, USMC
VMSB-232	Maj Richard C. Mangrum, USMC
11th Heavy Bombardment	
Group (at Espiritu Santo)	Col La Verne Saunders, USA
67th Pursuit Squadron	
(at Guadalcanal)	Capt Dale D. Brannon, USA

JAPANESE FORCES

Combined Fleet	Adm Isoroku Yamamoto (at Truk)
Guadalcanal Support Force	VAdm Nobutake Kondo (CinC 2nd Fleet)
Advance Force	VAdm Nobutake Kondo
Main Body	
Cruiser Division 4	
Atago (CA) (FF)	

Maya (CA)
Takao (CA)
Cruiser Division 5   VAdm Takeo Takagi
Myoko (CA) (F)
Haguro (CL)
Destroyer Squadron 4   RAdm Tomatsu Takama
Yura (CL) (F)
Oyashio (DD)
Hayashio (DD)
Asagumo (DD)
Yamagumo (DD)
Koroshio (DD)
Support Group
Mutsu (BB)
Harusame (DD)
Murasame (DD)
Samidare (DD)
Seaplane Group   RAdm Takaji Joshima
Chitose (CVL) (F)
Natsugumo (DD)

Carrier Striking Force   VAdm Chuichi Nagumo
                  (CinC 3rd Fleet)

Carrier Group
Shokaku (CV) (F)
Zuikaku (CV)
Akigumo (DD)
Shikinami (DD)
Yugumo (DD)
Kazegumo (DD)
Uranami (DD)

Vanguard Force   RAdm Hiroaki Abe

Battleship Division 11   RAdm Hiroaki Abe
Hiei (BB) (F)
Kirishima (BB)

Cruiser Division 7   RAdm Shoji Nishimura
    Suzuya (CA) (F)
    ' *Kumano* (CA)
    Chikuma (CA)
Destroyer Division 10   RAdm Susumu Kimura
    Nagara (CL) (F)
    Hatsukaze (DD)
    Nowaki (DD)
    Yukikaze (DD)
    Akizuki (DD)
    Maikaze (DD)
    Tanikaze (DD)

Mobile Force   RAdm Chuichi Hara

    Ryujo (CVL)
    Tone (CA) (F)
    Amatsukaze (DD)
    Tokitsukaze (DD)

Outer Seas Force   VAdm Gunichi Mikawa
    (CinC 8th Fleet)

Reinforcement Group   RAdm Raizo Tanaka
    Jintsu (CL) (F)
    Kagero (DD)
    Mutsuki (DD)
    Isokaze (DD)
    Umikaze (DD)
    Yayoi (DD)
    Uzuki (DD)
    Kawakaze (DD)
    Suzukaze (DD)
    Kinryu Maru
    PB-1
    PB-2
    PB-3
Covering Group   VAdm Gunichi Mikawa
    Chokai (CA) (F)

Cruiser Division 6   RAdm Aritomo Goto
   Aoba (CA) (F)
   Kinugasa (CA)
   Furutaka (CA)
Submarine Group
   I-121
   I-123
   RO-34

Land-Based Aircraft   VAdm Nishizo Tsukahara

11th Air Fleet
   (at Rabaul)

Advance Expeditionary   VAdm Teruhisa Komatsu
Force   (CinC 6th Fleet, at Truk)
Submarine Force
   I-9
   I-11
   I-15
   I-17
   I-19
   I-26
   I-31
   I-174
   I-175

APPENDIX B

BATTLE OF THE SANTA CRUZ ISLANDS
October 26, 1942

U.S. FORCES

Task Force 61	RAdm Thomas C. Kinkaid
Task Force 16	RAdm Thomas C. Kinkaid
Enterprise (CV) (FF)	Capt Osborne B. Hardison
Air Group 10	Cdr Richard K. Gaines
VF-10	LCdr James H. Flatley, Jr.
VB-10	LCdr James A. Thomas
VS-10	LCdr James R. Lee
VT-10	LCdr John A. Collett
TF 16 Screen	RAdm Mahlon S. Tisdale
South Dakota (BB)	Capt Thomas L. Gatch
Cruiser Division 4	RAdm Mahlon S. Tisdale
Portland (CA) (F)	Capt Laurance T. DuBose
San Juan (CLAA)	Capt James E. Maher
Destroyer Squadron 5	Capt Charles L. Cecil
Porter (DD)	LCdr David G. Roberts

Mahan (DD)	LCdr Roger W. Simpson
Destroyer Division 10	Cdr Thomas M. Stokes
Cushing (DD)	LCdr Edward N. Parker
Preston (DD)	LCdr Max C. Stormes
Smith (DD)	LCdr Hunter Wood, Jr.
Maury (DD)	LCdr Gelzer E. Sims
Conyngham (DD)	LCdr Henry C. Daniel
Shaw (DD)	LCdr Wilbur G. Jones

Task Force 17	RAdm George D. Murray
Hornet (CV) (F)	Capt Charles P. Mason
Air Group 8	Cdr Walter F. Rodee
VF-72	LCdr Henry G. Sanchez
VB-8	Lt James W. Vose
VS-8	LCdr William J. Widhelm
VT-6	Lt Edwin B. Parker, Jr.

TF 17 Screen	RAdm Howard H. Good
Cruiser Division 5	RAdm Howard H. Good
Northampton (CA) (F)	Capt Willard A. Kitts, III
Pensacola (CA)	Capt Frank L. Lowe
San Diego (CLAA)	Capt Benjamin F. Perry
Juneau (CLAA)	Capt Lyman K. Swenson
Destroyer Squadron 2	Cdr Arnold E. True
Morris (DD)	LCdr Randolph B. Boyer
Anderson (DD)	LCdr Richard A. Guthrie
Hughes (DD)	LCdr Donald J. Ramsey
Mustin (DD)	LCdr Wallis F. Peterson
Russell (DD)	LCdr Glenn R. Hartwig
Barton (DD)	LCdr Douglas H. Fox

Land-Based Aircraft

Task Force 63   RAdm Aubery W. Fitch

JAPANESE FORCES

Combined Fleet	Adm Isoroku Yamamoto (at Truk)
Guadalcanal Support Force	VAdm Nobutake Kondo (CinC 2nd Fleet)
Advance Force	VAdm Nobutake Kondo

Main Body
  Cruiser Division 4
    Atago (CA) (FF)
    Takao (CA)
  Cruiser Division 5   RAdm Sentaro Omori
    Myoko (CA) (F)
    Maya (CA)
  Destroyer Division 2   RAdm Raizo Tanaka
    Isuzu (CL) (F)
    Makinami (DD)
    Kawakaze (DD)
    Suzukaze (DD)
    Naganami (DD)
    Umikaze (DD)
    Takanami (DD)
Air Group   RAdm Kakuji Kakuta
  Carrier Division 2
    Junyo (CV) (F)
    Kuroshio (DD)
    Hayashio (DD)
Support Group   VAdm Takeo Kurita
  Battleship Division 3
    Kongo (BB) (F)
    Haruna (BB)
    Oyashio (DD)
    Kagero (DD)

Carrier Striking Force	VAdm Chuichi Nagumo (CinC 3rd Fleet)

Carrier Group

Carrier Division 1
  Shokaku (CV) (F)
  Zuikaku (CV)
  Zuiho (CVL)
Screen
  Kumano (CA)
  Hatsukaze (DD)
  Yukikaze (DD)
  Maikaze (DD)
  Hamakaze (DD)
  Amatsukaze (DD)
  Tokitsukaze (DD)
  Arashi (DD)
  Teruzuki (DD)
Vanguard Group   RAdm Hiroake Abe
  Battleship Division 11
  Hiei (BB) (F)
  Kirishima (BB)
  Cruiser Division 8   RAdm Chuichi Hara
  Tone (CA) (F)
  Chikuma (CA)
  Cruiser Division 7   RAdm Shoji Nishimura
  Suzuya (CA)
  Destroyer Division 10   RAdm Susumu Kimura
  Nagara (CL) (F)
  Makigumo (DD)
  Akigumo (DD)
  Urakaze (DD)
  Kazagumo (DD)
  Yugumo (DD)
  Tanikaze (DD)
  Isokaze (DD)
Supply Group
  Nowaki (DD)
  Toho Maru
  Kyokuto Maru

Kokuyo Maru
Toei Maru

Outer Seas Force

VAdm Gunichi Mikawa
(CinC 8th Fleet, at
Shortland Islands)

Assault Unit
  Akatsuki (DD)
  Ikazuchi (DD)
  Shiratsuya (DD)
Bombardment Unit   RAdm Tomatsu Takama
  Destroyer Division 4
  Yura (CL) (F)
  Akizuki (DD)
  Harusame (DD)
  Yudachi (DD)
  Murasame (DD)
  Samidare (DD)

Advance Expeditionary Force   VAdm Teruhisa Komatsu
(CinC 6th Fleet, at Truk)

Submarine Force
  I-4
  I-5
  I-7
  I-9
  I-15
  I-21
  I-22
  I-24
  I-174
  I-175
  I-176

BIBLIOGRAPHY

BOOKS

Belote, James H., and William M. Belote. *Titans of the Seas: The Development and Operations of Japanese and American Carrier Task Forces During World War II.* New York: Harper & Row, 1975.

Burns, Eugene. *Then There Was One: The U.S.S. Enterprise and the First Year of the War.* New York: Harcourt, Brace, 1943.

Dull, Paul S. *A Battle History of the Imperial Japanese Navy, 1941–1945.* Annapolis: Naval Institute Press, 1978.

Griffin, Alexander R. *A Ship to Remember: The Saga of the* Hornet. New York: Howell, Soskin, 1943.

Hammel, Eric. *Guadalcanal: Starvation Island.* New York: Crown Publishers, 1987.

Hara, Tameichi, Fred Saito, and Roger Pineau. *Japanese Destroyer Captain.* New York: Ballantine Books, 1961.

Johnston, Stanley. *The Grim Reapers.* New York: E. P. Dutton, 1943.

Knott, Richard C. *Black Cat Raiders of WWII.* Baltimore: Nautical & Aviation Publishing Company of America, 1981.

Lundstrom, John B. *The First Team: Pacific Naval Air Combat from Pearl Harbor to Midway.* Annapolis: Naval Institute Press, 1984.

Mears, Lt Frederick. *Carrier Combat.* Garden City: Doubleday, Doran and Co., 1944.

Miller, Thomas G., Jr. *The Cactus Air Force.* New York: Harper & Row, 1969.

Morison, RAdm Samuel Eliot. *History of United States Naval Operations in World War II.* Vol. 5: *The Struggle for Guadalcanal.* Boston: The Atlantic Monthly & Little, Brown, 1962.

Olynyk, Dr. Frank J. *USN Credits for Destruction of Enemy Aircraft in Air-to-Air Combat: World War II.* Aurora, Ohio: Frank J. Olynyk, 1982.

Okumiya, Masatake, and Jiro Horikoshi. *Zero! The Inside Story of Japan's Air War in the Pacific.* New York: E. P. Dutton, 1956.

Porter, Col R. Bruce, and Eric Hammel. *Ace! A Marine Night-Fighter Pilot in World War II.* Pacifica, Calif.: Pacifica Press, 1985.

Potter, E. B. *Nimitz.* Annapolis: Naval Institute Press, 1976.

Roscoe, Theodore. *United States Destroyer Operations in World War II.* Annapolis: Naval Institute Press, 1953.

Sakai, Saburo, Martin Caidin, and Fred Saito. *Samurai!* New York: E. P. Dutton, 1957.

Stafford, Cdr Edward P. *The Big E: The Story of the USS* Enterprise. New York: Random House, 1962.

Stover, E. T., and Clark G. Reynolds. *The Saga of Smokey Stover.* Charleston: Trad Street Press, 1978.

Tillman, Barrett. *The Dauntless Dive Bomber of World War II.* Annapolis: Naval Institute Press, 1976.

————. *The Wildcat in WWII.* Baltimore: Nautical & Aviation Publishing Company of America, 1983.

Toland, John. *The Rising Sun: The Decline and Fall of the Japanese Empire.* New York: Random House, 1970.

Wolfert, Ira. *Torpedo 8.* Boston: Houghton-Mifflin, 1943.

PERIODICALS

Blee, Capt Ben W. "Whodunnit?" *U.S. Naval Institute Proceedings* (July 1983).

Editors. "Capt Robin M. Lindsey, USN (Ret): The Last Cut for an LSO." *The Hook* (Summer 1984).

Gates, Thomas F. "Track of the Tomcatters: A History of VF-31, Part 2: Fighting Six at Guadalcanal." *The Hook* (Winter 1984).

Hammel, Eric. "Bogies at Angels Twelve." *World War II* (March–April 1986).

———. "Black Tuesday." *Marine Corps Gazette* (November 1986).

Lundstrom, John B. "Saburo Sakai over Guadalcanal." *Fighter Pilots in Aerial Combat* (Fall 1982).

———, and Henry Sakaida. "Saburo Sakai over Guadalcanal, Part 2." *Fighter Pilots in Aerial Combat* (Winter 1983).

Mason, RAdm Charles P., and Don Eddy. "How We Lost a Gallant Lady." *America* (November 1943).

Poulos, George. "Recollections of a VP Pilot." *Naval Aviation News* (September 1982).

Southerland, Lt J. J., II, USN. "One of the Many Personal Adventures in the Solomons." *U.S. Naval Institute Proceedings* (April 1943).

Tanaka, VAdm Raizo. "Japan's Losing Struggle for Guadalcanal, Parts 1 and 2." *U.S. Naval Institute Proceedings* (July and August 1956).

Toyama, Saburo. "Lessons from the Past." *U.S. Naval Institute Proceedings* (September 1982).

UNPUBLISHED

Norton, Mdn Douglas M. "The Battle of Santa Cruz." Research paper submitted to the faculty of the U.S. Naval Academy (1965).

Index

497

499

INDEX

Knight, ARM3 Paul W., 124, 190-191, 234-235
Knobel, S1 Edward, 388-389, 399-400, 458
Knuepfer, LCdr George, 362-363, 267, 274-276
Kokumbona, 290
Komatsu, VAdm Teruhisa, 311
Komura, Capt Keizo, 371
Kona, Ens Steve G., 383-384, 406-408
Kondo, VAdm Nobutake, 218, 226, 311, 313, 322-323, 329, 336-337, 440, 461, 478
Konig, Lt Rubin H., 148-149, 187, 212, 220-223, 233
Kraker, Lt(jg) James A., 317, 446
Krueger, Ens Fred J., 80
Krzeminski, AM3 Edmund, 171
Kukum, 10-15, 110
Kurita, VAdm Takeo, 440
Kusaka, RAdm Ryunosuke, 330
Kuykendall, EM1 Thomas S., 387-388, 400, 458

Lae, 17
Lamson, S1 Joyce W., 180
Landry, Lt(jg) DuPont P. (Paul), 380
Lane, ARM2 David H., 222
Lanvermeier, Pfc George E., 424, 430-431
Larsen, Lt Harold H. (Swede), 146-147, 218-220, 226, 258, 299
Leder, Ens William H. (Hank), 429
Lee, LCdr James R. (Bucky), 341-343, 345-346
Lee, Pfc Robert E., 174
Lee, RAdm Willis A., 320, 323
Lengo Channel, 5, 228
Leppla, Lt(jg) John A., 352-355, 374, 409, 431
Leslie, LCdr Maxwell F., 149, 176, 224-225
Lindley, TSgt Johnny, 116
Lindsey, Lt Robin M., 173, 205-206, 211, 407-410, 442-444, 449-453
Liska, ARM2 John, 344, 352
Livdahl, LCdr Orlin L., 167-168, 170, 172, 176-177, 316-317, 423
Loesch, Ens Richard L., 81, 157
Lowe, Lt John T., 125-126, 146, 211
Lunga, 7, 11-12, 14, 93, 254, 279, 280, 292-295, 298-299
Lunga Field, see Henderson Field
Lunga Perimeter, 97, 243, 245, 251-253, 256, 259, 284, 290, 294-298, 306-308, 311, 313, 320, 337
Lynch, Lt John J., 350, 370-372, 447-448

Machinsky, Carp Joseph, 275
MacNair, Lt Mark P., 78
Malaita Island, 75, 94, 96, 103-104, 112-113
Mangrum, Maj Richard C., 227-229
Mankin, AP1 Lee P. (Paul), 29-30. 159
March, Ens Harry A., Jr., 32, 159
Marcoux, MM2 William N., 216
Marianas Turkey Shoot, 479
Mason, Capt Charles P. (Perry), 386-387,

391-393, 395, 404, 463, 465-466, 468, 470, 473-476
Mason, Paul, 17
Matanikau River, 284
Mathews, Lt (Doc), 322
Maul, Ens Elmer, 99
McAteer, Lt(jg) Gerald H., 399
McCain, RAdm John S., 103
McCampbell, Lt David, 274-275
McCarthy, WT1 Charles P., 414-415
McConnaughhay, Lt James W., 370
McDaniel, Lt George T., 438
McDonald, Ens John B., 161
McGraw, Lt(jg) Bruce A., 340-341, 348
Mead, Ens Albert E., 353-354, 374
Mears, Ens Frederick, 65, 69, 119, 156, 189, 196, 211-212
Meredith, SM3 Dave, 417
Mester, Lt(jg) Charles, 79
Midway Battle, 5-6, 9, 43-44, 56, 83-84, 87-90, 106-107, 113, 118, 138, 140, 147, 150, 194-195, 230, 249, 283, 305, 310-314, 318, 344, 373, 385
Mikawa, VAdm Gunichi, 311, 321
Miller, Lt Frank D. (Don), 326-327
Miller, Lt(jg) Kenneth R., 343
Milner, Lt(jg) Robert M., 131
Miner, ARM3 T. H., 201
Moran, Cdr Henry G., 401, 404, 460-461, 470-471
Morgan, Ens Corwin F., 138, 140
Morgan, F3 Ralph C. (Don), 426-427
Mott, LCdr Elias B. II, 167-168, 174
Muccitelli, SM3 Albert G., 413
Murata, LCdr Shigeharu, 349, 419, 428, 432-433
Murray, RAdm George D., 245, 248, 257-258, 283, 287-288, 319, 385, 395-396, 457, 461, 476
Myers, Lt John N., 121, 123-125, 196-197, 211-212

Nadison, AM1 Stephen, Jr., 356
Nagle, Mach Patrick, 32
Nagumo, VAdm Chuichi, 93, 100, 103, 111, 125-126, 145, 154, 311-312, 323-324, 330-331, 336-337, 341, 346, 348-349, 440
Nakajima, LCdr Tadashi, 16-17, 19-20
Naval Aviation Cadet Program, 9
Naval Disarmament Conference of 1922, 39, 41-42
Naval Reserve Act of 1939, 55
Ndeni Island, 79, 94-95, 104-105, 107, 111, 125
Nelson, ARM1 Thomas C., 352, 355-357, 374
New Caledonia, 3, 75
New Georgia Island, 304
New Georgia Sound, see Slot, The
New Guinea, 5, 17, 296, 320, 344
    Japanese offensive, 254, 284, 290

INDEX